THE BROKEN CHINA DREAM

The Broken China Dream

HOW REFORM REVIVED TOTALITARIANISM

MINXIN PEI

PRINCETON UNIVERSITY PRESS
PRINCETON & OXFORD

Published by Princeton University Press
41 William Street, Princeton, New Jersey 08540
99 Banbury Road, Oxford OX2 6JX

press.princeton.edu

GPSR Authorized Representative: Easy Access System Europe - Mustamäe tee 50, 10621 Tallinn, Estonia, gpsr.requests@easproject.com

ISBN 9780691223339
ISBN (e-book) 9780691223346

British Library Cataloging-in-Publication Data is available

Editorial: Bridget Flannery-McCoy, Dave McBride, and Alena Chekanov
Production Editorial: Ali Parrington
Jacket Design: Ben Higgins
Production: Erin Suydam
Publicity: James Schneider and Kathryn Stevens
Copyeditor: Anita O'Brien

This book has been composed in Arno

Printed in the United States of America

10 9 8 7 6 5 4 3 2 1

MIX
Paper | Supporting responsible forestry
FSC® C008955

To Larry Diamond

CONTENTS

ABBREVIATIONS

A2/AD	anti-access/area denial
ADIZ	Air Defense Identification Zone
AIG	American International Group
BOT	build-operate-transfer (model)
BRI	Belt and Road Initiative
BRICS	Brazil, Russia, India, China, and South Africa
CCP	Chinese Communist Party
CCTV	China Central Television
CDIC	Central Discipline Inspection Commission
CMC	Central Military Commission
CNKI	China National Knowledge Infrastructure
CYL	Communist Youth League
DPP	Democratic Progressive Party
EPZ	export processing zone
EU	European Union
FAO	Food and Agriculture Organization
FDI	foreign direct investment
FTO	foreign trade organization
GATT	General Agreement on Tariffs and Trade
GFC	global financial crisis
HDI	Human Development Index
ICF	China Integrated Circuit Industry Investment Fund
ICOR	incremental capital output ratio
ILO	International Labour Organization
IMF	International Monetary Fund
IPO	initial public offering
KMT	Nationalists (Kuomintang)
LGFV	local government financing vehicle
MFN	most-favored nation

MOFERT	Ministry of Foreign Economic Relations and Trade
MPS	Ministry of Public Security
MSS	Ministry of State Security
NCW	new cold war
NPC	National People's Congress
ODA	Official Development Assistance
PAP	People's Armed Police
PAP	People's Action Party (Singapore)
PBOC	People's Bank of China
PLA	People's Liberation Army
PPP	purchasing power parity
PRC	People's Republic of China
PRI	Institutional Revolutionary Party (Mexico)
PSC	Politburo Standing Committee
ROC	Republic of China
SAIC	State Administration for Industry and Commerce
SARS	Severe Acute Respiratory Syndrome
SASAC	State Asset Supervision and Administration Commission
SCO	Shanghai Cooperation Organisation
SED	Strategic Economic Dialogue
SEZ	special economic zone
SOE	state-owned enterprise
SPP	Supreme People's Procuratorate
TFP	total factor productivity
TPP	Trans-Pacific Partnership
TVE	township and village enterprises
UNDP	United Nations Development Programme
UNHCR	United Nations High Commissioner for Refugees
UNICEF	United Nations Children's Fund
WEP	World Education Program
WTO	World Trade Organization
ZGTJNJ	*China Statistical Yearbook*

THE BROKEN CHINA DREAM

Introduction

THE CLOSING ceremony of the 20th National Congress of the Chinese Communist Party (CCP) on October 22, 2022, was supposed to be a festive occasion celebrating Xi Jinping's unprecedented third term as the party's general secretary. But something evidently went awry. Xi's predecessor, former party chief Hu Jintao, then 80 years old, was escorted off the podium, apparently against his will. The more than 2,300 delegates to the congress stared in stunned disbelief while Xi and the other top party leaders seated with Hu sat expressionless, pretending not to notice what was widely seen as an act of public humiliation of a former party chief.

What exactly happened remains a subject of fevered speculation. The most plausible explanation is that Hu noticed in the file given to him that his protégé and two-term member of the Politburo, Hu Chunhua (no relation), was not on the list of members to be appointed to the new Politburo, even though he was only 59 years old and had more experience than most other members of the Politburo. As Hu Jintao likely had not been notified of this last-minute change, he probably wanted to ask those seated around him (Xi Jinping sat to his right) why Hu Chunhua had been dropped from the Politburo. Apparently, this was too much for one of Xi's closest loyalists, Li Zhanshu, a retiring member of the Politburo Standing Committee. Li seized the file from Hu Jintao while Xi summoned an aide and appeared to instruct him to remove Hu from the podium.[1]

This incident, unanticipated by Xi as it may have been, nevertheless serves as a fitting marker of the total political dominance he had attained since becoming CCP chief in November 2012. During his decade in power, he had dismantled the political order constructed by his predecessors and had revived the central elements of totalitarianism: personalistic rule, a cult of personality, permanent purges, stifling social control, ideological indoctrination, and an aggressive foreign policy. The reinstitution of fear as a vital instrument of rule can be seen in a long list of acts previously thought to be inconceivable in the post-Mao era: the mass incarceration of millions of members of ethnic minorities (mostly Uighurs) in Xinjiang in the second half of the 2010s; the unilateral imposition of a national security law on Hong Kong in July 2020 that all but ended the "one country, two systems" governance model in the former British colony; the ferocious crackdown on civil society, the press, and social media that has raised repression to its worst level in the post-Mao era.

Within the regime, Xi made himself the most powerful—and most feared—Chinese ruler since the death of Mao Zedong in 1976, largely by deploying the tactics of the permanent purge and monopolization of decision-making power favored by totalitarian leaders. By the time he ordered that Hu Jintao be escorted off the podium, Xi had broken nearly all the norms and rules established by the party in the post-Mao era, including collective leadership, term limits, mandatory retirements, and security of political elites. (By late 2022, Xi's decade-long war on corruption had led to the investigation of 4.6 million party members, including more than 500 "centrally supervised" officials and more than 200,000 mid-level and local officials. About one in eight full and candidate members of the Central Committee had been investigated, prosecuted, and imprisoned.)[2]

The day after his display of raw political power in front of the officials who ran the country, the Central Committee duly elected Xi as general secretary for another five-year term, breaking the unwritten two-term limit and effectively making him the first lifelong ruler since Mao Zedong.

The return of a neo-totalitarian ruler and practices reminiscent of Stalinism was scarcely imaginable four decades earlier when survivors of Mao's Cultural Revolution had regrouped in Beijing to salvage a regime traumatized by its self-destructive policies. Prominent among them were Deng Xiaoping, who had the distinction of being purged thrice by the party (twice by Mao), and Chen Yun, another veteran revolutionary and the party's most respected economic planner. Although Deng and Chen would later clash over economic reform, they shared the same goal of restoring collective leadership and preventing the rise of a Mao-like figure who could again terrorize the party. They pushed through a series of reforms enshrining the principle of collective leadership, prohibiting the building of a personality cult, and introducing the practice of mandatory retirement and term limits.

In addition to such efforts to steer the party away from its totalitarian past, the party in the early 1980s also boasted liberal-leaning incumbent leaders running its day-to-day affairs (even though Deng and Chen would still call the ultimate shots). Hu Yaobang became party chief in June 1981 after Deng and Chen forced out Hua Guofeng, a transitional leader credited with the coup that led to the arrest of Mao's widow and three other radicals in early October 1976. Hu Yaobang oversaw the party's routine administration for the next five and half years and played a pivotal role in drafting some of the party's historic documents in the 1980s. On the economic side, Zhao Ziyang, the premier, worked tirelessly to turn Deng's vision of "reform and opening" into a reality. The reformist duo was instrumental in nudging the party in a kinder, gentler direction. Indeed, before Deng ordered the Chinese military to crush the peaceful prodemocracy protests in Beijing on June 4, 1989, China had experienced the most open and free decade in the post-1949 era.

Hopes that China would continue to evolve into a more prosperous and open society did not die even after the brutal suppression of the protesters in Beijing in June 1989. The collapse of the Soviet Union in December 1991 led Deng to launch his final attempt to revive the country's economic revolution in early 1992, as he knew that the CCP, like the former Soviet Union, would also lose legitimacy if it failed to deliver a better standard of living for the Chinese people.

During the following two decades, modernization on an unprecedented scale in human history completely transformed China, even though the party retained its power and continued to resist political liberalization. For those believing that growing economic prosperity and integration with the West through trade and investment would increase the odds of bringing democracy to the country, democratization through economic modernization seemed a feasible route for China in the post-Tiananmen era. In the twenty years between Deng's tour of South China in 1992 that reignited the economic reforms and the installation of Xi Jinping as the new party chief in late 2012, the Chinese economy grew at an average of 10 percent each year.[3] Per capita income measured in purchasing power rose nearly tenfold, from 1,262 purchasing power parity (PPP) to 11,169 PPP, during the same period.[4] In 1992, only 27.5 percent (or 322 million) of the population lived in urban areas. By 2012, 52.6 percent (or 712 million) of the population were urban residents.[5] The Chinese population had also become better educated. In 1992, 604,000 people graduated from college. In 2012, 6.24 million people graduated from college, representing a tenfold increase.[6] The globalization in the post–Cold War era helped make China an integral part of the global economy and also the world's largest manufacturing power. Between 1992 and 2012, more than $1.2 trillion in foreign direct investment (FDI) flowed into China, and foreign merchandise trade increased from $136 billion to $3.867 trillion.[7]

Before the rise of Xi, few could have imagined that a country that had made such tremendous progress through economic development and globalization could restore totalitarian rule at home and precipitate a new cold war with the West. Tragically, that is exactly what has happened. By the time that Xi effectively became China's new lifetime ruler, he not only had revived totalitarian rule at home but also had implemented an aggressive foreign policy that eventually contributed to the collapse of Sino-American relations and the rise of a new cold war.

What Happened?

No single theory in the existing social science literature can fully explain the revival of totalitarian rule in China despite decades of transformative socioeconomic modernization, the immense improvements in economic well-being, and integration with the global economy. To understand how China underwent a great political leap backward under Xi's rule, we must first appreciate the odds against a potential opposite outcome—political liberalization or even democratization in parallel with rapid economic development.

One of the greatest puzzles about China since the end of the Maoist era is the apparent disconnect between economic development and democracy. Contrary to the strong correlation between the level of economic development and the existence of democratic regimes that has long been observed, rising prosperity and social change in China since the 1980s have created many favorable preconditions for democracy but have not actually led to meaningful democratization of its political system.[8] Explanation of this puzzle may not be difficult to find. For starters, despite the observed correlation between wealth and democracy, the exact mechanisms by which economic development leads to democracy remain unclear.[9] Research on democratization since the mid-1970s shows that the choices made by authoritarian ruling elites play a far more important and direct role in the transition from authoritarian rule.[10] One of the most influential studies of the relationship between economic development and democracy finds no linear relationship between economic development and the transition to democracy. The single most important variable in a country's transition to democracy is not the attainment of a particular level of wealth but the demise of dictatorship.[11]

If the strategic choices made by China's leaders in the post-Mao era matter more than the structural changes of the country's society and economy in determining the evolution of its political system, then there may be a simpler and more straightforward explanation of the Chinese puzzle. One-party rule has persisted in China in spite of modernization mainly because the CCP not only has chosen to resist pressures for political liberalization but also has adopted effective measures to neutralize the political effects of economic development. Indeed, we do not need to look far to find evidence that Deng Xiaoping, the leader who almost single-handedly steered the party away from Maoism in the direction of modernization, had no intention of allowing his project of "reform and opening" to endanger the party's political monopoly. In March 1979, three months after he effectively became the paramount leader, Deng laid down the "Four Cardinal Principles"—upholding the socialist path, the people's democratic dictatorship, the CCP leadership, and Mao Zedong Thought and Marxism-Leninism—as the political limits not subject to challenge.[12] However hard he pushed for market reforms, integration with the West, and measures favorable to development during his rule, Deng made it abundantly clear that economic modernization was the means by which to perpetuate one-party rule, and nothing else. Although he fought the hardliners in the party who resisted his economic reforms, he consistently took their side, often wittingly, in lashing out against what he called "bourgeois liberalization"—his shorthand for societal pressures to advance political liberalism and democracy.

To be sure, there was perhaps a narrow and brief window for democratization in the 1980s, the most open period since 1949. During the decade, liberal reformers such as Hu Yaobang (party chief from 1981 to January 1987) and Zhao Ziyang (premier from 1980 to 1987 and party chief from 1987 to May 1989) did what they could to open up the political system. Taking advantage of Deng's support for administrative reforms to improve the efficiency of the state, in 1986–1987 Zhao even drafted a blueprint that had the potential of introducing a limited form of political pluralism into the Chinese party-state.[13] Despite their positions as the top leaders, these two reformers did not have ultimate decision-making authority. Deng Xiaoping and the other aging revolutionary veterans wielded such power and made sure that Hu and Zhao, whose limited mandate was to implement Deng's economic reforms, would not condone liberalizing trends that could endanger one-party rule. Indeed, Deng purged these two reformers when they supported prodemocracy forces in defiance of Deng's expressed hard-line views. As the balance of power in the 1980s consistently favored political hard-liners such as Deng and Chen Yun, the odds for genuine and sustained liberalization were never great.

After the thorough purge of the liberal reformers following the crackdown in June 1989, such odds evaporated. In the post-Tiananmen era, the regime adopted a sophisticated survival strategy that relied on a diverse set of tools to ensure that economic development and globalization would not endanger the party's hold on power.[14] The party maintained broad-based popular support mainly by delivering rising prosperity. Regime legitimacy was also reinforced with appeals to nationalism.[15] To expand its base, the party carried out a concerted program to recruit capitalists, professionals, and intellectuals—new social elites whose support would help it rule a more diverse and complex society and economy.[16] The post-Tiananmen period also saw the rise of a security state equipped with a vast network of informants and advanced technology, underwritten by a massive increase in fiscal resources generated by the economic boom.[17] As a result of the party's response, rapid economic development in the post-Tiananmen era strengthened party power instead of weakening it.

Furthermore, the critical choices made by top CCP leaders in the 1980s, the party's effective adaptation in the post-Tiananmen era, and the unique institutional features of the CCP increased the difficulties of transition to a more open political system. Unlike average authoritarian regimes, such as personal dictatorships, military juntas, or non-Leninist one-party regimes, for instance Singapore's People's Action Party (PAP) and Mexico's Institutional Revolutionary Party (PRI) before 2000, Communist totalitarian regimes have a programmatic ideology, better-organized ruling parties, a more systematic use of terror as a means of rule, greater influence over the economy through planning and state-owned enterprises, more effective control of military and security forces, and an unrivaled capacity to dominate society and restrict the flow of information.[18]

These institutional features make it much more difficult to democratize a totalitarian regime than an authoritarian one. The transition to democracy in a garden-variety dictatorship usually involves the ruling elites' exit from power and the establishment of civilian control over the military. But in the case of totalitarianism, such a transition requires changes in practically every facet of the political system, economy, and society because totalitarian rule itself is deeply embedded in them. Piecemeal reform in a totalitarian regime is unlikely to have much of an impact in terms of changing the nature of the system because the old system will retain its totalitarian essence unless the most important institutional features of totalitarianism—above all the Leninist party-state—are removed.

A quick review of democratization in the former Communist regimes beginning in the late 1980s and culminating in the fall of the Soviet Union in December 1991 shows that this process was accomplished almost exclusively through revolution—the rapid overthrow of the Communist regimes. To be sure, the Communist regimes in Eastern Europe and the former Soviet Union in the late 1980s were post-totalitarian regimes that had abandoned some of the essential practices of classic totalitarianism, in particular the permanent purge and mass terror, but they still retained other defining features of totalitarianism, especially the Leninist party-state, a command economy, and near-total control of the flow of information. However, once it became clear that the Soviet Union would no longer intervene militarily to keep the Communist regimes in its satellite states in power, spontaneous revolutionary movements overthrew these regimes and replaced them with democracy.[19]

If the rapid downfall of the Soviet-backed Communist regimes in Eastern Europe is easier to explain, the collapse of the Soviet Union itself perhaps shows that even an indigenous Communist regime becomes vulnerable to revolution if it attempts to reform and weaken the foundational institutions of totalitarianism as part of a gradual process of political reform. In the Soviet case, reformist leader Mikhail Gorbachev introduced *glasnost* and *perestroika* in an attempt to revitalize the moribund system. But Gorbachev's gamble on openness, pluralism, and competition to create a more humane system quickly unleashed revolutionary forces, in particular nationalism in the republics of the empire. As reform turned into revolution, Gorbachev ultimately lost control and became the gravedigger of Soviet communism.[20]

Although the fall of the Soviet Union is the only case of the overthrow of a Communist regime founded by an indigenous revolution, it raises the question whether totalitarian regimes can be transformed into a democracy through reform, not revolution. Admittedly, the Soviet Union under Gorbachev was the only indigenous Communist regime that attempted to save the crisis-ridden system with political reform, not economic reform. Yet, because Gorbachev's *glasnost* and *perestroika* succeeded in dismantling the foundations of post-totalitarian rule (most critically the Communist party's political monopoly), the Soviet case remains the only instance in which a post-totalitarian regime was replaced by another political regime (a weak democracy in the Russian case). Instructively, indigenous Communist regimes such as China and Vietnam that embraced capitalism but resisted political liberalization have gained unprecedented economic prosperity but have also retained the key political institutions of totalitarianism.[21] The absence of democratization in such regimes implies that economic modernization alone is unlikely to result in the transition to a different political regime. Political reform that fatally weakens the foundational institutions of totalitarianism, as in the case of the Soviet Union in the late 1980s, may be the only path to democracy for a totalitarian or a post-totalitarian regime.

The preservation of the foundational institutions of totalitarianism—the Leninist party-state, near-total control of information, direct control of the military and the security apparatus, and decisive influence over the economy—also suggests that the revival of totalitarian rule in such regimes is not only possible but also likely if a strongman holds political dominance and decides to return the regime to its totalitarian roots. As totalitarianism in such regimes has never really been uprooted and its principal institutions remain essentially intact, restoring totalitarian rule faces far fewer obstacles than it does in regimes where totalitarianism has been largely dismantled.

How the China Dream Was Broken

When Deng Xiaoping launched his "reform and opening" in 1979, China finally had a chance to realize its dream of becoming a rich and strong country after enduring a "century of humiliation," the period between the start of the First Opium War in 1839 and the founding of the People's Republic of China in October 1949. Economically, the country enjoyed favorable structural conditions to embark on a fast-paced modernization drive. Unlike the Soviet Union, the state-socialist economic system had shallower roots and a more tenuous hold on China. Most of the population lived in the countryside—outside the inefficient state sector. The potential of tapping into the productive capacity suppressed by communism was enormous if the CCP could relax its restrictions on economic freedoms.[22] Diverse local conditions forced the state to allow a more decentralized system with greater potential for experimentation, innovation, and private entrepreneurship.[23] Demographically, China could reap the immense benefits of a vast young and healthy labor force if it were to adopt policies to make it more productive.[24] Geographically, China is located in the world's most economically dynamic region—East Asia—and could not only benefit from trade and investment with Japan, then Asia's economic powerhouse, but also gain from the development experience of the four little dragons, Taiwan, South Korea, Singapore, and Hong Kong, all of which were success stories of globalization.[25] Geopolitically, by the end of the 1970s, China had become a strategic partner of the West in the Cold War. Supporting China's modernization drive served the West's security interests.

While the preconditions for China's economic take-off at the end of the Maoist period were overwhelmingly positive, the preconditions for political liberalization or democratization were mostly negative. It is true that, ideologically, the calamity of the Cultural Revolution had thoroughly discredited Maoism, weakened the party's hold on Chinese society, and motivated Deng Xiaoping to adopt pro-market economic policies.[26] But most preconditions for genuine political liberalization or democratization were either nonexistent or downright unfavorable.

Crucially, the strategic choice made by the dominant Chinese leaders, mainly Deng Xiaoping and his conservative rival Chen Yun, was to repair and preserve the rule of the CCP, albeit with more pragmatic economic policies. They not only viewed political liberalization, let alone democratization, with intense hostility, but also they had launched periodic crackdowns in the 1980s to rein in any trends threatening the party's hold on power. Although liberal reformers were represented in the top echelons of the regime, they lacked the power to push the party toward greater political openness.

If the unfavorable balance of power at the top precluded the possibility of an elite-led transition toward a more open society, the likelihood of a transition driven by societal forces was vanishingly small due to the legacies of three decades of totalitarian rule. As the most repressive form of dictatorship in human history, totalitarianism concentrates power and resources in the party-state and seeks to eliminate all potential threats to its rule. In totalitarian regimes established through revolution, the process of consolidating power typically entails the brutal destruction of social forces deemed to be threats to regime survival.[27] Consequently, societal groups, such as independent civic organizations, religious groups, and business associations, are not permitted in totalitarian regimes. The private sector is either strictly controlled by or beholden to the state (as in the case of Nazi Germany), or almost completely banned (as under Communist rule).[28] In the Chinese case, societal forces that might have pressured the CCP to liberalize the political system were too weak to become politically significant. Even though these groups grew as the result of economic development, the restrictions imposed by the Chinese regime prevented them from becoming truly autonomous and effective political actors.[29]

Thus the party's monopoly of power faced no real threats from within or without. The most important consequence of the post-Mao rulers' decision to rely on economic reform to save the party was the preservation of the key institutions of totalitarianism. Indeed, except for the decline of the orthodox Communist ideology and erosion of the party's control of the economy, practically all other components of totalitarianism remained intact throughout the post-Mao period. To be sure, Deng and other Chinese leaders sought to set up guardrails to prevent the return of a Mao-like figure who could restore personalistic rule and again terrorize the party. Unfortunately, the specific measures on term limits and protection of the rights of party members that had been introduced in the 1980s were too narrow and vague (for example, they set no explicit age or term limits for Politburo members or for the general secretary). As rules and norms are unenforceable in a dictatorship and Chinese leaders' resistance to democratization and the rule of law made it impossible for enforcement by independent third parties (such as the courts, the press, or voters), the limited reforms adopted by Deng in the 1980s were inherently incapable of preventing the return of totalitarian rule. Fortunately for the party, and for China, the fragile balance of power among rival leaders and their factions between 1979 and 2012 sustained collective leadership and ensured the continuation of Deng's pragmatic policies.

During the pre-Xi period, however, totalitarianism was merely lying dormant. The party had suspended or curtailed policies and practices associated with classic totalitarianism, most importantly the mass terror and the near-total control of the economy. But as long as the party kept intact the foundational institutions of totalitarianism, the possibility of its revival was both real and substantial. All it would take was the return of a leader who, driven both by his ideological beliefs and his personal ambitions, found that the restoration of totalitarian rule would best serve his goals and interests. Because the limited reforms introduced by Deng were too weak or too flawed to preclude this scenario, the return of totalitarian rule, however unthinkable to many, remained a real possibility. Once a strongman were to gain power in the party, he would face no real opposition from within to make himself into a Mao-like figure, while the preservation of the essential institutions of totalitarianism would enable him to revive such a regime with relative ease.

In addition to the dormant totalitarian institutions, the flaws of Deng's neo-authoritarian developmentalism—economic modernization under one-party rule—were also responsible for the return of totalitarianism. Neo-authoritarian developmentalism rests on two pillars: repression of organized opposition and civil liberties, and a single-minded focus on economic development. However appealing in theory, neo-authoritarian developmentalism not only is unsustainable in practice but also creates political conditions favorable for the return of a totalitarian leader. Economic development under autocratic rule faces two insurmountable obstacles. The first is the lack of rule of law—the foundation of property rights and a market economy. As dictatorships are unwilling to be constrained by the rule of law and have short time horizons due to their insecurity, state predation is a structural feature of dictatorship. Property rights will therefore remain permanently insecure in countries ruled by dictatorships, thus undermining investor confidence and inherently limiting the economic potential of these countries.[30] The second hurdle is the trap of partial economic reform. A dictatorship desperate to gain political legitimacy by improving economic performance may initially be willing to adopt radical reforms, but it will have decreasing incentives to pursue further radical reforms because the early success of its reform strengthens its legitimacy and reduces the pressures for further change. Critically, economic reforms under dictatorial rule tend to become more difficult politically as they progress because the most radical or thorough reforms require a full empowerment of market forces, decentralization of resources, and a concomitant curtailment of the power of the state. As complete market reforms threaten to limit the ability of the ruling elites to use their power to extract economic benefits, such reforms become less attractive to the ruling elites, who become more reluctant to undertake them. Economic stagnation, not sustained dynamism, will likely follow.[31]

A combination of autocracy and a partial reform trap inevitably produces crony capitalism characterized by collusion between political elites and capitalists who use their connections with political elites to gain access to privileges and opportunities unavailable to those outside such networks. This union allows political elites in an autocracy to convert their power into wealth. As crony capitalism exacerbates inequality and corruption by privileging only the well-connected, it stokes social tensions and accelerates regime decay, thus creating opportunities for a strongman to seize power by weaponizing anticorruption investigations to destroy his political rivals and their networks.[32] This is precisely what happened after Xi became party chief in late 2012.

In retrospect, the relative ease with which Xi could turn back the clock and restore a form of totalitarian rule few had thought would be possible was not a random outcome of Chinese history in the post-Mao era. To be sure, the leader responsible for this great leap backward—Xi Jinping—might have been an accident, as his rise to the top echelons of the CCP was by no means preordained or inevitable. But in the larger political context of the post-Mao era, in particular the deliberate choices made by Deng and other hard-liners to maintain and defend the party's political monopoly at all costs, the preservation of the foundational institutions of totalitarianism, and the inherent flaws of Deng's neo-authoritarian developmentalism, the conditions for the revival of totalitarian rule were both ever-present and highly favorable. In other words, that the post-Mao reforms ended with a new form of totalitarian rule reminiscent of Stalinism was an accident waiting to happen.

Argument in Brief

Post-Mao China has experienced three distinct eras: the reform era of the 1980s, the neo-authoritarian era (1992–2012), and neo-Stalinist era under Xi Jinping since 2013.[33] Despite the identifiable ruptures between these eras, they are all connected by the logic of path dependence. Chinese leadership's strategic choices in one era narrow the range of options and potential paths forward in the subsequent eras as these choices produce outcomes that increase the probability of certain developments and decrease the probability of other developments in later periods.

Specifically, path dependence means that China had the widest range of options in the 1980s. During that decade, unsurprisingly, the intense struggle at the highest level of the Chinese leadership centered on the three potential paths forward. Hard-liners advocated returning to a communist system without Maoist radicalism. Pragmatic Leninists wanted to embrace capitalism to save a crisis-ridden regime. Liberal reformers tried to institute both political and economic reforms to steer the party away from its totalitarian roots. The decisive defeat of the liberals in 1989 eliminated the third option. In the post-Tiananmen period, pragmatic Leninists led by Deng seized the fall of the Soviet Union in December 1991 to rally a demoralized party to a neo-authoritarian path of capitalist development under one-party rule. This strategy in the subsequent two decades initially produced unprecedented economic dynamism but gradually succumbed to rapacious autocratic cronyism. The legacy of the post-Tiananmen order—pervasive official corruption, moribund market reforms, and sophisticated and effective repressive capacity—opened a potential path for a strongman to gain dominance and revert to totalitarian rule. Although the party could conceivably continue to plod along its post-Tiananmen path under a different leader, it was just as likely that it could embark on an entirely different path—one toward a new form of totalitarian rule under a strongman. If anything, the odds of revival of totalitarianism were even greater because a potential strongman could easily purge corruption-tainted rivals to seek supremacy within the regime. The same strongman could deploy totalitarian repressive practices to reimpose strict control over society because the coercive institutions of totalitarianism, such as a party-controlled military, the secret police, mass surveillance, and networks of informants, not only had been preserved, but also had been significantly upgraded with technology and investments in the post-Tiananmen era.

The logic of path dependence similarly illuminates the trajectory of Chinese economic development in the post-Mao era. Thanks to its favorable demographic structure, pent-up entrepreneurial energy in society, and cooperative relations with the West, the economy was poised for a massive and rapid take-off if the party dismantled the old Communist economic institutions and adopted pro-market policies. Even though China indeed experienced an economic "miracle" that was marked by three decades of high economic growth, Deng's strategic choice of using economic reform and globalization to sustain one-party rule inevitably resulted in the loss of momentum of reform. Dictated by the political imperative of preserving one-party rule, Deng and his successors simply could not risk ceding the "commanding heights" to the private sector and foreign investors. The principle of preventing market reform from undermining one-party rule would severely limit the growth of the private sector and shield the state-owned enterprises from competition, resulting in a hybrid economy that would eventually stagnate. Even worse, the same principle could also lead to the rollback of the private sector if the regime wants to contain the threats of capitalism. Seen from this perspective, the reversal of post-Mao economic reform under Xi is no accident.

China's relationship with the West in the post-Mao era cannot escape the confines of path dependence, either. National weakness, the Soviet threat, and the party's desperate need for Western support necessitated a pragmatist foreign policy prioritizing economic development over ideological conflict with the West. The United States and its allies opened their arms to reintegrate China into the West-led economic order in the 1980s, motivated by shared security interests and the tantalizing prospects that Chinese reforms could promote both economic prosperity and political freedom in the country. When the Tiananmen crackdown in 1989 abruptly ended China's strategic partnership with the West and revealed their unbridgeable ideological divide, the path to full integration was nearly closed. The success of the post-Deng regime in pursuing a grand strategy of "hiding strength and biding time" in the post–Cold War era only increased the odds of a new cold war later as a far more powerful China began to assert its newly acquired power and challenge the US-led order. With the arrival of Xi in late 2012, the combination of his ideological hostility, geopolitical ambitions, and strategic miscalculations—all of them direct or indirect consequences of the revival of totalitarian rule—would lead to a series of confrontations with the United States and its allies that eventually escalated to a new cold war.

Organization of the Book

To understand how political and economic developments since 1979 gradually narrowed the range of alternatives and increased the probability of the revival of totalitarian rule, this book uses a chronological approach to describe and analyze the most critical events, decisions, and factors that shaped the political and economic trajectories during three distinct periods in post-Mao China: the 1980s, the post-Tiananmen era, and the era of Xi Jinping. Chapter 1 focuses on elite politics and factional struggles over the direction of reform in the 1980s, the most politically open decade that ended with the tragic crackdown on the prodemocracy movement in June 1989. Chapter 2 reexamines the introduction of market-oriented reforms in the 1980s, with a special focus on how the rapid decollectivization of agriculture unleashed pent-up entrepreneurship and created a fast-growing private sector. In chapter 3 we dissect the neo-authoritarian political order, which the CCP constructed during the first decade of the post-Tiananmen era under Jiang Zemin's leadership. We explore how the CCP's adaptation of this neo-authoritarian political order enabled the regime to survive the shocks of the fall of communism in the former Soviet bloc and to confront the threats of economic modernization. Chapter 4 examines the policies adopted by the party during the Hu Jintao era to address the social deficits produced by neo-authoritarian rule, and it probes the factors that contributed to the unraveling of the post-Tiananmen order. In chapter 5 we analyze the drivers of China's rapid economic growth in the post-Mao era. Chapter 6 traces the rise of Xi Jinping and the return of totalitarian rule. The story of the end of China's economic miracle is told in chapter 7. In chapter 8 we review and analyze how China's engagement with the West in the post-Mao era eventually ended in a new cold war.

1

The Decisive Decade

AFTER DENG Xiaoping and his coalition partners ousted the transitional leader Hua Guofeng at the end of 1978, they faced the momentous strategic choice of deciding on a path forward for the party and the country. Ideological differences within Deng's coalition over the direction of economic reform resulted in constant clashes over economic policy and political liberalization. As a result, politics in the 1980s was marked by persistent tensions and power struggle at the highest level of the leadership of the Chinese Communist Party, culminating in the Tiananmen crisis in June 1989. On the surface, fluidity of elite politics in this period may imply a wide range of outcomes, including simultaneous pro-market reforms and political liberalization. In hindsight, however, the forces arrayed against such an outcome were simply too powerful to overcome. Nevertheless, the decade of the 1980s presented a narrow window of opportunity for China to embark on a different political path. Indeed, during that decade, the party attempted a series of institutional reforms, some aimed to make the regime less totalitarian and others designed to open up the political process in a more pluralistic and accountable direction. Tragically, the Tiananmen crackdown foreclosed this narrow path toward an alternative—and arguably better—future. The purge of the liberals from the CCP leadership and Deng's success in forging an elite consensus on capitalist economic development under one-party rule put China on an entirely different path in the post-Tiananmen era.

Broadly speaking, this period can be divided into three phases, each marked with its distinct characteristics of struggle over power and policy among the party's top leaders. In the first phase (1979–1986), China's era of reform and opening was launched, and rapid progress in economic reform was made. It was also a period of relative political openness, in spite of one short-lived conservative backlash at the end of 1983. Assisted by two liberal reformers, Hu

Yaobang as CCP chief and Zhao Ziyang as premier, Deng was able to decollectivize agriculture, reintegrate China into the global economy, and implement the reforms to enable a private sector to emerge and grow. Politically, he also enacted modest changes to institute collective leadership, mandatory retirement, and measures to introduce fresh blood into the party.

But the informal coalition that toppled Hua Guofeng, the transitional leader who had seized power in October 1976 and effectively ended the Cultural Revolution, fractured during this phase because of incompatible visions about China's future. As he shared the conservative political values of the hard-liners led by Chen Yun but clashed with them on economic policy, Deng played a pivotal balancing role in this phase. As reform unleashed growing societal pressure for political liberalization, the rift between Deng and the liberal wing of the party widened, ultimately resulting in Deng's dismissal of Hu in January 1987.

In the second phase, 1987–1988, momentum of reform slowed down despite an abortive attempt to introduce comprehensive political reform in 1987. Hu's ouster not only weakened the liberals in the party but also undermined Deng's own ability to overcome resistance to further economic reform by the newly emboldened hard-liners. After Deng filled Hu's vacancy with Zhao, he effectively ceded the control of economic policy to the conservatives who took over the State Council. Even before the Tiananmen crisis in 1989, the third and final phase, Deng's reform and opening had stalled. Siding again with hard-liners during the most critical moments of the crisis, Deng stained his historical legacy by ordering the military to suppress the peaceful prodemocracy movement. Even worse, the wholesale purge of the liberals within the party and the worst rupture with the West in the wake of the crackdown threatened a premature demise of Deng's cherished project of reform and opening. As a result, the decade of the 1980s began with hope and optimism for a new future but ended with one of the darkest and bloodiest incidents in modern Chinese history.

Ideological Divisions in the Party

On October 6, 1976, a military-backed coup led to the arrest of the infamous "Gang of Four," a radical clique that included, among three others, the widow of Mao Zedong, the brutal dictator who had died less than a month earlier. The news of the fall of Mao's closest and most reviled followers quickly set off spontaneous celebrations throughout China. The victor in this succession struggle, Hua Guofeng, was immediately installed as China's new leader. He assumed positions as chairman of the Chinese Communist Party and of the Central Military Commission (CMC), as well as premier of the State Council (China's cabinet).[1]

When the 55-year-old Hua took over the party, his position seemed unassailable. Among the twelve voting members of the Politburo, none presented a potential threat. The group that could possibly dethrone Hua was nowhere near the center of power at the end of 1976. Many had already been purged, sidelined, incarcerated, or murdered by Mao during the Cultural Revolution (1966–1976). Among those who had survived physically, Deng Xiaoping, age 72, had been dismissed from all his positions in the party-state by Mao six months earlier. Chen Yun, age 71, a capable economic planner who had ranked number 5 in the party hierarchy in 1956, at the time of Mao's death was simply a member of the Central Committee after falling out of favor with Mao before the Cultural Revolution.

However, rule by the "wise leader," as Hua was then called, was brief. The writing was on the wall when revolutionary veterans forced him to bring back to office the victims of the Cultural Revolution. In July 1977 Deng regained all the leadership positions he had lost after the Tiananmen protests of April 1976, including membership on the Politburo Standing Committee (PSC), vice premier, and chief of the General Staff Department of the People's Liberation Army (PLA).[2] At a Central Committee plenum in December 1978, Hua lost a decisive power struggle to a coalition of revolutionary veterans and reformers.[3] Although he did not officially resign his position as chairman of the CCP until June 1981, the coup that brought him to the pinnacle of power had merely paved the way for the return of victims of the Cultural Revolution, who shared little else beyond a desire to depose Hua and to end Mao's self-destructive radicalism that had brought the country to the brink of ruin and endangered the party's hold on power.

The informal grand coalition that ousted Hua in December 1978 was led by Deng and Chen, both titans in the Communist revolution. Deng became the head of the Secretariat of the Central Committee in 1927 when he was only 23 years old. During the civil war (1945–1949), Deng co-commanded the Second Field Army that performed brilliantly in defeating the Nationalists. Between the establishment of the People's Republic in 1949 and the outbreak of the Cultural Revolution in 1966, he had served in a series of top-level party and government positions. In fact, as the seventh-ranked party leader on the eve of the Cultural Revolution, Deng had the dubious honor of being lumped together with Liu Shaoqi, Mao's designated successor, as one of China's top two "capitalist roaders" when Mao unleashed the Red Guards on his enemies in the party in the summer of 1966.

Chen Yun's revolutionary credentials were no less illustrious. He was made a member of the Politburo when he was 29. In fact, even though he was one year younger, he had greater seniority than Deng. After the party emerged victorious in the civil war in 1949, Chen became a vice premier, playing an instrumental role in crafting the First Five-Year Plan and constructing the basic framework for a command economy. However, he fell out of favor with Mao in 1958 because he cautioned against Mao's unrealistically ambitious economic targets. But being sidelined by Mao later turned out to be a blessing in disguise. While most of Mao's enemies were politically hounded or even physically liquidated during the Cultural Revolution, Chen escaped persecution and even managed to retain his seat on the Central Committee.

Although Deng and Chen played the most important roles in the decisive defeat of Hua and his supporters in December 1978, they were assisted by more liberal-leaning but lower-ranked leaders in the party. The two most prominent representatives of this wing were Hu Yaobang and Zhao Ziyang. Prior to the Cultural Revolution, Hu was the head of the Communist Youth League (CYL), an auxiliary organization of the party that had no real administrative responsibility. A victim of Mao's purge during the decade of chaos, Hu became a supporter of Deng when the latter briefly returned to power in 1973–1975. In the campaign to unseat Hua Guofeng as party leader, Hu made two crucial contributions. Wielding his administrative authority as the head of the party's organization department, he helped rehabilitate a large number of victims of Mao's purges and facilitated their return to positions of power within the party-state.[4] In addition, as Hua continued to rely on Maoism as his source of political legitimacy, Hu Yaobang organized a series of articles in 1978 debating the "criterion of truth." Behind this seemingly esoteric philosophical project was the intent to discredit Maoism as the guiding political doctrine of the party and weaken Hua's claim to rule.[5]

Zhao Ziyang, who had served as provincial party chief in Guangdong, Inner Mongolia, and Sichuan before and during the Cultural Revolution, did not play a direct role in the power struggle in 1978 that made Deng the paramount leader. Zhao had had little prior contact with Deng, but because he implemented bold and successful agricultural reforms in Sichuan in the late 1970s when he was the provincial party chief, Deng picked him to succeed Hua as premier in September 1980.[6]

In an illuminating history of elite conflict in the 1980s, Yang Jisheng persuasively argues that the grand coalition later collapsed into three forces, each with its own distinct ideological values and political agenda. The conflict among these three groups, in Yang's view, defines the politics and shapes the Chinese political and economic trajectories during the decade.[7] The forces represented by Chen Yun were hardcore conservatives seeking to maintain the orthodox Communist ideology and the Leninist one-party regime and to return to the pragmatic but essentially state-socialist economic policy and development strategy of the 1950s. The second group, led by Deng, shared the same political objective of preserving the Leninist party-state, but it differed from the conservatives in terms of the economic means by which to reach this goal. As Zhao Ziyang observed, although the elders, such as Deng and Chen, disagreed on economic reform, they had indistinguishable views on maintaining the existing political system. They feared "any real reform would challenge the Communist Party, undermine its power, and weaken its rule."[8] Unlike Chen Yun, who was enamored of the Soviet planned economy and took enormous pride in his own role in establishing China's command economy in the early 1950s, Deng was convinced that only an efficient market economy integrated with the capitalist West could save the party.

The third group, represented by a slightly younger cohort of more open-minded leaders, such as Hu Yaobang and Zhao Ziyang, sought both pro-market economic reforms and political liberalization because they believed that economic and political reforms were both needed to change a China that had been impoverished and brutalized by Maoism.[9]

Of these three groups, the most powerful were the first two factions: the conservatives led by Chen who wanted to return to the 1950s and the neo-authoritarians represented by Deng who believed that Chinese economic modernization, the sole means of regime survival, could succeed only with a combination of capitalism and autocracy. The political strength of the conservatives and the neo-authoritarians was derived mainly from the personal prestige of their most senior leaders, such as Deng, Chen, and other elderly revolutionaries. They wielded ultimate power on major policy and personnel decisions.

Another source of the political strength of the conservatives and neo-authoritarians was their extensive network of supporters in the bureaucracy of the party-state and the military. Because the conservatives had been in charge of the economy, propaganda, and organization before the Cultural Revolution, they had groomed a group of younger hard-liners whom they appointed to key positions in the party and government. Although Deng had fewer followers in the state and party bureaucracies, he had unrivaled control of the military because he had elevated many of his former subordinates in the Second Field Army to senior PLA positions, such as the General Staff Department and the Secretariat of the CMC, which oversaw the PLA's day-to-day affairs.

The sources of political support for the liberals were diverse. Within the party, they could count on a small number of (less influential) revolutionary veterans at the center of power, such as Xi Zhongxun (father of Xi Jinping and a member of the party's Central Secretariat), Wan Li (a vice premier credited with launching the agricultural reforms when he was party chief of Anhui province at the end of the 1970s), and provincial party chiefs in Guangdong and Fujian. The most vocal group of supporters of the liberals was made up of the intelligentsia. This group was extremely valuable to the liberals because they could provide ideas for reform and expose the ideological bankruptcy of the conservatives. However, the intelligentsia had no real political power and could, from time to time, create problems for the liberals in the party when they pushed too hard for political change.

The greatest weakness of the liberals is that they relied almost exclusively on Deng's support for their effectiveness and survival. If Deng sided with the liberals on economic reform, they could overcome the opposition from the conservatives. But when Deng threw his weight behind the conservatives in cracking down on "bourgeois liberalization" in 1987, the liberals were sure to lose (as in the downfall of Hu Yaobang in 1987 and the Tiananmen crisis in 1989). The liberals also likely underappreciated Deng's ruthlessness and unreliability at the most crucial junctures. To Deng, the liberal reformers were useful but ultimately dispensable. He needed them to fight the conservative opposition to pro-market reforms and an opening to the West. But Deng's support for them had a bottom line: When they defied him on the most important issue of preserving monopoly rule by the party, he would not hesitate to cast them aside.

The unfavorable balance of power among the conservatives, centrists, and liberals shaped the outcomes of the key battles over economic and political reform in the 1980s. Out of necessity, Deng had to rely on the liberal wing of the party to overcome conservative opposition to his economic reform agenda. As a result, he could form a winning coalition with the liberals in most battles over economic policy. At the same time, however, to defend against any threats to party rule, Deng consistently banded together with the hard-liners in lashing out against liberalizing trends and prodemocracy forces. Put another way, the differences between Deng and Chen were tactical, not fundamental. Both were determined to preserve one-party rule, but Deng believed that pro-market reform and opening to the West could better serve this ultimate objective than the closed command economy that Chen advocated. Obviously, post-Mao history vindicated Deng. Nevertheless, the differences between Deng and the liberals were fundamental and irreconcilable. The objective of the liberals was to build both a market economy and a political system in which party power would be curtailed by rule of law and would be withdrawn from the state. (Even though the liberal intelligentsia advocated a multiparty democracy, few liberal leaders, least of all Hu Yaobang and Zhao Ziyang, envisioned any replacement of CCP rule with a competitive democracy.) In retrospect, the fundamental agreement between the hard-liners and Deng made it inconceivable that the liberals, the weakest of the political forces in the party, could have prevailed in the most crucial battles over the direction of reform in the 1980s, such as the handling of the prodemocracy movements at the end of 1986 and during the Tiananmen protest movement in April and May of 1989.

Institutionalizing Elite Politics

High on the agenda of the grand coalition in the early 1980s was the implementation of institutional reforms to protect the party from the rise of another Mao-like figure and to reinvigorate party leadership. Deng initially summarized the overall framework for these reforms in a landmark speech at an enlarged Politburo meeting in August 1980.[10] Considered the most open-minded and searing diagnosis of the pathologies in China's political system, this speech laid out a set of measures to mitigate these flaws. From Deng's perspective, the most serious institutional flaws in the Chinese party-state and their manifestations included the "overconcentration of power, patriarchal methods, life tenure in leading posts, and privileges of various kinds."[11] Deng also decried "feudalism" (which really meant an autocratic mindset) and the phenomenon of "paternalism," which he defined as a form of despotism that led to the dominance of the individual over the party organization. Most likely Deng had Mao in mind because he blamed "paternalism" for the egregious harm that had been inflicted on the party.

Reforms to address these flaws, according to Deng, should include collective leadership, which meant the party chief would have to share decision-making authority with his colleagues. Another solution was to abolish lifetime tenure of cadres and to make improvements in the selection, appointment, evaluation, transfer, and dismissal of cadres. Intriguingly, although Deng said that reform of the political system could provide institutional safeguards for "democratization" of the political life of the party and the state, he stopped well short of calling for democratic reforms. Instead, he merely said that research and investigation were needed to learn from other countries' experiences and to produce practical plans. To underscore his belief in the centrality of the party-state, Deng said that "the reform of the system of party and state leadership is precisely to maintain and further strengthen party leadership and discipline, and not to weaken or relax them," because "without such a party, our country will split up and accomplish nothing."[12]

If anything, this speech revealed the limitations of Deng's vision of political reform. To be sure, he correctly identified the most serious symptoms of the pathologies of the Chinese political system. But the immediate solutions he proposed—abolishing lifetime tenure and improving the cadre management system—were purely technical or organizational. He focused almost exclusively on how to address the problems within the party but did not show much interest in dealing with the problems between the party-state and Chinese society caused by the lack of rule of law and democracy. Neither did he have a clear idea about how to establish enforceable mechanisms within the party to mitigate the overconcentration of power, feudalism, and paternalism. Most critically, by cautioning against reforms that would undermine the party's political monopoly, Deng effectively ruled out the empowerment of Chinese society or the establishment of rule of law as potential autonomous forces that could safeguard the new institutional rules and norms.

Such inherent limitations and contradictions notwithstanding, Deng's call for establishing the principle of collective leadership, norms of political conduct within the party, and formal rules on retirement age and term limits resonated with conservatives and liberals alike. As victims of Mao's tyrannical rule, they had no disagreement on the need to implement reforms to bring more stability and predictability into the inner workings of the party as an organization.

Thanks to the consensus within the party on collective leadership, security of elites, and rules on age and term limits, the post-Mao leadership quickly passed several historic documents that constituted the CCP's most serious effort to institutionalize. As we will see, however, these institutional reforms had severe limitations because Deng and the veteran revolutionaries did not observe them. Most key provisions were deliberately vague so as to grant top leaders sufficient discretion. Institutional reforms to separate the party from the state, which Deng sanctioned in late 1986, were doomed from the start because he was adamantly opposed to any reform that could weaken the party's power and result in some form of checks and balances. Taken together, the institutional reforms of the party-state in the 1980s were administrative in nature and largely superficial. They did not touch on the defining feature of a totalitarian regime: dominance and control of the state apparatus by the party. Consequently, instead of a transition from totalitarian to authoritarian rule, the institutional reforms of the party-state in the 1980s succeeded in preserving the core of a totalitarian regime.

The party laid out its most important principles and norms in a key document, "Guiding Principles for Inner-Party Political Life," in February 1980.[13] Besides reiterating the sacrosanct principle of loyalty to the party, this Central Committee document emphasized collective leadership and decried "personal arbitrary decision-making," obviously a veiled reference to Mao's personalistic rule. Thus it specified that all key decisions were to be discussed and approved by the party committee or standing committee at each level, and not by an individual—a provision Deng himself honored only in the breach. The resolution explicitly banned activities or rituals that could promote a "personality cult."

The document encouraged "democracy in the party" and called on the party to "correctly treat different views." It expressly prohibited the practice of exaggerating party members' mistakes or persecuting them under false pretenses. Party members had the right to participate in discussions of party policies (but only at meetings organized by the party or in party publications). They could make appeals and presentations to superior party organizations on disciplinary decisions related to themselves or other people.

In practical terms, perhaps the most important reform the party adopted in the early 1980s was the mandatory age limit for most party and government officials and term limits for top government positions. The party had urgent reason to persuade a large group of aging revolutionary veterans (roughly 2.5 million) to vacate their leadership positions to make way for younger and better-educated people. More important, the institution of mandatory retirement and term limits would also improve predictability of promotion and elite circulation, retain the loyalty of ambitious younger elites, and ensure vigor among the ruling elites.[14] In the party's February 1982 decision on establishing a retirement system for "veteran cadres," the retirement age limit of ministers, provincial party chiefs and governors, and heads of provincial high courts and procuratorates was set at 65. Their deputies were required to retire at age 60. Officials at the rank of director general (bureau-level) were not to serve beyond 60 under normal circumstances.[15] When the Chinese constitution was overhauled in 1982, it also instituted a two-term limit for the presidency (a largely symbolic position) and for the premier.

Although the institutional reforms in the early 1980s constituted a real and positive step toward making political life within the party-state less brutal and less arbitrary, they had serious limitations. In terms of age and term limits, it is notable that Deng and his colleagues deliberately exempted the most senior leaders. For instance, such limits were not imposed on members of the Central Committee, the Politburo, the PSC, or the chair of the CMC. This omission, as we will see later, was to have profound—and negative—consequences during the remainder of the post-Mao period. Another noteworthy loophole in the mandatory retirement system was that the age limit could be waived if continuing service by the official was "needed."

The most critical flaw of all the institutional reforms, whether in terms of the political norms within the party or the age and term limits, is the lack of credible enforcement mechanisms. For any rules or norms to be binding, the most effective institutional arrangement is the designation of a third party, in this case an organization independent of the CCP, to enforce them. However, none of the reforms implemented in the early 1980s contained provisions on third-party enforcement. Instructively, when the National People's Congress (NPC) was discussing a major overhaul of the constitution between September 1980 and October 1982, a key issue was whether to establish an institution to ensure compliance with the constitution. One proposal was to form a specialized constitutional committee within the NPC. However, Deng vetoed the idea. As a result, the Chinese constitution has no provisions for ensuring compliance.[16]

Two factors lay behind the limitations of the institutional reforms undertaken by the CCP in the early 1980s. Politically, Deng and the other aging leaders did not want to be bound by any rules in their own exercise of power. They not only wielded power behind the scenes but also openly violated the key provisions laid out in the "Guiding Principles for Inner-Party Political Life." For example, instead of convening meetings of the PSC, Deng spoke directly to key leaders to issue instructions, thus bypassing his archrival, Chen Yun. Important personnel decisions were made by party elders, not by the general secretary. Zhao Ziyang revealed that "leaders at my level could not make important personnel decisions. That was true when Yaobang was the general secretary. Sometimes we did not even have the opportunity to participate in discussing such decisions. Only a small number of elders were consulted. Such decisions could be made only when Xiaoping and Chen Yun reached an agreement between them."[17] Even though the guiding principles ostensibly permitted party members to voice different opinions and prohibited their persecution, after the start of the anti–bourgeois liberalization campaign in January 1987, Deng himself named several liberal party members who would be slated for punishment. It was only stalling by Zhao that allowed most of the people on Deng's list to be saved.[18]

An even more critical factor is the impossibility of enforcing any rules and norms in an autocracy. As many theorists have noted, institutions function only when the rulers' commitments to uphold them are enforceable.[19] Normally, the most effective mechanisms of enforcement are those that rely on third parties, such as independent courts, a free press, and civil society. Such third-party enforcers do not exist in autocratic regimes. Counting on autocrats to self-enforce their commitments is unreliable because the temptations to gain political advantage and power by violating the rules and norms are often too great to resist. Rules and norms may be enforceable in an autocracy only when the balance of power is equally distributed among dueling factions, making it costly for any one faction to violate them.

In the Chinese case, due to Deng's determination to suppress prodemocracy forces that could undermine the party's monopoly of power, it was impossible for third parties to emerge and help enforce the very rules and norms that Deng thought would help make political life inside the CCP more stable and predictable. The contradictions between Deng's goals of institutionalizing the CCP and his aversion to any reforms that might weaken CCP power ultimately would render his reforms partial, ineffective, and short-lived.

Clashing Visions of Economic Reform

Two fundamentally different visions of the future of the Chinese economy divided the conservatives, led by Chen Yun, and the Deng-liberal coalition. The reform agenda of the latter emphasized opening to the outside world and implementing market reforms, while the conservatives tried to preserve the command economy that had been established in the 1950s and maintained a skeptical attitude toward market reforms and integration with the West-dominated global economy.[20] In terms of policy, the two groups differed on the pace and scope of rural reform, domestic economic liberalization (such as development of a private sector), and economic growth rates.[21] Chen and

Deng also disagreed on foreign policy (Chen liked the Soviet Union and did not trust the United States, whereas Deng favored good ties with the United States and took a hard line toward the Soviet Union).[22]

Ideologically, Chen consistently advocated that central planning must determine economic activities, with the market playing only a secondary role. To use his famous analogy, the planned economy was the cage and the market was the bird living inside the cage. The market could operate freely—but only within the confines of the planned economy.[23] In contrast, Deng and the liberals saw a market-oriented economy as China's future.[24]

At the beginning of the 1980s, Chen's opposition to the economic reforms was more measured, even nuanced. As a fiscal hawk who preferred lower growth to deficit-spending, he repeatedly gave speeches affirming the dominant role of the planned economy, urging fiscal conservatism, and cautioning against hasty reforms.[25] But on occasion, he would show support for Zhao's reformist policies. Nevertheless, despite the early achievements of the economic reforms, Chen continued to insist on maintaining the dominant role of planning. Consequently, his opposition to the economic reforms—and his policy differences with the reformers—intensified.[26]

The area where Deng and Chen diverged and clashed the most was opening China to the capitalist West. As opening was key to the success of the domestic reforms, Deng strongly advocated policies welcoming foreign investment. He enthusiastically supported the proposal to establish special economic zones (SEZs) in Guangdong and Fujian in April 1979, and within a year he fast-tracked a package of policies granting Shenzhen, Xiamen, Shantou, and Zhuhai autonomy to attract foreign investment and trade.[27] In 1984 he visited some of the SEZs to show his support. As Deng said to Zhao and Hu in February 1982, "The SEZs are a window through which [we can] bring in technology, management, and knowledge."[28] In October 1984 Deng countered the conservatives' criticisms of his policy of opening, declaring, "Some of our comrades are always worried that if we open up, undesirable things may be brought into China. Above all, they worry that the country might go capitalist. . . . Of course, some negative elements will come in, and we must be aware of that. But it will not be difficult for us to overcome them. . . . If we isolate ourselves and close our doors again, it will be absolutely impossible for us to approach the level of the developed countries in fifty years."[29] Although Deng did not name Chen, he most likely was referring to him.

On the issue of opening, as Zhao observed, Chen Yun "was completely at odds with [Deng] Xiaoping. . . . Chen Yun was very cautious about foreign investments. The case file for the Shanghai-Volkswagen joint venture remained in his office for a long time before he finally gave his consent."[30] As reflected in his speeches on foreign trade and investment, Chen was consistently skeptical about, if not hostile to, the idea of economic engagement with the capitalist West. In December 1980 he opposed borrowing from the West or from the World Bank to finance imports of capital goods, and he called for "vigilance in welcoming foreign capitalists." On foreign trade, Chen had a zero-sum mindset, continuing to worry that competition among Chinese exporters would allow foreign trade partners to benefit. He therefore advocated retreating to a centralized foreign trade system to avoid "losses." Chen was especially skeptical about the SEZs. In 1982 he warned that if more SEZs were allowed, "foreign capitalists and domestic speculators will come out in droves, and speculation will be rampant. That must not be allowed."[31] Instead of promoting the SEZs, Chen urged a pause and, to show his opposition, never set foot in any of the SEZs. In all likelihood, Chen's opposition to opening arose from his fears of the ideological influence of the West, not just its economic clout. He called on the party to "pay attention to the negative things brought in by opening to the outside." In particular he worried that exposure to the developed capitalist West could lead people to believe that socialism is inferior to capitalism.[32]

Yet, despite Chen's consistent opposition to market reforms, he was constantly outmaneuvered by Deng and the liberals in the early 1980s because Zhao Ziyang was in direct charge of economic policy at the State Council and generally implemented Deng's policies, even though he would also consult with Chen out of deference.[33] Because of their sharp differences over the economic reforms, Deng developed a strategy to undercut Chen's role in economic policy making. He rarely held PSC meetings (which would have given Chen an opportunity to present his opposing views and potentially to force Deng to water down his reformist policies). Instead, Deng would approach Zhao and Hu Yaobang directly and give them instructions. At one point, a frustrated Chen asked Zhao why no PSC meetings were being held. Zhao, then serving as CCP acting general secretary, replied "I am only a big secretary. If you want to have meetings, you should first reach an agreement with Comrade Xiaoping."[34]

Partial Political Reforms

In addition to the institutional reforms focusing on party leadership, Deng also promoted two important reforms to modernize the legal system and restore the function of the NPC. He supported these reforms not because he intended to promote the rule of law and multiparty democracy but because he saw instrumental value in them. Specifically, restoring the legislative function of the NPC could give party policies a veneer of popular and procedural legitimacy. After all, CCP Central Committee resolutions were, strictly speaking, documents issued by a political party that lacked the same legal force as the national legislature. Much dearer to Deng's heart was the use of law to create a friendlier legal environment to attract foreign investment.

Therefore, from the very beginning, party efforts to introduce legal reforms were focused on passage of the essential commercial laws that underpinned a market economy, such as a contract law, foreign investment law, and company law.[35] Additionally, the legal profession, abolished during the Maoist era, was rebuilt. Law schools were reopened to train legal professionals. Courts and procuratorates, previously heavily staffed by discharged military officers with little legal training, were gradually filled with more qualified personnel. Citizens enjoyed better legal protections as the state was forced to observe some form of legal procedures.[36] Despite progress toward establishing a modern legal system, the party-sanctioned legal reforms in the 1980s were inherently limited. The supremacy of the CCP meant that the party continued to remain above the law and maintained tight control over the courts and procuratorates. Protection of human rights and property rights was spotty. Fragmented authoritarianism, a unique feature of the Chinese regime, meant that the implementation of law and the enforceability of judgments could not be ensured at local levels or across different jurisdictions.[37] To be sure, the reforms that took place in the legal arena during the 1980s marked a significant improvement over the lawlessness of the Mao era, but they made only modest progress toward establishing rule of law.[38]

In addition to these legal reforms, the party also gave the NPC a more prominent procedural role in policymaking. Institutionally, the NPC was strengthened by the formation of specialized committees, the establishment of formal legislative procedures, and the recruitment of a more professional staff. Politically, the NPC gained status with the appointment of heavyweight political figures as chairs of its Standing Committee. On occasion, delegates to the annual NPC sessions could voice their views on public policy and even register symbolic disapproval of government performance with "no" votes or abstentions to the work reports of the premier and the presidents of the People's Supreme Court and the People's Supreme Procuratorate. Similar institutional developments, albeit to a lesser degree, also occurred at the local levels.[39] Although these modest reforms made the NPC a more important actor in Chinese politics, they fell far short of establishing functional constraints on the power of the party, which controlled all key appointments to the NPC, set its legislative agenda, and used it mainly as an instrument to legitimatize its policies.

Attempt at Comprehensive Political Reform, 1986–1987

If there were one brief window of opportunity for the party to implement genuine political reforms to dismantle its totalitarian institutional foundations, it was an attempt undertaken by Zhao Ziyang in 1986–1987 with Deng's support. The paramount leader unexpectedly put political reform on the agenda in the summer of 1986 mainly because he was frustrated by the slow pace of reform in urban areas, which he attributed to obstruction by an inefficient party-dominated administrative apparatus, an assessment shared by Zhao as well.[40] In June 1986 Deng told leading members of the Central Committee: "Early in 1980 it was suggested that we reform the political structure, but no concrete measures to do so were worked out. Now it is time for us to place political reform on the agenda . . . to create the necessary conditions for sustained economic growth," warning that "otherwise economic restructuring and economic growth will be retarded."[41]

However, Deng's definition and objective of "political system reform" differed fundamentally from Zhao's. As Zhao pointed out, Deng's "political system reform was no more than a form of administrative reform." His idea of such a reform was not "real political modernization or democratization." As his goal of undertaking such reform was "to solidify further the CCP's one-party dictatorship," Deng resolutely rejected "any reform that could affect or weaken the CCP's one-party dictatorship."[42] By contrast, Zhao believed that the ultimate objective of political system reform was to "change the party's complete monopoly of power . . . so as to establish gradually a democratic and accountable system with the CCP as the ruling party." (Zhao also believed that Hu Yaobang shared the same vision even though Hu had not said much about political reform publicly.)[43] Even though Zhao's concept of political system reform fell short of full democratization, it was much more comprehensive and radical than anything Deng entertained. In Zhao's judgment, Deng's framing of political system reform represented a retreat from his famous speech of 1980 on the same subject because it narrowly confined reform to "separating the party from the government, decentralizing power, streamlining bureaucracy, and improving efficiency."[44]

Because Deng had lost trust in Hu Yaobang by the summer of 1986, he assigned Zhao the task of drawing up a comprehensive political system reform plan. In September Zhao formed a small group, innocuously called the "Central Research Small Group on Political System Reform," and chaired it himself. To carry out research and to draft the reform program, Zhao appointed his top aide, Bao Tong, to direct the special office supporting the "Small Group." Bao recruited a team of liberal intellectuals to staff this office.[45]

For the next twelve months, Bao's team labored in secrecy to produce a blueprint of a comprehensive reform that would be acceptable to Deng but would also accomplish Zhao's goal of introducing modest reforms that, in totality, could help the party-state make the transition from totalitarianism to authoritarianism. Despite Deng's restrictive remit, Zhao supported Bao's team in its exploration of a broad range of sensitive topics beyond the priorities laid out by Deng, in particular the "separation of the party from the government."

Ironically, Zhao's group had more freedom than it appeared mainly because Deng did not define what he meant by "separating the party from the government." For example, the group determined that "the party's supervision of cadres" did not mean that the party should make specific appointments. Instead, a civil service system needed to be established as soon as possible, a first step toward extricating the party from the state.[46] Besides defining the scope of "separating the party from the government" more broadly, Zhao's task force also veered off in more sensitive directions. It discussed how to institute "inner-party democracy," a topic not on Deng's list of reforms. In addition, the group explored the most sensitive issue of democratization by convening seminars on establishing channels through which various interest groups could engage in dialogue and consult with one another, and on the holding of competitive local elections to select delegates to local people's congresses.[47]

After Zhao delivered to Deng the blueprint of the reform, titled "Overall Design for Political System Reform," in late May 1987, Deng immediately spotted the potential in the plan to establish mechanisms of checks and balances that could undermine the party's monopoly of power. Reiterating his opposition to a "separation of powers," Deng chided Zhao for "introducing some separation of powers," even though the plan did not explicitly state this concept. Deng again emphasized that the Chinese system was superior because it did not have to face interference from interest groups and because decisions made by the leaders could be implemented immediately. Deng warned that this superiority must not be abandoned just to appease "sentiments for democracy."[48]

Deng's veiled but unmistakable criticism forced Zhao's group to scramble to revise the blueprint so that it could win his support. Two months later, Deng approved the revised draft of the "Overall Design"—but only after instructing Zhao to insert the following sentence: "[We] will never institute the Western practice of a tripartite separation of powers and rotation of powers among multiple parties."[49] In September 1987 the Politburo approved the final draft of the Overall Design "in principle." But even Deng's support failed to produce a resounding endorsement by the party (most likely because Deng did not actively promote the plan). When Zhao tabled the Overall Design for discussion at a Central Committee meeting in mid-October 1987, many members expressed reservations or different views. As a result, he decided not to have the plenum vote on the document because he feared a potential setback. Instead of "approving" it, the plenum's communiqué stated that the Central Committee "discussed and agreed in principle with the 'Overall Design.'"[50]

The text of the Overall Design was never made public. Based on the recollections of one of the drafters, this document likely stated the guiding principles for political reform and established its objectives in general terms.[51] After the Central Committee "agreed in principle" with the Overall Design in late October 1987, Zhao implemented several modest but substantive reforms. To promote inner-party democracy, he made the selection of members of the Central Committee at the Thirteenth Party Congress slightly more competitive. As a result, 185 candidates competed for the 175 slots on the committee. The archconservative Deng Liqun suffered a humiliating defeat when he was among the ten candidates who failed to get enough votes to serve. Competitive elections for provincial governors and the presidents of the provincial high courts and procuratorates were also introduced in some provinces, resulting in the defeat of a small number of CCP-nominated candidates.[52]

In an attempt to institutionalize the decision-making process, the Politburo supported Zhao's proposal to regularize meetings of the party's Central Committee, Politburo, and the PSC (two plenums of the Central Committee per year; a monthly Politburo meeting; and a weekly PSC meeting). Additionally, again at Zhao's suggestion, the Politburo formalized the procedural rules for voting in the Politburo, the PSC, and the Central Secretariat, and it mandated that the decisions of each Central Committee plenum and every meeting of the Politburo be made public via the media. (Remarkably, the party still follows some of these rules established by Zhao.)[53]

Unsurprisingly, the reform to "separate the party from the government" encountered strong opposition because it threatened both the power and the job security of a large number of apparatchiks. Nevertheless, local authorities began to carry out the leadership's guidelines on restructuring the party's role in government, such as reducing the number of party secretaries and full-time cadres and abolishing local party departments that were functionally redundant to their government counterparts. Zhao made only marginal progress in the central government. The party's "small groups" in finance, propaganda, foreign affairs, and political-legal work were kept intact, but they could no longer directly intervene or supervise the administrative tasks of the government. About half of the party groups in the State Council had been abolished by early 1989. Of all the measures to "separate the party from the government," the most important implemented by Zhao was abolition of the Central Political-Legal Committee, which oversaw law enforcement and the courts. To prevent this powerful body from interfering in the legal system, in 1988 Zhao downgraded it to a "small group." He also instituted an administrative leadership responsibility system by giving managers, presidents, and directors of state-owned enterprises (SOEs), universities, and public institutions sole administrative responsibilities, thus downsizing the role of the party chiefs.[54]

Liberalization and Backlash

Between 1978 and the Tiananmen crackdown in June 1989, Chinese writers, artists, and intellectuals experienced freedom unprecedented in the post-1949 period, like their counterparts in the former Soviet bloc after the beginning of the "thaw" that followed Nikita Khrushchev's denunciation of Joseph Stalin in 1956. This wave of liberalization in the literary, artistic, and ideological spheres occurred mainly because of the spontaneous efforts of China's long-repressed writers, artists, and intellectuals to seek freedom of expression, expose unspeakable suffering and trauma of the Chinese people under the Maoist regime, and challenge orthodox Communist ideology. Importantly, liberal leaders, in particular Hu Yaobang, provided political protection and helped sustain liberalization despite constant conservative backlash.

The awakening of Chinese society in the post-Mao period began with the emergence and popularity of the so-called scar literature—short stories, novellas, plays, and films based on fictional characters who were victimized during the Maoist period. This genre gets its name because one of its classics is a short story titled "Scar" (*Shanghen*), published in 1978 in a major Shanghai newspaper. Its heroine was a young woman who, brainwashed by party propaganda, broke off relations with her mother, who was wrongfully persecuted by the party as a "traitor" and "spy." But doubt, guilt, and pain tormented the heroine, who was sent to the countryside like many of her contemporaries during the Cultural Revolution. She finally sought reconciliation with her mother, who was exonerated after the Cultural Revolution. But before she could get home, her mother suddenly died. "Scar" became an overnight best-seller and inspired an entirely new genre of works exploring the collective trauma of Chinese society.[55]

The ostensibly philosophical debate over humanism and alienation under socialism in the early 1980s was another manifestation of the relative freedom of the period. Unlike the scar literature that sought to help a traumatized nation confront its darkest days, the discussion of humanism and alienation in socialist societies undermined the ideological legitimacy of Chinese communism. By emphasizing the humanism in Karl Marx's writings, participants in this debate—exclusively writers, journalists, and social scientists—attacked the brutal rule under Mao as an egregious deviation from Marxism. Even more important, the article launching this debate argued that alienation existed under socialism because the lack of democracy, economic mismanagement, and personality cult resulted in "alienation of power"—the abuse of the power by "the servants of the people."[56]

Even after the fall of Hu Yaobang in January 1987, the space for Chinese writers and social scientists did not disappear. Between early 1985 and the Tiananmen crackdown in June 1989, a "culture fever" swept over China. During this period, Chinese intellectuals explored a diverse set of topics, such as existentialism, the modernization theory, and contrasts between Chinese and Western cultures. On the whole, the culture fever consisted of a self-critical exploration of the reasons behind China's economic backwardness and displayed an eagerness to learn from the West even though one topic that emerged during this period was "neo-authoritarianism," the theory of successful economic development under autocratic rule.[57] The culture fever reached its peak with the airing of a six-part documentary, *River Elegy* (*Heshang*), in June 1988. Written by a leading liberal writer, this series critically examined the factors of China's failure to modernize and blamed its traditional inward-looking mindset. China Central Television (CCTV), the country's primary official media outlet, broadcast *River Elegy*, which became an instant success but also infuriated hard-liners because of its liberal tone and themes.[58]

These literary, ideological, and artistic efforts in the 1980s had the most profound impact on Chinese intellectuals and university students. Some even called this movement "enlightenment" because, collectively, the ideas and values promoted by these works were generally humanistic, cosmopolitan, and liberal.[59] In all likelihood, relative intellectual freedom in the 1980s allowed prodemocracy values to influence a generation of students to press for political openness and democracy, a struggle that would end in the tragic confrontation with the party in June 1989.[60]

Most accounts of the conservative backlash against liberalization in the 1980s focus on the role of two hard-liners in charge of the party's ideology and propaganda. One was Hu Qiaomu, a Politburo member (1982–1987) and Mao's former speech writer. The other was Deng Liqun (no relation to Deng Xiaoping), director of the CCP propaganda department between 1982 and 1987. On the surface, the backing by Chen Yun, their political patron, emboldened Hu Qiaomu and Deng Liqun to take the lead in attacking liberals, in particular Hu Yaobang.[61] In reality, they shared nearly identical views with Deng Xiaoping on the party's imperative to contain the trends of liberalization in the 1980s. A review of the key episodes of conservative backlash against liberalization in this decade shows that Deng Xiaoping, in fact, played a more prominent and direct role in launching the counterattacks on liberalization. Hu Qiaomu and Deng Liqun often acted with Deng Xiaoping's instructions and endorsement.

Deng Xiaoping demonstrated his staunch opposition to liberalization as soon as he gained political dominance at the end of 1978. When the Democracy Wall, the first major mass prodemocracy movement in the post-Mao era, emerged in Beijing in late 1978, he expressed some support, apparently because this movement could weaken Hua Guofeng, then the party leader. But Deng revealed his true stance on democracy after he dethroned Hua in December 1978. In March 1979 he not only shut down the Democracy Wall and sentenced its most prominent leader, Wei Jingsheng, to fifteen years in jail, but also announced his "four cardinal principles" reaffirming that the party's monopoly and its official ideology must not be challenged.[62]

As the trends of liberalization gathered pace in the 1980s, Deng either took the lead or backed the hard-liners in trying to suppressing them. Apparently alarmed by signs of liberalization at the end of 1980, he delivered a tough talk at a conference attended by all senior leaders. He lamented that the party had not put up a vigorous effort to "struggle against erroneous ideas that opposed the four cardinal principles." After warning against these trends, Deng emphasized the need to reaffirm the accomplishments and positive aspects of the Maoist era.[63] A month after Deng's speech, the party issued a document demanding stricter control of the media. Some of the words of the document were verbatim quotations from Deng's speech.[64]

In some instances, Deng would personally intervene to fight "bourgeois liberalization." The censorship of the movie *The Sun and the Man* [*Taiyang yuren*] in 1981 was one such example. This movie was based on a script, *Unrequited Love* [*Kulian*], published in September 1979. Its hero is an accomplished artist who returned to China from the West in 1950, only to suffer incessant political persecution during the Maoist period. He later froze to death in the wilderness while on the run. When *Unrequited Love* was turned into a movie in 1980, it enraged the hard-liners, including Deng Xiaoping. After watching the movie during its prescreening, Deng declared that "the movie smeared the socialist system. . . . Someone said its artistic achievement was high. But precisely because of this, its poisonous harm is all the greater. . . . Could you imagine the consequences if 'The Sun and the Man' were to be shown in public?"[65] Fortunately, resistance from the liberals prevented a full-scale crackdown on the intelligentsia in the wake of this incident.[66]

Deng Xiaoping's intervention during the debate on alienation would eventually result in the party's "anti–spiritual pollution" campaign in 1983, the first nationwide crackdown on liberalization in the post-Mao era. After liberal intellectuals launched the debate on alienation under socialism, the hard-liners, led by Hu Qiaomu and Deng Liqun, tried to suppress the debate and punish the proponents of "alienation under socialism." After Hu Yaobang thwarted their attempts, the two hard-liners went directly to Deng Xiaoping and apparently obtained his support to punish the liberals who started this debate in September 1983.[67]

The most important fallout from the controversy over "alienation under socialism" was the anti–spiritual pollution campaign. Backing the stance of the hard-liners on the debate in September 1983, Deng Xiaoping said "we must not do (*bugao*) spiritual pollution." At a Central Committee plenum on October 12, 1983, he reiterated his resolve, declaring that "spiritual pollution must not be allowed on the ideological front."[68] Deng's public stance instantly changed the political dynamics. The party's propaganda machine went into overdrive and launched a nationwide campaign against spiritual pollution. Although the conservatives initially targeted the liberal intelligentsia, they quickly expanded the scope of the campaign to crack down on pop culture, entertainment, and people's lifestyles, thus fanning fears of another Cultural Revolution.[69] Aware of the consequences of the conservative counterattack,

Hu Yaobang and Zhao Ziyang formed a united front to put the brakes on the campaign. After realizing the harmful effects of the campaign on his economic reform drive, Deng reversed course. As a result, the campaign died a quiet death within a month.[70]

The Road to Tiananmen

For the first half of the 1980s, Deng appeared to be successful in playing a role as the pivotal player. Economically, his alliance with the liberals achieved critical breakthroughs in the decollectivization of agriculture, liberalization of the economy, and opening to the West. Although he also aligned with the hardliners during this period in suppressing liberalizing trends, he would quickly reverse course once he realized that political retrogression would threaten economic reform, as shown in the short-lived campaign against spiritual pollution in 1983. Politically, he succeeded in containing the liberals with periodic crackdowns on prominent members of the intelligentsia and the causes they advocated without fatally undermining his alliance with them.

But starting in 1986 Deng began to find it increasingly difficult to perform this balancing act. As economic reforms in the urban areas turned out to be much tougher than those in the rural areas, Deng began to toy with the idea of endorsing limited political reforms to increase efficiency, but without introducing democracy or undermining the party's monopoly. His dalliance with political reforms occurred at a time when the intelligentsia and university students were growing more vocal in agitating for political liberalization. The result was that Deng's rhetoric on political reform unintentionally encouraged university students to take to the streets in several Chinese cities in late 1986 to demand democratic changes, thus triggering the first of the two major political crises facing Deng in the post-Mao era.

But the greatest mistake Deng made, and the one that fatally weakened his effectiveness as the pivotal player, was his decision to sack Hu Yaobang, who consistently resisted pressure from him to crack down on "bourgeois liberalization" in the early 1980s. When Deng removed Hu as party chief following the outbreak of the prodemocracy demonstrations in late 1986, he lost a capable ally. Even though Deng managed to appoint Zhao Ziyang, who was at that time a liberal economic reformer, the fall of Hu Yaobang shifted the balance of power decisively in favor of the conservatives.

The resultant unfavorable balance of power was likely the cause of the growing resistance Deng faced between 1987 and 1988 to his efforts to accelerate reforms in the urban areas and to open China's doors even wider to the West. Even though agricultural decollectivization and liberalization unleashed private entrepreneurs and gave birth to the "township and village enterprises" (TVEs), private firms disguised as collective firms, Deng could claim no progress in restructuring the unprofitable state-owned enterprises.[71] An ambitious but ill-timed effort to ram through price reforms in the summer of 1988 led to panic buying and run-away inflation, forcing Deng to retreat and leading to a weakening of Zhao's position.[72] Starting in the second half of the 1980s, the pace of opening up to the West also slowed down. Establishment of the Hainan Administrative District, with its expanded foreign trade authority, resulted in a smuggling scandal that the conservatives exploited to block Deng from creating a much larger SEZ.[73] In terms of economic reforms, Deng had little to show between 1987 and the outbreak of the Tiananmen protests in April 1989.

The Fall of Hu Yaobang and the Anti–Bourgeois Liberalization Campaign

The surprise dismissal of Hu Yaobang as CCP general secretary in January 1987 marked a political turning point in Chinese politics in the post-Mao era.[74] This event not only signaled Deng's resolve to defend the party's monopoly on power even at the cost of sacrificing a longtime ally but also foreshadowed his purge of Zhao Ziyang, another trusted supporter, nearly two and half years later. The fall of Hu Yaobang decisively strengthened the hard-liners and weakened both Deng and the liberals. The immediate political consequences of Hu's downfall consisted of a short-lived crackdown on "bourgeois liberalization" and the stalling of the economic reforms.

Given Hu's liberal political views, it may be difficult to understand why Deng, a staunch Leninist despite his pragmatist streaks, picked him for the position of CCP general secretary. One obvious explanation is their close personal relationship. After Deng returned to power in 1973, he appointed Hu to lead the Chinese Academy of Sciences. During Mao's campaign against Deng in late 1975, Hu refused to denounce Deng, thus proving his loyalty. Hu's contributions were also considerable during Deng's power play against Hua Guofeng in 1978, in particular his instrumental role in leading the debate on the criterion of truth and in rehabilitating many senior leaders whom Mao had persecuted during the Cultural Revolution.[75]

Despite their personal friendship and Hu's proven leadership abilities, the relationship between Deng and Hu began to fray over the issue of "bourgeois liberalization." Unlike Deng, who sought to restore CCP legitimacy through economic reforms, Hu envisioned reform as a more comprehensive process that entailed a high degree of democracy.[76] During his tenure, he was credited with a dramatic relaxation of the party's harsh policy toward ethnic minorities, and, in the case of Tibet, he almost single-handedly pushed through a policy that resulted in the withdrawal of many Han Chinese officials and improvements in the living conditions of Tibetans.[77] On foreign policy, Hu advocated improving ties with Japan. But as a politician in the CCP's Hobbesian world, Hu's integrity, tolerance, and openness that endeared him to the liberal intelligentsia turned out to be fatal political liabilities. After he was forced to resign, Hu painfully admitted his naiveté. "[I did] not know how duplicitous people could be," he told another senior liberal official. "I realized my folly only when I was dismissed at the beginning of 1987."[78]

According to Zhao Ziyang, Deng's erosion of trust in Hu grew gradually in the 1980s because Deng thought Hu was too weak to deal with the emerging liberalizing trends. Zhao believed that Deng and Hu held "genuinely different views" on "bourgeois liberalization," and the breakdown of their relationship was "unavoidable."[79] As early as July 1981, Deng revealed his dissatisfaction with Hu's resistance to cracking down on the liberal intelligentsia with his criticism that party work on the "theoretical front," an area for which Hu was responsible, was "lax and weak." Their rift widened further even before Deng launched the anti–spiritual pollution campaign in October 1983. Deng blamed Hu for tolerating the growing liberalizing trends among the intelligentsia.[80] Although Deng reluctantly called off the anti–spiritual pollution campaign at the end of 1983, Zhao believed that Hu's apparent resistance to the campaign "aggravated the conflict between them a great deal."[81] Based on Zhao's observation, Deng had made up his mind to remove Hu in 1986, if not earlier. In the summer of 1986, he privately told a group of veteran revolutionaries that he had made a big mistake in selecting Hu Yaobang and that Hu would not continue to serve as party chief when the Thirteenth Party Congress was convened in 1987. In other words, Hu's political fate had already been sealed several months before his formal ouster.[82]

Although Deng made his own decision to dismiss Hu without manipulation or pressure by the conservatives, his action could only have delighted the hard-liners who had been seeking Hu Yaobang's removal.[83] Deng launched a nationwide "anti–bourgeois liberalization" campaign after Hu's dismissal in January 1987, creating another golden opportunity for the conservatives to roll back economic reforms. Even though Deng wanted to limit the backlash against liberalism to the ideological sphere, the conservatives tried to expand the crackdown to culture, education, science, and the lifestyles of ordinary people. The crackdown had an immediate chilling effect on economic reform. The experiment to empower managers of SOEs ground to a halt, and foreign direct investment plummeted in the first half of 1987.[84]

To counter the conservative backlash and salvage economic reform, Zhao not only declared to senior officials in January 1987 that the party would not change its policy on comprehensive reform and opening but also warned against "leftist" excesses and another witch hunt.[85] Privately, he lobbied Deng in late April, warning him that "some people are trying to use the anti–bourgeois liberalization campaign to undermine reform and opening." An alarmed Deng immediately gave his personal support to Zhao's proposal to deliver a major speech that would constitute a counterattack against the conservatives. Shortly thereafter Zhao delivered his famous "May 13 speech" at a conference for high-level officials that effectively ended the anti–bourgeois liberalization campaign.[86]

The fall of Hu Yaobang in January 1987 dealt the liberals a near-fatal blow. They lost a powerful advocate for liberalization, and, more important, Hu's departure greatly strengthened the hard-liners. Because there were no suitable candidates to take over the position of party chief, Deng appointed Zhao to replace Hu, a move that entailed the promotion of Li Peng to the position of premier of the State Council and Yao Yilin to executive vice premier. Now wielding enormous influence over the economy, the two hard-liners were also elevated to the PSC at the party's Thirteenth Party Congress in fall of that year.

The emboldened conservatives soon set their sights on Zhao because he had used Deng's support to thwart the conservative counterattack against reform. Zhao further enraged the hard-liners by abolishing the Central Secretariat's Research Office, controlled by the hard-liner Deng Liqun, depriving him of the institutional base that had served as his platform for organizing ideological campaigns against reform. The relationship between the dwindling liberal forces represented by Zhao and the conservatives became so tense that, when Zhao was delivering his keynote speech at the Thirteenth Party Congress in October 1987, Chen Yun, the arch conservative and patron of Deng Liqun, stood up and left the stage, in a very public and calculated display of disapproval.[87]

But the fall of Hu Yaobang also weakened Deng politically because he could be a pivotal player only if the liberal wing in the party on which he had to rely to push through his economic agenda remained strong. Now Deng had a weaker ally to help him counter the conservatives. Between January 1987 and the outbreak of the Tiananmen prodemocracy movement in April 1989, Deng was unable to advance any ambitious economic reforms. The strategy of focusing on developing an export-oriented economy on China's coast, which Zhao proposed, did not become actual policy despite Deng's backing. The price reform Deng tried to rush through in the late summer of 1988 only succeeded in triggering an inflation crisis, which undercut Zhao's authority and enabled the conservatives to mount a retrenchment campaign to roll back the economic reforms.

The Tiananmen Crisis and the Fall of Zhao Ziyang

Before the fall of Hu Yaobang in January 1987, Zhao was not the primary target of the conservatives, who saw Hu, party general secretary responsible for day-to-day party affairs, as a much greater threat than Zhao. Zhao avoided direct attacks by the conservatives also because he seldom spoke out on sensitive ideological issues, and his effective implementation of reformist policies had earned Deng's strong support. However, after Deng replaced Hu with Zhao as party chief in January 1987, it did not take long for the conservatives to start trying to topple him. The campaign against Zhao gathered momentum in the summer of 1988 when a poorly timed proposal by Deng to implement price reform triggered a spike in inflation. Although Zhao had not proposed the idea, he took responsibility to avoid placing the blame on Deng.[88] The conservatives in charge of the State Council, Li Peng and Yao Yilin, seized this opportunity to sideline Zhao in economic policymaking. A group of retired leaders reportedly wrote a joint letter to Deng calling for Zhao's dismissal. However, Deng stood by Zhao, telling him that he wanted him to serve a second term as the party chief and even offering him the position of chairman of the CMC at one point.[89] Although Deng's support helped Zhao retain his job, his position had become increasingly untenable by early 1989.

After college students in Beijing went to Tiananmen Square to mourn the death of Hu Yaobang on April 15, 1989, the conservatives finally got their opportunity. By pure coincidence, Zhao Ziyang was scheduled to leave Beijing for an official visit to North Korea on April 24. Before Zhao left Beijing, however, he went to see Deng and obtained support for his proposal to take moderate measures to deal with the demonstrations. But immediately after Zhao left Beijing, the conservatives called a PSC meeting to discuss the situation in Beijing, even though the student-led demonstrations had all but died down by then. In Zhao's absence, the conservatives could turn Deng, a hard-line authoritarian, into an ally. Indeed, on April 25 Li Peng went to Deng's house to report on the discussions during the PSC meeting the previous night. Deng's reaction was predictable: He immediately declared that the events in the square were "not an ordinary student movement but a turmoil," and he called for a speedy and tough reaction, which completely contradicted his prior support for Zhao's proposed moderate approach.

Even though Deng's speech was not supposed to be publicized, Li Peng circulated it among senior party officials and then turned it into the infamous *People's Daily* editorial published on April 26, apparently without consulting Deng. Publication of this editorial, which was known to reflect Deng's hard-line stance, instantly fueled anger among the students and turned them against Deng. The next day, hundreds of thousands of students again took to the streets of Beijing, calling on the party to retract the editorial, an impossible demand because that would be a public humiliation for Deng. After Zhao's return from North Korea on April 30, he tried in vain to de-escalate the confrontation. By that time, however, Deng was no longer open to suggestions for a moderate solution. He refused to grant Zhao an audience, an indication of his loss of confidence in Zhao.

The final break between Deng and Zhao occurred on May 16, when Zhao disclosed at a meeting with visiting Soviet leader Mikhail Gorbachev that Deng remained the party's ultimate decision-maker. According to Zhao, he had made similar statements earlier to other Communist leaders, and, in this particular case, his intent was to affirm Deng's authority and prestige, not to undermine him. However, Deng apparently thought Zhao was trying to shift the blame to him, thus further enraging him, as Zhao later wrote. Deng must have viewed Zhao's action as treachery. The next day, May 17, Deng decided to impose martial law and fired Zhao.[90] On June 4, more than two weeks later, PLA tanks rolled into Beijing and crushed the Tiananmen prodemocracy movement, killing at least hundreds of students and ordinary citizens in both the capital and the provinces.[91]

In retrospect, the Tiananmen massacre and the fall of Zhao, a turning point in post-Mao history, appear to have been entirely avoidable. Obviously, had Zhao postponed or canceled his scheduled visit to North Korea, the conservatives could not have outmaneuvered him and turned Deng into their ally. Gorbachev's untimely visit to Beijing was another factor. The student movement had lost momentum by early May, but Gorbachev's scheduled visit on May 15–16 gave the sagging movement a second wind, as students took advantage of the international media spotlight to stage a mass hunger strike on Tiananmen Square to pressure Deng.

Historical contingencies, in this case, may not have played as critical a role as one might have wished. Today, one can make the case that by early 1989 Deng's reform and opening was in deep trouble, largely due to Deng's own mistakes. His hostility to democracy and liberalism led him to sack Hu Yaobang, fatally weakening the liberal wing that he had to rely on to prevail against the hard-liners. Although he managed to replace Hu with another reformer, Zhao Ziyang, the emboldened and strengthened conservatives took over the State Council and wasted no time in waging a campaign to topple Zhao. They succeeded all too soon, again thanks to help from Deng Xiaoping.

Reflections

The reforms undertaken by the party in the 1980s constituted a comprehensive political institutionalization effort aimed mainly at stabilizing a regime ravaged by the radicalism and brutality of the Cultural Revolution. On the whole, the party's reforms to reinstitute collective leadership, improve elite security, and establish rules on term and age limits marked an important step in the transition away from totalitarianism. Additional reforms, such as building a legal system and relaxing social control, helped create a more friendly business environment and greater space for personal freedom. However, these restorative reforms had serious limitations. The self-interests of the top leaders, especially Deng himself, diluted the application and effectiveness of the reforms. In practice, as these top leaders were exempt from the rules, the reforms failed to constrain them from violating the very rules and norms they were trying to enshrine. Most critically, the reforms were not backed by effective mechanisms of enforcement. This might not have been a problem when there was a rough balance of power among competing factions, as was the case in the 1980s and in the post-Tiananmen period (1992–2012). But when this balance of power broke down and a strongman re-emerged, the institutional reforms Deng had put in place crumbled quickly.

A feasible solution is to establish genuine institutional constraints within the regime, such as by introducing inner-party democracy, reducing the power of the Leninist party-state, and creating more political space for other autonomous social forces. Indeed, the political reform blueprint Zhao and his advisers conceived in 1986–1987 was intended to accomplish these objectives. In this sense, Zhao's attempted institutional reforms were transformative, not restorative. They were far more radical than the relatively modest steps Deng had taken earlier in the decade to repair the damage inflicted on the party by Mao. If Deng's reforms were designed to preserve the core features of Leninism and make party rule more stable and durable, Zhao's reforms sought to turn a post-totalitarian regime into a looser and more pluralistic authoritarian regime dominated by one party. Sadly, Zhao's efforts did not succeed. After making some real, although modest, initial progress, Zhao's reforms stalled. As he later admitted, "in reality, after the Thirteenth Party Congress, it became very difficult to implement or sustain political system reform."[92] When the PLA tanks rolled into Tiananmen Square on June 4, 1989, the party not only crushed the prodemocracy movement but also extinguished any hopes of a regime-initiated gradual transition.

In retrospect, however, the pathway to democracy via a party-sanctioned program of reform was too narrow to be viable. Regime-initiated reform, or "transformation," according to Samuel Huntington, requires that the reformers in the regime maintain political dominance.[93] But with Deng firmly aligned with the hard-liners in opposing any change that could undermine party power, the balance of power decisively favored the hard-liners. This balance grew even more lopsided after the dismissal of Hu Yaobang in January 1987.

The greatest negative legacy of the 1980s is the preservation of the core institutions of a totalitarian regime. The tenacious opposition to political liberalization by Deng and his hard-line allies shielded these institutions from even the moderate reforms envisioned by Zhao's task force in 1987. Throughout the 1980s, as would be the case in the post-Tiananmen period as well as in the Xi Jinping era, the CCP maintained a monopoly on violence through its direct control of the military and other coercive forces. It was the military that saved the party from the nationwide popular prodemocracy movement in the spring of 1989. The modest steps Zhao took to "separate the party from the government," most of which were reversed after his purge, hardly made a dent in the party's tight grip on the Chinese state. Throughout the post-Mao period, the party remained as deeply entrenched in the state as ever.

The party's control of information in the 1980s was weakened moderately, due partly to protection of the liberals by reformers such as Hu and Zhao, and partly to the impact of an increasingly commercially oriented media market.[94] But the mechanisms that enabled the party to limit access to information, such as state-owned television networks, newspapers, and publishing companies, the prohibitions against private ownership of media outlets, and the party's nationwide propaganda networks that censor news, were kept, allowing the party to tighten the control whenever needed. The use of terror, a hallmark of totalitarianism, declined significantly throughout the 1980s. However, the party retained its capacity to deploy terror against certain segments of the population (as during Deng's draconian anticrime drive in 1983) or to crush prodemocracy forces (as in the Tiananmen crackdown in 1989).

The only area in which the reforms of the 1980s substantially undermined party control was the economy. The rapid growth of the private sector broke the party-state's monopolistic control of the economy and fueled hopes that the growth and consolidation of a market economy would not only spur modernization but also deconcentrate vital resources away from the state. Yet, the experience of the post-Tiananmen decades reveals the limits of capitalist economic modernization in promoting political change. Despite sustained double-digit growth over a period of twenty years (1992–2012) and the emergence of the private sector as the largest contributor to economic output, the party's hold on power showed no signs of weakening. If anything, the party not only gained legitimacy from the ever-rising living standards but also acquired greater capabilities of control and coercion to defend its political monopoly.

2

Reform and Growth in the 1980s

MOST ACCOUNTS OF China's post-Mao economic history characterize gradualism as a deliberate decision made by its leaders to avoid initial costly mistakes.[1] As with most conventional wisdom, this observation is partly true. This narrative, however, obviously downplays the fact that the party decided to pursue a cautious and incremental course of reform because opposition by hard-liners made it impossible to undertake more radical reforms. More critically, once Deng Xiaoping decided to rely on capitalist tools to save the CCP, the actual range of choices for economic reform strategy was limited. Stated simply, a full and unconditional embrace of a market economy was out of the question politically because this would entail the demolition of the economic foundations of one-party rule. This danger did not deter Deng from courting capitalism in the 1980s because he was willing to try anything to salvage a regime devastated by three decades of Maoist misrule, but the threat of a decentralized market economy to one-party rule would mushroom decades later as the private sector overtook the state sector as the most dynamic economic force.

In the 1980s, fortunately, the prospect of a capitalist subversion of the CCP's political monopoly seemed so unreal that, despite staunch conservative opposition, the party went along with Deng and opened the door for domestic private entrepreneurs and foreign investors. What the party did not foresee was how fast capitalism would grow and thrive in a semihostile environment. Unfortunately, the logic of path dependence also means that the party's half-hearted embrace of capitalism would set firm boundaries for the reach of the market and preserve the regime's control of what Vladimir Lenin called the "commanding heights" of the economy. The resultant hybrid economy would eventually exhaust its initial dynamism and begin to ossify and stagnate.

The emergence of China's hybrid economic system in the 1980s can be divided into two phases. The most important achievement in first phase,

1979–1983, was the rapid decollectivization of agriculture. This breakthrough not only raised rural productivity and output dramatically but also paved the way for the rise of a dynamic private sector and established the foundations of China's dual-track economy: a highly efficient private sector alongside an inefficient state-owned sector. Reform of the urban sector, where the economy was dominated by the state-owned enterprises, began tentatively in this period and made no meaningful progress. In this phase, reformers led by Deng Xiaoping also launched "opening"—integration with the global economy through attracting foreign direct investment and promoting foreign trade. Compared with the successes of rural reform and the opening to the outside world achieved in the first phase, the second phase, 1984–1989, delivered far less impressive reform outcomes mainly because of the complex challenges of reforming SOEs, growing conservative resistance, and Deng Xiaoping's dismissal of the party's general secretary Hu Yaobang in January 1987, a move that seriously weakened the reformist camp at the top.

In spite of China's failure to reform its large and inefficient state-owned sector in the second phase, it built the foundations of sustained rapid growth in the 1980s, thanks to the rapid growth of the private sector and foreign-invested firms. Ironically, this development, especially the rise of a vibrant domestic private sector, was not the planned outcome of Deng's reform. Due to political opposition and the technical difficulties in reforming SOEs, reformers wisely opted for the path of least resistance: liberalizing the economy to bring into the marketplace far more efficient nonstate firms as the new engines of growth. Political expediency aside, this pragmatic approach to reform was also made possible by, paradoxically, the absence of a clear and comprehensive strategy to transform a state-socialist economy into a market-oriented one. Instead of following a rigid approach, Chinese reformers relied on learning-by-doing and avoided making costly mistakes in the early phase of the transition that could doom the entire enterprise.

Origins of Chinese Experimentalism

When China began to reform its economic system in the early 1980s, its leaders were in unchartered territory as they could not draw much guidance from economic theory or real-world examples.[2] The neoclassical economic literature was irrelevant for a country embarked on a transition from a nonmarket economy to another system. The experience of limited economic reform in Eastern Europe (mainly Hungary and Yugoslavia) in the 1960s and 1970s was only marginally useful because these efforts focused on SOEs and ultimately failed to produce meaningful economic improvements.

However, what Chinese policymakers lacked in theory was more than compensated for by their overriding political imperatives and pragmatic instincts. Politically, the top leaders knew they must produce higher growth to bolster CCP legitimacy after decades of economic mismanagement under Mao. Deng Xiaoping put it bluntly in October 1979: "Economic work is the greatest politics today. The economic issue is the overwhelming political issue."[3] As for how to achieve this objective, Deng's answer was straightforward, though it lacked specifics: "The goal of our revolution is to liberate and develop productivity."[4]

To "liberate productivity," China's initial efforts were focused on making the existing system more efficient mainly through decentralization, instead of replacing it altogether. Starting in 1979, decentralization consisted of granting local governments more autonomy in economic management and incentivizing them with "fiscal contracting." This allowed provincial governments to retain surplus revenues after they met the quota of tax revenues to be paid to the central government.[5] The pragmatic instincts of the Chinese leaders led them to prefer experimental measures to decisive but risky steps. This cautious approach was necessitated by both opposition from conservatives resisting full liberalization and a lack of the requisite knowledge or theoretical guidance. Consequently, reform measures were rolled out gradually, typically first in a small number of localities to gain valuable knowledge and avoid pitfalls.[6] One such example was the economic opening to the West, which occurred through a series of cautious reforms, such as the establishment of four SEZs in Guangdong and Fujian in the early 1980s, the gradual extension of policies to key coastal cities, and piecemeal reforms of the foreign trade regime. Another example is the price reform of the 1980s, which started with a unique "dual-track" pricing system featuring both government-mandated prices and market-determined prices.[7] The only big-bang reform breakthrough—in agriculture—occurred not because of a deliberate strategy by the top leadership but because of a combination of bottom-up peasant initiatives and support by reformers in a few key provinces in 1979.[8]

Although it is common to credit China's "learn-by-doing" strategy of the 1980s for the initial success of its economic reform, it would be unfair to dismiss the influence of ideas and lessons from Eastern Europe and the West in helping Chinese policymakers and economists gain a deeper and more sophisticated understanding of the nature, scope, and challenges of their tasks. If anything, one of China's initial moves was to dispatch a number of senior officials and economists to visit countries in Eastern Europe, Western Europe, and East Asia to gain useful lessons, insights, and knowledge about economic reform.[9] The World Bank, eager to help chart China's course, provided invaluable technical assistance. The head of the bank's office in Beijing organized seminars for technocrats and rising economists in the Chinese government. The most influential event was a seven-day seminar on a cruise along the Yangtze in September 1985 attended by prominent economists from Eastern Europe and the West. Many of the Chinese participants in the seminar later became influential players in the Chinese reform, such as Wu Jinglian, Gao Shangquan, Guo Shuqing, and Lou Jiwei. Impressed by the value of the World Bank's technical assistance, in 1983 Deng invited the bank to conduct a comprehensive study of the Chinese economy and identify the policy choices it faced. This led to a milestone study by the World Bank, published in 1985 and titled "Issues and Choices for Long-Term Development," which drew heavily on the bank's knowledge of developing economies.[10]

Gradually and cumulatively, these intellectual interactions, especially those with Eastern European economists (the most influential were Janos Kornai from Hungary, Włodzimierz Brus from Poland, and Ota Šik from Czechoslovakia), led some Chinese reformers to conclude that economic reform was "not a collection of random policies" but a "systemic transition."

Decentralization and liberalization, hallmarks of the gradualist reform in the 1980s, were too limited to achieve a transition to a different economic system. Consequently, Chinese reformers began to look elsewhere for insights and inspirations. Two models—the Western liberal model and the East Asian developmental state model—began to gain influence. For Deng, the East Asian model held stronger appeal because of the leading role played by an authoritarian state.[11]

This brief account of the evolution of China's economic reform strategy shows that in the 1980s China mainly followed an experimental and improvisational approach, appropriately captured by the idiom, "crossing the river by feeling for the stones." But Chinese leaders adopted this largely successful strategy out of necessity. The top leaders were divided about the goal and pace of reform, and even those committed to reform lacked the necessary intellectual tools or real-world models. Fortunately, interactions with their counterparts in the West and Eastern Europe helped Chinese economists realize the limits of piecemeal experiments and administrative decentralization and led them to gravitate toward a far more comprehensive and coherent strategy of transition. Because of the post-Tiananmen political turmoil and the brief conservative backlash against reform during 1990–1991, China would have to wait until after Deng's historic southern tour in 1992 to implement a full package of institutional reforms that marked the beginning of a qualitatively different phase of its transition.

Rural Breakthroughs

When CCP leaders pivoted away from Maoist class struggle to economic modernization in 1979, one of the strategic choices they faced was where economic reform should begin. At that time, the Chinese economic structure was severely distorted in terms of population and output. The countryside contained 82 percent of the population in 1978, but the rural sector accounted for only 28 percent of economic output. In other words, China was both under-urbanized and highly industrialized (with industry producing 48 percent of output in 1978).[12] Economically, it might appear that reforming the industrial sector, the largest contributor to economic output, could deliver faster and better results.

However, reform in China started not in the urban industrial sector but in the impoverished countryside. Reforming the industrial sector based in urban areas might have appeared to be a promising way to improve performance and produce a bigger bang, but political resistance to reform in the SOE-dominated industrial sector was strong. Technically, industrial reform was also far more complex, entailing not only changes in firm management and ownership but also a whole set of complementary institutional reforms involving prices, financial markets, and social safety nets.

If political opposition and technical challenges made rural reform more attractive than industrial reform, one might have expected the top party leaders to proactively pursue this route in 1979 or the early 1980s. But they did not. Rural reform began mainly as a bottom-up revolution waged by long-suffering peasants who received, in its early days, the support of only a small number of provincial party leaders, most notably Wan Li in Anhui and Zhao Ziyang in Sichuan. In fact, the CCP Central Committee issued a rural policy directive in September 1979 that explicitly discouraged decollectivization.[13] Opponents to rural reform included Hua Guofeng, who was still nominal party chairman, Li Xiannian and Hu Qiaomu, two hard-liners who consistently opposed economic reform in the 1980s, and a large number of provincial party chiefs. Chen Yun, the conservative standard bearer, was neutral, however. From the very beginning, Hu Yaobang was the most enthusiastic supporter of rural reform among the top leaders. Deng supported the "household responsibility system," the rural reform that effectively decollectivized agriculture, but he did not publicly endorse the reform until May 1980.[14] According to Zhao Ziyang, Deng's tacit support was critical to the success of the rural reform because it prevented the emergence of unified opposition among the party's top echelon.[15] The party did not formally approve the household responsibility system until the beginning of 1982.[16]

Judging by the speed and scope of agricultural decollectivization, which began in 1978 and was completed throughout the country by 1982, rural reform should be considered a radical big bang in one of the most important economic sectors.[17] Although China's post-Mao economic reform is often characterized as a case of "gradualism," in reality the country experienced both a "big bang" and a gradualist course of reform. China's big-bang approach to agricultural reform was feasible and successful mostly because the state-socialist system was less deeply entrenched in the countryside, and collectivized agriculture had victimized almost the entire rural population. By comparison, strong political opposition at the top, groups benefiting from a command economy (planners, managers, and workers in SOEs), and genuine technical difficulties of industrial reform compelled China to adopt a more cautious step-by-step approach in this area.

The end of collectivized agriculture produced an instant increase in productivity. Agricultural output, measured in constant prices, rose an average of 8.7 percent annually between 1979 and 1984.[18] Academic studies show that a radical institutional change—replacing the Maoist people's communes with private household farming—contributed at least half of output growth in the agricultural sector during this period.[19] The rural breakthrough in the early 1980s had vast—and positive—implications for Deng's reform. The rapid gains in productivity and standard of living due to agricultural decollectivization generated valuable political capital for the reformers as rural per capita income grew threefold from 1978 to 1985 in real terms.[20] Few appreciated the political benefits of the early success of reform in the rural sector as acutely as Deng, who said in 1985, "To make our domestic economy dynamic, we must start with the countryside. Eighty percent of the Chinese population is in the countryside. Whether Chinese society can be stable and the Chinese economy can develop depends on whether the countryside can develop and the life of peasants can improve."[21]

More important, liberation of the peasantry from the yokes of the people's communes was the first step in creating a private sector, which later became the most dynamic engine of growth. The connection between decollectivization and the private sector became obvious only in hindsight. In reality, the emergence of the private sector in the countryside during the post-Mao era was an inevitable outcome of the successful rural reform. Increased productivity and output freed up a huge amount of labor and allowed peasants to accumulate savings to finance nonagricultural activities, thus creating two necessary conditions for a nascent private sector: entrepreneurs and capital.

The dismantling of the communes opened up an unanticipated opportunity for rural entrepreneurs because the communes had accumulated considerable industrial assets during the Great Leap Forward (1958–1959) and the agricultural mechanization campaign in the Cultural Revolution. After the communes disappeared, some of these assets were effectively privatized (usually in the form of leasing), while others were transferred to newly formed collective firms that were nominally owned by township and village governments. This development laid the early foundations for China's township and village enterprises.[22]

Several other factors also contributed to the rapid growth of the TVEs. Due to fiscal decentralization in the early 1980s, local authorities had strong incentives to support industrial growth in their respective areas because nonagricultural activities generated more tax revenues.[23] The neglect of light industry and the service sector in favor of defense-related heavy industry during the Maoist period also meant that there was a severe shortage of consumer goods and services, which presented a huge opportunity to be exploited by rural entrepreneurs. Consequently, the market-oriented TVEs quickly gained a competitive edge over the SOEs in supplying consumer goods and services. They also began to contribute a rising share of Chinese exports.[24]

Policy support from Beijing mainly consisted of allowing rural entrepreneurs access to rural credit co-ops and informal financing.[25] The dual-track price reform, however imperfect, allowed TVEs to purchase vital inputs legally because this reform encouraged SOEs, which monopolized the production of steel, aluminum, chemicals, and other upstream materials used for the manufacturing of consumer goods, to sell their products to TVEs at higher, market-based prices.[26]

The explosive growth of TVEs in the 1980s (table 2.1) was a positive development totally unanticipated by even the most ardent reformers. Deng admitted in 1987 that "our greatest success—and it is one we had by no means anticipated—has been the emergence of a large number of enterprises run by

TABLE 2.1. Growth of the TVEs in the 1980s

Year	Number of TVEs	Employment	Gross Output (billion yuan)
1980	1,420,000	29,997,000	65.69
1984	6,065,000	52,081,000	170.99
1989	18,686,000	93,668,000	742.84

Source: *ZGTJNJ 1995*, 363–65.

villages and townships. They were like a new force that just came into being spontaneously. . . . The Central Committee takes no credit."[27]

Because the TVEs were officially designated as "collective" firms owned not by the state or private individuals but by a local collective entity, such as a village or township, one may have the impression that they were not genuine private firms. In fact, however, many were bona fide private firms despite the designation of "collective firms" because the latter provided more political protection in an era when private ownership of property was not officially endorsed by the party or legally protected by the Chinese constitution (the constitution was not amended until 2004 to protect private property). Research by Yasheng Huang shows that by 1987, private TVEs accounted for half of the output of all TVEs in eight provinces and 30–50 percent of the output of TVEs in fifteen provinces. In 1989 private TVEs contributed 58 percent of after-tax profits of all TVEs and accounted for 45 percent of the wage bill of all TVEs.[28]

Another far-reaching consequence of the TVEs is that they gave rise to a new generation of private entrepreneurs.[29] Those who leased the assets of TVEs or later assumed managerial responsibilities in them built thriving private businesses. The most successful became tycoons who led globally competitive firms, such as Fuyao Industrial Glass Group (a global leader of auto glass founded by Cao Dewang) and Wang Xiang Group (an auto parts maker founded by Lu Guanqiu). Entrepreneurs who did not lease or manage TVEs but were able to scrape together enough capital also started businesses that grew into thriving private companies, such as New Hope Group, which began as a small Sichuan company producing animal feed. A government-sponsored study of rural entrepreneurs in 1991 found that 19 percent were the heads of TVEs and 13 percent had at one time worked in TVEs. In other words, roughly one-third of all rural entrepreneurs were connected with the TVEs. Other studies show that between 17 percent and 47 percent of private entrepreneurs had been senior executives or workers in TVEs.[30]

Opening to the World

China's economic engagement with the world was miniscule relative to its size due to Mao's policy of "self-reliance." In 1978 total foreign trade was only $20.6 billion, or 10 percent of China's GDP.[31] But economic reintegration into the global trading system was crucial to the success of the country's modernization. Deng, who likely acquired a cosmopolitan outlook during his five-year sojourn in France (December 1920 to January 1926), viewed opening as a top priority and subsequently invested enormous political capital to push for reforms to attract foreign capital.[32] More than any other Chinese leader at the end of the 1970s, Deng recognized that a favorable external environment, in particular warming ties between China and the West, would provide a window of opportunity. In May 1979, shortly after he reached political supremacy, Deng told a French delegation that "now we enjoy relatively favorable international conditions and can introduce advanced technology, research products, and considerable international capital from the U.S., Europe and Japan. In the first twenty years of the [PRC] we did not have such international conditions. . . . We must adopt a policy of opening."[33]

In the early years of reform, Deng effectively made himself China's chief salesman to the West. His visits to the United States (in early 1979) and Japan (in October 1978 and February 1979) cemented diplomatic foundations with the two countries that were most critical to Chinese modernization. Deng also carried out a tireless campaign with visiting foreign dignitaries and businessmen to promote his policy of opening. The official chronology of Deng's activities in 1978 shows that during that single year he spoke to thirty-one visiting delegations of foreign businessmen and politicians about his policy of opening. In 1979 he delivered the same message to thirty-five visiting delegations.[34]

At the same time, Deng made it clear to the party that opening to the West was integral to his reform agenda, and he repeatedly emphasized that China had to seize this window of opportunity. Speaking to provincial party chiefs in October 1979, Deng devoted an entire section of his talk to foreign investment and trade. "We must utilize foreign capital in whatever form," he stressed. "This is such a rare opportunity and it would be a shame to pass it up. Utilizing foreign capital is a major policy. . . . I believe we should persist. . . . We must encourage exports."[35] He was even more explicit a month later: "Achieving the four modernizations requires a correct policy of opening to the outside. Although we will rely mainly on our own efforts, resources, and foundations, [the four modernizations] would not be possible without international cooperation."[36] An important reason why China had remained backward economically, according to Deng, was "its policy of closing the country to outside contact. Our experience shows that China cannot rebuild itself behind closed doors."[37]

Politically, it is not difficult to see why Deng prioritized opening. He was more directly involved personally in promoting policies to attract foreign investment and increase exports than he was in pushing for domestic reform. Also, domestic economic reform faced greater political resistance because it threatened entrenched interest groups, such as those in the state-owned sector. Outside the agricultural sector, which was quickly privatized, radical reform in urban areas would also encounter more practical difficulties and entail greater political risks. For example, restructuring the money-losing SOEs through bankruptcy or privatization would need new legal tools and a functioning capital market, which China still lacked in the early 1980s.[38] In the meantime, price reform, which could unleash temporary inflation, was politically risky. As an astute practitioner of geopolitics, Deng took full advantage of China's crucial role as a counterweight to the Soviet Union during the Cold War to reap substantive economic benefits from the West, in particular capital, technology, and access to markets. Given the overwhelming political logic for opening, Deng lent his support to a series of reforms to attract foreign investment and increase Chinese exports.

Legislation to Attract Foreign Direct Investment

Topping Deng's agenda to attract foreign capital was establishment of a legal framework. In May 1979 he told a delegation of Japanese legislators that China was considering setting up joint ventures with foreign investors and passing a law on foreign investment to underscore its policy of opening. He listed a set of laws on patents and international trade that would also need to be enacted.[39] In July 1979 the NPC passed the historic "Chinese-Foreign Equity Joint Ventures Law" to create a legal framework for allowing foreign investors to operate in China. Among other things, the law stipulated that a foreign partner had to put up at least 25 percent of the equity in a joint venture. Although the law did not limit the total amount of equity the foreign partners could invest, the practice was that their total contribution was not to exceed 50 percent of the equity. (The draft of the law sought to explicitly limit the amount of equity of foreign investors to 49 percent, thus making the foreign investors minority owners, but Deng quashed the idea after learning that such a provision was not an international norm.)[40] Foreign joint ventures were encouraged to source local materials, bring in advanced technology, and export their products in exchange for tax benefits. The Chinese partners could contribute land as part of their equity (the law would later be revised on three occasions before it was annulled in 2020).[41] Although it did not offer substantial benefits to foreign investors, who often found the law's provisions restrictive and vague, it nevertheless signaled China's desire to welcome foreign capital and opened the door slightly for foreign investors to enter a potentially huge market that had long been closed to the outside world. (Deng said that, despite its flaws, the law was a statement of "our political desires and goals.")[42]

The second law, promulgated by the NPC in 1986, most likely to make foreign investment even more attractive than joint ventures, was the "Foreign-Capital Enterprises Law," which allowed foreign investors to set up wholly owned firms in China. The law included only a small number of general provisions, but, like the law on joint ventures, it encouraged wholly owned foreign firms to introduce advanced technology, source locally, and export their products in exchange for tax benefits.[43] The State Council issued a far more detailed regulation on wholly owned foreign firms in 1990, with more specific, but also restrictive, provisions. Most important, foreign investors were allowed to set up wholly owned firms only if (1) they brought in advanced technology and equipment; (2) they could manufacture products to substitute imports; or (3) they could earn enough hard currency to cover their foreign exchange expenses.

China also kept many sectors—media, broadcasting, films, domestic retail, foreign trade, insurance, and telecommunications—off-limits to wholly owned foreign firms. Other sectors, such as public utilities, transportation, and real estate, were open to foreign investment but only with severe restrictions. Furthermore, all wholly owned foreign investment was subject to a national security review.[44]

In the late 1980s the Chinese government passed another law, the "Chinese-Foreign Contractual Joint Ventures Law," making it attractive for foreign companies to bring intellectual property rights and management know-how to China in lieu of capital.[45] These three laws, which were later revised several times to make them more liberal, laid a legal foundation to attract foreign capital and technology. But based on their still relatively restrictive provisions, which likely reflected both conservative opposition and lingering distrust of foreign capital, it is doubtful that these three laws on their own played a pivotal role in persuading foreign investors to bring their capital to a country that had yet to establish a record as a safe and welcoming place for outsiders. Despite Deng's heroic efforts to welcome foreign investment, only a modest amount of foreign capital actually flowed into China in the 1980s.

Special Economic Zones

A tentative but politically bold step taken by Deng and fellow reformers in the late 1970s was the establishment of SEZs. To be sure, the idea of attracting foreign investors by providing tax benefits and other privileges to set up shop in a designated jurisdiction for export-processing was not a Chinese invention. Taiwan, South Korea, Malaysia, and other countries in Asia had pioneered export-processing zones (EPZs) in the 1960s to promote labor-intensive exports.[46] However, for a country with fresh memories of Western "concessions" (areas within China where Westerners had exercised quasi-sovereign control) during the pre-1949 era, the creation of zones that would grant foreign investors privileges that were denied to Chinese people was fraught with political risks.

But the potential ideological and nationalist backlash did not deter Deng. In April 1979 he responded enthusiastically to a proposal made by Xi Zhongxun (then the party chief of Guangdong) and Yang Shangkun (a close ally of Deng) to set up EPZs in Shenzhen, Zhuhai, and Shantou, three underdeveloped areas close to Hong Kong. The only twist was Deng's suggestion that they be called "special zones" (*tequ*). According to him, the central government would give policy preferences instead of money to attract foreign businesses to these zones. Due to his intervention, in July 1979 the central leadership approved requests from Guangdong and Fujian for special policy treatment and flexibility, and by May 1980 the central government formally approved the establishment of four SEZs—in Shenzhen, Zhuhai, Shantou, and Xiamen.[47] Shenzhen was by far the largest: Even though at the time it was only a small fishing village with a population of thirty thousand, the entire territory of over 327 square kilometers was allocated for the SEZ. China made Shenzhen the largest SEZ because it bordered Hong Kong and could attract investment from the then-British colony. The other three SEZs were much smaller: Zhuhai, which bordered Macao, consisted of only 14 square kilometers, and Shantou was only 6 square kilometers. Initially, only one district in Xiamen was designated as an SEZ, but in 1985 the central government expanded the Xiamen SEZ to include the entire city, with 131 square kilometers of land.[48]

The primary objective in establishing the SEZs was to attract FDI and to set up export-processing factories to earn foreign exchange.[49] The NPC passed special legislation in August 1980 on Guangdong's SEZs that offered foreign investors favorable tax treatment and operational autonomy. For example, such investors could form wholly owned firms in the SEZs so as to retain full management control, a privilege denied to foreign investors elsewhere in the country. Those firms operating in the SEZs could import their equipment and materials duty-free. Furthermore, their profits would be taxed at only 15 percent, and additional tax subsidies would be made available for firms that invested more than $5 million or reinvested their profits in the SEZs. In return, firms in the SEZs were required to export their products.[50]

Despite the enormous attention given to the SEZs, their direct contribution to China's economic development in the 1980s was modest because they were established in underdeveloped jurisdictions (except for Xiamen). In 1980 the four SEZs accounted for only 0.2 percent of China's industrial output. In 1989, although their contribution had grown sixfold, it was still only 1.3 percent of the country's total industrial output. But in many ways the SEZs were stunning economic successes. Their growth was much higher than the national average at the time (Shenzhen's industrial output grew, on average, 20 percent per year between 1981 and 1992, compared with 14 percent for the national average). The SEZs also attracted $4.1 billion in utilized FDI between 1980 and 1989, roughly 26 percent of China's total utilized FDI during the same period.[51] Exports from the four SEZs recorded explosive growth in the 1980s. Between 1983 and 1989, exports from these areas rose seventeenfold. Their share of China's total exports grew from 1 percent in 1983 to 6.4 percent in 1989.[52] Of all the SEZs, Shenzhen is undoubtedly the greatest success story. Within three decades, it was transformed into a mega-city (with a population of over twelve million in 2020), a manufacturing center of electronics, and a high-tech cluster.[53]

Several factors, such as the preferential treatment of foreign capital, local autonomy, and proximity and historical ties to Hong Kong (in the case of Shenzhen) and Taiwan (in the case of Xiamen), lay behind the success of the SEZs. But perhaps the single most important favorable factor was the invisible institutional factor. Specifically, the institutions of the Leninist party-state, in particular the command economy, were the least embedded in the most successful SEZ. (In Shenzhen, the private sector accounted for more than three-quarters of economic output in 1992.) The private sector could flourish without the stifling control of the state, as illustrated by the contrast between two successful SEZs, Shenzhen and Xiamen. In 1980 Shenzhen's industrial output was only 84 million yuan, less than 10 percent of Xiamen's 943 million yuan. But by 1989 Shenzhen's industrial output had risen to 11.6 billion yuan, twice that of Xiamen's industrial output.[54]

In addition to FDI and exports, the SEZs generated substantial intangible and indirect benefits for China. This experiment in opening to the outside world yielded valuable lessons about how to integrate with the global economy via investment and trade. The knowledge gained from this learn-by-doing process gave the reformers, led by Zhao Ziyang, the confidence to turn the entire coastal area into de facto SEZs in the late 1980s (the plan was fully implemented in the 1990s, even after the ouster of Zhao in 1989).[55]

Foreign Trade Reform

Integration with the international economy—Deng's "opening"—meant a dramatic rise in China's foreign trade. The country's economic growth could be increased substantially if it took advantage of its comparative advantage in cheap labor and export labor-intensive manufactures.[56] During the Maoist era, however, China had pursued a development strategy that favored heavy industry and sought import substitution, contrary to its comparative advantage. More important, China's self-imposed isolation and hostility to both the capitalist West and the Soviet bloc isolated its economy from international trade. In 1978, on the eve of reform, China's foreign trade was only 10 percent of its GDP.[57] Even this figure exaggerated China's trade openness because of the significant overvaluation of the Chinese currency. In addition, China's GDP itself was undervalued. If both the GDP and the exchange rates were adjusted using market-based measures, China's trade openness at the start of the reform would have been 5–6 percent of GDP, nearly half of the nominal figure.[58]

Ironically, the closed nature of the Chinese economy and its inefficient development strategy that favored capital-intensive heavy industry implied that the country could boost its foreign trade and reap dramatic productivity gains if it reformed its foreign trade system. Parallel to the efforts to attract FDI, Chinese leaders also launched a series of reforms to promote exports and make the foreign trade system more efficient.

Because the state monopolized foreign trade through specialized central foreign trade organizations (FTOs), firms could conduct trade only through these monopolies. The first step was to dismantle these monopolies through

TABLE 2.2. Foreign Trade and Exports, 1978–1988 (in billion USD)

Year	1978	1980	1982	1984	1986	1988
Total foreign trade	20.6	38.1	41.6	53.5	73.8	102.7
Exports	9.7	18.1	22.3	26.1	30.9	47.5

Source: *ZGTJNJ 1990*, 641.

administrative decentralization. Provincial governments and their FTOs were thus allowed to directly engage in foreign trade. Once the central monopoly was broken, the impact of decentralization was instant and dramatic, as shown by the rapid increase in Chinese foreign trade (table 2.2).[59]

However, foreign trade reform was no smooth sailing. During the economic retrenchment campaign launched by Chen Yun in 1981–1983, foreign trade was recentralized with a permit system, ostensibly to regulate it and avoid excessive competition among provincial foreign trade firms that depressed the prices of Chinese exports.[60] But the conservative backlash fizzled out quickly, and a far more market-oriented round of foreign trade reforms took place in 1984–1986. New measures allowed large firms to directly engage in foreign trade by bypassing the state foreign trade organizations. Additionally, the Ministry of Foreign Economic Relations and Trade (MOFERT) was stripped of its authority to supervise the business activities of local FTOs, which could then become the real middlemen in foreign trade.

The number of FTOs therefore rose rapidly to about eight hundred in the country. Incentives for exports were enhanced by allowing firms to retain a larger share of their hard currency earnings and to swap their retained hard currency at designated foreign exchange swap centers at market rates instead of at the overvalued official rate, thus converting their hard currency at more favorable rates. In the second half of the 1980s, China restricted state planning of foreign trade to major commodities (such as crude oil, rice, minerals, poultry, and steel), allowing all other goods (mostly manufactures) to be traded without administrative controls. Even though the government set general export targets, MOFERT stopped making and issuing specific export plans.[61] Complementary market-oriented reforms were implemented as well. The (overvalued) Chinese currency was devalued repeatedly. Subsidies for foreign trade were reduced. A system of tax rebates was introduced to encourage processing trade (which involved the import of components without tariffs for assembly and re-export).[62] These initial reforms led to an instant and rapid increase in foreign trade (see table 2.2). Total foreign trade rose fivefold, from

$20 billion to $102 billion between 1978 and 1988. Exports registered an increase of similar magnitude. As manufactured goods began to account for a growing share of exports, China's foreign trade structure improved significantly. In 1980 manufactured goods accounted for about one-half of total exports; by 1989 manufactured goods constituted 71 percent of total exports.[63]

As a whole, after one decade of reform, the Chinese economy had become much more open. In 1978 foreign trade accounted for only about 10 percent of the economy based on the exchange rate; by 1988 it had risen to 27 percent.[64] Greater openness allowed the economy to grow faster. One study estimates that exports increased China's economic growth by one percentage point per year between 1981 and 1988.[65] Research on the benefits of China's opening to the world has also yielded evidence that the growth of foreign trade after 1979 led to the emergence of dynamic regional manufacturing clusters, technological upgrading, and improvements in productivity.[66]

However, China's reform of its foreign trade regime was far from complete. It maintained a dual-exchange-rate system that distorted prices (unification of exchange rates did not occur until 1994). Most firms still could not engage directly in foreign trade, hampering competition and efficiency. Nominal tariff rates remained high, although the effective tariff rate was lower because many imports—machinery and inputs for export processing—were tax exempt. Licenses and nontariff barriers were widely used to protect domestic industries (mainly SOEs).[67]

Rise of the Private Sector

The rapid emergence and expansion of the private sector in the 1980s was not the result of a planned or concerted effort by the party. In fact, the party did not anticipate the rise of the private sector, nor did it actively promote the sector, due to conservative opposition. Instead, reformers took tentative steps to enable the private sector gradually to gain legal status and economic freedom. Unlike in the former Soviet bloc, where the private sector emerged mostly as the result of the privatization of SOEs after the fall of communism, the emergence of the private sector in China was marked by the entry of a huge number of small firms and "creeping privatization" of state-owned assets.[68] Throughout the 1980s the dynamism of the private sector, which was practically nonexistent on the eve of reform, created a new engine of economic growth that fundamentally reshaped the Chinese economy and contributed to its long-term success, arguably more than any other policy or reform. As a result, it is reasonable to claim that China's economic success was more one of "growing out of the plan" than of reforming inefficient SOEs.[69]

The best summary of this process of growing out of the plan was provided by Zhao Ziyang, the premier in charge of the economy during most of the 1980s. According to Zhao, one of the most important aspects of China's economic reform in the decade was the gradual growth and strengthening of a new market economy that consisted of TVEs, private firms, and foreign-invested firms. The new market economy existed outside the planned economy and operated according to market rules. Due to their efficiency and dynamism, such firms grew much faster than the state-owned firms. Consequently, even as the planned economy remained fundamentally unreformed, the share of the market economy continued to rise, and over time this development changed the nature of the Chinese economy.[70]

In hindsight, the benefits of growing out of the plan are self-evident. The dynamics are simple but powerful. Because private firms are more efficient, they grow faster and can, over time, take market share away from state firms and account for a higher proportion of economic output.[71] The growth of the private sector and the commensurate decline of the state sector—the defining characteristic of growing out of the plan—can be seen in the economic statistics of the 1980s (and subsequent decades). In absolute terms, the state sector grew in the 1980s, but because the nonstate sector (mostly private firms) grew much faster, the latter gained a greater share of economic output. Official data show that the industrial output of SOEs rose from 367 billion to 1.234 trillion yuan from 1979 to 1989, while the nonstate sector grew from 100 billion yuan to 967 billion yuan.[72] As a result, the share of industrial output attributed to SOEs declined from nearly 78 percent to 56 percent between 1979 and 1989 (table 2.3).

TABLE 2.3. Contribution of the Nonstate Sector to Industrial Output, 1978–1989 (%)

Year	SOEs	Nonstate Sector
1978	77.63	22.37
1980	75.97	23.54
1983	73.36	25.74
1986	62.27	33.51
1989	56.06	35.69

Source: *ZGTJNJ 1990*, 416.

Economically, growing out of the plan helped sustain growth and avoid the decline in economic output that had characterized the transition experience in the former Soviet bloc. The superior economic efficiency of the private sector also created competitive pressures on the state sector and accelerated its relative decline in the post-Mao era. Politically, growing out of the plan allowed Chinese reformers in the 1980s to build up political capital quickly while shelving the more difficult task of reforming the SOEs, a step almost certain to precipitate a confrontation with conservatives opposed to dismantling the economic foundation of the party-state. At the same time, it created winners and avoided making powerful groups losers, at least at the crucial initial stage of reform.[73]

However, growing out of the plan had serious limitations. Because the party continued to favor inefficient SOEs and failed to provide secure property rights and a level playing field for the private sector, China's private entrepreneurs operated in an unfavorable regulatory and institutional environment that severely constrained their potential. The economic benefits generated by the rapid growth of the private sector reduced pressures to reform the inefficient SOEs until the end of the 1990s, resulting in ever-increasing subsidies to SOEs that ultimately contributed to an accumulation of bad loans in the state-owned banking system. China's hybrid economy also generated abundant opportunities for rent-seeking because the resources under the control of the state sector, such as the regulatory approvals, land, and bank credits, could be allocated through administrative means to well-connected private entrepreneurs and families of officials.[74] As Zhao Ziyang observed after his downfall, the coexistence of two fundamentally different economic systems—a favored state sector and a dynamic private sector—produced significant negative effects on the economy. Although it was wise to adopt growing out of the plan as a transitional strategy, it would stop working in the long term.[75]

Emergence of the Private Sector

The party's primary focus of economic reform in urban areas in the 1980s was on the SOEs. Ironically, the private sector thrived during the decade, even though the party did not provide meaningful economic incentives to promote it. The most the party did was to create the minimal legal or policy space needed for the private sector to emerge and exist, even though this process was slow, gradual, and tentative. The party opened the door slightly for the private sector in July 1981 when the State Council issued a document permitting the establishment of individually operated businesses (*geti jingji*) in the urban areas. The document, "Several Policy Provisions on Nonagricultural Individually Operated Economic Activities in Urban Areas," allowed private entrepreneurs to hire up to seven employees and operate mainly micro service businesses, such as retail, restaurants, handicrafts, and residential renovation.[76] Shortly thereafter, with its major overhaul of the Chinese constitution in 1982, the party officially recognized the legal existence of the *geti jingji*. Article 11 of the amended constitution states that "economic activities of individual laborers conducted within legally permitted scopes are an auxiliary of the socialist state-owned economy. The state protects the legal rights and interests of individually operated economic activities. The state, through administrative means, guides, assists, and supervises such economic activities."[77] (The constitution was amended again in 1988, 1993, 1999, and 2004 to provide greater protections for the private sector.) At the beginning of 1983, the party took another small step by allowing rural residents to engage in nonagricultural activities and, more important, to purchase tractors, motor vehicles, and boats to operate in transportation businesses.[78]

As the private sector began to grow and prosper, the conservatives pushed back. Chen Yun, Deng's ideological rival who was adamantly opposed to the rise of a private sector, launched a campaign against "economic crimes" in 1982.[79] In 1985 he and his followers manufactured a national scandal, the so-called Case of Fake Medicines in Jinjiang. Private entrepreneurs producing food supplements in Jinjiang, Fujian province, were falsely accused of turning out counterfeit medicines on a massive scale. Shortly thereafter, Chen engineered the ouster of the reformist provincial party chief, Xiang Nan, blaming him for the scandal.[80]

The most potent tactic deployed by the conservatives was attacking the widespread practice of private firms employing more than seven workers (the legal limit was up to and including seven workers). As they thrived, private entrepreneurs had to expand by employing more workers, thus running up against the legal limit imposed by the State Council's 1981 document on *geti jingji*. It was Deng's personal intervention in 1984 that apparently prevented the conservatives from cracking down on the private sector.

At a meeting with revolutionary veterans on the Central Advisory Committee in 1984, the conservatives clamored for punishment of successful private entrepreneurs (in particular, a flamboyant private entrepreneur who had hired over a hundred workers and had made a fortune by selling snacks). But Deng pushed back hard. "Based on my view," he declared, "we should not deal with the issue of hiring labor [above the limit of seven] for two years. Can [allowing the private entrepreneur to do business] upset our overall situation? But if you touch him [the entrepreneur], the people will say that [our] policy has changed. Confidence would be shaken. Let 'Idiot Seeds' [the brand of snacks sold by the entrepreneur] do its business for a period. What is there to be afraid of?"[81]

It was not until April 1988 that the party formally endorsed private businesses (*siying qiye*), when the NPC amended the constitution to permit the private sector to exist and develop. Compared with the constitutional amendment passed in 1982, which allowed only individually run private businesses (*geti jingji*), the constitutional recognition and protection of the private sector in 1988 represented a major ideological breakthrough, even though by that time the private sector had already been thriving in a vast legal gray area for the better part of the decade.[82] In June 1988 the State Council issued a landmark document granting private businesses most of the rights they needed to operate and grow. The key provisions of the document, known as "The PRC Interim Regulations on Private Businesses," include permission to hire more than eight workers, limited liability, an expanded scope of business, the right to hire and fire workers and to set their compensation, and the right to enter into joint ventures, to engage in transactions with foreign companies, to conduct foreign trade, and to have access to bank credit.[83]

Due to political support from the reformers, the private sector grew at an astonishing rate in the 1980s. At the end of 1978, the private sector, which employed only 150,000 individuals in household-run, or *geti*, micro businesses, was a negligible economic force. But by 1988 such micro businesses had mushroomed into 14.5 million firms, employing 23 million people.[84] TVEs, most of which were private firms despite their official "collective" label, saw their employment grow from 28.3 million to 93.7 million between 1978 and 1989.[85] As table 2.4 indicates, growth of the private sector in the 1980s was truly phenomenal.

Both individually owned businesses and foreign-invested businesses grew rapidly in the 1978–1989 decade (the contribution of firms in these two categories to industrial output grew from zero to more than 8 percent in just one decade). But the star performers in the private sector in the 1980s were undoubtedly the TVEs. Their output rose from 49 billion yuan to 742 billion yuan from 1978 to 1989, accounting for 21 percent of "total social output" in China in 1989.[86]

Aside from the necessary political protection and regulatory framework that allowed the nascent private sector to exist and expand, several other

TABLE 2.4. Share of Industrial Output, 1978–1989 (%)

Year	State-Owned	Nonstate Sector	TVEs	*Geti* (Individually Owned)	Cooperative	Other (Foreign-Invested)
1978	77.63	22.37				
1985	64.86		14.65	1.85	1.56	1.21
1989	56.06		19.58	4.80	2.25	3.44

Source: *ZGTJNJ 1990*, 413, 416.

factors also facilitated the rapid growth of the private sector. Some scholars attribute this phenomenon to the self-interests of the key actors, in particular the entrepreneurs themselves and the local officials. While the growing private businesses enabled entrepreneurs to build and accumulate wealth, the same development also helped local officials expand the sources of revenue, burnish their performance in employment and growth, and acquire private wealth from previously nonexistent opportunities for rent-seeking and self-enrichment.[87]

However, other economic and political factors likely played a far more important and direct role in turbo-charging growth of the private sector. The most critical factor is the success of the decollectivization of agriculture. The virtuous cycle created by the rural reforms produced the essential conditions for the private sector to take root and thrive. On the supply side, higher productivity in the rural areas increased overall income, which boosted private savings for investment and in turn then allowed a small number of entrepreneurs to raise capital, either by borrowing from family, relatives, and friends or by tapping into their savings. Greater efficiency in rural production also freed up the surplus or the underutilized vast labor pool in the countryside, channeling them into the more productive manufacturing and service sectors.

On the demand side, higher rural productivity raised farmers' income and boosted their demand for consumer goods. At the same time, the economic distortions of the Maoist era had led to serious shortages of consumer goods and services, thus creating a huge backlog of demand that the private sector could meet. The demand for employment in the modern sector, which (the already bloated) SOEs could not meet, also forced the party to liberalize the economy so that the new private firms could absorb new entrants into the labor market (between 1980 and 1985 alone, more than thirty-seven million people in the urban areas needed employment).[88]

Yet, despite such favorable conditions, private entrepreneurs nevertheless hedged their bets by disguising the ownership of their businesses. A popular method was to register as "collective enterprises" rather than as "private," or *siying*, firms (legally, the state did not formally endorse *siying* firms until 1988). In addition to the political protection, private businesses registered as "collective enterprises," in a practice known as "wearing red hats," so they could navigate the many regulatory obstacles to obtain business licenses and secure access to banking services and credit as well as to government contracts. To be sure, donning a "red hat" had its disadvantages as well because such private firms were effectively paying for political protection, and they had to bear extra financial burdens (such as forced contributions to local budgets and employment). Private entrepreneurs resorting to this survival strategy also exposed themselves to legal risks, such as disputes over the ownership of their assets and even criminal prosecution.[89]

Although wearing a "red hat" was widespread, the exact share of private firms among the TVEs is a matter of dispute.[90] According to a 1995 survey conducted by the State Administration for Industry and Commerce (SAIC), of 178,000 "collective firms," roughly one in five of them had private majority ownership.[91] This number almost certainly underestimates the share of private firms among collective firms. Yasheng Huang's research uncovers more convincing evidence that, based on data collected by the Ministry of Agriculture, nearly 90 percent of TVEs in 1985 were actually private firms.[92]

Entrepreneurs blazing the trail in the 1980s came from a wide range of social backgrounds, but a majority hailed from the countryside, again affirming the critical contribution of the rural reform to the transformation of the Chinese economy. According to a national survey of 1,187 owners of private firms in the countryside in 1991, 42 percent had served as village cadres, 19 percent had been principal officials of TVEs, 13 percent had been workers in TVEs, and 9 percent were former PLA soldiers. Another survey of 1,853 owners of private businesses (apparently based in urban areas), also conducted in 1991, shows that 30 percent had resigned from SOEs, 31 percent had been peasants, 16 percent had been self-employed, and 12 percent had been unemployed.[93] In other words, most pioneers in the private sector came from outside the state sector.

Reform of the SOEs

On the eve of Deng's reform, SOEs dominated the modern sectors of the Chinese economy, accounting for 87 percent of the fiscal revenue of the state, 77.6 percent of industrial output, and 78 percent of urban employment.[94]

However, like their counterparts in the former Soviet bloc, Chinese SOEs were plagued by systemic inefficiencies.[95] As economic organizations, these firms were more like government bureaucracies than profit-seeking economic actors because they were administered by the government through directives governing nearly all operational matters. As part of a planned economy, they did not have the basic freedoms for business operations, such as determining what or how much to produce. Nor did the SOEs have control in matters such as the amount of labor to employ, the appointment of management, and compensation of workers and management, because it was the supervising government bureaucracies that made these decisions. Like the SOEs in the Communist regimes of the former Soviet bloc, Chinese SOEs had two critical institutional flaws: an absence of real owners and soft budget constraints. Nominally, the "state" owned these firms. In reality, there were no real owners but instead multiple bureaucracies (such as government agencies in charge of production planning, fiscal revenue, and labor-related issues) exercising control over them. This situation not only created conflicts of interest among stakeholders but also made it impossible for the SOEs to pursue economically efficient goals. The "soft budget constraints" meant that these firms were not responsible for their failure because they could always count on the state to bail them out.[96]

The last systemic flaw of Chinese SOEs was their so-called policy burden. As an essential component of the party-state, SOEs had to perform many non-economic roles that served the needs of the party, such as maintaining employment regardless of costs and providing social services, including healthcare, housing, childcare, and retirement income.[97]

Given the centrality of the SOEs in the Chinese economy and the daunting technical difficulties of restructuring these firms (practically all attempts to reform SOEs in the former Soviet bloc and Yugoslavia had ended in failure), reformers were forced to adopt a far more cautious and incremental approach.[98] Their first step was to expand the autonomy of the SOEs and to grant more financial incentives to SOE management in the belief that greater operational freedoms and material rewards could improve their efficiency. After localized experiments in Sichuan and Beijing in early 1979 produced promising results, the State Council formally endorsed measures to expand the autonomy of SOEs in July 1979.[99] According to "Several Provisions on Expanding Management Autonomy of State-owned Industrial Enterprises," the management of the SOEs could retain a portion of the profits, hire workers, appoint executives, and exercise a wide range of executive authority provided they fulfilled the targets set by the state.[100]

However, the expanded autonomy quickly created its own problems, especially as the managers of the SOEs gamed the new policy to retain more profits, which led to less income for the state and an increase in budget deficits.[101] To liberal economists, expansion of SOE management autonomy alone was unlikely to produce sustained improvements in SOE performance. Real SOE autonomy was impossible to achieve because the state kept most of the power that directly affected the performance and operations of the enterprises. Expanding SOE autonomy also worsened the "principal-agent" problem in the state-socialist system because it allowed managers to behave more opportunistically.[102] Most important, because SOEs were part of the market, giving the enterprises autonomy when the market itself had systemic flaws was unlikely to work. Specifically, when prices were distorted, even enterprises with full autonomy could not respond to distorted markets or be responsible for profits and losses.[103]

Once it became clear that expanding the autonomy of the SOEs was an unpromising proposition, Chinese leaders began to look for alternatives. Liberal economists argued that a successful reform of SOEs would be possible only when it was part of a package of reforms of other institutions, such as prices, taxation, wages, social security, and the financial system, that directly affected the SOEs. But the party did not adopt their proposal for comprehensive reform.[104]

The alternative, which the party eventually settled on in 1986, was the "contract responsibility system" (*chengbao zerenzhi*). In essence, the contract responsibility system was an updated version of a 1981 government attempt to attach conditions to the autonomy of the SOEs.[105] What made the reform proposed in 1986 different was its granting of full operational autonomy in return for commitments to fulfill fixed financial targets. A document issued by the State Council in February 1988 formalized this system (implementation had begun in 1987).[106]

In terms of specifics, the "contract responsibility" of the SOEs consisted of meeting financial targets, such as profitability, growth, reduction of losses, capital investments, technological innovations, and tax payments. SOEs that reached these goals could retain more profits to provide higher compensation to workers.[107] However, the contract responsibility system quickly proved to be a disappointment. Because of the heterogeneity of firms and their vastly different structural conditions (such as competition, supply, and demand) among industrial sectors, it was nearly impossible for the government to stipulate standard contracting terms or to set performance standards.[108]

Even worse, the contract responsibility system rewarded short-term SOE behavior because the length of a typical contract was three years, which encouraged SOE managers to cut spending on capital investments and technological upgrading in order to reach their profit targets. SOEs also had powerful incentives to raise prices to increase their profit margins—an easy thing to do in sectors where incumbent SOEs faced little competition. Despite the formal contracts signed between SOE management and supervising government agencies, SOEs continued to enjoy soft budget constraints and, as a result, were not responsible for failing to fulfill the terms of their contracts. As the contract responsibility system did not touch the core issue of "state ownership," it was obviously incapable of addressing all the pathologies of such ownership.[109]

Despite the flaws in China's approaches to reforming the SOEs in the 1980s, some economists endorsed these limited measures but with qualifications, arguing that they helped improve the SOEs' financial performance, output, and innovative capacity.[110] But evidence supports the consensus opinion among Chinese policymakers and economists that the SOE reforms in the 1980s essentially were failures.[111] The early experiment to expand SOE autonomy was short-lived; it was replaced by the contract responsibility system, which itself was abandoned in the early 1990s when the post-Tiananmen leadership introduced a new round of reforms that sought to "establish a modern corporate system." By then, most SOEs were mired in crisis because they simply could not compete with private firms or imports. By the end of the 1990s, the government, no longer able to keep loss-making SOEs afloat without endangering the banking system, was forced to adopt a new strategy of "grasp the big and let go of the small," by which it retained only the large SOEs in critical sectors (banking, telecommunications, transportation, and energy) and allowed small and medium-sized SOEs to go bankrupt en masse.[112] Zhao Ziyang, the reformist premier in charge of the economy in the 1980s, was perhaps the most authoritative person to render a verdict on this issue. Reflecting on China's reform when he was under house arrest in the 1990s, Zhao said: "Reform of the mechanisms of SOEs did not touch the fundamentals." By "fundamentals," he likely meant the most critical institutional factors affecting the performance of the SOEs, such as state ownership, the pricing system, capital markets, and the social safety net. However, Zhao believed that, ironically, the failure to reform the SOEs had a positive impact during China's transition to a market economy.[113] Although he did not elaborate on this point, he was likely thinking of the potential political risks and costs of more aggressive reforms that might have made SOEs far more efficient but would have also triggered strong opposition from both the ideological conservatives and the affected interest groups.

Dual-Track Price Reform

As in Soviet-type economies, prices in China during the prereform era were set by the state, not by the market (although as a more decentralized economy, some prices in China were set by local, not central, authorities).[114] Theoretically, price reform should be a top priority during a country's transition from state-socialism to a market economy. But as the experience of the former Soviet bloc in the early 1990s shows, price reform could only be completed with a "big bang" that freed all prices at once—at the cost of hyperinflation that would be economically disruptive and politically destructive for the reformers.[115]

By comparison, China adopted a far more gradual and cautious approach to price reform in the 1980s, for two reasons. Economically, unlike the Soviet bloc after the fall of communism, China did not face high inflation in the early 1980s and therefore had no need for the stabilization program that all Soviet bloc countries had to adopt. Politically, Chinese reformers in the early 1980s had to share power with conservatives, so they did not have the ability to push through radical reforms, such as the freeing up of prices. Even more important, Chinese reformers likely realized that a failed price reform could spell calamity for the entire reform program (such fears were realized when mere *talk* of price reform triggered panic buying and high inflation in the summer of 1988).

As a result, China did not start to reform the pricing system until 1984, when the government implemented an experimental program of "dual-track pricing." Instead of ending mandatory pricing set by the state, dual-track pricing retained mandatory pricing but also introduced a second set of parallel prices determined by the market. The initial concept was proposed by a graduate student at an academic conference in 1984. Economists advocating dual-track pricing argued that since the prices of most products cannot be liberalized without eviscerating the command economy, the only way to reform a planned economy without abandoning it right away is to introduce pricing that allows both plan-mandated and liberalized prices to operate alongside each other to bring supply and demand into balance.[116]

The government quickly embraced this alluring concept. In May 1984 the State Council formally permitted SOEs to adopt dual-track pricing. Specifically, SOEs could sell excess output at prices they set by themselves (but only

20 percent above or below the state-mandated prices).[117] Leading economists have since hailed dual-track pricing reform as an innovative measure that produced winners but no losers.[118] It likely also gave the SOEs a greater incentive to increase production because they could charge higher prices for products exceeding the planned target. Such marked-up products also provided a vital source of inputs for the nonstate sector, in particular the TVEs that otherwise could not purchase products made by SOEs outside the plan.[119]

But the dual-track pricing system also facilitated rent-seeking behavior and corruption because the SOEs and well-connected individuals could easily make a quick profit by obtaining products at lower state-mandated prices within the plan and then selling them at higher prices. Many SOEs also gamed the new system by trying to get more "fixed-price" (below-market price) inputs from the plan and to underreport their production so they could sell more at above-plan prices.[120]

For all the attention the dual-track pricing in the 1980s received, it is impossible to evaluate its contribution to China's price reform. Although the share of products subject to state-mandated prices continued to fall, it was most likely the result of increased production that can be credited to other factors, especially the rapid increase in industrial output by nonstate firms.[121] Instructively, when nearly all prices were fully liberalized in the 1990s, this achievement was not due to any price reform. By that time, China was no longer a shortage economy. The liberalization of prices was almost certainly the result of sufficient supply made possible by the explosive growth of the private sector and foreign trade.

Summary

Measured by key indicators of economic performance, China achieved unqualified success in the 1980s. Through domestic reform and integration with the global economy, the country scored its best growth rates since 1949. Per capita income, which was 315 yuan in 1978, rose to 1,189 yuan in 1989. Adjusted for inflation, real per capita income nearly tripled during the period. The gross social product (a proximate measure of the gross national product) rose from 677.6 billion yuan in 1978 to 3.46 trillion yuan in 1989, representing a 3,600 percent increase after adjusting for inflation. Despite high inflation in 1988–1989, China maintained overall macroeconomic stability, with inflation averaging 6.8 percent per year between 1979 and 1989. The economic structure improved as well. Household consumption averaged 65 percent of national income during the period, reflecting a relatively balanced economy. The rapid growth of the nonstate sector reduced the role of the state in the economy, as indicated by the fall of its share in industrial output from 78 percent in 1978 to 56 percent in 1989.[122]

China's integration with the world economy proceeded at a rapid pace as well. Foreign trade rose from $20.6 billion in 1978 to $111.6 billion in 1989, averaging an annual growth rate of 49 percent. Exports increased from $9.75 billion to $52.5 billion during the same period. The inflow of FDI totaled $15.4 billion during the decade.[123] Even though China would attract far more FDI in the 1990s, this amount still represents foreign investors' vote of confidence in Deng's economic revolution.

Aside from these measurable achievements, reform in the 1980s also scored major political and institutional breakthroughs. Obviously, by delivering a proverbial "early harvest" of the fruits of reform, Deng and his supporters reaped immense political capital to bolster their case for more reform. Thus the most important success of the reform in the 1980s was the laying of the foundations for China's economic take-off in the subsequent two decades.

As this chapter shows, Deng's reform and opening in the decade substantially weakened the command economy by growing out of the plan. Rural decollectivization not only dismantled a key pillar of the Maoist economic system but also unleashed pent-up entrepreneurial energy and created a virtuous cycle that powered the emergence and growth of a new and dynamic private sector. At the same time, integrating China into the global economy through trade and investment enabled a previously self-isolated economy to capitalize on its comparative advantage of cheap labor. The combination of an efficient domestic private sector and integration with the global economy quickly became the engine of Chinese growth.

To be sure, growing out of the plan avoided tackling the thorny issue of SOE reform. Indeed, China's attempts to reform these dinosaurs of totalitarianism in the 1980s were largely unsuccessful. It would take another decade and a pending banking crisis for the party to muster the courage to push through major SOE reforms. But this particular failure must be understood in the political context of the times. With powerful conservative forces led by Chen Yun entrenched at the top of the party's leadership, it was inconceivable that Deng and his fellow reformers would risk a confrontation in order to enact far more radical SOE reforms (such as mass bankruptcy and privatization—the approach the party eventually adopted at the end of the 1990s). Given the complete lack of knowledge in the 1980s about how to reform the SOEs and the far superior alternative of cultivating new and more efficient economic forces, such as domestic private firms and foreign-invested firms, it made perfect political and economic sense to prioritize growing out of the plan over reforming the plan itself.

Nevertheless, the success of growing out of the plan during the decade was achieved at the expense of not dismantling, once and for all, the economic foundations of totalitarianism—the SOEs through which the party-state controlled the "commanding heights" of the economy. Even though the output of the private sector eventually exceeded that of these firms, they continued to dominate some of the most important sectors of the economy, in particular finance, energy, telecommunications, and transportation. The party-state's control of these firms not only allowed the regime access to bountiful economic resources but also necessitated costly protection of these firms that distorted markets and undercut economic efficiency. Zhao Ziyang, the reformer in charge of economic policy in the 1980s, foresaw the long-term danger of a "dual-track" transition characterized by rapid growth of the private sector and continuing state dominance in a large segment of the economy. "The long-term coexistence of two systems and two tracks," he warned in the 1990s, "ultimately will produce enormous negative effects. It was right to resort to gradual transition initially, but this approach must not continue in the long run."[124] If anything, the deposed former premier and CCP general secretary likely underestimated the economic and political costs of the dual-track transition. The dual-track transition would ultimately lose momentum, and the party-state would be forced to use its power to support a hugely inefficient state sector at the expense of the private sector.[125]

3

Building Neo-Authoritarianism, 1992–2002

THE BLOODY end of the Tiananmen crisis closed off, at least for the foreseeable future, China's path to a more open and free society. But the neo-authoritarian order—capitalist economic development under one-party rule—did not emerge in the immediate aftermath of the crackdown. Indeed, the party still had two plausible pathways to choose. One was to reverse the economic reforms of the 1980s, reassert the party's control over the economy and society, and reconstitute a system embodying most of the institutional characteristics of the early 1950s. The other was to fully embrace neo-authoritarian developmentalism. Initially, between mid-1989 to the end of 1991, hard-liners who had gained power after the crackdown attempted to resuscitate the old communist system. Even though their efforts largely failed, a prolonged political stasis during which the regime would be stuck in a transitional no-man's land was a distinct possibility.

The event galvanizing the party into unreservedly endorsing neo-authoritarian developmentalism was the fall of the Soviet Union in December 1991. Less than a month later, Deng Xiaoping started his tour of southern China that, in substance though not in name, launched the post-Tiananmen era of neo-authoritarian rule. Due to the purge of the liberal wing from the party in 1989 and the demoralization of the hard-liners by the dissolution of the Soviet Union, party leadership became ideologically more homogenous. However reluctantly, hard-liners bought into Deng's vision of capitalist economic modernization under one-party rule because this was the only feasible survival strategy despite their past resistance to this path.

After he rallied the party to his neo-authoritarian vision and installed a new leadership team in the fall of 1992, Deng gradually faded away from the political scene. Jiang Zemin, the compromise choice for the CCP general secretary the elders picked during the Tiananmen crisis, became an effective implementer of Dengist neo-authoritarian strategy. Under Jiang's leadership, the party was laser-focused on economic development while adopting novel tactics to keep its grip on a fast-changing society. The individual components of the party's survival strategy, such as performance-based legitimacy, an implicit security pact among elites, nationalism, social co-optation, and selective repression, evolved into the key pillars of the post-1989 neo-authoritarian order.

Judging by the economic boom and political tranquility at both the elite and mass levels in the post-Tiananmen era (1992–2012), Deng's neo-authoritarian vision had to be credited with bringing about the party's golden period and enabling the regime to weather the shocks of the Tiananmen debacle and the collapse of the Soviet Union. Behind the façade of stability and prosperity, however, new dangers began to emerge. The party's success in delivering rising standards of living, albeit on an investment-led growth model that would soon produce diminishing returns, reduced incentives for deeper and more difficult economic reforms. At the same time, the party's control of immense and fast-growing economic resources fueled corruption, exposing the fundamental flaws of Dengist neo-authoritarianism.

A Family "Vacation" That Changed History

The brutal crushing of the Tiananmen protests on June 4, 1989, severely damaged Deng politically. The purge of Zhao Ziyang and other liberal reformers meant Deng could no longer rely on members of this group to implement his agenda of reform and opening. The octogenarian was said to be very depressed, and, after having given up smoking for several years, he began to smoke again.[1] The only consolation for Deng was that he managed to install a compromise choice, Jiang Zemin, former party chief of Shanghai, as Zhao's replacement, thus preventing an ideological hard-liner from taking over the party's top leadership position. But Deng's power play failed to prevent the hard-liners from implementing policies to roll back the reforms of the 1980s as Jiang, a risk-averse opportunist with no power base of his own, lacked both the inclination and the ability to put up any resistance.

Li Peng and Yao Yilin, the two arch conservatives in charge of economic policy, doubled down on an austerity program adopted in late 1988 to contain inflation. Although initially it prioritized reducing investment, in the wake of the Tiananmen crackdown they aggressively pushed for a recentralization of power and a reinvigoration of economic planning. These measures favored the SOEs at the expense of the nascent private sector.[2] Consequently, the economy registered its weakest growth in a decade. GDP rose only 4.1 percent in 1989 and 3.9 percent in 1990, even though it rebounded to 9.5 percent in 1991.[3] The TVEs, the largest component of the private sector, averaged an annual growth rate of 40 percent from 1985 to 1988, but in 1989 and 1990 they grew only 15 percent and 14 percent, respectively.[4] Hard-liners had less success in recentralizing the economy, however, as such efforts encountered strong resistance from the large and economically important provinces, such as Shanghai and Shandong.[5]

The political crackdown launched by the hard-liners targeting the participants in the prodemocracy movement produced mixed results at best. The regime successfully restored political control on university campuses.[6] But its witch hunt for prodemocracy activists at the grassroots level largely failed due to resistance by sympathetic local officials.[7] The hard-liners' thinly veiled ideological attacks on Deng's policy of reform and opening instantly encountered pushback from Deng himself.[8] The overall political situation in the year and a half following the Tiananmen crackdown can be best described as a political stalemate.[9] Although ascendant hard-liners had momentum to reverse Deng's reform and regain the party's eroded control over society, they were not fully successful. At the same time, the reformist camp led by Deng, now structurally weakened as the result of his purge of the liberals at the top, lacked strength to breathe new life into reform and opening. To outside observers, the Chinese regime in 1990 "showed many of the classic signs of a moribund system."[10]

Deng, whose legacy was hanging in the balance, was reluctant to see his project of modernizing China wither in midcourse. In 1991 he began to take actions to revive his reform and opening.[11] He first visited Shanghai in January 1991 and gave a series of speeches calling for "emancipating the mind" and taking bolder steps in reform and opening.[12] Shortly after he returned from his visit, Deng elevated Zhu Rongji, the no-nonsense party chief and mayor of Shanghai, to the position of vice premier, even though Zhu was only an alternate member of the Central Committee (traditionally vice premiers were also Politburo members). The promotion of Zhu in April 1991 marked the beginning of the erosion of control of economic policy by the hard-liners in the State Council.

However useful these political maneuvers might have been for Deng, they were insufficient to change the political dynamics decisively in his favor. What really made the difference was the shock of the fall of the Soviet Union in late 1991. Judging by the rebound of the Chinese economy that year, the primary motivation behind Deng's last-ditch effort to salvage his legacy at the beginning of 1992 was not China's economic difficulties but the geopolitical and ideological environments that had been altered beyond recognition by the events in the Soviet Union.[13]

On August 19, 1991, diehard conservatives in Moscow, in a desperate attempt to save the imploding Soviet Union, launched a coup. Initially, their counterparts in Beijing were thrilled. Some of them even proposed that they should publicly support the coup, but Deng quashed the idea and urged caution.[14] If anything, the crisis in the Soviet Union reinforced Deng's conviction that only economic success could keep the CCP in power. The day after the coup, Deng stressed that the party's survival would largely depend on reform and opening. Instead of seeing the pending Soviet collapse as a crisis, he warned leading members of the Central Committee that "great changes are taking place in the world, and this gives us an opportunity. . . . If we don't seize this opportunity to raise the economy to a higher level, other countries will leap ahead of us, leaving us far behind."[15]

How Deng personally reacted to the dissolution of the USSR at the end of 1991 is unknown. However, three weeks after Gorbachev signed away the USSR, Deng embarked on his historic southern tour that would usher in the post-Tiananmen era of neo-authoritarianism. Ostensibly, the thirty-six-day trip that took Deng, then 87 years old, to several cities in the South was a family vacation. Before his train rolled out of Beijing on January 17, 1992, there was no indication that the political stalemate after the Tiananmen crackdown would end anytime soon. But by the time Deng returned to Beijing on February 21, he was on the verge of relaunching an economic revolution that would establish a new order: capitalist economic development under one-party rule and the route to modernization that Deng had consistently advocated since the late 1970s.[16] Within a week of Deng's return, as a gesture of endorsing his views, the party distributed summaries of the speeches he had given during his tour. On March 9 and 10 the Politburo convened a rare two-day meeting (Politburo meetings usually last one day) and decided to implement the "spirit" of Deng's speeches.[17] The political atmosphere in the country changed instantly afterward. After it became clear that Deng had regained dominance, provincial leaders vied with one another in calling for more rapid economic reform. Growth immediately exploded (GDP would rise 14 percent in 1992).[18] By October 1992 Deng had installed a Politburo Standing Committee dominated by a new group of leaders who shared his neo-authoritarian vision (Li Peng, the premier, was the only surviving hard-liner in the top leadership).

There is no single answer to the question of how a monthlong "family trip" by a retired 87-year-old leader, whose only title at that time was "honorary chairman of the China Bridge Association," could change the course of Chinese history.

At the level of elite politics, the most important impact of Deng's tour was to force Jiang Zemin, who had toed a more conservative line since his appointment as party chief in June 1989, to fully embrace Deng's policy. Based on one unofficial, but apparently authentic, version of the summaries of the talks by Deng during his tour, Deng could barely conceal his deep dissatisfaction with the post-Tiananmen leadership, and he implicitly threatened to sack Jiang.[19] In addition, Deng talked at length about the fall of the Soviet Union. "What I have been thinking about the most these days," Deng allegedly told his audience in Shenzhen, "is the Soviet Union. This is a country with such bountiful natural resources, a deep cultural tradition, a powerful state, and a huge Communist Party. But it collapsed overnight." (Ironically, Xi Jinping would be reflecting on the Soviet collapse in nearly identical language two decades later after he assumed the position of party chief in November 2012.) Deng's diagnosis of the Soviet collapse was its economic failure ("it could not even fill up the bellies of its people," to use his colorful language). If China failed economically, Deng warned, "today's Soviet Union will be tomorrow's China."[20]

Deng's threat to dismiss Jiang in early 1992 seems credible. A well-connected Chinese journalist, Yang Jisheng, writes that Deng was disappointed with Jiang, and he implied that Jiang should step aside if he would not support reform more aggressively. Later, Deng did not sack Jiang, but this was only because he was dissuaded by a close associate, veteran revolutionary Bo Yibo. Ezra Vogel also claims that Jiang, in February 1992, was aware that Deng was "determined" to fire him if he did not support reform.[21]

With his job on the line, Jiang decided to back Deng's agenda wholeheartedly. Even though in 1992 Jiang had not yet consolidated power, the shift in his position from a fence-sitting opportunist to a supporter of Deng's renewed call for economic reform decisively tipped the balance at the top of the leadership in favor of Deng's policy. In addition, by early 1992 the major aging hard-liners were either in poor health or dying. The eighty-six-year-old Chen Yun, the leader of the conservative camp who might have been able to resist Deng's offensive, was apparently in poor health and politically inactive. (Chen died in April 1995.)[22]

In terms of policy, the conservative forces could not put up any resistance because by 1992 they had no credibility left. Their retrograde economic policies had produced the worst two-year growth record since 1979. The implosion of the Soviet Union, the party's model, fully revealed the ideological bankruptcy of orthodox communism. While Deng had laid out a strategy to keep the CCP in power in the changed world that was becoming implacably hostile to communism, the hard-liners simply had no alternatives to offer. Deng's call for accelerated economic development also resonated with the public. One alternative to this path—reversion to a planned economy and totalitarian social control—hardly sounded attractive to people who still remembered the dark era of Maoism. The other alternative—economic modernization concurrent with political liberalization—was impractical. The Tiananmen crackdown had dealt a fatal blow to the (already weak) prodemocracy forces at all levels. Their patron in the top leadership, Zhao Ziyang, had been purged. Leading liberal intellectuals and activists had been either exiled or imprisoned. The political control imposed after the Tiananmen crackdown eliminated any public space for advocating political change.[23]

Under these circumstances, a neo-authoritarian path appeared to offer something for everybody. For those determined to perpetuate one-party rule, this survival strategy was the most pragmatic and promising. For those seeking to reform the one-party regime, economic modernization could be a roundabout way to liberalize or even democratize the dictatorship. For the vast majority of Chinese people, with a per capita income of only 1,262 in purchasing power parity in 1992, a ruling regime bent on economic development appeared to be much better than one that was not.[24]

Lastly, the Soviet factor likely had a major, albeit difficult to measure, impact on the attitudes of ordinary Chinese people toward their government. The chaos in the wake of the Soviet collapse, which the Chinese government portrayed in apocalyptic terms through official propaganda, probably made ordinary Chinese, for whom the turmoil of the Cultural Revolution was recent memory, prefer order and stability to change that might bring about a calamity on the order of the Soviet collapse. Indeed, opinion surveys conducted in the early 1990s show a surprisingly high level of support for the CCP. In addition to the party's satisfactory economic performance, an important source of support was fear of social instability.[25]

After turning the tide with his southern tour, Deng immediately set about to rearrange the party's top leadership to ensure that his neo-authoritarian survival strategy would be faithfully implemented. Because Chen Yun had largely abandoned his opposition to Deng's policy, partially due to his poor health, Deng had near-complete freedom to pick the top leaders at the Fourteenth Party Congress in October 1992.[26] Judging by the line-up of the top leadership chosen at the congress, Deng scored a total political triumph. The Central Committee featured a number of technocrats who could be trusted with the mission of supercharging economic development.[27] Of the seven members of the PSC, Deng could count on six to carry out his policy, including Jiang Zemin (general secretary), Zhu Rongji (executive vice premier), and Hu Jintao (a rising star whom Deng anointed as Jiang's successor). The only conservative on the PSC was Premier Li Peng.

Deng's anointment of Hu Jintao, then 50 years old, as Jiang's successor likely reflected his fear that there might be a succession struggle after Jiang completed his second full term as party chief in 2002. Such a fight not only would be destabilizing but would probably result in elevating a leader to the top who could threaten Deng's legacies. Deng's choice of Hu, a party apparatchik with a thin record of accomplishments, remains a puzzle. Since Deng hardly knew Hu personally because Hu was nearly forty years younger and had not worked under him directly, it is very likely that Deng had relied on the recommendation of close associate and Hu's lifelong patron Song Ping, a conservative and member of the PSC (1989–1992). Deng might have also been reassured by Hu's loyalty to the party because, as party chief in Tibet beginning in 1988, he had ordered martial law and had crushed the protests by Tibetans in March 1989, several months before the Tiananmen massacre. At the same time, Hu had not demonstrated any opposition to market-oriented reforms. Under these circumstances, Hu Jintao apparently was the safest choice as a future leader.[28]

Intellectual Foundations of the Post-Tiananmen Order

Intellectually, the CCP's survival strategy in the post-Tiananmen era was derived, in most part, from the developmental successes of the East Asian countries (in particular South Korea, Taiwan, and Singapore) under authoritarian rule from the 1960s to the 1980s and, after the Soviet collapse, from their own interpretation of the causes of the failure of the Soviet regime. "Neo-authoritarian developmentalism"—a combination of pro-market reforms, integration with the West-dominated global economy, and authoritarian rule—probably best summarizes the essence of Deng's strategy of economic modernization. As indicated by his speeches emphasizing both economic development and preservation of the CCP's political monopoly (the most important of his "four cardinal principles"), from the outset neo-authoritarian developmentalism was the ideological inspiration of Deng's reform and opening, even though he never invoked the term in his public speeches. The only credible piece of evidence that Deng embraced the concept is provided by Zhao Ziyang, who said that Deng commented to him in a meeting in 1988 that "neo-authoritarianism"—economic development in a stable environment under the rule of a strongman—"is my position, but there is no need to frame it in such a way."[29]

Indeed, the concept of "neo-authoritarianism" had become a hot topic in 1988 in China's intellectual circles due to advocacy by a group of young and middle-aged scholars with conservative leanings participating in a larger debate on China's optimal path forward. Although there is no evidence that hard-liners were behind the proponents of neo-authoritarianism at the time, the idea of an authoritarian regime committed to economic development held tremendous appeal and was seen among its advocates as an alternative to the model of development under a liberal political regime.[30] In terms of real-world examples, champions of neo-authoritarianism could find persuasive cases supporting their argument. South Korea, Taiwan, Singapore, and to a less extent Thailand, Indonesia, and Malaysia had achieved spectacular developmental successes since the 1960s under authoritarian rule. Even though no academic research explicitly argues that authoritarian rule made such economic success possible, the connection between authoritarianism and rapid economic development appears intuitively obvious.[31] Although neo-authoritarianism was the guiding principle of Deng's reform and opening prior to its ascendance in scholarly circles in 1987–1988, Deng had encountered great difficulty completely translating this vision into policy because of opposition, primarily from the hard-liners and secondarily from the liberals. The hard-liners, led by Chen Yun, steadfastly resisted Deng's efforts to liberalize the Chinese economy, while the liberals advocated political reform even though they supported Deng on economic policy. The decimation of the liberals as a political force after the Tiananmen crackdown in 1989 eliminated one set of obstacles to Deng's neo-authoritarian vision. After the Soviet collapse in 1991, hard-liner opposition to a survival strategy that would rely on capitalist economic development to perpetuate one-party rule also melted away.

Besides bolstering Deng's neo-authoritarian strategy, the Soviet collapse also informed the CCP's survival strategy in many important ways.[32] In the

1990s the Chinese leadership tasked the country's social scientists with carrying out a number of studies probing the factors responsible for the Soviet collapse. Not surprisingly, these studies reached very different and contradictory conclusions. In general, the liberal scholars pinned the blame on the inefficient economic system, imperial overreach, corruption, and the rigidity of the Soviet regime, but the conservative academics attributed the Soviet collapse mainly to Mikhail Gorbachev's policies of *glasnost* and *perestroika* and to the "peaceful evolution" advocated by the West.[33] The conservative interpretation of the Soviet collapse would become the dominant official narrative and would influence the CCP's strategy of suppressing domestic dissent and guarding against Western influence in the post-Tiananmen era. But two conclusions drawn by liberal scholars—the Soviet regime's failure to reform its economy and its imperial overreach—had a profound impact on the party's survival strategy during this period. To be sure, credit for these two observations should go first to Deng himself because he not only had pointed out that economic failure would doom the party but also had insisted that China "must never take the lead" in confronting the West.[34]

The lessons the Chinese leadership derived from the Soviet collapse, albeit eclectically, complemented Deng's neo-authoritarian vision almost perfectly and guided the party's domestic and foreign policies until the rise of Xi Jinping at the end of 2012. Domestically, the Soviet collapse underscored the centrality of economic development for the party's performance-based legitimacy, thus justifying bold market-oriented reforms and integration with the global economy. In foreign relations, the post-Tiananmen leadership faithfully followed Deng's dictum of *taoguan yanghui* (hiding your brightness and building up strength) and took great pains to avoid conflict with the United States. At the same time, however, the party also methodically strengthened social control to guard against "peaceful evolution," systematically cultivated nationalism to augment regime legitimacy, carried out a campaign of co-opting the social elites to expand its base of support, and consistently maintained control of the key sectors of the economy to prevent the market reforms from undermining the economic foundations of one-party rule. To be sure, the party's post-Deng leadership arrived at this comprehensive survival strategy mainly through learning and adaptation.[35] Yet, judging by the party's success in economic growth and regime survival in the two decades following Deng's southern tour, the core ideas of neo-authoritarianism and the lessons from the Soviet collapse can claim a great deal of credit for the golden age of one-party rule in China from 1992 to 2012.

Key Pillars of the Post-Tiananmen Order

The neo-authoritarian order, beginning with Deng's historic southern tour in 1992 and ending with Xi Jinping's takeover as party chief in November 2012, lasted about two decades. In addition to producing the Chinese economic "miracle" during this period, the post-Tiananmen order was characterized by ideological consensus among the elite on policy, collective leadership and power-sharing at the top, an implicit security pact among the rulers, and recruitment and promotion of elites apparently based on established rules and norms. These observed features of elite politics deviated substantially from those that had characterized all other periods in post-1949 China. During the Maoist period (1949–1976), personalist strongman rule and constant purges dominated elite politics, as has been the case in Xi's "new era" since 2013. During the 1980s, ideological differences led to bitter conflicts over policy and triggered the fall of two general secretaries. What made post-Tiananmen elite politics relatively stable has fueled a vigorous debate about the role of institutions and power in the post-Deng era.

One obvious factor behind this development was the smooth exit of the revolutionary veterans, which began in the early 1990s and ended with Deng's death in February 1997. The transition from revolutionary veterans to a new and younger generation of well-educated technocrats (Jiang Zemin was the first party chief with a college education) took place without incident, mainly due to Deng's political maneuvering in 1992. The meltdown of opposition to his neo-authoritarian vision allowed him to appoint a leadership team that could implement his agenda of keeping the party in power through supercharged economic development. By pure coincidence, but crucially, nearly all the heavyweight hard-liners died before Deng. Their departure removed a potential threat to the new leadership to which Deng had entrusted his unfinished agenda. To be sure, a small number of slightly younger hard-liners were still alive. But shorn of powerful patrons and official positions, they could do little more than occasionally rail against a "capitalist restoration."[36] The marginalization of the hard-liners after 1992 and the purge of the liberals in 1989 allowed the new leadership to pursue Deng's agenda without distraction or debilitating infighting.

After Deng selected the new leadership team at the Fourteenth Party Congress in October 1992, he receded from the scene. According to his official chronology, his last public appearance was in February 1994, about three years before his death on February 19, 1997. It was during this period that the foundations of the post-Tiananmen political order were laid. Despite his reputation as an opportunist, Jiang Zemin had by then become fully committed to Deng's vision and started to implement Deng's neo-authoritarian agenda with few reservations.

In November 1993 Jiang shepherded approval of a landmark document at the Third Plenum of the Fourteenth Central Committee. "The CCP Center's Resolution on Several Questions on Establishing Institutions of a Socialist Market Economy" legitimized, for the first time, the status of the market economy, representing the ideological breakthrough that had eluded Deng throughout the 1980s. The resolution also laid out a blueprint for the radical economic reforms that the hard-liners had bitterly opposed in the prior decade. The fifty provisions of the resolution include plans to reform the SOEs, develop the underlying institutions of a market economy, encourage the growth of the private sector, establish mechanisms of macroeconomic management, expand the opening to the world economy, and build a modern legal system.[37]

Institutionalization of the Party and the Balance of Power

Compared with the preceding Maoist and Dengist periods as well as the subsequent Xi era, the post-Tiananmen era stands out for its normality and stability. No earth-shaking political events on the order of the Cultural Revolution, the Tiananmen crackdown, or Xi's unrelenting purge took place during this period. Although Jiang Zemin and Hu Jintao each sent a rival Politburo member to prison, these incidents are notable mainly because they were so rare. Throughout this period, China's rulers conducted their business seemingly according to a set of written rules and unwritten norms, of which the most important and effective appear to have been those governing the recruitment and promotion of officials on the basis of their age, educational qualifications, and administrative record and the disciplining and punishment of party members suspected of corruption.

To be sure, the idea of making elite politics more rule-based originated in the early 1980s, as exemplified by "Guidelines on Political Life in the Party" passed by the Central Committee in 1980.[38] However, few specific rules on governance within the party were formulated in the 1980s. One of Jiang's top priorities in the early to mid-1990s was to promulgate specific rules and regulations governing key procedures for appointment, promotion, discipline, and administration of local party committees. Some of the party's most important regulations, such as the Trial Regulations on the Selection and Appointment of Party and Government Leading Cadres (1995) and the Regulations on Chinese Communist Party Discipline and Sanctions (1997), were promulgated under Jiang's leadership. (The project of subjecting politics within the party to more rules continued under Hu Jintao, who updated the interim rules passed by Jiang and rolled out new ones.)[39]

The stipulations in these rules and norms provided the party with significant benefits. Making certain measurable qualifications—such as age, education attainment, and record of administrative competence (mainly in terms of economic management)—some of the considerations for recruiting and promoting officials helped add youthful vigor and technocratic capabilities to the party's local apparatus. The value placed on administrative experience in different capacities and different sectors enabled the party to train and promote well-rounded officials. The concomitant de-emphasis on ideology allowed the party to confine disagreements to policy and personality, not to polarizing debate over ideological values.

Nonetheless, rules on "meritocracy" and administrative accomplishments could be gamed by clever local officials. For instance, officials without a genuine four-year college education could burnish their credentials with degrees obtained through less rigorous college or graduate programs. Xi Jinping, for example, received a doctorate from the prestigious Tsinghua University via a correspondence program in the late 1990s while he served as the governor of Fujian province. The practice of faking economic data to embellish one's record was widespread. Cultivating ties with superiors, often through illicit means such as bribes, could advance an official's career.[40] Such meritocracy appeared to apply to the promotion of local officials more strictly than to national-level officials as patronage—personal ties to senior leaders in the party—played a decisive role in the selection of members of the Central Committee who typically staff the most important political and administrative positions in the party-state.[41]

Yet, despite these flaws, codified rules and implicit norms on elite politics helped the party recruit more talented individuals and keep them committed to the party out of self-interest. At a minimum, these rules and norms provided them with a career road map for upward mobility inside the party-state. Enforced limits on term (usually two terms in the same position) and age (the mandatory retirement age was 60 for officials with the rank of vice minister or deputy provincial governor, while ministers and governors were required to retire at 65) accelerated elite circulation as officials reaching these limits were forced to retire and give way to a younger cohort. This allowed the party to avoid the Maoist-era problem when the absence of age and term limits enabled the revolutionary veterans to stay in office indefinitely, blocking the careers of younger officials. These frustrated followers of the party played an outsized role in toppling the old guard at the beginning of the Cultural Revolution.[42]

To avoid alienating a large group of officials forced into mandatory retirement, the party appointed them as deputies to local people's congresses or people's political consultative conferences (an advisory body). Those officials who retired from frontline responsibilities also retained their perks, such as generous retirement benefits, government-provided housing, and access to high-quality healthcare. They could count on support and services provided by a special bureaucracy, the "Veteran Cadres Bureau," which originally had been set up in the central government in the 1980s to cater to the needs of the octogenarian revolutionaries but had been expanded to all levels of the party-state in the 1990s. Although maintaining an ever-growing number of officials in their early sixties consumed enormous resources, the party had no trouble covering the expenses because the coffers of the state were flush with tax revenues generated from the rapidly expanding economy.

Unlike during the Maoist and the Dengist eras, elite politics during the period when Jiang was effectively in charge (1993–2002) was marked by a degree of stability and collective leadership that was unmatched in all other periods of PRC history, except for the Hu era (2003–2012). When Mao ruled the party, he conducted ceaseless purges to get rid of his enemies, including his two designated successors (Liu Shaoqi and Lin Biao). In the 1980s Deng's disenchantment with his own protégés, Hu Yaobang and Zhao Ziyang, ultimately led to their ouster from power.

By contrast, the end of bitter ideological feuding after 1992 dramatically bolstered elite unity in the post-Tiananmen era. Jiang did not carry out any mass purges during his time as general secretary, even though he occasionally did conduct half-hearted anticorruption campaigns, mainly targeting mid-level officials.[43] Only a personal rival, Politburo member Chen Xitong, was imprisoned on corruption charges in 1995 (an act of poetic justice in the eyes of many because Chen had played a dark role in the Tiananmen crackdown). To be sure, in the post-Tiananmen era personal vendettas and naked power struggles likely replaced ideological conflicts as the main cause of conflict among elites. This change may not seem to be much of an improvement. However, the presence of explicit rules for approval of the penalties to officials accused of corruption most likely constrained discretion among most party officials who would have liked to see their rivals sent to prison. It is worth noting that anticorruption investigations were not weaponized on a meaningful scale until after the rise of Xi Jinping. The party established procedures for approving penalties for senior officials found guilty of corruption in 1983. Normally, expulsion from the party had to be blessed by the standing committee of a party organization. So a member of the Central Committee could not be punished without the approval of the PSC.[44]

At the highest level of the party, however, what most likely helped curb the weaponization of corruption investigations against political rivals was not merely the presence of such rules but the delicate balance of power in the PSC.[45] During the Jiang era, Jiang had to share power with formidable rivals. Li Peng, the hard-line premier (and later chairman of the Standing Committee of the NPC) who occupied the second most senior position in the party, had a strong base of support among conservatives. Qiao Shi, the third-ranked leader until 1997, had enjoyed a more illustrious career than Jiang, having overseen the party's Organization Department and security apparatus. Zhu Rongji, who joined the PSC in 1992 and became premier in 1998, was no pushover, either. In 1993, after poor health and high inflation forced Li Peng, then the premier, to cede much of the executive authority of the State Council to Zhu, the former hard-charging mayor of Shanghai quickly established his credentials as the country's economic czar and served as the most influential economic policymaker in the post-Tiananmen era until his retirement in 2003.

In addition to these three political heavyweights, Jiang also had to contend with Li Ruihuan, the fourth-ranked member of the PSC, whom Deng had promoted after the Tiananmen crackdown to counter the hard-liners. Even though they allegedly did not get along, Jiang could do little more than maneuver Li into retirement at the Fifteenth Party Congress in 1997.[46] The presence of Hu Jintao, Jiang's successor designated by Deng in 1992, further tied Jiang's hands. The leader-in-waiting could not be counted as a Jiang ally. If anything, Hu had a stake in preserving the balance of power to prevent Jiang from becoming a strongman and threatening his ascension to the top party position after Jiang served out his full second term in 2002.

This analysis suggests that, perhaps more critical than any formal rules, the finely tuned balance of power during the Jiang era (and later in the Hu era) preserved elite stability and collective leadership. Rules are effective only when they can be enforced with coercive power. In the post-Tiananmen era, the appearance of institutionalization and relative stability in elite politics led some to conclude that the party had successfully established binding rules and norms, and politics in the erstwhile Hobbesian world had become "normal."[47] But skeptics questioned whether, in the absence of a third-party enforcer, elites in an autocracy can be counted on to exercise self-restraint and abide by any rules and norms.[48] What stands out in the post-Tiananmen era is the total absence of a third party—such as an empowered electorate, an independent judiciary, or a free press—that could enforce party rules and norms. The absence of third-party enforcers was by design rather than by accident. It was Deng's firm opposition to the political liberalization and to the checks and balances proposed by Zhao in 1987 that blocked the establishment of potential third-party enforcers.

The fragile balance of power in the post-Tiananmen era enabled the party to adhere to its rules of succession. But a closer look at the two successions, in 2002 and 2012, shows that these two cases were close calls, and they reveal that the institutionalization of elite politics in the post-Tiananmen era was mostly an optical illusion. In the case of Hu's succession in 2002, Jiang most likely resented Deng's appointment of Hu as his successor, but he lacked the power to remove him. Yet Jiang still tried to hang on to power by keeping his position as chairman of the party's Central Military Commission, ostensibly following the precedent set by Deng (who retained the same position after giving up his seat on the PSC in 1987). In Chinese vernacular, Jiang did not retire "naked" (*luotui*) by giving up all his official titles, as Hu would later do in 2012.

The shallowness of the party's institutionalization was again on display at its Seventeenth Party Congress in 2007, when Hu's successor was to be selected. Deng's far-sighted, if not preemptive, move to designate Jiang's successor in 1992 may have spared the party a brutal power struggle in 2002, but in 2007 the party was forced to reach agreement on who should succeed Hu. As will be discussed later in this chapter, there were no rules for the party to follow. Xi Jinping—the eventual victor emerging from a contest between Jiang and Hu—was unaffiliated with either faction. But it was this relatively unknown princeling who, after his rise to power in November 2012, wasted little time in purging his political rivals and destroying the fragile balance of power at the top. Xi's success in expanding and perpetuating his personal power reconfirmed that the many rules and norms the party had instituted in the post-Mao era were no match to the political ruthlessness and machinations of a strongman. If anything, the relative tranquility in elite politics during the post-Tiananmen era was the exception that proves the rule of the impossibility of institutionalizing politics in a dictatorship.

The Patriotic Education Campaign and the Resurgence of Nationalism

On June 9, 1989, five days after the PLA crushed the Tiananmen prodemocracy movement, Deng Xiaoping met with senior military officers responsible for the crackdown. As he thanked them for their "hard work," Deng also admitted that "the biggest mistake [we] have made in the last decade was . . . [neglecting] ideological and political education."[49] To remedy this mistake, his successors in the 1990s launched a comprehensive campaign to revive nationalism as a means of cultivating mass support for the party. The core component of this campaign was patriotic education—a program utilizing party control of the education system, media, and cultural facilities to instill in the Chinese public, especially the younger generations, national pride, resentment against Western imperialism, and loyalty to the party.

The patriotic education campaign slightly predated Deng's historic southern tour. In late August 1991, prodded by newly installed party general secretary Jiang Zemin, the State Education Commission issued two important documents. One required a strengthening of the history curriculum in primary and middle schools so that pupils would learn more about China's modern and contemporary history. The document explicitly stated that this undertaking aimed to "smash the plot of 'peaceful evolution' by domestic and foreign hostile forces." To ensure that students would have an incentive to study the party's version of history, the document also mandated that starting in 1992, the college entrance examinations, or *gaokao*, would test knowledge of party history. The second document directed schools and universities to organize visits to museums and revolutionary monuments as part of a program to foster "patriotism and a revolutionary spirit."[50]

The most important policy document on patriotic education, "Outline on the Implementation of Patriotic Education," was issued by the CCP Central Propaganda Department in August 1994.[51] It laid out the specific provisions for this campaign. Among other things, patriotic education was to focus on Chinese history, China's contributions to civilization, Chinese resistance to foreign aggression and oppression, and CCP policy and accomplishments in economic development. The younger generations were to be the target audience of the patriotic education campaign, and schools were to be the primary venue for this endeavor. Textbooks in primary and middle schools were required to include content on patriotic education. Additionally, films, television, publications, and music would be utilized to disseminate patriotic education. The government would also fund the establishment of "patriotic education bases"—museums, historical monuments, sites of major battles during the civil war, and well-known cultural heritage sites. Patriotic rituals, such as singing the national anthem and flag-raising, would be required at graduation commencement ceremonies and at large sports events. Patriotic education also included promotion of patriotic models—party leaders, artists, poets, and revolutionary martyrs—who had made outstanding contributions to China.

The motivation behind Jiang's push for patriotic education is easy to identify. Politically, he wanted to establish his bona fides as an ideological conservative faithfully implementing Deng's edicts. In the aftermath of the Tiananmen debacle of 1989 and the disintegration of the Soviet Union, cultivating Chinese nationalism also served party interests because it could rally the public behind the party after orthodox Communist ideology had lost its popular appeal.[52]

Following promulgation of the "Outline" in 1994, the party mobilized its propaganda apparatus and the entire education system to implement patriotic education. Judging from official publications, universities and schools carried out the specific instructions laid out in the "Outline." Curricula were revised to include the required patriotic education content, such as the history of Western imperial aggression and Chinese culture, tradition, and patriotism. Schools began to hold regular flag-raising ceremonies, sing the national anthem at major events, and hang national flags in classrooms, lecture halls, and offices.[53] "Patriotic education bases"—newly designated revolutionary monuments, sites of major battles during the second Sino-Japanese war (1937–1945), history museums, and birthplaces of major revolutionary and cultural figures—were established throughout the country. The narratives in the majority of these bases explicitly glorified the role of the CCP in regaining the country's sovereignty, independence, and dignity after a century of national weakness and humiliation.[54]

University students were the chief target of patriotic education because the party viewed them as more deeply corrupted by Western ideas and potentially more threatening to CCP rule than any other social groups. Students were required to take two courses: "Theories of Marxism and Leninism" and the "Current Situation and Policy" (*xingshi zhengce jiaoyu*). Although the campaign was labeled "patriotic education," its primary objective, according to a senior official in the State Education Commission, was to ensure loyalty to Deng's "four cardinal principles" and to the party mission of constructing "socialism with Chinese characteristics under the leadership of the Communist Party."[55] Some university officials explicitly stated that the "basic component" of patriotic education was "love for the party and socialism."[56]

In a major departure from the party's triumphalist tone in promoting Chinese nationalism during the Mao era, the post-Tiananmen leadership opted for a victimhood narrative emphasizing imperial bullying of China and portraying the party as the greatest defender of China's honor.[57] The party deliberately picked this theme because, after the Tiananmen crackdown and the Soviet collapse, China was isolated from the West, and it was easy to portray the West as again attempting to subjugate China.

By coincidence, a series of incidents in the 1990s helped lend credibility to the party's victimhood narrative and reinforce its message that the United States, then the world's sole superpower, was intent on containing China. In 1993 the so-called *Yinhe* incident enraged the Chinese public. US intelligence agencies accused the *Yinhe*, a Chinese container ship, of carrying materials to be used in Iran's chemical weapons, and, likely due to American diplomatic intervention, the United Arab Emirates prevented it from docking in its ports. Even after an inspection revealed that the *Yinhe* was not carrying any contraband, the United States refused to apologize. In 1995, under pressure from Congress, the Clinton administration was forced to grant a visa to Lee Teng-hui to visit the United States. Lee was at the time the president of Taiwan, who was reviled in Beijing for his pro-independence aspirations. In response to the pro-independence remarks Lee had made in the United States, China staged a series of military exercises as a warning to Taiwan. But Washington responded in March 1996 by dispatching two carrier battle groups to the waters surrounding Taiwan as China was conducting its largest military exercises thus far, which included the firing of missiles into the waters near Taiwan. Although no military conflict broke out, America's show of support for Taiwan once again angered the Chinese public.[58]

The event that perhaps did more than anything else to help reinforce the party's narrative of Chinese victimhood is the accidental bombing of the Chinese Embassy in Belgrade by an American stealth fighter during a NATO bombing campaign against Serbia in May 1999. Despite Washington's explanations and apologies, Chinese leaders insisted that this was a deliberate act, and ordinary Chinese took part in nationwide anti-American demonstrations. Angry protestors in Beijing, many of whom were university students, trashed the American Embassy with rocks and other projectiles. In Chengdu, mobs set on fire the residence of the US consul-general.[59]

Judging by such a virulent outpouring of anti-Americanism, exactly one decade after prodemocracy students had erected a miniature Statue of Liberty in Tiananmen Square, the party's patriotic education campaign obviously succeeded beyond its own expectations. Indeed, most scholarly research on the rise of Chinese nationalism in the 1990s finds that the attitudes of the Chinese public at the time, in particular the attitudes of the younger generations, became more patriotic and more progovernment.[60]

Selective Repression

One of the key lessons learned by the party leadership from the Tiananmen crisis was the need for a more effective coercive apparatus. As a result, the party undertook a comprehensive campaign in the 1990s to invest in the state's coercive capacity.[61] In April 1990 the party issued a key policy document on strengthening domestic security. Its provisions included restoration of the Central Political and Legal Affairs Commission, a specialized party bureaucracy in charge of law enforcement that had been abolished by reformist party chief Zhao Ziyang in 1988. This resurrected commission was to supervise the strengthening of law enforcement and to coordinate implementation of the party's security agenda. The document vows to wage a merciless struggle against "hostile forces, infiltration, and subversion." It explicitly orders the establishment of urban mobile antiriot forces to quell demonstrations (China had not had specialized antiriot police to deal with the prodemocracy protesters in 1989).[62]

Ten months after the issuance of this document, the party released a second directive on domestic security, "Decision on Strengthening Comprehensive Management of Public Security." On paper, this document appears to emphasize law and order as well as social stability, but it also includes provisions for tightening social control, such as monitoring the "floating population" (people without fixed household registrations) and surveillance of dance halls, printed materials, and venues for showing videos. It calls on local governments to increase funding for law enforcement.[63]

Investment in China's coercive apparatus—police, courts, and procuratorates—rose dramatically in the years after these documents were issued. From 1991 to 1995 the amount spent on these three branches of the state rose threefold in absolute terms (from 10 billion yuan in 1991 to 30 billion yuan in 1995). By 2002, a decade after Deng's southern tour, spending on these three branches would rise to 110 billion yuan, ten times the amount in 1991 (unadjusted for inflation).[64]

The size of the police force more than doubled from 1989 to 2010 (from 769,000 to at least 2 million).[65] Starting in the early 2000s, the party expanded the police units responsible for domestic surveillance and political repression ("domestic security protection"), adding probably more than ten thousand police devoted solely to dealing with political dissidents, underground religious believers, and cult members.[66] In mid-1990 the People's Armed Police (PAP) began to form specialized antiriot units. By the end of the 1990s, most local police departments had established similar units.[67]

In the 1990s the party launched a series of initiatives to upgrade the capabilities of the surveillance state. In November 1991 the powerful Ministry of Public Security (MPS) issued new rules on surveillance of "key populations" (such as dissidents, activists in underground religious groups, and ex-convicts). In December 1991 the ministry established covert operations on university campuses. In May 1992 it directed local police to increase manpower to target Western "infiltration," underground Catholic groups, and cults. At the direction of the party, police intensified internet surveillance in July 1997, and in October 1997 it tightened control over foreign funding of Chinese social science research organizations.[68] The decade saw a major expansion of the network of informants recruited by the police to act as the "eyes and ears" of law enforcement. For example, the number of "special intelligence personnel" (informers) employed by police in Shaanxi province nearly doubled between 1988 and 2001.[69]

The 1990s also saw the beginning of a well-funded program to upgrade the technological capabilities of the coercive capacity of the party-state. In November 1991 the MPS convened a national conference on the modernization of law enforcement technology, marking the beginning of a drive to upgrade law enforcement with advanced surveillance technology.[70] In 1998 the party formally approved the Golden Shield Project (the IT modernization program of the MPS that includes the "Great Firewall of China").[71]

In addition to its sustained and massive investment in coercive capacity, during the Jiang era the party constantly refined its tactics of repression, often deploying methods used in soft-authoritarian regimes in other East Asian countries.[72] Inviting known dissidents to "tea" as a subtle form of intimidation became a routine tactic, as was the use of family relatives and friends to engage in emotional blackmail against ordinary citizens who participated in peaceful petitioning. When brutal force was needed, local authorities would hire thugs to beat up the protesters. Aware that major public holidays, key anniversaries (such as the anniversary of the June 4 massacre), or visits by foreign dignitaries could become rallying points for collective protests, police would tighten security measures on those sensitive dates to prevent such disturbances from occurring.[73]

The regime became more selective in picking its targets. It prosecuted and jailed fewer dissidents, often preferring to charge dissidents with nonpolitical crimes (such as disturbing public order) instead of "subverting state power." To decapitate political opposition at home and to placate Western governments, which the post-1989 regime sought to woo in order to maintain access to capital, technology, and markets, the party forced into exile nearly all the best-known dissidents, such as Wei Jingsheng (the symbol of the Democracy Wall Movement in 1978–1979) and Wang Dan and Wang Juntao (leaders of the Tiananmen protests in 1989).[74]

Several key factors motivated the post-Tiananmen regime to massively increase investment in its coercive capacity but at the same time also to adopt more refined tactics of repression. Due to the party's near-death experience during the Tiananmen crisis, it came to appreciate that its coercive capacity was the ultimate guarantor of regime survival and that prevention of a similar crisis was far preferable to a brutal crackdown. The rapid growth of fiscal revenue during the booming 1990s also enabled the state to channel more resources into law enforcement and surveillance. The switch to soft-authoritarian tactics of repression allowed the party to target fewer political threats more effectively and to leave most of the population unaffected. Politically, selective repression served the party well. Most ordinary people enjoyed continual expansion of their personal freedoms as the economy thrived. This was translated into mass support for the regime. Geopolitically, soft-authoritarian repression helped reduce tensions between China and its key trading partners in the West, justifying that engagement with China offered tangible evidence that economic liberalization might lead to a political opening in the future.

Despite adoption of more refined tactics of repression, the essential bureaucratic organizations of totalitarianism and the mechanisms of deploying them for mass terror remained intact. The party could quickly mobilize these organizations when confronted with a direct and forceful challenge to its authority, as in the case of the protests staged by the Falungong spiritual group in 1999. After the party leadership issued an order banning this group, which allegedly had tens of millions nationwide followers, Chinese police resorted to extremely brutal methods to arrest, imprison, and torture its leaders and followers, effectively destroying the group as an organized force within only a few years.[75] The near-total destruction of Falungong foreshadowed the return of totalitarian rule under Xi Jinping more than a decade later.

Co-optation of Social Elites

A distinct feature of the post-1989 neo-authoritarian order is the successful effort by the party to expand its social base beyond workers and peasants, the two groups that made up the majority of party members but that had lost huge economic ground and political influence during the post-Mao era. In 1978, on the eve of Deng's reform, peasants constituted 47 percent of party members, while workers accounted for nearly 19 percent. Only 1.6 percent of the 37 million party members were classified as "professionals, cadres, and students."[76] The majority of party members were poorly educated. In 1980, 11 percent of party members were illiterate, 45 percent had only a primary-school education, and a mere 3 percent had received a college-level education.[77] As the party pivoted to a survival strategy centered on economic development, it needed to recruit individuals with better educational and professional qualifications. Beyond the requirement for expertise that would be useful in managing a complex economy, the party's strategy was to co-opt the very social elites whom it had viewed as enemies or threats during the Maoist era. This tactic also contained a Machiavellian element: preempting elite-based opposition in Chinese society. Exclusion of elites with a higher social status and more economic resources could antagonize and even turn such social elites into opponents of the regime. Because repression of the intelligentsia and private entrepreneurs could endanger the party's economic agenda, it therefore was no longer attractive, and co-optation became a preferred option.

The broad outline of the party's strategy of co-opting social elites was laid out in a September 1994 Central Committee decision on party building. Among the top priorities identified by the party were the appointment and promotion of a large number of loyal and talented young officials and recruitment of "outstanding elements" among young people and women.[78] Initially, the focus of the co-optation strategy was the recruitment and promotion of well-educated individuals, in particular university students, a group the party had a strong incentive to win over given its role in leading the prodemocracy movements in the 1980s.[79] (The party issued a specific directive in 2005 on strengthening recruitment of university students.)[80] For example, the share of party members among undergraduates at prestigious Tsinghua University doubled from 8.3 percent to 16.5 percent between 1995 and 2005 (the share would rise to 29 percent in 2011).[81] As the party controlled access to career opportunities, it had no difficulty luring talented and ambitious university students to join its ranks.[82]

The drive to recruit well-educated individuals made rapid progress in the 1990s, and toward the end of the post-Tiananmen era it had dramatically transformed the composition of the party. In 1990 only 10.3 percent of party members had received a college-level education or higher. A decade later, 21 percent of party members had a college-level education or higher.[83] By 2000 the party would be unrecognizable to its founders. Of the 64.5 million members, workers and peasants accounted for about 44 percent (compared with 66 percent in 1979). The share of professionals had risen to 19 percent (from 1.6 percent in 1978).[84] The share of workers and peasants in the party would continue to fall as the party recruited more college graduates and professionals. In 2011 workers and peasants made up 39 percent of party members, while managers (excluding full-time party and government officials), professionals, and college students accounted for 27 percent. Close to 40 percent of party members had a college-level education or higher.[85]

After the party's efforts to co-opt the well-educated yielded impressive results, it shifted its attention to private entrepreneurs who had gained social status and enormous resources during the booming 1990s. The milestone was Jiang Zemin's theory of the "Three Represents," unveiled with great fanfare on July 1, 2001, the eightieth anniversary of the founding of the party.[86] Ostensibly, Jiang was trying to advance a new ideological theory spelling out what the party stood for (or represented) to replace the party's orthodox ideological doctrine that had emphasized revolution and struggle against capitalism. Ideologically, the "Three Represents" implicitly endorsed capitalism, which Jiang euphemistically but awkwardly termed "advanced social productive forces." In practice, this framing opened the door for the party to admit as members private entrepreneurs—the very exploiting class whose destruction theoretically is the goal of orthodox communism.

Even though Jiang's "Three Represents," which the party enshrined in its charter in November 2002 as "important thought," do not appear to have done much to rejuvenate the party ideologically, the green light to recruit capitalists quickly had a notable impact on co-opting a new social group that was in control of a growing portion of the national economy. By 2000, private firms (excluding micro household businesses) employed over 24 million workers.[87] Obviously, the party was eager to gain the support of this group of social elites.

Based on surveys conducted in the early 2000s of owners of private firms, in 1999 only 18 percent of them were party members.[88]

Following Jiang's call to admit capitalists into the party, the share of private entrepreneurs who were party members rose rapidly. Survey results show that in 2002 that share had risen to 30 percent, compared with only 20 percent in 2000.[89] Toward the end of the 2000s, the party was recruiting about 80,000 "managers and technical personnel" of private firms each year.[90] To be sure, private entrepreneurs had mixed motives for joining the party. Many, if not most, sought the political status that came with party membership as a layer of protection of their wealth, or they believed that they could have more access to opportunities via membership. Additionally, having this new social group inside the party was, on the whole, a successful move to shore up support for the party in the rapidly changing society.[91]

Party membership was not the only enticement used to co-opt social elites. In the post-Tiananmen era, a select group of eminent intellectuals, professionals, and private entrepreneurs were picked to be delegates to the local people's congresses and the people's political consultative conferences. The inclusion of these successful and well-known individuals conveyed the impression to the public that the party enjoyed their support.[92]

False Dawn: The Limits of Neo-Authoritarianism

As illustrated, within a decade of Deng's southern tour in 1992, the collective leadership under Jiang Zemin had successfully transformed Deng's neo-authoritarian vision into a comprehensive strategy of regime survival. Its key pillars consisted of performance legitimacy, collective leadership underpinned by a fragile balance of power, expansion of popular support through the cultivation of Chinese nationalism, selective repression, and co-optation of social elites. By and large, the party showed a remarkable degree of adaptation in the 1990s, and its new strategy served it well.

Ideologically, the party was far more homogenous than perhaps at any time in its history. The purge after the Tiananmen crackdown eliminated the liberals at the top of the leadership. Ever fearful of elevating China's equivalent of a Gorbachev to the top, the party, dominated by conservative technocrats, denied power to those with liberal leanings. At the same time, ultra-conservatives who resisted the market reforms were sidelined as well because their ideological orthodoxy was incompatible with the party's conviction that its survival depended on performance legitimacy, which could be delivered by business-friendly policies. In terms of elite politics, ideological homogeneity was translated into relative elite stability. In contrast to the 1980s, the Jiang era—as well as the Hu Jintao era—stands out mainly because of the absence of bitter ideological clashes such as those that ended with the purge of Hu Yaobang, Zhao Ziyang, and their close associates. To be sure, conflicts among senior leaders existed, but they were over personality and power, not ideology. More important, such conflicts were contained, as evidenced by the fact that during the Jiang era, only one Politburo member was jailed on charges of corruption.

The timing of the party's pivot to neo-authoritarian rule in the 1990s could not have been more fortuitous. Economically, the reforms in the 1980s had built the foundations of a market economy—privatization of agriculture, a fast-growing private sector, and linkages with the global economy. The massive rural-urban migration coupled with the young population (nearly 90 percent of the population was under the age of 59 in 1990) became a sustained and powerful driver of growth during the subsequent two decades.[93] Despite a few episodes of tensions between the United States and China, the external environment was relatively benign. Instead of efforts by Washington to contain China after the end of the Cold War, as Beijing feared, the United States promoted globalization as an instrument to integrate China into the global economy, thus giving China unprecedented access to Western markets, capital, and technology.

The tools deployed by the party to guard against domestic threats to its power proved surprisingly effective. The nationalism cultivated by the party generated a new source of mass support. Co-optation of social elites broadened the party's base and improved the educational and professional qualifications of party officials. More sophisticated tactics of political repression enabled the party to contain emerging threats to its power. In the 1990s surveillance, intimidation, imprisonment, and exile neutralized the prodemocracy movement as a serious danger, and the party's investment in a coercive apparatus paid off handsomely, as shown by the suppression of ethnic minority unrest in Tibet and Xinjiang, the banning of Falungong, and the suppression of worker unrest in the aftermath of the mass layoffs by bankrupt SOEs at the end of the decade.[94]

However, the neo-authoritarian order constructed in the 1990s under Jiang Zemin's leadership had inherent flaws, which would become both more visible and more serious during the Hu era. Elite security was ensured not by rules and norms enforceable by a third party but by a fragile balance of power among rivals. Senior leaders with their respective extensive power bases in the party-state prevented the two party chiefs, Jiang and Hu, from turning collective leadership into strongman rule, as Xi Jinping was able to do shortly after his rise in late 2012. Without durable institutional constraints, which are difficult to establish and preserve even in democracies, elite security was certain to vanish once the underlying balance of power ceased to exist.

In addition, the post-Tiananmen neo-authoritarian order was fundamentally incompatible with genuine political liberalization, democratization, and rule of law, thus diminishing the possibility that economic development under one-party rule could result in a transition to democracy. The reforms championed by liberals and moderates in the party laid the foundation for a modern legal system. Landmark legislation such as the Criminal Procedure Law (1980), Economic Contract Law (1981), Foreign Company Law (1986), and Administrative Litigation Law (1989) were all passed in the 1980s. Despite their flaws, they marked a promising first step toward rule of law. Even with the booming economy, however, the progress in legal reform in the 1990s was mixed at best. The NPC enacted many more laws than it did in the 1980s, and judges and lawyers were also better educated and trained. But the party steadfastly resisted any reforms that would make the judiciary more independent, and it frequently ignored or even violated the laws passed by the NPC. Consequently, by the end of the Jiang era, China's legal system remained firmly under the control of the party despite its ostensible modern appearance of robed judges presiding over proceedings in newly built courtrooms.[95]

Substantive progress in developing a basic system of accountability was also minimal. With the support of the party, the NPC enacted an interim law permitting rural residents to elect "village committees" and their directors in 1987. Even though the "village committees" were civic organizations and thus lacked formal political authority or power, this move was initially hailed as another tentative step in the direction of grassroots democracy. By the 1990s, however, this route had turned out to be a dead end. The party allowed such elections throughout rural China, but it refused to take the next step of permitting competitive elections for township governments. (Townships constitute the lowest administrative units in the Chinese state.) Eventually, this experimental effort to build grassroots democracy in rural China fizzled out.[96]

Without rule of law and accountability enforced by a civil society or a free press, economic development under autocratic rule inevitably breeds systemic corruption. Although corruption in the 1990s appeared to be less rampant than it would be in the 2000s, the decade saw several major cases of corruption that were unprecedented in terms of the number of people and the amount of bribes involved.[97] In the infamous Xiamen smuggling scandal, anticorruption investigators found that a criminal group had managed to smuggle into China more than 53 billion yuan worth of goods between 1996 and 1999 with the help of dozens of government officials, including a vice minister of public security and other senior officials in Fujian's police and customs systems.[98]

Toward the end of the 1990s, cracks began to appear in the party's survival strategy that had centered on economic performance, as evidenced by the rising social unrest.[99] Among the drivers linked to the social unrest were the brutal enforcement of the party's "one-child policy," regressive tax-collection policies, illegal evictions in urban areas, seizure of the farmers' land by local officials, factory closures, and unpaid wages.[100] Even though most social protests were small, isolated, and short-lived, this growing trend not only dented the party's image of competence but also indicated that the pro-growth policies pursued by the post-Tiananmen regime were harming a significant portion of the Chinese population, and the regime would likely lose support if inequality, corruption, and abuses of the rights of ordinary people continued to fuel popular resentment.

Ultimately, economic reform pursued by a neo-authoritarian regime is likely to fall into the trap of a "partial reform equilibrium." In a transition from a planned economy to a market economy, reform tends to stall after some initial efforts have been completed but more critical measures have yet to be undertaken.[101] At the midpoint in the transition process, regimes initiating a transition will lose incentives to go all the way because, although partial reforms improve economic efficiency and bolster party legitimacy, any further reforms are certain to weaken the regime's control over the economy and undermine its power.[102] To be sure, the full symptoms of this "trapped transition" were not yet plainly visible, at least in the economic realm, until Hu Jintao came to power in 2002, but the political logic behind a "trapped transition" was firmly embedded in the very neo-authoritarian vision that Deng bequeathed to Jiang in 1992.

4

Stagnation in the Hu Jintao Era

DENG XIAOPING, who had doggedly pursued his neo-authoritarian vision in the 1980s, almost certainly believed that this political order would have more staying power than orthodox communism. His immediate successor, Jiang Zemin, who had translated Deng's rather abstract vision into actual party policies in the 1990s with great success, also likely thought the post-Tiananmen order could endure. It is true that, in the wake of the Tiananmen crisis and the collapse of the Soviet Union, the party's decision to embrace capitalism with no ideological reservations in order to save its rule was wiser than the only other alternative of returning to the orthodox communist system of the early 1950s. But Deng, Jiang, and other post-Tiananmen party leaders overlooked the most serious flaws of neo-authoritarian developmentalism: the gradual but inevitable loss of momentum of economic reform and corruption-induced regime decay. If anything, the post-Tiananmen neo-authoritarian order turned out to be more fragile and less durable than its architects had thought. When Hu Jintao succeeded Jiang in late 2002, signs of pathologies of neo-authoritarian developmentalism such as rampant official corruption, rising socioeconomic inequality, deteriorating governance, and growing social unrest had become inescapable. By the time Hu left office in November 2012, the rot inside the regime was so advanced that Xi Jinping, who succeeded Hu, was able to dismantle it with relative ease.

On the surface, however, the post-Tiananmen order persisted without much change during the decade when Hu Jintao served as the party chief, 2002–2012. The Chinese economy sustained its rapid ascent mainly because China's entry into the World Trade Organization (WTO) at the end of 2001 generated a boom in foreign direct investment and trade, while urbanization continued to funnel tens of millions of rural migrants into the manufacturing and service sectors. Despite rising incidents of social unrest, the party managed to use a mixture of carrots and sticks to maintain stability. Collective leadership was preserved, ensuring a high degree of security for the ruling elites at the top (with the exception of a politically motivated corruption investigation of a Politburo member). By and large, the party stuck with the same domestic policies that had delivered unprecedented economic prosperity and political stability in the 1990s. If anything, it was during Hu's decade that China marked its spectacular rise as a global power with the hosting of the Olympics in Beijing in August 2008.

But a closer look at the Hu era reveals the growing cracks in the post-Tiananmen order. Economic reform lost its momentum because the party under Hu introduced no new measures to accelerate the building of a market economy. Instead, it doubled down on a flawed growth model that relied excessively on investment at the expense of consumption. Inefficient state-owned enterprises retained their privileged positions in the economy. Growth was maintained largely thanks to the massive increase in foreign trade following the WTO entry and the rise of the real estate sector as a major domestic driver. In the meantime, the combination of repression of the freedom of the press, the lack of rule of law, and the party's control of immense economic resources fueled corruption and made Dengist neo-authoritarian developmentalism increasingly look like crony capitalism. Practices symptomatic of regime decay, such as collusive corruption and bribing superiors for government office, became endemic.

To be sure, the party under Hu's leadership did try to address some of the social problems created by its single-minded focus on economic development during the Jiang era. The issues included rising inequality, inadequate social protection, and environmental degradation. Hu Jintao and Wen Jiabao, the premier, also attempted to make the economy less reliant on investment for growth. But their efforts were too little and too late. To make matters worse, the party responded to the global financial crisis in 2008 with a massive injection of credit. Although the stimulus sustained growth temporarily, it blew a colossal debt bubble that would create huge financial risks and constrain growth in the future.

It is tempting to blame Jiang Zemin for the stagnation of reform under Hu. Although he nominally retired in November 2002, Jiang retained his post as chairman (commander-in-chief) of the Central Military Commission. In addition, he elevated at least four supporters to the PSC, which was expanded from seven persons to nine to accommodate Jiang's scheme.[1] Jiang continued to wield enormous influence even after giving up the position of chairman of the CMC in 2004. Tellingly, judging by the fact that Hu did not succeed in obtaining the moniker "core leader," which Deng had conferred on Jiang and Xi bestowed on himself, he failed to establish uncontested authority as party chief during his tenure in office. But Jiang's political maneuvering was not the sole, or even the most important, cause of the effective demise of post-Mao reform in the Hu era. By all accounts, the neo-authoritarian model, which the party adopted fully in the wake of the crises of the Tiananmen crackdown in 1989 and the fall of the USSR in 1991, could no longer provide the intellectual guidance needed to perpetuate regime survival. With the selection of Xi Jinping as Hu's successor in November 2007, the writing was already on the wall for the post-Tiananmen order.

Building a Harmonious Society

By the time Hu succeeded Jiang as general secretary of the CCP, the project of building the foundations of Deng's neo-authoritarian order had largely been completed. On the economic front, Hu took over at a propitious time. After China's formal accession to the WTO in 2001, FDI began to pour into China, and exports grew explosively. The powerful economic momentum meant that, unlike Jiang in the early 1990s, Hu faced little pressure to launch new reform initiatives.

As a new leader, however, Hu needed to advance a political agenda that would bolster his authority and differentiate his performance from that of his predecessor. His challenge was to formulate and implement such an agenda without reversing Jiang's policies or clashing with Jiang directly. Practically, the consensus-based decision-making process gave a veto to Jiang's proxies on the PSC, making it difficult for Hu to effect a radical shift. These factors meant that policy change would occur only on the margins, with modest outcomes.

At first glance, Hu seemed to have inherited a booming economy. But daunting socioeconomic challenges lurked underneath. Economically, growth had become more dependent on investment. In 1992 consumption and investment accounted for 61.6 and 37.2 percent of GDP, respectively. By 2002, investment accounted for 39.4 percent of GDP, while the share of consumption fell to 58 percent.[2] This unbalanced growth model threatened future sustainability because ever-increasing investment would lead to excess capacity and diminishing returns, whereas surging exports generated large trade surpluses but also tensions with China's trading partners. Socially, the party's obsessive focus on growth during the post-Tiananmen era had neglected environmental protection, income equality, and social services. Income inequality, perhaps the single most important indicator of the health of a society, worsened dramatically from 1990 to 2002, with the Gini index rising from 0.322 to 0.42.[3]

The government also underinvested in healthcare during the Jiang era. The data in table 4.1 show that the share of health spending funded by the state fell from 20.8 percent to 15.7 percent between 1992 and 2002. During the same period, employers were also paying less for workers' healthcare. This resulted in a significant increase in personal out-of-pocket spending on healthcare. In 1992 such spending accounted for about 40 percent of total healthcare spending. A decade later, this ratio had risen to 57.7 percent, representing an increase of nearly 45 percent. As this ratio is used to measure access to healthcare, people have less access to healthcare in countries where personal out-of-pocket spending on healthcare is high. In comparative terms, personal out-of-pocket spending on healthcare in China in 2002 was about three times the global average (19.3 percent).[4]

Education is another area that fell victim to government neglect under Jiang Zemin. Public spending on education from 1992 to 2002 dropped during most of the decade, and by 2002 it had barely recovered to the level it had reached a decade earlier as a share of GDP. Measured as a share of total government spending, education outlays stagnated throughout this decade (table 4.2).

During the Jiang era, environmental protection was not a priority, either. Spending on environmental projects was woefully low throughout the 1990s—consistently less than 0.24 percent of GDP. Only in the 2000s did spending on the environment exceed 1 percent of GDP (1.13 percent in 2000 and 1.30 percent in 2002).[5]

To Hu and Wen Jiabao, the new premier who succeeded Zhu Rongji in 2003, these socioeconomic challenges presented an opportunity to offer a

TABLE 4.1. Share of Healthcare Spending, 1992–2002

Year	Government	Employers	Personal Out-of-Pocket
1992	20.8	39.3	39.8
1994	19.4	36.6	44
1996	17.0	32.3	50.6
1998	16.0	29.1	54.9
2000	15.5	25.6	59
2002	15.7	26.6	57.7

Source: *ZGTJNJ*, various years.

TABLE 4.2. Government Spending on Education, 1992–2002

Year	As Share of Total Government Spending (%)	As Share of GDP (%)
1992	15.1	2.71
1994	16.1	2.44
1996	16.2	2.35
1998	15.3	2.41
2000	13.8	2.58
2002	14.8	2.90

Source: *ZGTJNJ 2014*, e-book.

different agenda that would ameliorate these imbalances. Although Hu and Wen did not have close ties to each other before their rise to the top, they became temporary political allies because they shared an interest in countering the influence of Jiang's faction.

The outbreak of SARS in early 2003, which occurred just months after Hu became CCP chief, provided both Hu and Wen with an opportunity to show that their agenda would be an improvement. Their pitch for a kinder and gentler China apparently was well received because the SARS crisis had exposed the dark side of the party's policy of growth at any cost. When the epidemic broke out, China lacked a basic public health infrastructure to provide an adequate response, such as early detection and warning, data analysis, and treatment facilities.[6] Although the party relied on draconian measures to suppress a rapid spread of the virus, Hu and Wen followed up with a more comprehensive plan to address the country's mounting social deficit.

Hu spelled out its substance comprehensively at a July 2003 national conference reviewing party performance during the SARS crisis. Calling for "coordinated development of the economy and society," Hu maintained that even though economic development remained the party's central task, it had to be sustainable and measured not only in terms of growth but also in terms of indices such as environmental health and human development. He singled out the development of rural areas, ground zero of government neglect. Hu also pledged to invest more in public health, reform the poorly resourced healthcare system, and strengthen state capacity for order, stability, and crisis management.[7]

In October 2003, Hu's agenda was given the fancy title, "Scientific Outlook of Development," which, in 2007, the party enshrined into its charter as one of its ideological tenets. Its essence was sustainable or, in Hu's signature phrase, "harmonious" development that maintains the right balance between speed and quality of economic development. In an important speech to high-ranking officials in February 2005, Hu further defined the party's goal of building a "socialist harmonious society."[8]

The highest-profile—and much applauded—step Hu took to achieve a "socialist harmonious society" was abolition of the agricultural tax in December 2005. The amount of revenue generated by this tax—a levy on agricultural produce calculated on the basis of the land leased to farmers—was small, so the government could easily absorb the fiscal costs. Total revenue from various rural taxes (such as levies on tobacco leaves or on the nonagricultural use of arable land) was 93.6 billion yuan in 2005, the year before abolition of the agricultural tax. In 2006 tax revenue from rural sources amounted to 108.4 billion yuan. This suggests that the unpopular agricultural tax generated a relatively small amount of revenue (tax revenues from all rural sources accounted for only 3.2 percent of total tax receipts in 2005).[9] Hu's reform also ended other regressive nontax levies that funded public services (such as education, public health, and law enforcement). Lost revenue was made up for with subsidies from the central government.[10] Even though these measures did not significantly increase farmers' net income, they were welcomed by Chinese farmers who had long resented paying the agricultural tax and other assorted administrative fees that were collected by rural officials using brutal methods.[11]

Another high-profile reform enacted in the early phase of Hu's tenure was abolition of a draconian regulation allowing local authorities to detain undocumented vagrants found in cities, based on the "Procedures for Detaining and the Repatriation of Vagrants and Beggars in Cities," issued by the State Council in 1982. Local authorities routinely abused this administrative rule to extort money from migrants, who were frequently maltreated and beaten in detention centers run by local governments. In March 2003, at the height of the SARS crisis, a college graduate, Sun Zhigang, was detained by police as a vagrant in Guangzhou because he was not carrying the proper identification papers. Sun was beaten to death a few days after he had been transferred to a detention center for vagrants.

This scandal shocked the country because college graduates were considered elite members of society, and Sun's horrific death was a devastating illustration of the cruelty of the regulation and the lawlessness of local law enforcement officials. Seizing the opportunity, in May 2003 three liberal legal scholars petitioned the Standing Committee of the NPC to review the constitutionality of the regulation. The combined political pressure from public

TABLE 4.3. Estimates of the Gini Coefficient by the National Bureau of Statistics

Year	2003	2005	2007	2009	2011	2012
Gini Coefficient	0.479	0.485	0.484	0.490	0.477	0.474

Source: *China Yearbook of Household Survey 2018* (Beijing: China Statistics Press, 2018), 523.

TABLE 4.4. Government Spending on Environmental Protection, 2003–2012

Year	2003	2004	2006	2008	2010	2012
Environmental spending as share of GDP (%)	1.2	1.19	1.22	1.57	1.9	1.59

Source: *ZGTJNJ 2008*, e-book; *ZGTJNJ 2013*, e-book.

opinion and the legal challenge probably would not have been enough to force the new leadership to embrace a radical solution, such as abolishing the regulation. After all, the party could resort to strict censorship, and the NPC Standing Committee controlled by the party could reject the petition summarily. However, the Hu-Wen administration surprisingly announced abolition of the regulation five weeks after the legal challenge. The most likely explanation is that the new leaders were looking to burnish their public image.[12]

Judging by available data, Hu's project of building a "socialist harmonious society" achieved mixed results. His administration scored greater success in some areas than in others. The level of income inequality did not fall during his tenure, mainly because he failed to take any substantive measures, such as tax reforms or meaningful income support for the poor. Data collected by the National Bureau of Statistics show that income inequality rose slightly during Hu's decade in power. When Hu left office in 2012, income inequality had already returned to the 2002 level (table 4.3).

Hu scored moderately better results in the area of environmental protection, at least measured in terms of investment. Government spending on the environment steadily increased during his decade in office. Although spending stagnated during his first term, it rose meaningfully during his second term (table 4.4).

Like spending on the environment, public expenditures on education stagnated during Hu's first term, but they rose measurably as a share of GDP during his second term. In 2003 education spending was 2.84 percent of GDP. In 2006 it was still only 2.93 percent. But it rose steadily from 2009 to 2012, and

TABLE 4.5. Spending on Healthcare by Source, 2003–2012 (%)

Year	Government	Employers	Personal Out-of-Pocket	As Share of GDP (%)
2003	17	27	56	4.85
2004	17	29	54	4.75
2006	18	33	49	4.55
2008	25	35	40	4.63
2010	29	36	35	4.98
2012	30	36	34	5.4

Source: ZGTJNJ 2013, e-book.

by the time Hu left office in 2012, government spending on education had reached 4.28 percent of GDP.[13]

Hu made the greatest mark in terms of improving access to healthcare during his second term in power. He implemented a package of reforms in 2009 that significantly expanded access. In 2002, 45 percent of urban residents and 79 percent of rural residents had no health insurance. In 2010, a year after Hu's healthcare reform, 95 percent of the population was covered by various health insurance schemes. This was achieved mainly through large government subsidies to cover premiums and to reimburse hospitalization costs.[14] As a result, access to healthcare increased significantly, as measured by the dramatic decline in personal out-of-pocket spending on health. Hu's reforms increased the share of spending covered by the government from 17 to 30 percent of total spending. The share of personal out-of-pocket spending on health fell from 56 percent in 2003 to 34 percent in 2012 (table 4.5).

However, by the more commonly used measure of human welfare—the Human Development Index (HDI) developed by the United Nations Development Program (UNDP)—the progress made by Hu's project to build a "socialist harmonious society" achieved a magnitude of improvement in China's HDI from 2003 to 2012 that was similar to that gained during the Jiang period. The HDI rose 8 basis points, or an improvement of 15.7 percent under Jiang. During the 2003–2012 period, China's HDI rose 9 basis points, representing an improvement of 14.8 percent (table 4.6).

Based on his record in addressing China's social deficit, Hu's decade in power may be divided into two phases. He scored marginal progress during his first term, most likely due to his lack of authority and the residual influence of Jiang Zemin. Since any substantial modification of Jiang's policies that

TABLE 4.6. China's Human Development Index, 1993–2012

Year	Health Development	Education Development	Human Development Index
1993	0.762	0.424	0.527
2002	0.809	0.495	0.610
2003	0.815	0.507	0.621
2012	0.852	0.599	0.713

Source: UNDP, *China National Human Development Report* (2019), https://hdr.undp.org/system/files/documents/nhdrcnpdf.pdf, 271–72.

prioritized growth would have been perceived as a repudiation of Jiang, Jiang's proxies on the PSC and Jiang himself would not have supported such a course correction. Hu managed to do more to implement his agenda of building a "socialist harmonious society" during his second term, likely because of the dilution of Jiang's power on the PSC after the fall 2007 Seventeenth Party Congress, which elevated Xi Jinping and Li Keqiang to the PSC and as designated successors to Hu and Wen, respectively. The fiscal windfall produced by China's rapid growth following WTO entry (government revenue grew at an annual average of 21 percent during 2002–2007) also allowed the party to allocate more resources to social spending.[15]

Nevertheless, Hu's "socialist harmonious society" was at best a modest success because the program adopted only partial measures that relied on moderate increases in government spending but did not change the underlying political incentives or institutional factors behind the rise in the social deficit. For example, promotion of party officials continued to depend on their meeting specific economic or fiscal targets, not their record in improving the livelihoods of citizens.[16] Notably, Hu made no attempts to give ordinary people a stronger voice in determining government priorities, nor did he enact reforms that would hurt the interests of the powerful constituencies, such as SOEs, state-controlled health providers, education bureaucracies, and the party-state itself, all of which benefited from policies that channeled resources to the haves from the have-nots.[17] This explains why Hu's "socialist harmonious society" project had no impact on reducing China's high-income inequality, which reached a peak during his tenure and remained unchanged upon his departure from office. The party under Hu did make the slice of the pie for ordinary people slightly bigger, but the bulk of the economic benefits from growth was still accessible only to an exclusive elite—most important, party and government officials and their family members.

Social Unrest and the Rise of the Security State

After the crushing of the prodemocracy movement in June 1989, the party faced negligible overt political opposition to its rule as most of leaders of the movement were either jailed or exiled. In the two decades after the Tiananmen crisis, however, a new source of threat emerged: various forms of collective protests by ordinary people who were being victimized by government policies and official abuses of power.[18] In the early 1990s the number of such protests, officially labeled "mass incidents," was in the thousands each year (for example, 8,700 "mass incidents" allegedly took place in 1993). Over time, such incidents grew more frequent and attracted more participants. In the public domain, there are few reliable official data on the number, size, and duration of mass incidents. In 2003, the beginning of the Hu-Wen era, around 60,000 mass incidents were reported. In 2006 the number of such incidents exceeded 90,000. The total number of participants in these incidents rose from an estimated 730,000 to over 3 million.[19]

Despite the catch-all label of "mass incidents," these acts of protest and resistance had divergent causes, ranging from labor disputes, illegal land seizures, forced evictions, and environmental pollution to draconian enforcement of the one-child policy, oppression of ethnic minorities, and other conflicts between the state and ordinary people. Data on collective petitions (considered one type of mass incidents) in Hunan for 1994–1995 and 2000–2001 show that labor disputes accounted for the largest share of such incidents (roughly one-half). The second category of collective disputes (around 15 percent) involved rural issues (land seizures and brutal enforcement of government policies). Conflicts between workers and employers (mainly SOEs) made up the lion's share of the collective protests in 2000–2001 mainly because the SOEs were struggling financially and their mass bankruptcies at the end of the 1990s had left millions of workers without minimal social protections.[20] A study examining only large-scale social protests (that included more than five hundred participants) from 2000 to 2010 reached similar conclusions. Labor disputes in state and nonstate firms accounted for 53 percent of such incidents. Conflicts over land seizures and land use made up 16 percent. Protests over environmental pollution and ethnic oppression represented a very small share (4 and 2 percent of total reported incidents, respectively).[21]

Although specific incidents of abuses of power or lawlessness by government officials might have triggered such protests, underlying flaws in the

Chinese system of governance were the deeper causes. One clear culprit was the system the party had developed to evaluate officials' performance, which gave disproportional weight to economic growth and consequently incentivized officials to favor actions that would boost growth in the short term regardless of the social costs. Illegal land seizures or urban evictions might harm a large number of ordinary people, but the economic gains from developing real estate projects on the land could boost a local official's chances for juicing up growth and making that official a more competitive candidate for promotion.[22] Another institutional cause of the collective protests is the lack of peaceful channels of conflict resolution, especially when the state is party to the conflict. Despite the existence of a law allowing citizens to sue local officials and to seek judicial relief, it seldom produces the desired outcomes because local officials effectively control the courts (and the party is literally above the law since it cannot be sued).[23] Ironically, the party's own efforts to improve governance may have even fueled the popular protests. In an effort to make post-Mao governance less arbitrary, the party has promulgated a large number of rules that ostensibly set boundaries on the exercise of power by government officials. But instead of improved governance, the existence of this large body of rules seems to have produced the worst of two worlds: Local officials ignore or violate these rules because they restrict their freedom of action, while ordinary people, aware of the rights annunciated by the rules, are more emboldened to assert their claims. This combination lies behind the rise of China's "rightful resistance."[24]

Even though the dramatic increase in the number of collective protests in the Hu-Wen era attracted extensive attention from journalists and researchers and alarmed the Chinese government, the immediate political impact of these incidents was limited. Most were set off by specific socioeconomic, not political, grievances. The demands of the participants were specific, such as requests for payment of back wages or return of illegally seized property. Despite the label of "mass incidents," large-scale protests were relatively rare. Because they were either poorly organized or unorganized altogether, the duration of such protests was short, with most incidents lasting only one to several days. Notably, such protests were geographically isolated and seldom spread beyond the boundaries of a county or district, thus limiting their impact.[25] In addition, the party quickly learned how to quell such collective protests by mixing repressive tactics (severe punishment of the protest leaders) with concessions (such as wholly or partially meeting the demands of the protesters).[26]

The rise of incidents of social unrest nevertheless prompted the party to embrace a comprehensive strategy to strengthen regime security, ushering in an era of "stability maintenance" (*weiwen*). To be sure, the party began to bolster its repressive capacity immediately after the Tiananmen crackdown in 1989, but it subsequently developed more refined tactics of repression. In the face of growing social unrest, the party doubled down on its investment in its repressive capacity.

In November 2003 the party issued a key directive on domestic security, "The CCP Decision on Further Strengthening and Improving Public Security Work."[27] This directive lists a broad range of threats: "infiltration" by external and internal hostile forces, ethnic splittist forces, sabotage activities by religious extremists and terrorist groups, illegal activities by Falungong and other "evil sects," individuals with the potential of endangering state security and social stability, and mass incidents. The document pledges increases in funding, an expansion of security forces, and adoption of advanced policing and surveillance technologies.

During the Hu-Wen period, two hard-liners were put in charge of domestic security. Luo Gan, a protégé of former premier Li Peng, concurrently also served from 2002 to 2007 on the PSC as well as the party's Central Political and Legal Commission (as director), responsible for domestic security. He was succeeded by Zhou Yongkang, who oversaw domestic security affairs from 2007 to 2012 (Zhou would be the most prominent victim of Xi Jinping's purge in 2013).

Due to the rapid increase in government revenue during the Hu-Wen era, the party was able to invest immense resources in its coercive apparatus. Nominal spending on law enforcement (police, procuratorate, and courts) rose from 110 billion yuan in 2002 to 711 billion yuan in 2012. Adjusted for inflation, this represents a real increase of 400 percent.[28]

Generous funding enabled the party to acquire new technological capabilities for surveillance. The first phase of the "Golden Shield" project was unveiled in 1998. The program, designed to modernize the information technology systems of the Chinese police, was completed in 2005. According to the Ministry of Public Security, the Golden Shield contains basic population information, DNA data, and specialized software programs performing dedicated tasks. The infamous "Great Fire Wall of China," a system of filtering and blocking information the party deems to be harmful or subversive, was part of the Golden Shield.[29] However, the party's strategy of neutralizing the threats of the information revolution went beyond the adoption of technology. It also heavily relied on other tools, such as regulations (mandating real-name registration of users of social media and requiring users of internet cafes to scan their national identification cards to gain access to the web) and organization (establishing a party-state bureaucracy, the Cyberspace Administration, and a specialized internet police unit).[30] Tactically, the party learned to censor the internet with greater sophistication by prioritizing prevention of dissemination of information likely to encourage collective actions.[31] The Chinese model of "networked authoritarianism" has been remarkably effective in addressing a novel threat that prominent observers, including former American president Bill Clinton, thought would be impossible to contain.[32]

Another key component of China's techno-surveillance state, consisting mainly of ubiquitous video cameras and sensors, was also built during the Hu era. In 2004 the government launched the Skynet project (formally known as the "City Alert and Surveillance Technological System"), a hi-tech video and sensor surveillance program.[33] As revealed in an official document, Skynet consists of an elaborate system of surveillance using high-definition cameras, fiber-optic cables, sensors, servers, special software applications, and data resources. It is capable of conducting real-time visual surveillance of streets, highways, and other public venues, and of storing images for various purposes. Repeated technological upgrades later provided Skynet invisible electronic checkpoints equipped with cameras, license plate readers, Wi-Fi sniffers (to collect mobile phone information), and facial recognition technology.[34] In addition to adopting advanced surveillance technologies, in the mid-2000s the party established more specialized bureaucracies to oversee "stability-maintenance offices," with a full-time staff and a large network of informants.[35]

Conceptually and institutionally, the party under Jiang Zemin can possibly be credited with introducing the essential framework of selective repression. Operationally, selective repression was significantly upgraded with financial resources and technological capabilities under Hu Jintao. Even though Hu's rule is considered a period of political stagnation, this characterization obviously does not apply to the case of strengthening the coercive capacity of the Chinese state.

Civil Society and "Rights Defense"

The party's ability to maintain its political monopoly in spite of the rapid economic development in the post-Tiananmen era has raised doubts about the validity and applicability of modernization theory to China. The association between high levels of income and democracy, which is found in nearly all societies (with the exception of the oil-rich dictatorships), remains missing in China.[36] However, it is both oversimplistic and untrue to claim that, even in the case of post-Tiananmen China, sustained and rapid economic development did not contribute to the growth of forces and movements normally associated with civil society and democratization. Influential studies on the process of democratizing authoritarian regimes demonstrate that bottom-up pressures produced by economic modernization alone do not lead to democratic transitions. The most critical factor is the emergence of elites favoring political liberalization within the authoritarian regime.[37] As I show in this section, sustained economic development in the post-Tiananmen era contributed to the rise of a broad but unorganized social movement that challenged one-party rule using flexible and sophisticated tactics. This "rights defense" movement featured activist lawyers and liberal journalists who could generate substantial political pressure on the party. To be sure, the party's successful prevention of the growth of this movement into a broad organized political opposition was mainly the result of the regime's coercive capacity and not of a failure of economic development to produce prodemocracy social forces.

The rights defense movement can be traced to the tragedy of Sun Zhigang, a college graduate beaten to death in a detention center for vagrants in Guangzhou, in March 2003. Shortly after this incident, public pressure forced the government to abrogate the notorious regulation blamed for causing Sun's death, marking the first major victory of the rights defense movement.[38] Although individual acts of defiance against one-party rule occurred frequently during the Jiang era, they lacked the two defining characteristics of the rights defense movement of the Hu era: the role played by an informal coalition of lawyers, journalists, and human rights activists in asserting the constitutional rights of Chinese citizens, and the impact of public opinion that was amplified by the internet. Leaders of the rights defense movement were mainly activist lawyers who had received formal legal education in the post-Mao era and become the public face of the movement.[39] The number of lawyers participating in the movement is unknown. Teng Biao, one of the leading human rights lawyers associated with the movement, estimates that, when it began in 2003, no more than three dozen lawyers were actively engaged in "rights defense." But by 2015, perhaps as many as a thousand lawyers were associated with the movement.[40] Yu Zhengsheng, the Shanghai party boss (2007–2012), has claimed that about 3 percent of China's 270,000 lawyers were "rebellious," implying that as many as 8,000 might have been engaging in activities the party disliked.[41]

Compared with the Jiang era, the Hu era was a more favorable period for a social movement, such as the rights defense movement, to grow and gain influence. The soft-authoritarian rule practiced by Jiang and Hu relied more on intimidation than on brute force, allowing a large gray area in which human rights activists could test the boundaries set by the regime. Because the party had promulgated a large body of laws and regulations that ostensibly claimed to protect the rights of ordinary people and, toward the end of his rule, Jiang himself promoted the slogan of "ruling the country according to law" (not the "rule of law"), human rights lawyers could take advantage of the very laws issued by the party to engage in activities that challenged its exercise of power.[42] Additionally, the advent of the internet created a new and powerful platform for "rights defenders" to rally public opinion. When Hu became party chief at the end of 2002, the number of Chinese citizens with access to the internet was 59 million. By the end of 2012, 564 million Chinese people had access.[43]

Public Interest Litigation

A core strategy of the activists in the "rights defense" movement was to challenge the government on issues that resonated with the public, such as environmental pollution, employment discrimination, and food safety. Because suing the government in Chinese courts or advocating on behalf of the rights of victims of pollution and unsafe food was the only feasible option, public interest litigation became the most frequently used tactic of the "rights defenders" during the Hu era. One representative case illustrating how the rights defenders utilized public interest litigation to challenge the party is that of discrimination against individuals carrying the hepatitis-B virus.

Hepatitis-B is one of the most prevalent diseases in China. Based on a survey of blood samples collected at the end of 2014, it is estimated that 86 million Chinese carried the hepatitis-B virus at that time.[44] But people infected with the virus were ineligible for employment regardless of their qualifications. In December 2003, a college graduate sued the government of Wuhu city in Anhui for determining that he was ineligible to take the civil service exam because he had tested positive for the hepatitis-B virus. His lawyer, a legal scholar specializing in human rights law, convincingly argued that the provincial government's prohibition against hepatitis-B virus carriers violated a national law and the constitutional rights of the applicant. The court of first instance ruled in favor of the applicant.[45] The rare legal victory paved the way for removal of this discriminatory rule in 2005.

Another representative case is the "Sanlu poisonous baby formula" case. In early September 2008 the government acknowledged that the Sanlu Group, one of the country's largest producers of baby formula, had been adding a hazardous substance, melamine, to its products to raise their protein content. The contaminated baby formula made more than 300,000 children sick and caused at least six deaths.[46] In the wake of the scandal, a group of human rights lawyers offered legal representation to the families of the children harmed by the tainted formula. Many lawsuits were subsequently filed against Sanlu. Under public pressure, the government punished some of the individuals directly implicated in the scandal and launched a nationwide campaign to check future levels of melamine in baby formula.[47]

Advocating for the Voiceless

The progrowth policies of the party in the post-Tiananmen era created both winners and losers. While the winners enjoyed a standard of living few could have imagined merely a decade earlier, the losers lacked advocates for their rights—until the emergence of the "rights defenders" in the early 2000s. Human rights activists and lawyers relied on the same playbook to advance their cause: After the emergence of a major scandal, they would offer legal representation to the victims and rally public opinion to pressure the government. In some cases, their efforts succeeded in forcing the government to take remedial actions. Even in cases where they failed to help the victims gain compensation or judicial relief, human rights activists managed to expose the callousness, incompetence, and corruption of the local authorities and to puncture the myth of the superiority of a prodevelopment autocracy.

One such example is the case of slave labor in Shanxi. In May 2007 investigative journalists uncovered a scandal that shocked the nation. Several politically connected operators of brick kilns were employing dozens of enslaved laborers, including kidnapped underage boys and mentally handicapped persons, and making them work under inhumane conditions. The ensuing public outrage forced the government to send a special investigation team from Beijing to punish the kiln operators and their political patrons. In the wake of the scandal, several human rights lawyers represented some of the victims in a civil suit seeking compensation. Although the court rejected the lawsuit, the publicity surrounding the scandal helped raise public awareness of labor rights and shine an unflattering spotlight on the image-conscious Chinese government.[48]

Another representative case is the Henan HIV/AIDS scandal. In the 1990s poor rural residents in Henan province sold blood plasma to shady operations run by well-connected individuals. Because these individuals used the same but undisinfected needle to collect blood plasma, the practice resulted in transmitting the HIV virus to the sellers of the blood plasma. Worse still, the virus-carrying blood plasma was later used to treat other patients. In total an estimated 150,000 people were infected through these two transmission mechanisms. But the Henan provincial government covered up the scandal. Leading rights defenders tirelessly championed the cause of the victims and called on the government to take urgent action. Human rights lawyers also defended those victims who were demanding medical treatment.[49]

High-Profile Sensitive Cases

Rights defenders—mainly lawyers and human rights activists—were prominent players in the most politically sensitive legal cases during the Hu era. They employed a well-honed strategy to assert the rights of Chinese citizens and expose the dark side of the post-Tiananmen order. Typically, activist lawyers would offer their services to victims of political persecution, corruption, environmental pollution, and violators of food safety rules and labor laws. Once retained, the lawyers would vigorously assert the legal rights of these victims and contest, in criminal proceedings, the charges being leveled against them by the government. At the same time, the rights defenders used the media and the internet to rally public opinion to their cause. Although these efforts did not always succeed in winning justice in a legal system in the firm grip of the party, rights defenders sometimes managed to help their clients avoid harsher penalties when acquittal was impossible. In the court of public opinion, the rights defenders seemed to be clear winners since their involvement generated popular support for their clients and undermined the party's moral authority.

One of the most high-profile cases that such rights defenders represented is that of the "Taishi village incident." In July 2005 residents of Taishi village, near Guangzhou, started a process to impeach the director of the village committee because of his mismanagement of village finances and suspected corruption. However, the party viewed this incident as a direct challenge to its authority and dispatched riot police to the village to clear the protesting villagers from the offices of the village committee. During the two-month standoff between police and villagers, several human rights activists and lawyers went to the village to provide moral support and legal advice. The incident reportedly raised alarms at the highest level of the Chinese leadership. Although the government eventually relied on high-pressure tactics to quash the protest and restore control in the village, the incident represents another milestone in the rights defense movement during the post-Tiananmen era.[50]

The "Shaanbei oilfield litigation" is another high-profile case that demonstrates the potential of the rights defenders. After the Shaanxi provincial government seized oil wells operated by private investors in 2003 and provided only nominal compensation, activist lawyers and several liberal publications came to the defense of the private investors. Despite government intimidation and threats, a number of human rights lawyers represented the investors in their lawsuit against the provincial government. The incident produced an unwelcome spotlight on the party. Although the lawsuit ultimately failed, the act of confiscation of private property discredited the regime's pledge to respect private property rights.[51]

On occasion, rights defenders would score a rare victory, as in the case of Sun Dawu, a rural entrepreneur in Hebei province. In May 2003 Sun was arrested on charges of "illegal fund-raising." Prosecution of Sun was based on a broad and vague legal provision that effectively prohibited private entrepreneurs from raising private funds. Sensing an opportunity to defend the rights of private entrepreneurs, activist lawyers served as his defense counsel. With the support of liberal publications, the rights defenders created enormous public support for Sun and, at the same time, also discredited the government's charges against him. Ultimately, he received a suspended light sentence.[52] (Sun later became an outspoken critic of the government. In 2022 the Xi regime sentenced him to eighteen years in prison on made-up charges.)

Judging by its measurable accomplishments, such as court victories, favorable administrative actions, and reversal of unjust government policies, the rights defense movement during the Hu era achieved only modest successes. But its accomplishments reveal several important aspects of state-society relations in that era. First, rapid economic progress in the post-Tiananmen era did create favorable socioeconomic conditions—in particular, an expansion of the middle class (represented by the human rights activists, liberal lawyers, and journalists in the rights defense movement) and access to new information technologies. These conditions enabled those grassroots champions of freedom and rule of law to mount a sustained, albeit unorganized, social movement to assert the rights of the Chinese people. Second, the party's attempt to burnish its image and promote economic growth with an ostensibly improved legal system opened up the legal arena as a contested space for advocates of human rights and rule of law to challenge the party and test its boundaries. Third, the rights defense movement was part of the growth of Chinese civil society and had the potential of becoming a more organized and coherent force for democratization, as demonstrated by the rise of the New Citizens Movement, a 2003 civic group founded by the civil rights lawyer Xu Zhiyong that attracted a diverse group of supporters and played a leading role in the rights defense movement until the government banned it in 2013.[53] Finally, bottom-up pressures for liberalization without the support of the reformers within the regime could win small battles in some instances but were insufficient to promote systemic change. The absence of reformers in the top leadership of the party during the post-Tiananmen era made it impossible for this movement to realize its potential.

Crony Capitalism and Corruption

Official corruption is widely thought to have become more pervasive in the post-Mao era and, in particular, the Hu era.[54] During the Jiang period, China was typically ranked among the bottom third of the countries surveyed (although the number of countries surveyed was smaller than that in later periods). Corruption appeared to have abated modestly during the Hu period. China's ranking rose to the median of the countries surveyed, most probably because the surveys included more (and likely more corrupt) countries.[55]

Even though the Corruption Perception Index may not help us ascertain whether corruption grew worse in the Hu era than it was in the Jiang era, it is possible to rely on another measure to gauge corruption. Official data on the prosecution of bribery cases disclosed in *Zhongguo falü nianjian* (Law yearbook of China) give us a more detailed picture of the intensity of corruption. We here include only bribery cases because China almost exclusively punishes bribe-takers who are party and government officials. Data on major bribery cases provide more convincing evidence that corruption intensified during this period (see table 4.7). The number of major bribery cases rose 6.7 times from 1998 to 2012, far outpacing the increase in the Consumer Price Index (1.4 times during the same period), indicating that inflation was a negligible factor in the dramatic increase in the number of major bribery cases.[56]

Data on the number of officials at the county level and above prosecuted for corruption may give us a glimpse of the scope of official corruption, i.e., the number of officials implicated in corruption cases. The annual reports of

TABLE 4.7. Number of Major Bribery Cases Prosecuted, 1998–2012

Year	Number of Major Bribery Cases
1998	1,847
1999	2,552
2000	3,658
2002	4,871
2003	5,424
2004	5,690
2005	6,042
2006	7,033
2007	8,045
2008	8,805
2009	9,875
2010	10,586
2011	10,927
2012	12,326

Note: Major bribery cases involve over 50,000 yuan.
Source: *Zhongguo falü nianjian*, various years (Beijing: Zhongguo falü nianjian chubanshe).

the Supreme People's Procuratorate (SPP) show that the scope of corruption by this measure has expanded dramatically since the late 1980s (see table 4.8). Particularly notable is the significant increase in the number of higher-ranking officials (bureau level and above). The data for the 2013–2017 period, Xi's first term, also show that his anticorruption campaign targeted far more higher-level officials than were targeted during previous periods, while lower-level officials (at the county level) were less affected. This may be interpreted as evidence of Xi's weaponization of anticorruption prosecution to destroy political rivals and consolidate power.[57]

In addition to a measurable increase in the intensity and scope of corruption, corruption during the Hu era acquired characteristics normally associated with regime decay. Collusive corruption—cases involving multiple individuals—became widespread, as did the practice of bribing superiors for appointments and promotions. Government officials and businesspeople forged close relationships that allowed the latter to bribe the former for lucrative government contracts, cheap land, underpriced state assets, and bank loans.[58]

In retrospect, the intensification of corruption during the Hu era was the result of a convergence of several factors, most of which were embedded in the

TABLE 4.8. Number of Officials Criminally Prosecuted

Period	County Level	Bureau Level	Provincial-Ministerial Level
1988–1992	4,451	173	5
1993–1997	2,903	265	7
1998–2002	12,830 (all three levels)		
2003–2007	12,964	930	35
2008–2012	12,193	950	30
2013–2017	15,234	2,405	122

Source: "Work Report of the Supreme People's Procuratorate," https://www.spp.gov.cn/spp/gzbg/index.shtml.

nature of the post-Tiananmen political economy. The ruling elites had abundant opportunities to abuse their political power to engage in rent-seeking or self-enriching activities.[59] Despite the regime's unabashed endorsement of the pro-market reforms in the 1990s, the state continued to retain enormous influence over the economy. It owned large commercial entities with trillions of yuan in assets. In 2002 state-owned and state majority-controlled industrial firms held 8.9 trillion yuan in assets (nearly two-thirds of total industrial assets). By 2012, the end of the Hu era, the state-owned or state-controlled industrial assets in these firms reached 31.2 trillion yuan (about 41 percent of total industrial assets).[60] Despite the relative decline in their share, SOEs still directly controlled enormous assets, creating plentiful opportunities for officials to convert their political power into illicit income. Aside from industrial assets, the state also monopolized land rights, which it could lease to private entrepreneurs for commercial development. Unsurprisingly, sweetheart deals between private developers and local officials turned real estate into one of the most corrupt sectors in China during the Hu era.[61] China's government-funded infrastructure boom that began in the 1990s also spawned sector-wide corruption because local officials in charge of building highways could dole out contracts to construction companies in return for bribes. Between 1995 and 2014, seventeen directors of provincial transportation departments were arrested on charges of corruption. The vast amounts of bribes that they received necessitated severe punishment: One was executed, another received a suspended death sentence, and five were imprisoned for life.[62]

The sectors singled out by China's top prosecutor for bribery investigations in 2008—infrastructure projects, sale of land rights, transfer of property rights (of SOEs), purchase and sale of medicine, government procurement, and development of natural resources—illustrate that state control of assets, regulatory approvals, and project financing are some of the root causes of corruption.[63] Politically, two factors likely fueled official corruption in the post-Tiananmen era. First, the neo-authoritarian model of development that combines political repression with capitalism can make corruption more difficult to control because of the suppression of a civil society and the lack of press freedom. One of the most effective approaches to combatting official corruption is to rely on civil society and a free press to act as public watchdogs.[64] However, the space for civil society in the post-Tiananmen era was extremely compressed due to the party's paranoia about the emergence of an organized opposition. The regime also maintained tight press censorship (although it would become even worse during the Xi era).

Second, the party's primary approach to fighting corruption—waging periodic political campaigns—was largely ineffective. The sole bureaucratic organizations charged with the task, the party's own discipline inspection committees, lacked independence and were easily politicized.[65] The effects of the anticorruption campaigns were short-lived also because the officials on the take would simply lie low during the campaigns and then resume stealing once the political heat had subsided.[66] The fragile balance of factional power at the top levels of the leadership similarly constrained the party's ability to combat corruption because of the implicit mutual security pact among top leaders. No single leader was powerful enough to launch a sustained anticorruption drive that could potentially send his rivals and their followers to jail (as Xi did immediately after gaining power). Because the collective leadership in the post-Tiananmen era made decisions through consensus, prosecuting senior officials (those at or above the ministerial or provincial level) likely required unanimous agreement among the members of the Politburo or the PSC. This arrangement may explain why relatively few ministerial-level and provincial-level officials were prosecuted in the post-Tiananmen era and why the number jumped in the Xi era. Although the unspoken mutual security pact at the top of the regime probably helped maintain leadership cohesion and limited the weaponization of anticorruption investigations, it also made it more difficult to contain corruption.

Even though corruption in the Hu era was widespread, it is difficult to calculate its economic costs. On the surface, the pervasive corruption did not lead to a slowdown of growth.[67] But the economic costs of corruption were likely reflected in performance data that are not captured by growth. For instance, the costs of "white elephant" infrastructure projects and inflated prices of goods procured by the government actually boosted GDP growth because of the use of expenditures in growth accounting. Since goods and services tainted by corruption are typically of inferior quality, measuring the economic costs is methodologically difficult. Research on corruption nevertheless shows that most of its costs tend to be indirect and manifested in high income inequality, inadequate social services, poor food safety, environmental degradation, and social unrest—exactly the socioeconomic pathologies widely observed during the Hu era.[68]

Politically, endemic official corruption during the Hu era created favorable conditions for the return of a ruthless strongman such as Xi Jinping. As corruption permeated the regime and a large number of officials were tainted, they became easy targets for a potential strongman who could purge rivals and amass huge power under the guise of cleansing the party. This is precisely what occurred during Xi's first term.

The Beginning of the End of the Post-Tiananmen Order

On the surface, the Hu era seems to be almost a seamless continuation of the Jiang period. With the exception of the purge of one Politburo member, Shanghai's party boss Chen Liangyu, elite politics was relatively stable. But trouble was brewing beneath the façade of elite unity. The two major factions—the "Shanghai Gang," led by the retired Jiang Zemin, and the "Youth League faction" (*tuanpai*), under the aegis of Hu Jintao—had no real ideological differences over policy as they both were committed adherents to Deng's neo-authoritarian vision. But at the same time they were fierce rivals for power over personnel appointments. This rivalry would peak in 2007 with the party selection of Hu's successor. The impasse between the two factions ended with the anointment of a dark horse, Xi Jinping—who was unaffiliated with either faction—as future party chief. This fateful decision would later change the course of history. The designation of Xi, however, did not completely settle the issue of succession. As Xi was seen as a potentially weak leader because he lacked his own power base, ambitious party apparatchiks, in particular Bo Xilai, who was promoted to the Politburo in 2007, began to maneuver for more power in the run-up to the leadership transition scheduled for late 2012. The ultimate outcome of Bo's power grab was a spectacular and sordid scandal that not only ended his political career but also put a fitting end to the two-decade-long post-Tiananmen era, fully exposing the rot and decay that had been accumulating beneath the ever-prospering economy.

The rivalry between the Shanghai Gang and the Youth League faction reached its peak ahead of the Seventeenth Party Congress in 2007, which was scheduled to select Hu's successor. The most widely circulated rumor is that in that year the deadlocked party leadership conducted an informal poll of more than four hundred top officials, and Xi came up on top of his rival, Li Keqiang, a former CYL leader and Hu's protégé.[69] Xi was subsequently promoted to the Politburo Standing Committee in 2007 and was slated to succeed Hu in 2012. Li Keqiang, also elevated to the PSC, was ranked below Xi and would be the future premier.

Although this version of the events of 2007 lacks documented evidence, several factors apparently converged to produce this surprise outcome. The most important factor in Xi's favor was that the Shanghai Gang could not put forward a competitive candidate. Chen Liangyu, a protégé of Jiang and former Shanghai party chief, might have been a plausible candidate even though he would be 61 in 2007, six years older than Xi, and he would be 66 if he were to succeed Hu in 2012. But he was purged by Hu on corruption charges in 2006, most likely as a preemptive move to clear the path to the top for Li Keqiang.[70] With no candidate of its own, the strategic goal of the Shanghai Gang was to deny the Youth League faction the top prize, even if it had to consent to picking someone who was not part of its network.

In terms of his "princeling" family background and political career, Xi had no prior contact with the Shanghai Gang. But his political prospects brightened significantly on the eve of Jiang's retirement as party chief in 2002. Although Xi had spent seventeen years in Fujian province, climbing from the position of deputy mayor of Xiamen (in 1985) to Fujian's governor (in 2000), he had a lackluster record as an administrator.[71] Nevertheless, Jiang gave Xi a critical career boost by making him party chief of Zhejiang in late 2002 and placing him in a favored position for promotion to the Politburo in 2007. Jiang's role in Xi's rise in 2002 indicates that he probably saw Xi as a potential ally despite his lack of ties with Jiang's Shanghai Gang.

The inherent weakness of the Youth League faction in general, and the weak leadership of Hu Jintao in particular, further contributed to the faction's 2007 defeat in the succession struggle, to Xi's benefit. On paper, the Communist Youth League seems to be an impressive political organization. With more than 73 million members (in 2023) and branch organizations spanning the entire country, CYL officials are on a fast track to promotions in the party's organizational hierarchy.[72] In the post-Mao era, two national leaders of the league, Hu Yaobang and Hu Jintao, became the party's general secretary. The third, Hu Qili, was made a PSC member and a future successor before he was dismissed after the Tiananmen crackdown.

However, senior leaders promoted from the CYL have one glaring weakness. With the exception of Hu Yaobang, who climbed to the top of the CYL by starting as a local official in Sichuan, most league members who ascended to the top lacked local administrative experience as party chiefs. Typically, they began their political careers inside the CYL and then helicoptered to provincial governments to gain the requisite experience before they could be promoted to national-level leadership. This path to the top may have put some CYL officials on a faster track to the top than most CCP officials, but it also tended to produce weaker leaders.[73] First, the CYL as an ancillary organization of the party does not have real administrative authority, so its leaders have few opportunities to gain executive experience at the local levels. When the lucky few are promoted to the top, they are untested and unproven leaders. Second, due to the status of the CYL as an ancillary organization of the party, the league has no say in the distribution of government resources, making it impossible for its officials to trade favors with local party officials or other elites or to build up their own networks. As a consequence, CYL stars such as Hu Qili, Hu Jintao, and Li Keqiang rose to the top mainly due to the support of powerful patrons. Hu Jintao, the only former head of the CYL to become CCP chief after the fall of Hu Yaobang, owed his good fortune to Deng Xiaoping, who designated him as Jiang's successor—an arrangement Jiang could not undo.

But when the party had to pick Hu's successor, the weakness of the CYL became evident. Its power could not match that of the Shanghai Gang, which was determined to prevent another former CYL leader from taking over the party's top post. Li Keqiang, the CYL candidate, appeared to be a clone of Hu. Like Hu, he had risen to the top of the CYL, and later he had helicoptered to Henan and Liaoning to burnish his credibility and experience. Also like Hu, Li was colorless and had no track record as a dynamic and capable leader. Furthermore, Li's patron was Hu Jintao, not Deng Xiaoping. Deng's support and authority ensured Hu's appointment as Jiang's successor, but in 2007 Hu had nowhere near the same amount of prestige and power as Deng had in 1992 to pick a successor.

Hu Jintao is commonly believed to be the weakest of all Chinese leaders in the post-Mao era.[74] He had no close allies on the powerful PSC during his first term, and he could count on only one member (Li Keqiang) during his second term. By contrast, his predecessor Jiang, with at least four supporters on the PSC during Hu's decade in power, could constrain Hu's exercise of power.[75] In retrospect, however much Hu might have wanted Li to be his heir, he lacked the clout to make it happen.

Even though the details of the succession struggle in 2007 may never be fully known, its outcome—the selection of Xi Jinping—would change China's trajectory decisively, and disastrously, after 2012. To be sure, before Xi was made Shanghai party chief in 2007 after the fall of Chen Liangyu, he was a plausible successor but not in the top tier. If it is indeed true that Hu Jintao's purge of Chen was intended to remove a potential obstacle to Li Keqiang, he achieved just the opposite: He actually paved the way for Xi to move to the front row. When the party was forced to pick a successor, the impasse between the Shanghai Gang and the Youth League faction resulted in an apparent compromise—a successor seen as unaffiliated with either group.

After the Sixteenth Party Congress ended in November 2007, the struggle for power at the top only intensified. By that time, the influence of the Shanghai Gang was beginning to wane because its chief patron, Jiang Zemin, was 81 and had been in retirement for five years. His associates on the PSC were all expected to step down in 2012. In the meantime, Xi, the designated successor, was perceived to be a weak leader because he had no faction of his own. The political landscape at the top of the regime appeared to open up opportunities for ambitious apparatchiks to jockey for power in the post-Hu era.

As with other power struggles in dictatorships, the political maneuvering during Hu's second term is shrouded in secrecy and spiced up with unsubstantiated rumors. But two characters feature prominently during this period. The first and most well-known is Bo Xilai, another princeling and newly promoted member of the Politburo and party chief of Chongqing. The second and more obscure figure is Ling Jihua, the director of the powerful General Office of the Central Committee and Hu's long-serving chief of staff. The salacious allegations about Ling's machinations are impossible to verify,[76] but because he is one of the four "biggest tigers" (senior officials) whom Xi arrested at the height of his anticorruption campaign, it is reasonable to believe that Xi saw Ling as a lethal threat.

By comparison, the scandal involving Bo Xilai and his family is well-known. The most revealing part of Bo's saga, for the purpose of understanding elite politics during the second half of Hu's rule, is not Bo's spectacular fall in early 2012 or the sleazy details of the corruption in his family, but his attention-grabbing antics to brand himself as a new type of leader during his tenure as Chongqing's party chief.

Almost as soon as Bo Xilai became Chongqing's party chief in late 2002, he embarked on a risky strategy of promoting himself as a future member of the PSC (mainly because the top two slots—the party chief and the premier—had already been assigned to Xi and Li Keqiang). Unlike Xi, who had shunned the limelight so he would not be seen as an ambitious and potentially dangerous leader, Bo gambled that his only path to the party's most powerful body was to market himself as a more dynamic and creative leader, far different from the risk-averse and colorless apparatchiks who had made up the overwhelming majority of the party's senior echelons in the post-Tiananmen era.

Bo's campaign consisted of two tracks, both with a populist touch. Ideologically, he revived Maoist symbols with a campaign of "singing red" by organizing mass performances of revolutionary songs popular during the Maoist era. Given his family's suffering under Mao, Bo might not have been a real Maoist. But he apparently calculated that invoking Maoist symbols would resonate with a population concerned about high socioeconomic inequalities and rampant materialism. As no other senior apparatchiks dared to flaunt Maoist symbols, Bo's strategy succeeded in attracting enormous publicity and made him into an instant political star. Simultaneously, Bo launched a ferocious crackdown on alleged "organized crime" (*dahei*, literally smashing black). This drive led to the arrest and execution of local officials and private businesspeople accused of "organized crime." He dramatically expanded the police force as part of his "Safe Chongqing" campaign. This combination of Maoist ideological revival and cultivation of a public image as a strongman made Bo a popular figure among the local population.[77] But Bo's unabashed campaign of self-promotion also earned him many enemies. Liberal scholars and private entrepreneurs saw him as a dangerous ultra-leftist. His rivals in the party were alarmed by the prospect of having this ambitious and ruthless man as one of the top leaders in the post-Hu era.

The most remarkable—and revealing—aspect of Bo's attempted power grab before his fall in March 2012 is that he almost succeeded. During his campaign of "singing red and smashing black," not a single senior leader dared to criticize him. Nearly all members of the PSC, including Xi, visited Chongqing as an endorsement of Bo's "Chongqing model." Only Hu and Wen did not go to Chongqing. Bo might have secured one of the seats on the PSC at the Eighteenth Party Congress in November 2012 if his police chief, Wang Lijun, had not exposed the murder of a British businessman by Bo's wife in November 2011.[78]

In retrospect, the greatest beneficiary of Bo's political demise was Xi (who allegedly played a crucial role in urging the PSC to pursue a thorough investigation of Wang Lijun in hopes of implicating Bo).[79] Had Bo been promoted to the PSC in fall 2012, he would have made a formidable rival to Xi, likely complicating the latter's efforts to consolidate power. Ironically, although Xi sent Bo to prison for life in August 2013, he has copied the tactics Bo had used in building up his authority and image in Chongqing. Instead of an anticrime drive, Xi launched a wide-ranging crackdown on corruption to destroy political rivals and amass power. Ideologically, Xi went even further than "singing red"—he launched a comprehensive movement of orthodox ideological indoctrination to return the party, which he believed had become too corrupted by materialism, to its revolutionary roots.

Fatal Flaws of Dengism

The fall of Bo Xilai is a fitting coda of the post-Tiananmen political order. By the time the once-swaggering princeling was brought down by his own hubris and political enemies, the foundations of the neo-authoritarian order, envisioned by Deng and constructed during the Jiang era, had begun to crack. Elite unity was fraying as power struggles assumed an increasingly vicious nature. The fragile balance of power was on the verge of collapse as the Shanghai Gang was losing influence due to the advanced age of its principal patron, Jiang Zemin, while the Youth League faction lacked the strength to become an effective countervailing force. A new generation of politicians unaffiliated with either faction, such as Xi and many others, was poised to rise to the top and to fundamentally reshape the elite landscape. Because of the unsustainable investment-driven growth model and the lack of economic reforms during the Hu era, the economy was beginning to lose steam, threatening to undercut the party's claim to performance legitimacy. If the incidence of mass protests is a measurement, tensions between the state and society were greater than at any time since the Tiananmen crackdown. Co-optation of elites might have secured some support from wealthy private businesspeople, but at the price of rampant corruption as ruling elites and well-connected entrepreneurs forged a self-serving alliance. Chinese leaders also appeared to have abandoned Deng's dictum of "keeping a low profile" on foreign policy as they began to flex their muscles abroad in the belief that their moment in the sun had arrived. The only pillars of the post-Tiananmen order that remained intact were the party's security apparatus, now equipped with the most advanced surveillance technologies, and Chinese nationalism.

To be sure, the post-Tiananmen order could conceivably have lasted longer if Li Keqiang, instead of Xi Jinping, had become party chief in November 2012. It was Xi who demolished the post-Tiananmen order. Before the rise of a neo-Stalinist figure like Xi, few would have imagined that Hu's successor could reverse Deng's policy of reform and opening and reimpose totalitarian control on the party and on a Chinese society that had been so thoroughly transformed by two decades of economic modernization.

In retrospect, Xi's speedy dismantling of the post-Tiananmen order—without much resistance in the party to boot—suggests that forces larger than the ambitions and ideological visions of a princeling were at work. In other words, the post-Tiananmen order contained the seeds of its own destruction. Under Xi, it came to a quick and abrupt end. Had a different leader succeeded Hu, the decaying order might have experienced a slower death, but it would nevertheless have met its end.

Like other dictatorships, the party in the post-Tiananmen era could not evade the law of negative selection: Its power and privileges mainly attracted opportunists who embraced the regime for personal gain, not out of genuine ideological commitment. As patronage and corruption became the principal means to get ahead in the regime, only apparatchiks with fewer scruples had a better chance to gain power, thus creating a dynamic of bad money driving out good money. Over time, less capable but more venal and sycophantic apparatchiks came to dominate the ranks of the regime. Institutionally, the degeneration of elites created favorable conditions for the rise of a ruthless personalistic ruler because they were too compromised by their record of corruption or too cowardly to put up a fight.[80]

The post-Tiananmen order unraveled also because of the inherent limitations of Deng's neo-authoritarian model. Transition from a centrally planned economy to a market economy under a Leninist regime faces impossible odds because such a transition will necessitate a near-total withdrawal of the state from the economy, fatally weakening a Leninist party-state's control of the economy. It is worth recalling that market reform was Deng's tactic to save the party, not his ultimate goal. As a pragmatic Leninist, he embraced capitalism out of necessity, not out of ideological conviction.

Toward the end of the Hu era, however, the logic of a "partial reform equilibrium" set in. The remarkable economic achievements after the Tiananmen debacle, likely unanticipated by the regime (or anyone else, for that matter), boosted the party's legitimacy and confidence but also perversely diminished incentives to carry out further reforms.[81] The most insidious aspect of a "partial reform equilibrium" is that this status quo offered maximum benefits to the party if it could be preserved. As a partially reformed economy was far more efficient than a centrally planned economy, the party could claim a higher degree of performance legitimacy. At the same time, this equilibrium also allowed the party to maintain a substantial degree of control over the economy and enabled the ruling elites to wield their political influence to extract personal benefits. Consequently, the regime had no desire either to return to a Maoist system or to advance to a full market system. But a "partial reform equilibrium" cannot be sustained forever. The combination of corruption and systemic inefficiency in the partial reform economy began to sap China's economic dynamism on the eve of Xi's takeover.

The growth of private wealth, expansion of a middle class, and emergence of a nascent civil society constituted yet another existential threat to the post-Tiananmen order. Although the party had invested massive resources in surveillance and had acquired an unprecedented coercive capacity toward the end of the Hu era, it also began to encounter more direct and well-organized challenges to its authority from many directions—ethnic minorities in Tibet (which in 2008 experienced the region's most violent uprising in two decades) and Xinjiang (which saw China's most deadly ethnic riot in July 2009), underground religious and cult groups, human rights activists, environmental movements, and ordinary people victimized by government policies and abusive officials. Despite the regime's formidable capacity to quell these challenges, it would have to resort to more brutal tactics to deter and suppress societal opposition forces.

On the external front, the durability of the post-Tiananmen order critically depended on stable and largely cooperative relations with the West, its primary source of technology, market access, and capital. The strategic restraint urged by Deng served China well. However, there were two fundamental flaws in Deng's "hide and bide" strategy. First, ideological hostility toward the West's capitalist democracy was deeply embedded in the party, which saw the US-led West as an existential political threat and its economic engagement with China simply as an instrument of "peaceful evolution" or regime change. Such insecurity, if not paranoia, limited the extent of the West's economic engagement with China because China would prioritize regime security over economic benefits, and the West would understandably erect safeguards against a potential geopolitical adversary that was rapidly gaining strength through globalization. Second, China's rapid growth in the post-Tiananmen era radically transformed the global balance of power and changed its leaders' strategic calculus. When Deng prescribed strategic restraint in the wake of the Soviet collapse, it was not so much a stroke of geopolitical genius as a concession to reality: China was simply too weak to be assertive. All this would change toward the end of the Hu era. Finally, due to its growing power, China felt confident enough to take steps to extend its global influence, even at the risk of antagonizing the West, particularly the United States. Xi Jinping would later adopt a far more systematic and aggressive foreign policy, but China's strategic overreach actually began under the leadership of Hu Jintao.[82]

5

China's Economic Miracle

BASED ON CHINA'S rapid growth in the post-Tiananmen era, it is tempting to think that this was primarily due to the party's neo-authoritarian development model. But such a conclusion is at most just partly correct because many other factors likely played a greater role in supercharging economic growth in the two decades following Deng Xiaoping's southern tour in early 1992.[1] Certainly, the party's single-minded focus on economic development gave rise to an incentive structure that motivated local officials to prioritize growth. Reforms carried out in the 1990s helped lay some of the critical institutional foundations of a market economy. Additionally, the Chinese state's unrivaled capacity for mobilizing resources enabled the country to invest in physical capital, such as factories and infrastructure, on an unprecedented scale. However, a closer look at the underlying drivers of sustained economic growth in the post-Tiananmen era makes it clear that the most important foundations had actually been laid in the 1980s. A dynamic private sector that would evolve into the most powerful and efficient productive force in the post-Tiananmen era was created in the 1980s. The opening to the outside world, another critical step taken in the 1980s, allowed China to capitalize on the globalization boom in the post–Cold War era. The highly favorable demographic structure enabled China to benefit from an abundant supply of young workers and a low old-age dependency ratio. Cooperative relations with the West helped China gain support for accession to the World Trade Organization and become a trading superpower.

Unfortunately, favorable economic and geopolitical factors seldom last forever. China's post-Tiananmen economic miracle conceivably could have become even more spectacular and endure longer had its leaders undertaken more radical reforms to complete the country's march to a full market economy. Yet, the logic of path dependence again precluded this possibility. Instead of taking advantage of favorable structural factors to implement the difficult reforms, the party in the Hu Jintao era was trapped in a "partial reform equilibrium." The hybrid economy that emerged in the 1980s turned out to be far more difficult to reform. Strong economic performance reduced the party's incentive to risk tougher reforms. Its choice of an investment-driven development model became an addiction despite evidence of its diminishing returns in the Hu era. Further reduction of the state's influence over the market, especially through the privatization of state-owned enterprises, was politically unthinkable because the party saw them as the economic foundations of its monopoly of power. When China's economic momentum began to decelerate in the second half of Hu's decade in power, the party took the easy way out. Instead of painful structural reforms, it turned to credit-funded stimulus and blew an epic investment bubble that would burst and mire the economy in stagnation a dozen years later. In retrospect, party supremacy over market—the sine qua non of Dengism and the ultimate destiny of neo-authoritarian developmentalism—meant that the party would not permit considerations of economic efficiency to subvert its goal of regime survival. In this light, China's economic miracle in the post-Tiananmen era could not last.

Economic Achievements

Judging by measurable data, China's economic performance from the time between Deng's historic southern tour in 1992 and the end of Hu Jintao's rule in 2012 was among the most impressive in the annals of development. Although the quality of Chinese growth is marred by extensive environmental degradation, high income inequality, and rampant corruption, its quantitative achievements are undeniable. Factoring in the economic accomplishments of the 1980s, China transformed itself from an impoverished agrarian society to a moderately prosperous one within one generation. The main driver of this economic revolution was sustained growth in the post-Tiananmen period (table 5.1). During the two "miracle decades" (1993–2012), the Chinese economy grew at an annualized rate of 10.2 percent. The size of the Chinese economy in 2012 was nearly twenty times larger than that in 1992 in dollar terms (from $0.427 trillion to $8.53 trillion) and ten times larger in purchasing power parity (PPP) (from 1.47 trillion to 15.12 trillion).[2]

During this period, China also became a foreign trade powerhouse. The volume of exports rose more than elevenfold, and imports increased by the same order of magnitude (table 5.2). The explosive growth of Chinese foreign

TABLE 5.1. GDP Growth, 1993–2012

Period	Average Annual GDP Growth Rate (%)
1993–1997	13.1
1998–2002	8.2
2003–2007	11.7
2008–2012	9.2
Entire period	10.2

Source: Calculated from data in *ZGTJNJ 2013*, e-book, https://www.stats.gov.cn/sj/ndsj/.

TABLE 5.2. Foreign Trade (in billion USD)

Period	Imports	Exports	Total
1993–1997	633	696	1,329
1998–2002	1,070	1,220	2,290
2003–2007	3,983	3,381	7,364
2008–2012	7,096	8,140	15,236

Source: Calculated from data in *ZGTJNJ 2013*, e-book.

trade turned the country into the world's largest exporting economy within the two decades after the end of the Cold War. In 1992 China's share of global exports of goods (including Hong Kong) was 5.2 percent, placing it behind the United States, Germany, Japan, and France as the world's fifth-largest exporter. By 2012, China's share of global exports of goods (including Hong Kong) reached 13.9 percent, making it the world's largest exporter (a position it continued to hold in the mid-2020s).[3] As a result of government support, Chinese exports included a large share of electronics and manufactured goods that were technologically more sophisticated than those of other economies at a comparable income level.[4] Burgeoning exports filled China's foreign exchange coffers to the brim. In 1992 the country had only $19 billion in hard currency reserves. Two decades later, it boasted the world's largest foreign exchange reserves ($3.3 trillion).[5]

Economic growth in the post-Tiananmen period also urbanized a predominantly rural society. In 1992 only 27.5 percent (or 322 million) of the population lived in urban areas. By 2012, 52.6 percent (or 712 million) of the population were urban residents.[6] The structure of the economy was transformed beyond recognition as the modern sectors (industry and services) dominated economic activities by 2012. In 1992 agriculture, industry, and services accounted for 21.8, 43.5, and 34.8 percent of GDP, respectively. By 2012, the share of agriculture had declined to 10.1 percent, while the shares of industry and services were 45.3 and 44.5 percent, respectively.[7]

The standard of living for the average Chinese rose from 1,262 in PPP in 1992 to 11,169 in PPP in 2012, a nearly tenfold improvement.[8] Due to sustained high growth, the scale of the reduction in poverty during this period was unprecedented. On the eve of Deng's reform and opening, China had 770 million people living in poverty, of whom 658 million were living in rural areas. By 2013, the number of rural poor had fallen to 82 million (8.5 percent of the rural population). In other words, economic growth reduced the number of rural poor by 576 million between 1990 and 2013.[9]

Economic Reform and the Chinese Miracle

The post-Tiananmen leadership benefited enormously from the legacy of reform implemented by Zhao Ziyang and the other liberal reformers in the 1980s. When Deng reignited reform in 1992, most of the basic institutional framework for a market-oriented economy had already been laid. Agriculture, for example, had been privatized, freeing up an immense pool of surplus labor to engage in more productive activities in manufacturing and services. A dynamic private sector had firmly established itself as a new engine of growth. (In 1991 nonstate firms were generating 47 percent of industrial output.)[10] China's linkages to the world economy through trade and investment were fully restored by the beginning of the 1990s. Geopolitically, China's ties with the West survived the shock of the Tiananmen crackdown despite the (mostly symbolic) sanctions imposed by its main trading partners in protest. With the end of the Cold War in 1991, China managed to preserve its commercial ties with the West. Instead of being cast aside or isolated, China joined the high tide of globalization championed by the United States, then the world's sole superpower.

Conservative resistance to more radical economic reforms collapsed after Deng's southern tour in early 1992. In November 1993 the party issued a comprehensive package of reform, "Resolution on Several Questions on the Construction of a Socialist Market Economic System."[11] With Jiang Zemin's support, Executive Vice Premier Zhu Rongji sidelined the conservative premier Li Peng and supervised the major institutional reforms laid out in the resolution.

The first measure—unification of exchange rates and a major devaluation—went into effect on January 1, 1994. Prior to this reform, China had two exchange rates, with a highly overvalued official exchange rate. Yi Gang, who later became China's central bank governor, has recalled that the average official rate in 1993 was 5.6 yuan to the dollar, while the average market rate was 9.04 yuan to the dollar, implying an overvaluation of roughly 60 percent.[12] The dual exchange rates encouraged Chinese firms to withhold their foreign exchange earnings from the central government, fueling black market transactions and disincentivizing exports. The positive impact of the exchange rate reform was felt instantly. The Chinese yuan was effectively devalued by 60 percent, thus making exports highly competitive. The unification of the exchange rates also simplified the administration of foreign exchange and encouraged firms to export.[13] Chinese exports in 1994 rose 32 percent vis-à-vis 1993 (in 1993, exports had grown only 8 percent over 1992). China's foreign exchange reserves more than doubled in 1994 (from $21.1 billion in 1993 to $51.6 billion in 1994).[14]

A revamped fiscal system that recentralized government revenues was also put in place on January 1, 1994. In the 1980s Beijing had resorted to a form of "fiscal contracting"—or tax-farming—to incentivize local governments to increase economic output. Under fiscal contracting, local governments could keep surplus revenues after meeting their previously negotiated quota with Beijing. Although fiscal contracting contributed to local economic dynamism, it also had several major shortcomings. The most serious was a decline in the share of revenue collected by the central government because this arrangement ensured that local governments reaped more benefits of the growth than did Beijing. As a result, the share of the central government was only 22 percent of total government revenue in 1993.[15] Lack of fiscal resources limited Beijing's ability to fund infrastructure and other expensive capital projects. Fiscal contracting also encouraged "local protectionism" as provincial governments erected trade barriers to products from other regions so as to protect their local industries.[16]

In 1993 Zhu Rongji personally negotiated with provincial leaders an agreement on a new fiscal system that would recentralize revenue. At the heart of the reform was the introduction of a national value-added tax, which dramatically broadened the tax base. The central government would receive 75 percent of the value-added tax, with the remainder going to local governments. Local governments could also collect other taxes, but they contributed a much smaller share of taxes. In 1995, one year after the new system went into effect, the value-added tax accounted for 43 percent of total tax revenue.[17] To sweeten the deal, the central government allowed local authorities to keep income from the leasing of land, thus giving birth to the so-called land-based fiscal system (*tudi caizheng*).

In subsequent years, the central government's share of fiscal revenue rose dramatically. (During 1996–2000, it shot up to 50 percent.)[18] Like all reforms, the fiscal recentralization in 1994 produced winners and losers. In this case, the winner was clearly the central government, which was able to capture the lion's share of the tax revenue generated by China's fast-growing economy in the post-Tiananmen era. Its abundant revenue allowed Beijing to invest in infrastructure, military modernization, and domestic security. The losers were the local governments that subsequently experienced chronic budgetary shortfalls and had to rely increasingly on income from the sale of land-user rights and bank loans to fund their investments and operations. A lack of fiscal resources also limited the local governments' ability to pay for social services.[19] On balance, however, the fiscal reform of 1994 largely accomplished Beijing's objectives, despite the mixed outcomes. The fiscal system became more stable, and the lower budget deficits helped contain inflation (from 1980 to 1990 the consumer price index rose 11.6 percent on average annually, but in the decade following implementation of the new fiscal regime the increase averaged only 6.8 percent per annum).[20] The central government acquired ever-increasing resources to invest in high-priority projects. The negative effects of the new fiscal system did not become clear until roughly two decades later, when local governments began to borrow heavily from banks to finance their capital projects, thus accumulating a huge amount of debt that they could not repay.[21]

A third major reform in the 1990s was the establishment of a modern financial system and increased independence of the central bank, the People's Bank of China (PBOC). At the end of 1993, the State Council announced a comprehensive overhaul of the financial system.[22] During the Maoist period, China had no commercial banks. Few financial reforms were carried out in the 1980s as such reforms were technically too complicated and too risky to undertake in a transition economy. But because a modern financial sector is critical to mobilizing savings and allocating capital, the party identified reform of the financial sector, in particular the establishment of a modern banking sector, as a priority in its resolution on pro-market reform issued at the November 1993 Central Committee plenum.

Financial sector reform encompassed three subsectors: banking, insurance, and capital markets (equity and bonds). Because the insurance industry was relatively small and the tightly regulated capital markets played only a minor role in channeling savings into investments, the most critical sector was banking, the largest component of China's financial system.

The most successful part of the financial reform carried out in the 1990s, also led by Zhu Rongji, was the reform of the PBOC. Local governments had wielded substantial influence over the central bank, whose local branches were set up according to the administrative hierarchy of the state (for example, the PBOC had a branch office in each province and city). Since local governments appointed the leadership and staff of these offices, they could influence the PBOC. Zhu's reform established larger regional PBOC offices responsible for multiple provinces and filled them with officials appointed by the PBOC, making the central bank less dependent on local governments and increasing the technocratic capabilities of its local staff.[23] (Xi Jinping would reverse this reform in 2023 and increase party control of monetary policy.)

However, the other components of the banking-sector reform achieved mixed results. On the positive side, the reform increased competition in the banking sector and improved supervision, albeit from a very low level. Although the five largest state-owned banks (the Industrial and Commercial Bank of China, Construction Bank of China, Bank of China, Agricultural Bank of China, and Communications Bank) continued to dominate, reform in the 1990s brought in a large number of smaller banks with a diverse set of owners (mostly local governments, state-owned companies, and private and foreign investors), thus moderately increasing competition.[24] Separating policy lending from commercial lending, at least technically, the reform created a better division of labor in the financial sector. The policy to allow major Western banks, such as Bank of America, HSBC, and Singapore Development Bank, to purchase up to 20 percent of equity ownership in Chinese banks in the early 2000s was another positive step toward strengthening the financial health of the banking sector and introducing more sophisticated banking practices.

At the same time, the banking reform in the post-Tiananmen era did not create a truly market-based system. The state-controlled banks continued to channel a disproportionate amount of credit to the SOEs and to discriminate against the more efficient private firms. One survey of private firms at the end of the 1990s found that bank loans provided only 4 percent of the start-up capital and about 9 percent of the operating funds of private firms.[25] Consequently, private firms often had to resort to bribery to gain bank credit or had to tap into the more costly and less stable shadow banking system for credit.[26]

Progress in developing other parts of the financial system, such as equity and debt markets, was similarly uneven. China established these markets in the early 1990s, but initially it limited access only to state-owned enterprises and other state entities. Even after private firms were allowed access, an effective quota system led to a complex and time-consuming process to obtain approvals to raise capital. Foreign investors could only invest in B-class shares, which had far less liquidity than the A-class shares that were available to domestic investors. Although China's equity markets grew significantly in the post-Tiananmen era and would boast about 2,500 listed companies, with a total market value of 23 trillion yuan (over $3 trillion) in 2012, they remained a secondary channel through which firms could raise capital. By comparison, the outstanding credit of the banking system in the same year was 63 trillion yuan, nearly three times larger than the total market value of Chinese stocks.[27]

Reform of the SOEs, which made little progress in the 1980s, was another priority of the government in the 1990s. However, because the party initially resisted large-scale privatization and mass bankruptcy of unprofitable SOEs due to ideological concerns and worries about social unrest, it preferred mostly half-measures, such as leasing, mergers, and a comprehensive program of "establishing a modern enterprise system based primarily on state ownership."[28] The party's conception of a "modern enterprise system" appeared to be inspired by the corporate governance system prevalent in the West. Chinese reformers hoped that by adopting a Western-style corporate governance system they could make SOEs more efficient without changing their ownership.

As a consequence, many large SOEs went through mostly cosmetic changes, such as establishment of a board of directors, regular financial disclosures, and audits conducted by professional firms. Some were listed on domestic and international stock exchanges to attract nonstate minority investments and to create external pressures and oversight as tools to increase SOE efficiency. Yet, these reforms did not divest the state of complete or partial ownership. Most crucially but logically, the SOEs continued to serve the interests of the party, which retained effective control over these firms through management appointments. In theory, the party's "modern enterprise system" was supposed to maximize efficiency and improve the financial performance of the SOEs. In reality, the party's most important objective in retaining control over the SOEs was not to increase their economic value but to use them as tools to maintain a patronage system to reward loyalists, to implement industrial policy for regime and national security purposes, and to allocate SOE investments to balance factional and regional competition for resources. The subordination of economic efficiency to the party's self-interests inevitably meant that efforts to build a "modern enterprise system" would unlikely succeed in turning the SOEs into truly efficient and competitive firms. Indeed, the cosmetic reforms implemented in the 1990s failed to address most of the long-standing SOE problems, such as soft-budget constraints, low profitability, bloated employment, and excess wages and benefits.[29]

In 2003 the party tried a different approach—it decided to imitate Singapore's model of managing state-owned assets. As in China, Singapore's largest firms are state-owned or state-controlled. But the city-state established an agency—Temasek—to which the state transferred its shares so it could function as a more independent and effective supervisor. China thus set up its own version of Temasek—the State Asset Supervision and Administration Commission (SASAC)—in 2003. Its mandate was to exercise the power of the owner of the asset and monitor SOE operations and financial performance. Initially it was responsible for overseeing about two hundred large "centrally owned SOEs," whose state-owned shares were transferred to SASAC. Provinces also formed their SASAC equivalents to oversee provincially owned enterprises. Theoretically, this new bureaucracy would assume sole responsibility for management and prevent other state bureaucracies from interfering. Unlike Temasek, however, SASAC had one fatal design flaw. In Singapore, the ruling People's Action Party does not appoint management of the country's SOEs, leaving the responsibility to Temasek. But in China, the CCP's Organization Department, not SASAC, is empowered to appoint or remove SOE management, thus significantly weakening the supervisory role of SASAC.[30] Consequently, the setting up of SASAC produced no meaningful improvement in efficiency, as demonstrated by the persistent underperformance of SOEs relative to private firms in terms of profitability, generation of employment, and debt levels.[31]

Ironically, the most successful measure implemented by the party to reform the SOEs was the one it wanted to talk about the least: privatization and mass bankruptcy of loss-making small and medium-sized enterprises. In the mid-1990s the overall strategy of reforming SOEs was to "grasp the large and release the small"—focusing on improving the large SOEs but letting the smaller SOEs sink or swim. "Grasping the large" achieved at best modest results, as illustrated by the outcomes of corporatization and the experience of SASAC. "Releasing the small" meant, literally, allowing small and medium-sized SOEs to be restructured or liquidated through whatever means that could take these zombie firms off the hands of the government. Initially, releasing the small proceeded slowly and cautiously, and it appeared to take the form of management buyouts (insider privatization), mergers, and leasing. This process created opportunities for SOE management and well-connected private entrepreneurs to obtain state assets at steep discounts.[32]

After the East Asian financial crisis of 1997, Chinese leaders endorsed a drastic solution: the mass bankruptcy of small and medium-sized SOEs that could no longer be sustained without endangering the undercapitalized banking system. Judging by official data, this was carried out in 1998 quickly and most probably with no prior planning. The number of industrial SOEs in 1997 was 110,000, representing a moderate decline of about 17,000 over 1996, and with the overall number of SOEs peaking at 127,600. This indicates that releasing the small began in 1997 but proceeded slowly. However, the shock of the East Asian financial crisis, which led to the collapse of currencies in Thailand, South Korea, and Indonesia and the fall of the long-ruling Suharto regime in Indonesia, forced Chinese leaders to take the unprecedented step of closing, in the industrial sector alone, nearly 55,000 SOEs and laying off 13 million workers in 1998. In 1999 they shuttered an additional 3,400 firms and laid off roughly 12 million workers.[33]

Economically, releasing the small definitely achieved its desired objective of ridding the state of massive liabilities. But this achievement came with enormous social costs, as tens of millions of workers in the bankrupt SOEs were cast out on their own, most with no social safety net. Many fell into poverty.[34] Even though the government faced waves of demonstrations by the large number of laid-off workers, it managed to contain and ultimately suppress them through coercive means.[35]

The housing reform launched in the mid-1990s created a powerful new engine of growth. In July 1994 the State Council released a package of policies to privatize state-owned housing. Subsequently, state-owned housing units rented to employees in government-affiliated entities were privatized at heavily subsidized prices. Four years later the State Council issued a document promoting development of a private real estate market to address the housing shortages. In retrospect, the real estate boom during the subsequent two decades constituted a powerful engine of growth before it began to lose steam in the mid-2010s.[36]

On balance, the reforms of the 1990s achieved mixed results. On the positive side, they strengthened the fiscal system significantly and made the financial system moderately more market-oriented. Policies to privatize housing and promote the real estate market unleashed a powerful source of growth. But the efforts to reform the SOEs were largely unsuccessful. The strategy of "grasping the large and releasing the small" preserved state control over big firms in strategic sectors, such as telecommunications, energy, transportation, and finance, but did not improve their efficiency. The mass bankruptcy of small and medium-sized SOEs did succeed in shutting down the loss-making firms that the state could no longer support, thus producing an improvement in efficiency, but this was carried out in a hasty and chaotic manner that impoverished tens of millions of workers.

Ascendance of the Private Sector

If the party's efforts to reform the SOEs in the post-Tiananmen era ended mostly in failure, an unintended consequence of this setback was the rapid rise of the private sector, which consisted of private domestic and foreign-invested firms. As described earlier, the government's inability to turn around the inefficient SOEs with half measures finally forced it to embrace mass bankruptcy of the small and medium SOEs in 1998–1999. This solution, adopted out of desperation to avoid wrecking China's banking system, caused massive losses of jobs and income for those workers employed in these firms. However, the exit of tens of thousands of SOEs also created opportunities for the private sector. The fire sale of the assets of the bankrupt SOEs allowed their managers to obtain them cheaply and to set up their own businesses, often in controversial if not illicit collaboration with private entrepreneurs.

Ironically, the lack of a comprehensive program of privatization conceived and approved by the central government enabled local authorities and SOE management to adopt flexible, innovative, and often questionable methods of transferring the assets of the struggling or bankrupt SOEs to private entities.[37] Because most of these transactions were conducted opaquely and the purchasers of the SOE assets were managers and well-connected private entrepreneurs, conservatives and the so-called new left—scholars opposing neoliberal reforms because they were exploitative—vociferously denounced the deals as an "erosion and loss of state assets," insisting that assets sold to management and private entrepreneurs were deliberately and significantly underpriced at the expense of the Chinese people, who nominally owned these assets.[38] Academic research, indeed, provides evidence that these assets were sold cheaply during privatization. Large-scale, officially sanctioned national surveys of private firms conducted in the early 2000s reveal that, on average, the assets of the SOEs were underpriced by about 20 percent. Managers who bought these assets enjoyed a discount of 30 percent.[39]

However, critics decrying privatization as a process in which state-owned assets were sold too cheaply apparently ignored two crucial factors. First, those willing to buy the assets of the underperforming or nearly bankrupt SOEs took enormous risks and understandably demanded deep discounts. Second, China had no functioning institutions that could price such assets correctly. It was impossible to determine the appropriate price at which such assets should be sold.

In any case, the mass bankruptcy of tens of thousands of SOEs and the quick disposal of their discounted assets most likely boosted economic performance during the Hu era. With one stroke, privatization achieved three objectives: ending the waste of precious resources on zombie firms, saving the banking system, and transferring underperforming assets to private firms that could deploy them more productively. One study shows that, after privatization, private firms utilizing the same assets that were previously owned by collective firms could increase their output on average by 5–7 percent. Since private firms were more efficient than collective firms, it is reasonable to assume that the assets of SOEs in the hands of private firms would be utilized even more productively.[40]

Parallel to the privatization of small and medium SOEs was the conversion of TVEs into private firms. Since a large number of these were private firms that had disguised themselves as TVEs when they were first established in the 1980s, part of this process was not privatization but normalization. The real owners—rural entrepreneurs who had established them—simply gained formal legal title to their property. Another part of the process involved the privatization of collectively owned assets. The transformation of TVEs into private firms began in southern Jiangsu in 1994 and quickly spread to other parts of the country. Nearly all TVEs had been converted to private firms by the end of the Jiang era.[41] This is evidenced by the rapid decline of employment in "collectively owned" firms (in all sectors) and the corresponding rise of employment in private firms from the mid-1990s to 2002 (table 5.3).

The positive impact of the privatization of TVEs was the emergence of some of China's largest and most successful private corporations, such as Fuyao Glass (which later became one of the world's leading makers of automobile glass, as featured in the Oscar-winning documentary, *American Factory*), Wanxiang Group (maker of auto parts), and Hope Group (agrobusiness).

Privatization in the 1990s enabled the private sector to eclipse the state sector as the most important engine of economic growth and job creation during

TABLE 5.3. Employment in the Post-Tiananmen Era (in millions)

Year	SOEs	Collectively Owned Firms	Private Firms*
1990	103.5	35.5	1.7
1995	112.6	31.5	9.6
1997	110.4	28.8	13.5
1998	90.5	19.6	17.0
1999	85.7	17.1	20.2
2002	71.6	11.2	34.1
2012	68.4	5.9	113.0

* Both urban and rural; private firms do not include individual (*geti*) businesses.

Source: *ZGTJNJ 2013*, e-book.

TABLE 5.4. Utilized FDI, 1993–2012 (in billion USD)

Period	Utilized FDI
1993–1997	187
1998–2002	226
2003–2007	313
2008–2012	516
Total	1,242

Source: Calculated from *ZGTJNJ 2013*, e-book.

the post-Tiananmen period. In terms of employment, the state sector employed 103.5 million people in 1990, compared to only 1.7 million in private firms. By 2012, employment in the state sector had declined to 68.4 million, while that in private firms had increased to 113 million (table 5.4). The decline in the number of SOEs in industrial sectors was most pronounced. For example, SOEs in the manufacturing sector employed 34.4 million people in 1993. By 2002, their employment had fallen to 9.8 million, a decrease of more than two-thirds. SOEs in mining and construction saw their employment fall by more than half during the same period.[42] The output of SOEs plummeted correspondingly. In 1993 SOEs accounted for 43 percent of China's total industrial output. By 2011, their share had fallen to 26 percent.[43]

Fast-growing domestic private firms became a powerful force in China's industrial sector. In 1993 the share of industrial output by domestic nonstate firms reached 47 percent. By 2011, private firms contributed 46.6 percent of industrial output, and foreign-invested firms accounted for 25.8 percent (about the same as the SOEs), while the share of collectively owned firms fell to 1.3 percent.[44] Even though the party did not actively promote the private sector, it deserves credit for taking the crucial political steps to give it legitimacy and protection. In March 1999 the party-controlled National People's Congress passed a constitutional amendment that formally recognized the legal status of nonstate economic entities. Jiang's theory of the "Three Represents," first unveiled in early 2000 and written into the party's charter in 2002, elevated the political status of private entrepreneurs by identifying them as a group the party should represent and recruit.

Globalization

China's opening in the post-Tiananmen era was more aggressive and far-reaching than its domestic reforms. Policies to attract FDI and increase exports in the post–Cold War era were necessary for China to build commercial ties with the triumphant West and to avoid geopolitical isolation. At the same time, the globalization championed by the United States and its allies after the end of the Cold War provided China with an unprecedented opportunity to utilize its comparative advantage of cheap labor to compete for a larger share in the global marketplace. Zhao Ziyang should receive credit for the strategy of closely integrating China into the world economy in the late 1980s when he proposed prioritizing development of the coastal areas as platforms to connect with the global economy. Although Zhao was purged during the Tiananmen crisis, his economic strategy not only survived him but also yielded spectacular outcomes few Chinese leaders could have imagined in the 1980s.

One measurement of China's embrace of globalization in the post-Tiananmen era is its success in attracting FDI. Between 1979 and 1989, foreign firms invested about $16 billion in China. But starting in 1992, foreign investors dramatically increased their bets on China. In 1992 alone, they invested $11 billion in China.[45] In the subsequent two decades, the amount of FDI would reach a staggering $1.24 trillion (table 5.4).

Several factors turned China into a favored destination for direct investments by foreign companies. In the early 1990s the government opened up more cities, including the major cities along the Yangtze River (such as Chongqing and Wuhan) and all inland provincial capitals, to foreign investors and allowed them to offer the same preferential terms as were initially made available only to foreign investors in the SEZs. To compete for foreign capital, local governments built large industrial parks and provided subsidies, such as cheap land and tax holidays. The most important city to become a giant SEZ in the early 1990s was Shanghai's Pudong area. With Deng's constant prodding, the government approved the city's proposal to open up Pudong to foreign investors in the 1990s. Within a few years, the area was transformed into a high-tech manufacturing hub built mainly with foreign direct investment.[46] Furthermore, the process to approve FDI projects was simplified and decentralized. In Guangdong, for example, the government allowed cities to approve projects under $30 million and counties to approve projects under $15 million.[47] Liberalized rules were adopted so that FDI projects not on the "restricted" or "prohibited" lists were all allowed.[48] Further liberalization measures implemented in the early 1990s included amendments to the laws on joint ventures and wholly foreign-owned enterprises and passage of new laws and regulations on income tax, intellectual property, and foreign exchange that made it easier for foreign investors to conduct business.[49] As a result, foreign firms were permitted to form retail joint ventures in several major cities and to become involved in natural resource exploration. They could also invest in power generation and infrastructure using the build-operate-transfer model. American International Group (AIG) was given a coveted license to sell some insurance products in Shanghai, and foreign banks could conduct local currency transactions.[50]

Although the government's policies definitely helped make China an attractive destination for FDI, other factors were in its favor as well. Perhaps the most important was timing. The revival of the country's reform and opening after the Tiananmen crackdown occurred just after the end of the Cold War and the beginning of the high tide of globalization. In East Asia, Japan and the four little dragons—Hong Kong, Taiwan, Korea, and Singapore—began to lose their competitiveness in labor-intensive manufacturing, forcing their companies to relocate elsewhere. Because of its vast pool of cheap labor and its geographical proximity, China was an ideal destination. In 1992 the average hourly wage of a Chinese manufacturing worker was a mere 1.27 yuan, or $0.16 at the unofficial exchange rate of 8 yuan to one dollar.[51] By one estimate, the wage of Chinese manufacturing workers in the early 1990s was the lowest in Asia.[52]

China enjoyed an additional unique advantage: its huge diaspora in the region. Successful ethnic Chinese entrepreneurs in Hong Kong and Taiwan, in particular, were eager to utilize their cultural and social connections to the mainland as a competitive edge in identifying investment opportunities.[53] Official data for 1997–2006, for example, show that investors from Hong Kong alone accounted for about 35 percent of total FDI utilized during this period, with Taiwan contributing about 6 percent.[54] The amount of FDI flowing from Hong Kong was likely inflated due to the practice of "round-tripping"—mainland Chinese firms would first transfer their capital to the former British colony and then use the same capital to invest in the mainland as FDI so they could enjoy greater legal protections and take advantage of the preferential treatment Beijing had granted to foreign investors.[55]

China also had a geopolitical turn of good fortune in the early 1990s. The United States and its allies decided to continue their policy of engagement and integration with China despite the Tiananmen crackdown and the end of the Cold War, which overnight had reduced China's strategic value to the West. President Bill Clinton's 1994 decision to stop linking China's most-favored nation (MFN) trading status to its human rights record lifted a dark shadow over Sino-American commercial ties.

Additionally, the party's renewed commitment to reform and opening after Deng's southern tour in 1992 and the explosive growth momentum unleashed thereafter significantly brightened China's economic future, making the country not only a cost-competitive and business-friendly export platform but also a fast-growing market for Western goods and services. The fierce competitive dynamics that pitted Western firms against one another in outsourcing their production to low-cost manufacturers benefited China immensely, since companies reluctant to invest in China would likely be outcompeted by their rivals that could take advantage of China's lower labor costs and large market. In the 1990s domestic Chinese firms were not strong enough to compete against foreign firms. With government policies giving foreign firms many advantages denied to domestic firms, foreign investors could count on capturing a significant share of the Chinese market.[56]

Massive inflows of FDI brought China bountiful benefits. In 1993 foreign-invested firms employed 2.87 million people. By 2012, more than 22 million Chinese were working in these companies.[57] In addition to the employment, capital, and technology that came with FDI, such investments generated significant spillover effects and improved the efficiency of Chinese firms. Foreign-invested firms allowed to sell goods inside of China increased competition in the marketplace, forcing domestic firms to improve their productivity and services. FDI firms also added to China's human capital by training a large pool of skilled labor and management. Once they reached a critical mass, such firms helped create local supply chains and form clusters of specialized industrial ecosystems, such as electronics in Shenzhen and Kunshan (near Shanghai).

The transfer of tangible and intangible know-how to domestic Chinese firms via the FDI process was invaluable, albeit difficult to calculate.[58]

The most significant impact of FDI in the post-Tiananmen era was on China's foreign trade. As part of the global trend of outsourcing manufacturing to countries with low labor costs, the majority of foreign firms used China as a processing center that assembled imported components to make products for export. Called "processing trade," this model served the interests of foreign investors well because they could utilize China's ultra-cheap labor and thus reduce costs. For China, FDI made the country a global foreign trade juggernaut. In 1992 foreign-invested firms accounted for 26 percent of China's total foreign trade in goods and 20 percent of its exports. By 2012, the share of foreign-invested firms in China's total foreign merchandise trade rose to 50 percent.[59] The rapid increase of foreign-invested firms in imports and exports reflects the role of "processing trade." Indeed, the share of processing trade rose steadily during the post-Tiananmen era, hovering between 50 and 57 percent of total exports from 1996 to 2006. FDI-funded firms accounted for 75–85 percent of China's processing trade between 2002 and 2008. Processing trade began to decline slightly toward the end of the Hu era. In 2012, 47 percent of China's merchandise trade was processing trade.[60]

Foreign Trade and the WTO

The explosive growth of foreign trade in the post-Tiananmen era was one of the most important factors behind the Chinese economic miracle. Although China began to liberalize its foreign trade in the 1980s, the pace was greatly accelerated in the 1990s, resulting in sustained growth in that trade. The volume of merchandise trade grew more than tenfold from 1993 to 2012 due to a combination of government-initiated reforms, luck, and specific policies (table 5.5). The State Council radically liberalized foreign trade with a set of new policies in 1994, including a series of tariff reductions that brought down the average import tariffs from well over 50 percent in the early 1980s to 17 percent in 1998.[61] The tariffs would be cut even further after China's entry into the WTO in 2001.[62] The government also ended subsidies to exporters to create a more level playing field, lowered entry barriers to foreign trade, and made the renminbi freely convertible for the purpose of foreign trade. The government passed a new Foreign Trade Law in 1994, authorizing any company to engage in such trade if it registered with the government and could find an agent to serve as intermediary. This measure significantly increased

TABLE 5.5. Foreign Trade (in billion USD)

Period	Imports	Exports	Total
1993–1997	633	696	1,329
1998–2002	1,070	1,220	2,290
2003–2007	3,983	3,381	7,364
2008–2012	*7,096*	*8,140*	*15,236*

Source: *ZGTJNJ 2013*, e-book.

competition in foreign trade because previously only firms approved by the government could engage in that trade. As a result of this reform, nonstate (mainly private) domestic firms gained a growing share of foreign trade. In 1992 they accounted for only 1 percent of total foreign trade (SOEs accounted for 72.5 percent). By 2000, their share had risen to 4.7 percent (compared with a SOE share of 45 percent).[63] At the end of the Hu era, domestic private firms accounted for 31.6 percent of China's foreign trade, second only to the share of foreign-invested firms at 49 percent (the share of SOEs had fallen to 19.4 percent).[64] In 2019 domestic private firms overtook foreign-invested firms as the largest contributor to foreign trade.[65]

To promote exports, China sweetened the incentives for exporters. The new foreign exchange policy that became effective in January 1994 allowed exporters to buy and sell foreign currency freely through the banking system. Exporters could also get a rebate from the VAT on their goods, a common international practice, to be more competitive. The Export-Import Bank of China was established in 1994 to finance foreign trade. Although both increasing competition and making exports more attractive were useful, the single most effective export-promotion policy was undoubtedly the one-time major devaluation of Chinese currency in January 1994 that not only unified exchange rates but also made Chinese exports much less expensive. In 1993 the official exchange rate of the renminbi was 5.77 yuan to the dollar. In 1994, the rate was 8.7 yuan to the dollar, representing a devaluation of over 50 percent.[66]

Taken together, these factors vaulted China to the front row of global trading nations. In 1993 China (including Hong Kong) was the world's fourth largest trading nation, with 6.1 percent of world trade. By 2012, China and Hong Kong accounted for 14 percent of global trade and claimed the number one spot.[67]

China's formal entry into the WTO in December 2001 was the most important event after Deng's southern tour in 1992 that altered the country's economic trajectory. China applied to join the General Agreement on Tariffs and

Trade (GATT), the predecessor of the WTO, in 1987. But the country's non-market economy, protectionist trading practices, and enormous potential to disrupt global trade due to its size made it difficult for the United States and Europe to support the application. China's bid languished until the late 1990s, when Jiang Zemin and Zhu Rongji put their support behind a renewed drive to gain accession, most likely to use WTO entry to spur a new round of economic reform at home and to seek further integration with the global economy. Although Zhu personally led the critical negotiations toward the end of the process in 2000, Jiang's political support was crucial because China's trade partners were demanding many concessions as conditions for Chinese entry. The most important concession was that China had to forgo the preferential terms accorded to developing country members of the WTO. To assuage fears of a flood of Chinese exports, China also accepted the "safeguards" demanded by its key partners, such as the United States and the European Union, allowing them to take unilateral measures against Chinese exports to protect their industries.

The timing of China's renewed bid was propitious because President Clinton, a strong US proponent of engagement with China, saw China's accession to the WTO as a strategic opportunity to bind China closer to the West-led economic order and to advance America's own economic interests. Sensing the enormous potential of a more liberalized China market after WTO entry, corporate America furiously lobbied a skeptical Congress, which reluctantly passed a bill in late 2000 granting China permanent normal trading status to pave the way for its WTO accession.[68]

China's entry into the WTO has remained a hotly debated issue. Geopolitically, after US-China relations turned completely adversarial toward the end of the first administration of Donald Trump, some argued that US economic engagement with China in the post–Cold War era, including support for its entry into the WTO, had been an epic strategic blunder.[69] In 2023 several hard-line senators introduced legislation to strip China of its permanent normal trading status. Whether China has lived up to its commitments remains similarly controversial.[70] What is not controversial is that China's WTO entry radically reshaped the landscape of global trade and supercharged its domestic economic development until the momentum dissipated toward the end of the post-Tiananmen era.

The impact of WTO accession on FDI and foreign trade was instant and dramatic as foreign investors rushed to China to take advantage of its commitments to open its domestic market for services and to build manufacturing facilities for exports. In the five years (2002–2006) immediately following WTO entry, inbound FDI grew at an annualized rate of 36 percent, averaging $59 billion a year. Even more FDI flowed into China thereafter. During 2007–2011, foreign investors poured $478 billion into China. Altogether, FDI totaled $775 billion in the first decade following China's WTO accession.[71]

The inflow of FDI and China's greater access to global markets granted under WTO rules precipitated explosive growth in foreign trade and, within a decade, made China (excluding Hong Kong) the world's second largest trading nation after the United States. In 2001, on the eve of China's WTO entry, its total foreign merchandise trade was $509.6 billion (exporting $266 billion in goods). A decade later, China's total merchandise trade had skyrocketed to $3.64 trillion. Its exports reached $1.9 trillion, surpassing Germany as the world's largest exporter by volume (but not by value-added).[72]

The most beneficial impact of China's WTO entry has been to make its economy more efficient and able to grow faster through three channels: an increase in foreign trade due to liberalization, a dramatic rise in FDI, and efficiency gains produced by implementation of the reforms China pledged to undertake and by the rising competition from greater access to the Chinese market by foreign manufacturers and service companies (such as retail).[73] Areas more exposed to WTO entry experienced greater productivity growth due to accelerated development of the modern sector (manufacturing and services) and a more rapid shrinking of the agricultural sector.[74] The magnitude of the boost in growth delivered by WTO accession is substantial but difficult to measure precisely. One study comparing China's growth performance from 2002 to 2007 with that of a group of developed and developing countries finds that accession increased China's real growth rate by 2.5 percentage points each year, implying that without WTO accession, China's average growth rate during this period would have been 8 percent, instead of 10.5 percent.[75]

However beneficial, WTO accession was a one-off event, and the momentum it generated gradually petered out. Instead of taking advantage of the favorable economic environment after WTO accession to implement more market-oriented reforms, the government continued to protect SOEs, maintain hidden barriers to critical sectors (such as financial services and energy), and pursue industrial policies prioritizing technological self-sufficiency.[76] Debate over whether China fulfilled its accession commitments also began to surface almost immediately after it became a WTO member. Trade tensions with its key trading partners, in particular the United States, rose as Chinese exports surged and the promised economic bounties to Western firms in terms of market access failed to fully materialize. The most contentious issues were China's poor protection of Western intellectual property rights, industrial policy, and regulatory restrictions on services and agricultural imports.[77]

Globalization might have been more beneficial for China than it was for any other developing country. But it was not all good news for the developed economies. The combination of technological progress and globalization was responsible for a significant reduction of manufacturing employment in high-income countries. Because after its WTO accession China had become the world's largest exporter of manufactured goods, and because it maintained huge trade surpluses with the advanced economies, in particular the United States, China was blamed for the loss of millions of blue-collar jobs. President Barack Obama managed to contain trade tensions with China, but China's rise as a global manufacturing superpower has had a lasting impact on America's political landscape. Research by labor economists shows that trade exposure drove American working-class voters, who had turned against globalization, to the Republican Party and put Donald Trump in the White House in 2016 (and brought him back to power in 2024).[78]

Strong Economic Fundamentals

The Demographic Dividend

Among the strong economic fundamentals that contributed to the Chinese "economic miracle" in the post-Mao era, the so-called demographic dividend is likely the most important. "Demographic dividend" refers to the gains from a decades-long period during which a country's labor force grows more rapidly than its population, resulting in more producers than consumers. However, not all countries with a favorable population structure (a large working-age population and a relatively small population of retirees) can reap this dividend because the productive utilization of a large labor force depends crucially on appropriate government policies affecting human capital accumulation through education and healthcare, savings, investments, and trade. Countries with the right policies during this window of demographic opportunity, as the countries in East Asia had, achieve higher rates of growth than those who do not have such policies. During the 1960–2000 period, the demographic dividend in Korea, Singapore, and Thailand contributed roughly one-third of the rise of per capita income, compared with only 16 percent of the rise of per capita income in the Latin American region.[79] China's population transition to an era of low birth and death rates actually began in the late 1960s. But during the Maoist era, the demographic dividend was wasted due to the radical economic policies and political turmoil. The favorable structural factors did not begin to drive economic development until the reform era.[80]

A population with low dependency ratios (more workers than both the old-age and young populations) contributes to economic development through two mechanisms. The first is the accumulation of savings due to the low dependency ratio and the extra savings that can fund investments in physical and human capital. The second mechanism is the development of capital markets because workers need to save for their retirement and thus require a more sophisticated financial system.[81]

Evidence of China's population transition can be seen in the dramatic fall in its birth rate starting in the mid-1960s. The country's birth rate peaked at 4.3 percent in 1963. By 1969, the birth rate had fallen to 3.4 percent, and in the 1970s the birth rate averaged 2.4 percent per year.[82] The sustained lower birth rate coupled with the low mortality, following a period of high birth and low mortality rates (the 1950s and early 1960s), resulted in a population structure with a low dependency ratio. According to the 1990 census, China's working-age population was 60 percent of its 1.13 billion people, while its old-age population (age 60 for men and 55 for women) was only 10 percent of the population, making the old-age dependency ratio 6 to 1 (six workers supporting one retiree). Those under 14 years of age accounted for 28 percent of the total population. So the total dependency ratio was slightly less than 3 to 1.[83] Studies of the magnitude of the effect of China's demographic dividend on economic growth show a substantial positive impact. One frequently cited article estimates that between 1982 and 2000, the demographic dividend contributed about 27 percent of China's per capita GDP growth. Another study finds that changes in the age structure of the Chinese population added about 20 percent to its per capita GDP growth between 1990 and 2005.[84]

One unique characteristic of China's demographic dividend is the massive transfer of surplus labor from rural areas to the cities. This process was set in motion in the 1980s by the decollectivization of agriculture, which raised productivity in the agricultural sector significantly and freed up a huge pool of surplus labor. In the 1980s the rural surplus labor was transferred mainly to the TVEs. Starting in the 1990s the boom in coastal areas and large cities attracted even more rural laborers who were migrating from villages to urban areas where they could earn higher wages in manufacturing, construction, and services. Estimates vary about the exact number of rural laborers transferred from the agricultural sector to manufacturing and services. The National Bureau of Statistics reports that 268.9 million rural laborers had transferred to the modern sector by the end of 2013.[85]

The infusion of a labor force that was larger than the population of most countries into manufacturing and services enabled China to keep wages low and maintain its competitiveness. More important, because the transfer of labor from a sector in which labor productivity is low to one in which one unit of labor can produce more value delivers a one-time improvement in labor productivity. The epic transfer of hundreds of millions of rural laborers to the modern sector in the post-Mao era (with most of this transfer taking place in the post-Tiananmen era due to the relaxation of restrictions on internal migration) accounted for a significant rise in productivity.[86] Estimates of the one-off boost in productivity due to the transfer of labor from less productive sectors (agriculture and SOEs) vary. According to one study, labor transfers from agriculture to nonagricultural sectors during 1978–1998 contributed about one-fifth of per capita GDP growth in China. Another study shows that relocating labor from agriculture to the nonagricultural sectors during 1991–2003 accounted for roughly 26 percent of Chinese growth in labor productivity. For the 1978–2015 period, the transfer of labor from less productive sectors to more productive sectors was responsible for 45 percent of the increase in labor productivity.[87]

However, China's demographic window of opportunity began to close toward the end of the post-Tiananmen era. By 2012, the country had reached the "Lewis Turning Point," whereby rural surplus labor was exhausted and wages were beginning to rise rapidly.[88] Due to the party's draconian one-child policy, which restricted urban families to one child and rural families to two, China quickly confronted a far more adverse demographic landscape—low birth rates and a rapid rise in aging—in the 2010s. In 1990 the total dependency ratio was 3 to 1. But the population structure indicates a continuation of the demographic dividend because roughly two-thirds of dependents were under age 15 and the elderly population constituted only 9 percent of the working population. By 2012, the share of the population under age 14 had fallen to 223 million (compared with 323 million in 1992), while the number of those aged 65 and above had risen to 127 million (in 1992 there were 72 million people in this age-group), raising the old-age population dependency ratio to nearly 13 percent.[89] Therefore, demographic aging began to act as a drag on future economic growth.

High Savings and Investments

The positive impact of the demographic dividend on China's growth in the post-Mao period is a much less disputed factor than the role of savings and investment. Like other fast-growing economies in East Asia, the story of the Chinese "economic miracle" also features high savings and investment rates. As an influential World Bank study of the East Asian development experience argues, high savings and high investment rates were the most important factors behind the region's post–World War II developmental success.[90] Even those economists who maintain that there was no such thing as an economic miracle in East Asia acknowledge that high investment rates made the region an economic development star after World War II.[91]

Not surprisingly, economists examining the sources of growth in post-Mao China also disagree on whether an increase in total factor productivity (TFP) or an increase in investment played a more important role in the Chinese economic miracle. Some insist that TFP growth in the private sector and agriculture after reform began accounted for most of the increase in per capita GDP growth because the state sector, which had invested more than half of the capital during the period covered by the study (1978–2007), wasted a significant amount of its investment.[92] Other economists, however, give more credit to investment. One study covering the 1978–2004 period finds that investment contributed 44 percent of the output of each worker, and TFP accounted for 49 percent. Another study examining the sources of growth during the 1978–2005 period produces similar results.[93]

At the heart of this esoteric debate is the sustainability of China's growth. If China's growth is driven primarily by investment and not by growth in productivity, it will eventually grind to a halt because of the law of diminishing returns (each additional unit of investment will produce less of an increase in output). But if China's growth is due more to rising productivity than it is to investment, its growth will be more sustainable.

What is not disputed, however, are the sustained high levels of savings and investment in the post-Tiananmen era. Even though the sources of growth—whether productivity growth or high investments—will remain a subject of academic debate, the undeniable fact is that China could not have achieved its sustained high growth without an abundant source of capital. As table 5.6 shows, its savings and investment rates were extremely high throughout the post-Tiananmen period, reaching a peak toward the end of the Hu era.

TABLE 5.6. Savings and Investment Rates (as a share of GDP)

Period	Average Gross Domestic Savings (%)	Average Gross Domestic Capital Formation (%)
1993–1997	40.9	33.3
1998–2002	38.1	33.3
2003–2007	45.8	38.8
2008–2012	50.0	43

Source: World Bank, https://databank.worldbank.org/source/world-development-indicators#.

Even compared with its neighbors in East Asia that are known for high savings and investment rates, China stands out during this period. In the Jiang era, its savings rate was 25 percent more than the regional average, and its investment rate was 12 percent higher. This gap would grow even further in the Hu era. On average, China saved a whopping 43 percent more than its neighbors and invested 35 percent more.[94] China was able to maintain high rates of investment mainly because of its abundant domestic savings, not because of FDI. Although utilized FDI totaled $1.24 trillion during 1993–2012, it was only a fraction of China's total investment. In 2012 alone, China invested $5.3 trillion in fixed assets. In the same year, inbound FDI was $111 billion, roughly 2 percent of total fixed asset investments.[95]

The reasons for China's high savings rate are not only hotly debated but also reflective of some of the flaws in the Chinese political and economic systems. In terms of the positive factors contributing to high savings, the most obvious is the combination of high growth and the demographic dividend. China experienced a virtuous cycle during most of the reform era—the reforms increased productivity and growth, resulting in higher income. Reinforced by the demographic dividend, more income was saved.[96] Another factor is simply rational human behavior. According to the life-cycle hypothesis, people save when their income is high so they will have money to spend when they have no income. Indeed, China's reform and opening produced higher growth and hence higher income, and as a result individuals rationally saved more.[97] This explanation is intuitively persuasive, but it does not address the unique and largely adverse circumstances in China's transitional economy during the post-Mao era. One casualty of the reforms is the (limited) socialist welfare state and the employment security of workers in urban areas. Uncertainty about future income in a transition economy motivated Chinese households to save more.[98] The theory of "precautionary savings" appears to make more sense in the Chinese context because, during much of the reform era, China did not provide sufficient social services (such as publicly funded healthcare or education) or a social safety net (pensions or unemployment insurance), forcing individuals to set aside a portion of their income for such future expenditures. Another factor unique to China that also forced people to save more was the high housing prices that motivated potential home purchasers to save for down payments.[99]

Although high domestic savings are critical to funding China's massive investment in infrastructure, alone they cannot sustain its economic development. Savings are expected to fall as China exhausts its demographic dividend and must provide for its rapidly aging society. If savings are not productively invested, they will not generate sufficient returns to cover pensions. The latter probably is far more challenging because China's state-dominated financial system and capital controls (which prevent Chinese households from investing abroad) limit investment options and potential returns. Instructively, the only class of assets that appears to have generated high returns is housing, in contrast to the equity market that has not delivered any returns despite its high volatility between 2008 and 2016.[100]

Losing Momentum

No one was in a better position to sound the alarm about the Chinese economy than China's premier, the country's chief economic manager. While the rest of the world was admiring China's economic miracle, Premier Wen Jiabao, uncharacteristically frank for a senior party official, told journalists at a press conference after the conclusion of the annual session of the NPC in March 2007 that the Chinese economy had "huge" (*juda*) problems—"the same persistent problems of instability, imbalances, lack of coordination, and unsustainability." In particular, Wen singled out the excessive investment growth rate, amount of credit, and liquidity; the large imbalances in foreign trade and the current account and between investment and consumption; excessive dependence on investment and exports to generate growth; and unsustainable environmental degradation.[101] When he delivered his work report to the NPC in March 2013 before retiring as premier, he reiterated his warning that economic imbalances, lack of coordination, and unsustainability continued to be prominent problems.[102]

The premier's warning reveals the weaknesses of China's economic development model in the post-Tiananmen era. Even though the party delivered two decades of spectacular growth, exceeding its own expectations, many of the factors that contributed to this economic miracle either were one-off or began to yield diminishing returns toward the end of the Hu era. If the party had adopted substantive reforms to correct these imbalances when Wen first sounded the alarm in 2007, the Chinese economy would likely have been in better shape than it was when Hu and Wen left office in 2012/2013.

But that did not happen. Instead of addressing the worsening macroeconomic imbalances through reform, the party under Hu merely rode the momentum generated by China's WTO entry, the housing boom, and the demographic dividend. When the global financial crisis (GFC) of 2008 hit, the leadership reacted with a massive credit-fueled stimulus package that avoided a recession over the short term. But the price was high. The party's panicked response to the GFC drastically increased the overall level of debt in the economy and led to a gigantic housing bubble. This credit-fueled investment cycle began to unwind around 2021 when the housing bubble popped and local government debt threatened to unleash a financial crisis. In retrospect, the party's stimulus package at the end of the Hu era merely delayed China's economic reckoning.

Macroeconomic Imbalances and Falling Productivity

By the end of the Hu era, most economic indicators were flashing yellow, or even red, signaling the end of the Chinese economic miracle. GDP recorded its last double-digit growth rate (10.3 percent) in 2010. Growth would fall to 6.4 percent in 2019, the year before the Covid-19 pandemic.[103] Judging by the structure of the Chinese economy, growth had become excessively dependent on investment (table 5.7). An economy that relies too much on one of the three drivers of growth—consumption, investment, and trade—can become vulnerable if this main driver loses momentum. In the Chinese case, the economy was most balanced in the 1980s, when Zhao Ziyang was the premier in charge of it. Consumption contributed, on average, 64 percent of the growth, and investment accounted for 31 percent. The ratio began to shift toward investment in the Jiang era, during which time foreign trade also claimed a much higher share of the source of growth. Nicholas Lardy, a leading authority on the Chinese economy, argues that macroeconomic data show that the Chinese economy became "highly imbalanced" in about 2003, the year Hu began his decade in power.[104]

At the end of the Hu era, the economy was less dependent on trade, as the contribution of trade to growth had fallen to 3.4 percent, most probably due to the decline in external demand following the GFC. But the domestic imbalances in the economy deteriorated, with investment contributing on average 52.4 percent of the growth during Hu's decade in power and consumption falling to 44.2 percent. Data from Hu's second term reveal even worse imbalances. During 2008–2012 investment accounted for an average of 56.5 percent of GDP growth, while trade brought down 6.2 percent of the growth because of the slump in world trade after the 2008 GFC.[105]

An economy overly reliant on investment as a source of growth faces two problems. First, investment typically yields diminishing returns: More capital is needed to generate an additional unit of output. This phenomenon is usually captured by the term "incremental capital output ratio" (ICOR). This ratio measures the unit of capital needed to generate an additional unit of output. Higher ICOR numbers indicate a greater need for capital investment to sustain growth. One estimate shows that China's average ICOR was 3.6 during 1983–1992, 4.0 during 1993–2002, and 4.3 during 2003–2012. Although it is debatable whether China's ICOR is too high, the upward trend is self-evident. In the Xi period, China's ICOR would rise even more rapidly (averaging 5.8 in 2010–2019).[106] A more nuanced analysis of China's rising ICOR finds that capital-intensive housing and infrastructure investment accounted for the bulk of this increase.[107] This explanation contains both good news and bad news. The positive interpretation is that China may have room to invest in the more productive sectors of the economy, such as manufacturing and services. The bad news is that the two engines behind the country's economic miracle—infrastructure and housing—cannot be sustained due to their high capital intensity coupled with their lower returns.

Second, excessive investment raises the risk of waste. High investment can lead to excess capacity, a chronic problem plaguing industries such as coal, steel, automobile, construction, and solar panels in China.[108] If SOEs undertake investment, the return on capital is much lower than it is in the private sector (private firms produced returns on capital that were roughly 50 percent higher than returns on capital in SOEs during the 2000s). Indeed, Chinese SOEs consistently have higher debt and report far lower returns on invested capital than do private and foreign firms. In the second half of the Hu period, the performance of SOEs relative to private and foreign firms became even worse. During the entire Hu period, SOEs recorded losses averaging 0.5 percent of GDP each year, indicating an inefficient use of capital.[109]

In addition to dramatic structural imbalances and a rising capital intensity, a third indicator of the flagging economic momentum that appeared at the end

TABLE 5.7. Contributions to GDP Growth (%)

Period	Consumption	Capital Formation	Foreign Trade
1980–1989	64.3	31.0	4.7
1993–2002	52.2	40.2	7.6
2003–2012	44.2	52.4	3.4

Note: Average contributions during each period.
Sources: *ZGTJNJ 2008* (Beijing: Zhongguo tongji chubanshe, 2009), 57; *ZGTJNJ 2013*, e-book.

of the Hu era is the slowing of productivity. One study of the sources of growth during the post-Mao period indicates that the increase in TFP accounted for 20 percent or more of the growth of output before 2008. However, the contribution of TFP to GDP growth became negative after 2009.[110] Another study shows that the contribution to GDP growth from the rise in TFP averaged 15 percent from 1980 to 2007, but TFP did not contribute to GDP growth from 2007 to 2012; in fact, TFP growth itself was negative in this period, implying declining economic efficiency.[111] Several factors likely led to the fall in productivity during the second half of the Hu era. The principal culprits were the party's failure to adopt more reforms to improve economic efficiency and its massive stimulus package in response to the GFC that channeled investments into the inefficient state sector and the unproductive infrastructure.[112]

Party Response to Global Financial Crisis in 2008

The GFC occurred at a time when the Chinese economy was at a crossroads. Its economic structure had become even more unbalanced than when Hu began as premier six years earlier. In 2007 consumption and investment contributed 40 percent to GDP growth, respectively, while foreign trade, due to China's whopping trade surplus of $261.8 billion, accounted for 20 percent. The boom in foreign trade following China's WTO entry made the Chinese economy heavily dependent on exports prior to the GFC. The positive effects of China's WTO entry took about three years to show up in China's trade data, most likely because of the time lag between the relocation of manufacturing facilities to China and their exports. During 2002–2004 foreign trade contributed an average of only 5 percent of GDP growth. But between 2005 and 2007 it accounted for an average of 21 percent of growth.[113]

Due to tight regulations and capital controls, the Chinese financial system was insulated from the turmoil in global financial markets. However, China's foreign trade immediately felt the impact of the GFC as demand for Chinese exports in the crisis-ridden Western economies declined dramatically. In response, the party rolled out a massive stimulus package to avoid a recession. This package consisted of two sources of funding. The fiscal spending that was announced in November 2008 amounted to 4 trillion yuan (about $486 billion, or 14 percent of GDP). Most of the stimulus targeted infrastructure projects. Despite its nominally large size, it is difficult to determine the actual amount of the fiscal stimulus because cash-strapped local governments were supposed to cover the bulk of the spending.[114] The other source of funding was bank loans, which provided most of the stimulus. Between December 2008 and December 2009 alone, Chinese banks lent out 11 trillion yuan in new loans, almost triple the amount of the announced fiscal stimulus.[115]

Judging by China's macroeconomic performance in the immediate aftermath of the GFC, the party appears to have made the right call. Exports in 2009 fell 16 percent from 2008, but they recovered strongly in 2010. Nevertheless, the GFC marked the end of China's export-driven growth. Foreign trade was a negative contributor to growth between 2008 and 2011, and it would not resume its role as an engine of growth until 2019.[116] The injection of massive credit into the economy did succeed in achieving the party's goal of maintaining growth. In 2008 the country reported growth of 9.6 percent (a significant fall from the 14.2 percent growth in 2007). Growth in 2009 and 2010 was 9.2 and 10.4 percent, respectively.[117]

Even though some economists hailed the party's response, in retrospect it was a costly mistake that led to a rapid buildup of debt in the economy, a worsening misallocation of resources, and the subsequent decline in productivity.[118] Arguably the greatest—and most negative—legacy of China's response to the GFC is the rapid increase in debt. According to the Bank of International Settlements, the debt of China's nonfinancial sector averaged 140 percent of GDP from 2000 to 2008 (it was 139 percent of GDP at the end of 2008). But the debt of the nonfinancial sector reached 175 percent of GDP at the end of 2009, a net increase of 36 percentage points. This implies that China's credit-fueled stimulus package was more than one-third of its GDP—probably the largest in peacetime history. Although the pace of credit slowed in 2010 and 2011, by the time Hu left his position as CCP general secretary at the end of 2012, total outstanding debt had risen to 192 percent of GDP, a historic record. Judging by the sustained buildup of debt in the Xi era, as will be discussed later, the party's debt-driven stimulus seems to have opened the door for Xi, during his first term, to rely on credit expansion to keep growth from falling from a cliff as a substitute for reform. (Debt to GDP would reach 297 percent by the end of Xi's second term in December 2022.)[119]

The rapid buildup of debt most likely created a large amount of nonperforming loans because SOEs and local governments had borrowed the bulk of the new credit created in 2009.[120] Researchers at the International Monetary Fund estimate that half of the new credit made available after 2008 went to SOEs.[121] Of all the outstanding debt to the nonfinancial sectors at the end of 2012, SOEs and local government financing vehicles (LGFVs) accounted for 37 percent.[122] Because inefficient SOEs do not generate enough profits to repay their loans and local governments frequently invest in wasteful projects, relying on revenue from the leasing of land to cover their financial liabilities, it is reasonable to assume that a significant portion of the borrowing after the GFC ended up as nonperforming loans in the financial system. In addition to misallocating massive amounts of resources to inefficient producers and dragging down productivity, the party's response to the GFC limited the space for future monetary policy and made the financial sector more vulnerable to a debt crisis.

One lasting legacy of the stimulus package is the housing bubble that it created. Data on floor space under construction reveal a massive increase of construction in both commercial and residential real estate. In the four years before implementation of the stimulus package (2005–2008), the total amount of space under construction was 177 million square meters. In the four years following the stimulus package, floor space under construction ballooned to 313 million square meters. Floor space under construction between 2009 and 2012 exceeded the combined total in the prior eight years.[123] Although the bubble would grow even bigger during the Xi era, it was a dark cloud hanging over the Chinese economy. When the real estate sector crashed during the Covid-19 pandemic in 2021–2022, a powerful engine of growth became the heaviest drag on the Chinese economy.

Summary

This account of the unprecedented economic growth that China achieved in the two decades following Deng Xiaoping's tour of southern China in 1992 illustrates the diverse factors that made this "miracle" possible and the obstacles to its sustainability. The reforms implemented by the party played a positive role. Even though these measures, rolled out mostly in the 1990s, were partial and oriented toward strengthening state control over the financial sector and the fiscal system, they helped make the economy more open, market-oriented, and productive.[124] At the same time, however, these partial reforms did not fundamentally change China's economic system. The state—in reality, the party—retained control over the most vital economic sectors. The share of SOEs in the economy remained too large to make China qualify as a market economy. Most of the growth during this period should be credited to the private sector, globalization, and favorable structural factors.

The post-Tiananmen economic model began to unravel during Hu Jintao's second term, as indicated by falling productivity growth and worsening economic imbalances. This process coincided with the emergence of cracks in the post-Tiananmen political model. In retrospect, the end of the Chinese miracle was almost inevitable. The beneficial effects of the demographic dividend and globalization had either dissipated or disappeared toward the end of the Hu era. In the meantime, the lack of reforms to address high income inequality, inefficient SOEs, macroeconomic imbalances, and the insufficient provision of social services made the economy less dynamic.[125]

In the aftermath of the GFC, the party took the path of least resistance: It opened the spigot of credit to fund infrastructure and to inflate a gigantic housing bubble. Even though the party managed to sustain high growth for the short term, its stimulus package worsened the economic imbalances, channeled resources to the least productive sectors, and saddled the economy with a heavy debt burden that would eviscerate its vitality during the subsequent decade. Fittingly, the end of the Chinese miracle also marked the end of the post-Tiananmen neo-authoritarian order and the beginning of a new, and darker, era of neo-Stalinist rule.

6

Revival of Totalitarianism Under Xi Jinping

BEFORE XI Jinping officially became the general secretary of the CCP in November 2012, few would have thought that he could reverse most of Deng's reforms and bring back a form of totalitarian rule within only a few years after his rise. Given the transformative socioeconomic changes China had experienced in the post-Mao era, such a scenario was simply unthinkable. Yet, like most inconceivable events in history, the revival of totalitarianism under Xi becomes almost self-evident only in hindsight. By the time he assumed power, as discussed at the end of chapter 4, the post-Tiananmen order was beginning to unravel. But the political reality of the early 2010s precluded a potential path to democracy through elite-initiated reform. Although fraying elite unity, pervasive corruption, and dissipation of economic dynamism indicated that the party was in trouble, the regime was not in a serious enough legitimacy crisis to precipitate a split between soft-liners and hard-liners, a prerequisite for an elite-led transition.[1] Even more important, the absence of liberal reformers in senior leadership positions made this prospect unrealistic.

Politically, the path of least resistance for Xi would have been muddling through, as Hu had done throughout his decade in power. This would have required the party to continue its post-Tiananmen survival strategy, but with greater tactical dexterity. The party was not facing an imminent existential threat, so it did not need to adopt dramatic reforms. It seemed to make sense to keep a strategy that had enabled it to enjoy two decades of unprecedented peace, prosperity, and stability. Hu articulated the rationale of playing it safe more succinctly than anyone else. In his last political report to the party on the opening day of the Eighteenth Party Congress in November 2012, he bluntly stated that as long as the party does not *zheteng* (a colloquial expression best translated as "engage in useless and self-destructive actions"), it would reach its goal of making China a "prosperous, strong, democratic, civilized, and harmonious modern socialist nation."[2] At the time, Hu's use of *zheteng* on such a formal party occasion raised eyebrows. Although Hu's invocation of this phrase was treated as a lame excuse for doing little during his tenure, his political wisdom became clear soon after Xi began to do precisely the opposite, plunging the party into its most turbulent era since the end of the Maoist period.

If insecurity motivated risk-averse leaders like Hu to prefer muddling through, the same sense of insecurity could also drive someone like Xi to opt for a radically different course—confronting perceived threats by reviving totalitarianism and reasserting party control over Chinese society. Even though few had thought Xi would embark on such a path, it was this new survival strategy that he started to implement immediately after taking office. The only part of his strategy incongruent with the regime's sense of insecurity was an expansionist foreign policy. Although one might expect an insecure regime to avoid provoking powerful external foes, Xi did the opposite. Most likely he sensed strategic opportunities created by the global financial crisis and America's relative decline in the 2000s. The rapid rise in Chinese power likely made Xi confident that the West would not push back, even if China jettisoned Deng's dictum to "keep a low profile."

Xi's personal ambitions and commitment to the preservation of CCP rule most likely had motivated him. Motives alone, however, could not explain the ease with which he dismantled the post-Tiananmen order and reestablished a form of neo-Stalinist rule. He needed enablers—not just shrewd and ruthless henchmen, but also institutional tools—to bring back totalitarian rule. It turned out that such tools were readily available, as more than three decades of economic reform had left the fundamental institutions of totalitarianism largely untouched. To reimpose strict control on Chinese society, Xi could mobilize the regime's potent repressive apparatus, modernized and strengthened by huge investments and advanced technology in the post-Tiananmen era. To reestablish strongman rule, he could weaponize anticorruption investigations to purge political rivals, most of them made vulnerable by their involvement in shady deals. With no civil society, rule of law, or genuine "inner-party" democracy, Xi faced no institutional constraints in exercising his newly acquired power. Only with the revival of totalitarian rule under Xi can we appreciate the tragic consequences of Deng Xiaoping's steadfast resistance to political reform in the 1980s when a narrow path toward a more open and free China existed.

The Xi Jinping Manifesto

Before he rose to the pinnacle of power in November 2012, Xi was a consummate practitioner of "hiding your strength and biding your time," except that he applied this Dengist foreign policy strategy to politics within the CCP. Xi had carefully maintained a low profile and kept his ideas to himself. But once he attained supreme power, he wasted no time in articulating his vision. On a tour of Guangdong in December 2012, about one month after his appointment as party general secretary, he gave a speech to local officials on the greatest threats facing the party. Although the speech was never made public, its leaked content reveals a man whose political agenda had been decidedly shaped by the lessons he had drawn from the fall of the Soviet Union.

Notably, Xi made no reference to the abysmal economic performance of the Soviet regime, its imperial overreach, or the Cold War with the United States. Instead, he attributed the collapse of the Soviet Union to the loss of "ideals and convictions" among its elites. He lamented that, when the Soviet Union was dissolved, "in the end nobody was a real man, nobody came out to resist," apparently forgetting about the failed coup staged by the hard-liners in August 1991. His choice of words—"real man"—was especially significant because it appeared to imply that Xi thought the Soviet regime was too soft and cowardly. Unlike Deng, who sent in the military to crush the prodemocracy movement in 1989, Soviet leaders were too squeamish to use mass violence against their own people.[3]

These fragments of Xi's informal conversation with local officials in 2012 give us a glimpse of the two main components of his strategy to prevent the party from following the Soviet path: reviving ideological indoctrination within the regime and escalating repression against its opponents. On January 5, 2013, shortly after his trip to Guangdong, Xi delivered what appeared to be a political manifesto to new members of the CCP Central Committee at a special training class at the Central Party School in Beijing. Significantly, the party released only a brief summary of this speech in January 2013.[4] It did not publish its full content until April 2019, most probably because the fuller version of Xi's speech not only signaled a fundamental deviation from Dengism but also because it unabashedly advocated views closely associated with ideological "ultra-leftism."[5]

Xi's political manifesto, like the leaked content of his talk in Guangdong in December 2012, contained few references to the importance of economic development as the party's fundamental guiding principle. Instead, Xi reminded his audience that "socialism with Chinese characteristics" was socialism and not "other isms." This system, according to Xi, would demonstrate its superiority as it became more mature and allowed China to prosper and exercise more influence in the world. Xi also mentioned the Soviet collapse, albeit without impugning the "manhood" of the Soviet regime. Xi castigated "historical nihilism," which later became Xi's favorite phrase whenever he referred to any efforts to establish the historical truth. In his judgment, the Soviet regime had been negligent in controlling the ideological domain and allowing hostile forces to comprehensively "negate" Soviet history and the Soviet leaders, such as Lenin and Stalin, thus "causing confused thinking." He used the Soviet example to warn against "negating" the Maoist period. This section of his speech represented the strongest endorsement of Mao by a top Chinese leader in the post-Tiananmen era. It also signaled Xi's intention to tighten party control over the ideological sphere.

Xi concluded his speech by underscoring the imperative to reinvigorate the regime's ideological commitment to communism as its ultimate goal. The loss of this goal, Xi warned, would lead the party astray ideologically, causing it to degenerate into "utilitarianism and pragmatism." He singled out the new ideological doubts, materialism, self-centeredness, passivity, and loss of faith in communism among party members as completely incompatible with the ideological values and historical mission of communism.

Unlike his predecessors, such as Jiang Zemin and Hu Jintao, who routinely recited Communist ideological clichés but seldom allowed them to dictate policy, Xi turned out to be a true believer who meant what he said. When the full text of this political manifesto was released in the party's flagship ideological publication, *Qiushi*, in April 2019, Xi had been in power for six and half years and had already succeeded in turning the abstract ideas expressed in the manifesto into actual policy. In retrospect, Xi's speech in January 2013 marked the return of orthodox ideology as the party's guiding principle and the end of an era during which the party's top leadership treated economic performance as vital to regime survival.[6]

The specific components of the political order Xi envisioned in early 2013 and later constructed differed qualitatively from the post-Tiananmen neo-authoritarian order. Under Jiang and Hu, the party relied on a diverse set of tools to maintain elite unity and popular support at home and stable ties with the West abroad. In contrast, the new political order under Xi's rule rests on different pillars: centralized one-man rule built on personality cult, rule of fear through constant purges and repression, prioritization of regime security over economic performance, revival of orthodox ideology and political rituals, and an expansionist foreign policy reinforced by a triumphant nationalist narrative—"the China dream."[7] As this new order relies on the regime's coercive apparatus more than mass movements, it resembles classic Stalinist bureaucratic totalitarian rule, not Maoist antibureaucratic totalitarian rule.[8]

Xi's neo-Stalinist agenda was ambitious, risky, and, around the time of his ascent to the top, apparently unpromising. As a compromise choice to succeed Hu, Xi was selected most likely because he was seen as a weak leader without an extensive network of powerful allies. Taking on the entrenched factions headed by Jiang and Hu could be dangerous because they had planted their supporters in key party positions during their two decades in power. Adopting more repressive tactics and reverting to statist economic policies would likely encounter resistance from below. Indeed, before Xi's formal appointment as party chief in late 2012, there was debate whether Xi was a closet reformer with a more liberal agenda than his predecessors.[9] Only after his (manhood) talk about the fall of the Soviet Union was leaked in February 2013 did some begin to develop a sense of foreboding. Fears that Xi was taking the party in a more hard-line and anti-Western direction were reinforced when the leaked content of a key document issued by the General Office of the Central Committee in April—known as Document No. 9—received widespread attention (more on this later).[10] By the summer of 2013, when Xi launched a massive crackdown on social media, it was clear that his neo-Stalinist project was well under way.[11]

War on Corruption

Prior to Xi's rise, the party had frequently launched anticorruption campaigns to discipline its officials. These campaigns were relatively short in duration, targeting mostly mid- to lower-level functionaries to reestablish party authority and to appease public anger. Although these campaigns seemed to curb corruption for a brief period of time as officials tended to lay low to avoid being caught, their long-term impact was modest at best.[12] Politically, the top leaders were careful not to weaponize corruption investigations against their rivals. The two exceptions—the fall of Politburo members Chen Xitong (in 1995) and Chen Liangyu (in 2006) on corruption charges—proved the rule.

The apparent infrequent weaponization of corruption in elite rivalry was most likely the result of the fragile balance of elite power in the post-Mao era, which prevented the top leader—Deng, Jiang, or Hu—from resorting to this tool, except on rare occasions (Deng did not touch it at all). According to the

CCP charter, only the Politburo has the power to expel a member of the Central Committee for violation of party discipline.[13] This meant that a top leader had to win support from rival factions to topple any senior official on corruption charges. The presence of rival factions on the Politburo raised this procedural hurdle as all members shared a similar interest in preventing one faction from dominance through the subterfuge of anticorruption investigations.

In practice, the party's procedural stipulations grant enormous investigative authority to the head of the Central Discipline Inspection Commission (CDIC), the sole body empowered to investigate senior officials.[14] Instructively, to prevent the party chief from using anticorruption investigations to purge his rivals, top leaders in the post-Mao era usually picked for this position someone who was not a close ally of the top leader. Chen Yun, the first chief of the CDIC, was actually Deng's rival. During the Jiang period, the head of the CDIC was someone from a rival faction. In Hu's first term, the CDIC was led by an apparatchik perceived to be close to Jiang. In his second term, another official who had quickly risen under Jiang was in charge of the CDIC. Even though the Politburo or the PSC must approve the opening of a formal investigation into a senior official, the head of the CDIC could play a critical role in this process. As the CDIC would conduct "preliminary verification" of alleged violations, it was in a position to gather sufficient evidence to make it difficult for the Politburo to block an investigation.

The practice of appointing someone who was not an ally of the party chief to be the head of the CDIC ended in November 2012 when Xi's close associate, Wang Qishan, was chosen to take it over. Xi likely had insisted on giving Wang the anticorruption portfolio so that he would have a trusted ally to supervise his war on corruption. With his direct control of the CDIC's investigative capabilities, Wang could be counted on to produce dossiers containing incriminating evidence against rivals that was too strong for the Politburo members to reject.

In terms of objectives, targets, ferocity, and duration, Xi's anticorruption campaign differed qualitatively from all previous such efforts. What defines Xi's war on corruption is its objective of systematically dismantling the networks of power formed under Jiang and Hu, neutralizing rivals, and establishing his dominance.[15] Also notable is the fact that Xi's campaign focused on high-level officials and their allies in local governments, whereas previous campaigns had ensnared mostly mid-level or junior officials. Tactically, Xi opted for much harsher penalties. Disgraced top leaders, including a former PSC member (Zhou Yongkang), four former Politburo members (Bo Xilai,

Guo Boxiong, Xu Caihou, and Sun Zhengcai), and Hu Jintao's former chief of staff (Ling Jihua) were given life sentences. In terms of duration, previous anticorruption drives were short-lived, but Xi's campaign was open-ended. In 2022, for example, a decade after the beginning of his campaign, the party claimed to have investigated (in reality, detained) 32 "centrally supervised" (*zhongguan*) high-ranking officials, the most since 2018, and 410 mid-level officials.[16] Because 2022 was the year of the scheduled Twentieth Party Congress at which Xi planned to secure an unprecedented third term, it seemed likely that he dialed up the anticorruption campaign to deter potential opposition. Xi escalated the purge further in 2023 and 2024, likely to shore up his authority during a period when the Chinese economy was struggling with deflation and an epic real estate crash. In 2023, 47 "centrally supervised" officials were investigated; in 2024, 60 such officials, including two retired provincial party chiefs, were investigated.[17] Anticorruption investigations thus became Xi's potent weapon to intimidate and purge rivals and potential threats.

A review of the course of Xi's anticorruption drive shows that, from the outset, he had clear political priorities. The first was to neutralize any threat to his power posed by those with ties to the domestic security apparatus and the military. Consequently, the first prominent target of Xi's purge was Zhou Yongkang, a former PSC member and a powerful domestic security chief with close ties to Jiang. An investigation into Zhou began almost as soon as Xi rose to the top. To build a case against Zhou, the CDIC detained several senior officials who had worked with him and could provide incriminating materials. The CDIC also cast a wider net, investigating family members and relatives of the main targets because they could be forced to cooperate. In the case against Zhou Yongkang, it took roughly one year for the CDIC to complete its investigations. The PSC formally placed him under investigation in July 2014; eleven months later, he was convicted of accepting bribes totaling 130 million yuan and leaking state secrets to his personal fortune teller, for which he received a life sentence.[18]

The fall of Zhou, the first former PSC member to be jailed in the post-Mao era, sent shockwaves throughout the party-state as it showed that no one was safe under Xi's rule. But that was just the beginning. In March 2014, shortly after the PSC approved an investigation into Zhou's activities, Xu Caihou, a former Politburo member and vice chairman of the CMC, was placed under investigation as well. Several months later, Xu was expelled from the party and transferred to a military court for prosecution. He died in March 2015, before his trial. Xu's colleague and fellow Jiang ally, former Politburo member and CMC vice chairman Guo Boxiong, was investigated for corruption in April 2015 and received a life sentence in July of the following year.

The purge of Xu and Guo served another one of Xi's critical objectives—to seize control of the military. Aware that his own survival would be imperiled without the support of the PLA, Xi launched the most far-ranging purge of the senior ranks of the military since the 1971 fall of Lin Biao, a legendary general and Mao's main ally during the Cultural Revolution. By November 2015, Xi's campaign had ensnared forty-five generals for alleged corruption.[19] The purge of generals suspected of being disloyal became a constant feature of Xi's rule. In subsequent years, more high-ranking generals, including a former chief of the General Staff and head of the PLA's Political Department, fell victim to Xi's anticorruption investigations. According to a tally by the highly respected journal *Caixin*, seventy-five generals were arrested between November 2012 and October 2019.[20] The removal of generals who had been promoted when Guo and Xu were effectively in charge of military personnel matters (2002–2012) accomplished two goals for Xi: With one stroke, he neutralized the potential threat posed by their supporters in the military and paved the way to appoint his own supporters to those positions.

Xi deployed the same tactic to purge senior officials and their supporters in local governments. As shown by the number of officials ranked at bureau level or above who were criminally prosecuted during Xi's first term, his campaign evidently was focusing on senior and mid-level officials in order to destroy entire networks.[21] Because the party did not disclose the ranks of those officials who had been criminally prosecuted during the Hu era, we have to use data from the Jiang era as a comparison. According to the CDIC, between October 1992 and June 1997, 1,673 bureau-level and 78 ministerial- or provincial-level officials were prosecuted for corruption. Between October 1997 and September 2002, Jiang's last term in office, 2,422 bureau-level and 98 ministerial- or provincial-level officials were prosecuted for corruption. During Xi's first term, by comparison, 8,900 bureau-level and 440 ministerial- or provincial-level officials were prosecuted for corruption, representing a huge increase in each category.[22]

A close examination of the highest-ranking targets of Xi's anticorruption campaign reveals that he prioritized the purge of full and alternate members of the Central Committee who typically occupied the most important provincial and ministerial positions. Again, the contrast with his predecessors is illuminating. Between 1992 and 2012, only seventeen full and alternate members of the Central Committee were prosecuted for corruption. During Xi's first decade in power, forty-nine full and alternate members of the Central Committee were punished for corruption (and most sentenced to long prison terms).[23]

In his second term, Xi's top priority was to purge the domestic security apparatus of officials who were suspected of political disloyalty. As a complementary effort, the purge of the so-called political-legal sector would completely cement Xi's control of the coercive apparatus. In January 2018, two months after Xi got a second term, he launched a campaign ostensibly to root out organized crime and its "protective umbrellas"—officials in the domestic security apparatus suspected of shielding criminals from the law.[24] The campaign quickly claimed several high-ranking officials, including secretaries of CCP provincial political-legal committees (who typically had served as provincial police chiefs) and an incumbent vice minister of public security, Sun Lijun, who was allegedly the ringleader of a cabal of corrupt officials in the security apparatus.[25]

In February 2021 Xi launched a separate campaign, "Education and Rectification of the Nation's Political-Legal Ranks," explicitly targeting officials in the domestic security sector. As this purge was overseen by Xi's loyal ally Chen Yixin and launched roughly twenty months before the Twentieth Party Congress, at which Xi was expected to seek a third term, its political objectives—removing security officials suspected of disloyalty and intimidating potential threats—were self-evident. A large number of officials fell victim to this round of purges, and many had held senior positions. Fu Zhenghua, a former Central Committee member and executive vice minister of public security, was given a suspended death sentence in September 2022. Another former vice minister of public security who had overseen anticorruption in the Ministry of State Security (MSS), China's secret police, was detained in March 2022 and given a suspended death sentence in January 2023. By July 2022 this campaign had brought down nearly three dozen senior local law enforcement officials, including nine secretaries and deputy secretaries of the provincial legal-political committees.[26] Many lower-ranking law enforcement officials also fell into the dragnet. Within the first six months of the campaign, 12,576 police officers had turned themselves in.[27] Following this purge, Xi was able to install his loyalist, Wang Xiaohong, as the new minister of public security. Chen Yixin became minister of the MSS in March 2023, thus giving Xi total control over the security apparatus.

Despite the scale of the purges, Xi introduced institutional changes to make anticorruption investigations an even more powerful instrument against potential threats. Three weeks after his installation as party chief, the Politburo issued a set of rules limiting official entertainment, meetings, issuance of documents, use of government vehicles, and media coverage of the activities of party leaders.[28] Violators would be punished (although these rules apparently do not apply to Xi, who has received lavish media coverage).

In addition, Xi revised the party's disciplinary code and the procedures for anticorruption investigations to bolster his personal authority and to make any expression of dissent against the top party leadership a punishable infraction of the law. A comparison of the party's disciplinary code formalized under Hu in December 2003 and its revised version published in October 2015 reveals several crucial changes made to suppress potential opposition to Xi's authority. Most notably, the revision added several punishable *political* violations, such as "wantonly discussing major policies of the party-state and undermining the party's centralized unity, smearing the images of the party and the state, denigrating the top leadership of the party and the state, or distorting the history of the party or of the military." Unauthorized public statements on major policy issues that should be within the "purview of the party center" could result in severe penalties as well.[29]

To expand the party's disciplinary reach beyond party members, Xi set up a super agency—the National Supervisory Commission—in March 2018. Even though this commission was to be staffed by the same personnel as the CDIC, the law establishing it gave it power to investigate and punish nonparty members who work in SOEs and in publicly funded entities, such as hospitals, universities, cultural institutions, and nongovernmental organizations. The commission and its local agencies were also empowered to detain the subjects of investigation for up to six months without court approval or judicial review.[30]

It is tempting to credit Xi's unrelenting crackdown for curbing official corruption. But the continuous stream of disgraced officials accused of corruption years after the beginning of Xi's campaign suggests that his war on corruption had at most a partial impact on curbing corruption. In all likelihood, Xi's other policies—such as suppressing press freedoms and civil society and shifting resources to the state sector—either facilitated or made it difficult to fight corruption.[31] This outcome should not be surprising because the principal objective of Xi's crackdown on corruption was for him to gain political dominance. In this regard, the campaign has evidently served him well.

Power Grab

Taking advantage of the momentum of his anticorruption drive, Xi wasted little time to consolidate power. He scored his greatest victory in October 2016 when the Central Committee formally granted him the title of "core leader." (Jiang's designation, conferred on him by Deng, was a less significant achievement.)[32] Underscoring Xi's newly obtained political supremacy, the Central Committee communiqué announcing the elevation of his status called on the party to "firmly and unswervingly preserve and defend the authority of the party center and its centralized and unified leadership," an obvious reference to Xi.[33]

Besides gaining this coveted title, Xi had scored other major victories. He successfully grabbed power that normally would belong to the premier. This was accomplished by establishing "leading small groups" that effectively took away power to make policy on specific issues from the State Council. For instance, he formed the "Central Leading Small Group on Comprehensively Deepening Reform" in November 2013 and appointed himself as its chairman. Because of its broad mandate, any new reform or policy change required its approval, thus allowing Xi to control more directly the overall political and economic agendas. Other new leading small groups Xi established and also headed at the beginning of his first term oversaw cybersecurity and military reform. In addition, he chaired preexisting leading small groups on foreign policy, Taiwan affairs, and finance.[34]

Another tactic he used to amass power was a systematic revision of the party's organizational rules and the updating of its resolutions on history to formalize and legitimize his personal authority and expand his power. Immediately after the conclusion of the Nineteenth Party Congress in October 2017, the Politburo issued the "Regulations on Strengthening and Maintaining the Party Center's Centralized and Unified Leadership." Although the full text of this document has not been made public, the official media have disclosed some of its key points. First, the regulations emphasize absolute loyalty to Xi, as indicated by the statement that the Politburo must "resolutely maintain General Secretary Xi Jinping's status as the core of the party center and the entire party." In addition, the regulations require Politburo members to "proactively report major issues to the party center for deliberation, studiously implement decisions and plans of the party center, and make timely reports on their significant progress . . . (and) self-consciously struggle against words and acts that . . . harm the party center's centralized leadership and unity." To enforce these rather abstract requirements, the regulations include an unprecedented rule mandating that Politburo members must submit annual written self-evaluations of their job performance to the general secretary (i.e., Xi). This provision, which recalls the Maoist "self-criticisms" the late dictator regularly forced his colleagues to make, grants Xi additional leverage over Politburo members, who must perform this annual exercise in full awareness of the adverse consequences of an unfavorable evaluation of their performance. In addition to the Politburo members, other senior leaders, such as the members of the Secretariat of the Central Committee, the CDIC, the party organizations within the Standing Committee of the NPC, the State Council, the Chinese People's Political Consultative Conference, the Supreme People's Court, and the Supreme People's Procuratorate, are required to submit similar self-evaluations to the PSC and the Politburo, thus allowing Xi to more directly control the critical central organs of the regime.[35]

To bolster the legitimacy of his personal authority, Xi undertook to rewrite a landmark document issued under Deng to prevent the return of a Mao-like figure. In February 1980 the Central Committee had approved a historic document, the "Guiding Principles for Inner-Party Political Life" that explicitly established collective leadership and prohibited personality cults.[36] As this document would stand in the way of Xi's goal of replacing collective leadership with one-man rule and fortifying his power with a personality cult, the Central Committee, most likely under pressure from Xi, revised it at the same plenum that granted Xi the title of "core leader" in October 2016. A comparison of the two documents shows that the revision completely removes the prohibition against personality cults and downplays the principle of collective leadership, while, in an obvious reference to Xi, placing strong emphasis on the authority of the "core leadership."[37]

The party's celebration of its centennial in 2021 provided another opportunity for Xi to burnish his credentials as a great leader. The Central Committee issued a historic resolution in November of that year, ostensibly to summarize the party's experiences during the past century. But in a comparison of two similar documents, the one issued by Mao in 1945 and the other by Deng in 1981, Xi's version focuses mostly on the party's self-proclaimed accomplishments during Xi's nine years in power—the so-called "New Era." Roughly 19,000 of the resolution's 36,200 characters are devoted to Xi's period in power, while the sections covering the prior ninety-one years of party history contain only 10,000 characters.[38]

Xi's efforts to revive a personality cult go well beyond passing resolutions glorifying his leadership. Coverage of his activities dominates the official media. His published works are on prominent display in bookstores. Judging by the number of published volumes of his collected works, those by Xi exceed those by all other Chinese leaders, including Mao. In February 2022 the first volume of *Selected Letters of Xi Jinping* was published, implying that future volumes would be forthcoming (among Xi's predecessors, only one volume of Mao's *Selected Letters* was published). This honor was not accorded to Deng or any other revolutionary leader. By June 2022, four volumes of Xi's speeches on governance had been published, equaling the number of volumes of Mao's *Selected Works* released during Mao's time in office (Deng, Jiang, and Hu were limited to three volumes each). In 2023 the party released two additional volumes, *Selected Readings of Xi Jinping's Works* as well as a college textbook, *Xi Jinping Thought on Socialism with Chinese Characteristics in the New Era*.

Judging by the outcome of the Nineteenth Party Congress in October 2017, Xi's neo-Stalinist tactics evidently paid off. On the eve of the gathering, Xi arrested Sun Zhengcai, a Politburo member affiliated with the Jiang faction who had been seen as a potential candidate for the position of party chief. (Sun was later sentenced to life in prison for alleged corruption.) The prosecution of Sun was evidently carried out to intimidate rival factions that might have been standing in the way of Xi's plans to remake the top party leadership at the upcoming party congress.

As expected, the congress cemented Xi's political dominance: Two-thirds of the twenty-five Politburo members were his acolytes. Of the six other members of the PSC, Xi could count at least four as allies (one of them was in charge of the powerful CDIC). His loyalists were also made party chiefs of the most important provinces, such as Beijing, Shanghai, Guangdong, Chongqing, and Xinjiang.

Most important, at the same party congress Xi revealed his intention of breaking the implicit two-term limit for the general secretary. At the Seventeenth Party Congress in 2007, when Hu was about to start his second term, the party designated his successor, Xi, after intense internal jockeying. A decade later, however, Xi prevented the designation of an heir-apparent since no newly promoted members of the PSC were under 55 (the ideal age for a potential successor because that person would be 60 when appointed party chief at the next party congress and then could serve two five-year terms).

Having stacked the Politburo with supporters, Xi immediately took the required procedural steps to break the implicit term limits. Of his three positions—CCP general secretary, chairman of the CMC, and state president—only one, the state president—was subject to an explicit constitutional limit.

Even though this position is largely ceremonial, the party chief must also hold the title of state president to engage in top-level foreign affairs. Diplomatic protocols usually do not allow foreign heads of state to meet the leader of a political party. Xi thus had to abolish the constitutional term limit for the state president as a first step to extend his rule indefinitely.

In January 2018 the Politburo approved a package of constitutional amendments that contained the abolition of the presidential term limit even though the meeting's press release did not refer to this particular amendment. In March the annual NPC meeting, the rubber-stamp parliament, duly approved the abolition of presidential term limits, signaling Xi's intention to serve indefinitely.[39]

At the Twentieth Party Congress in October 2022, Xi easily obtained a third term as CCP general secretary, and by the time of the conclusion of the congress, he had achieved total political dominance. Implicit norms on term and age limits no longer applied to him or to his followers. In addition to giving himself a third term, Xi kept on the Politburo two supporters who were over the implicit mandatory retirement age of 68, but he also forced out two rivals, Premier Li Keqiang and PSC member Wang Yang, who were under 68. A former Politburo member, 59-year-old Hu Chunhua, was not reappointed because he was a protégé of Hu Jintao (no relation) and a possible contender for future party chief. At the Twentieth Party Congress, Xi also prevented the designation of a potential successor.

Flash the Sword

Shortly after Xi delivered his political manifesto, "Some Questions on Maintaining and Developing Socialism with Chinese Characteristics," at the Central Party School in January 2013, the General Office of the Central Committee, which at that time was directed by Xi's close ally, Li Zhanshu, issued the now-infamous Document No. 9, "Communiqué on the Current State of the Ideological Sphere." The document identifies "erroneous ideological trends" that must be "watched." The document was issued on April 22, 2013, but it was never made public, most likely because it would reveal Xi's hard-line ideological stance. When it was leaked in August 2013, its contents confirmed Xi's hostility to liberal ideas.

According to Document No. 9, the party must tighten control over the media and guard against seven subversive ideas—Western constitutional democracy, universal values, civil society, economic neo-liberalism, the Western concept of press freedom, historical nihilism (exposing the party's dark past), and questioning the nature of socialism with Chinese characteristics. In addition to listing these ideas that could directly undermine party legitimacy, Document No. 9 also sounds an alarm about subversive dissident activities, such as agitation for political reform, human rights, press freedom, and public disclosure of officials' assets. It warns that Western diplomatic missions, media, and NGOs were engaging in various activities inside of China to cultivate opposition forces and to conduct "cyber infiltration." According to the authors of Document No. 9, the West represents an existential threat because it seeks regime change through "Westernizing, splitting, and color revolutions."[40] Despite the dire warnings in Document No. 9, the party waited until August 2013 before launching a full-scale crackdown on the dangerous trends identified in the document.

Liangjian, or flash your sword, is an apt metaphor for Xi's get-tough-on-dissent approach, and, unsurprisingly, it quickly became a popular phrase in the official media despite its association with intimidation and violence. In all likelihood, Xi first invoked this phrase at the National Meeting on Publicity and Theoretical Work in August 2013, even though the phrase cannot be found in the published version of his speech. Nevertheless, two clues suggest Xi himself likely used this phrase at this conference. First, the published official version of Xi's speech, most probably sanitized, urges the party to "maintain an initiative and fight successful offensive battles" (*zhudong zhang*) on fundamental political issues.[41] Second, the official media published summaries of the reflections by all thirty-one provincial propaganda chiefs (who almost certainly attended the conference) on Xi's speech. Notably, ten used the phrase "dare to flash your sword" (*ganyu liangjian*). As it is customary for provincial propaganda chiefs to regurgitate key points made by the party chief (in this case, Xi), it is reasonable to conclude that they were merely parroting one of the most emphatic points Xi made at the conference.[42]

Events that transpired subsequently show what *liangjian* meant—it was a concerted preemptive campaign against a potential "color revolution," marking a fundamental shift from the party's stance toward dissent in the post-Tiananmen era. Both Jiang and Hu had adopted a defensive or reactive strategy of repression: They usually cracked down on dissent in response to overt challenges to party authority or actions by the country's small community of dissidents who crossed the regime's threshold of tolerance. From the very beginning, however, Xi's campaign assumed a preemptive or offensive nature. Instead of responding to overly aggressive challenges to one-party rule, his campaign targeted the very sources that could generate, maintain, and reproduce such threats: social media, human rights activists, lawyers, liberal academics, ethnic minorities, NGOs and their foreign supporters, and protest movements in Hong Kong. This campaign is also notable for its blitzkrieg tactics: The crackdown was carried out at lightning speed. Targets of the repression received harsh punishments, extra-judicial mass incarcerations, or long prison sentences, which the party had eschewed during the pre-Xi period. In another qualitative departure from his predecessors' tactics in dealing with threats to the party, Xi sought to reinforce his metaphoric "sword" through institutionalization and the party-controlled legal system. As a result, new bureaucracies overseeing cybersecurity and national security were established. New laws and regulations, such as those governing foreign NGOs, cybersecurity, and internet use, were issued to add a veneer of legality to the emerging neo-Stalinist order.

The first target of this preemptive campaign was social media, which had gained unprecedented reach and influence due to the popularization of smart phones. Not coincidentally, the crackdown on social media began on August 20, 2013, the same day that the national publicity conference ended. Police in Beijing arrested Qin Zhihui, a well-known blogger with a mass following, on charges of fabricating online rumors. Three of his colleagues were arrested as well. Charles Xue, a Chinese American businessman with over twelve million verified followers on *Weibo* (a Chinese microblogging website), was detained on August 23 for "patronizing a prostitute." He later appeared on national TV confessing his crime, evidently against his own will. Several hundred netizens were arrested, detained, or punished between August 20 and 31 in this nationwide crackdown, which was carried out to implement Xi's order for a "serious blow" against internet "rumors."[43] On September 6 the party-controlled Supreme People's Court and Supreme People's Procuratorate issued a joint "legal interpretation" that made "internet libel" a criminal offense. If a piece of "libelous information" receives more than five thousand clicks or is forwarded more than five hundred times, its author will receive severe punishment.[44] The effect of "flashing" this metaphorical "sword" was instant: by singling out well-known social media influencers, the party tamed China's once-vibrant social media practically overnight, a feat few had thought was either conceivable or feasible.[45]

To institutionalize the party's strict control over cyberspace, Xi established the "Central Leading Small Group on Cybersecurity and Informatization" in February 2014. He personally chaired this committee and appointed a party propaganda official, Lu Wei, to direct its daily operations. (In March 2018 Xi elevated the "leading group" to the status of a central commission and made himself its chairman.) Lu Wei, a ruthless apparatchik, faithfully implemented Xi's orders and instituted a series of new censorship measures (including a requirement that all social media users register their accounts with their real names so the authorities could identify them).[46] The Cyber Security Law passed in November 2016 is another attempt to solidify party control of the internet as it strictly forbids anyone from "using the internet to engage in activities that endanger state security, reputation, and interests, or instigate the subversion of state power, the socialist system . . . fabricate and disseminate false information."[47]

Around the same time as the crackdown on social media, the party began a separate campaign against well-known human rights activists and dissidents. During the Jiang and Hu periods, the regime had dealt with most dissidents using less repressive tactics. They were placed under routine surveillance and occasionally harassed, but most remained free. However, under Xi's new policy of "flashing your sword," they were not only arrested but sentenced to long prison terms under trumped-up charges, such as "picking quarrels and provoking trouble" and "disturbing public order"—the two criminal charges the regime favored using against its opponents. In July 2013 Xu Zhiyong, a Beijing-based legal scholar who had gained fame a decade earlier for petitioning the NPC to abolish the harsh antivagrancy regulation, was arrested for "disturbing public order." Xu had founded the New Citizens Movement in 2010 to promote constitutional rule, equal rights, and government transparency. During the Hu period, the authorities largely left him alone, even allowing him to run for—and win two times—a seat in a district people's congress in Beijing. Apparently to make Xu an example, the party sentenced him to four years in prison in 2014. (In 2020 he was rearrested and later received a sentence of fourteen years.)

The party flashed its biggest metaphoric sword on July 9, 2015, when it conducted a nationwide crackdown on human rights lawyers. Police detained more than three hundred lawyers who had been active in the rights defense movement. Many were later debarred and imprisoned. Like the campaign to silence social media in August 2013, the blitzkrieg against human rights lawyers instantly destroyed a nascent but largely informal political movement seeking modest incremental change through the legal system that the party itself had established and controlled. Based on the limited success of these lawyers in seeking judicial relief for their clients during the less repressive Hu era, they did not present a serious threat to one-party rule. But in Xi's "new era," no form or degree of dissent could be tolerated. Indeed, in the eyes of Xi's regime, human rights lawyers exploiting the loopholes and formal procedures of China's legal system were far more dangerous because they were more resourceful, sophisticated, and difficult to deal with than the less well-educated workers and farmers. They could not only expose the regime's hypocrisy and brutality but also set examples for challenging its rule peacefully and, on occasion, successfully.[48]

Labor organizers came under attack in April 2014 when a court in Guangzhou convicted eleven labor activists for "disturbing public order." In December 2015 at least three leaders of the workers' rights movement in Guangzhou were arrested for "gathering a crowd to disturb social order."[49] Supporters of labor rights were not left alone, either. In the fall of 2018, police conducted a nationwide crackdown on self-proclaimed Marxist students involved in protesting against violations of labor rights.[50] Compared with the repressive tactics previously used by the party against labor organizers, which mainly consisted of intimidation and harassment, Xi's campaign against labor rights activists was decidedly an escalation in terms of state-sponsored violence as it used criminal charges, such as "picking quarrels and provoking trouble," to convict and imprison them.[51] The crackdown on other civil society organizations similarly followed this new approach of "authoritarian legality."[52]

Liberal academics were not spared in the crackdown. Academics whose lectures or online speech contained views contradicting or violating official orthodoxy were either warned or dismissed. Based on a partial record of academics fired under Xi's rule, this campaign started in late 2013 when a law professor at the prestigious East China University of Political Science and Law in Shanghai was fired for posting an online article critical of the party.[53] Although the precise number of academics fired thereafter is unknown, as of the end of 2019, dozens of university faculty had reportedly lost their jobs because of their political views.[54] A small number of professors received even more severe punishment. A prominent law professor at Tsinghua University who had published an open letter critical of Xi and the party's handling of the Covid-19 pandemic in early 2020 was arrested on a trumped-up charge of "patronizing a prostitute" in July 2020 and subsequently fired.[55] In Guizhou, an academic was sentenced to four and half years in prison in August 2023 for his outspoken views.[56]

To ensure the routinization of ideological control on university campuses, the party increased its use of student informants and installed video cameras in classrooms to record professors' lectures. Again, even though the authorities began to deploy student informants after the crushing of the student-led prodemocracy movement in 1989, the use of student informants under Xi is far more systematic, extensive, and aggressive.[57] Another measure of institutionalizing ideological repression on university campuses is the issuance of the "Ten Professional Principles" by the Ministry of Education in November 2018. Principle no. 3 explicitly prohibits faculty from "using classrooms, forums, lectures, information networks, and other channels to express and share erroneous views or to fabricate false or unhealthy information."[58] Obviously, this "principle" gives the authorities a handy tool to punish academics for their political views.

Despite official restrictions, Western NGOs were able to establish a modest presence inside China prior to Xi's rise. After Xi became party chief, however, the regime's paranoia about foreign NGOs, perceived to be potential instigators of "color revolutions," reached a new level. In April 2016 the NPC passed a new law on foreign NGOs that imposed onerous administrative burdens and significantly raised security risks for operating in China. Among other things, the law orders foreign NGOs to register with Chinese police, the designated enforcement agency that has broad authority over nearly all aspects of the operations of foreign NGOs. For example, the requirement that foreign NGOs must provide the police with advance notice of their planned activities is obviously intended to discourage their activities.[59] The law, which affected more than seven thousand foreign NGOs when it went into effect, allowed no grace period, forcing many to suspend operations immediately. By early 2018, only 350 foreign NGOs had reregistered under the new law, suggesting that 95 percent of the foreign NGOs might have exited the country.[60] Judging by this metric, the law has evidently achieved its objective.

As surveillance of the population constitutes a key pillar of Xi's neo-Stalinist order, the party has made the upgrading of mass surveillance a top state priority. In the post-Tiananmen era, the regime had rolled out two high-tech surveillance programs, Golden Shield and Skynet, that allowed police to utilize a vast digital database, a cyber surveillance apparatus, and networked cameras and sensors to keep track of the activities and speeches of Chinese people. After Xi came to power, the surveillance state received several technological and organizational upgrades. The first program singled out for upgrading was grid management, which divides a community into several grids, each with roughly a thousand residents. The grid is supervised by an official and patrolled by a grid attendant, each equipped with a mobile device to report any incidents. This program was listed as a key task at the Central Committee plenum in November 2013.[61] In June 2014 the State Council issued an outline to build a "social credit" system.[62] Although this technologically challenging system remains a work in progress, its potential surveillance capabilities can make the dystopia depicted in George Orwell's *1984* a reality in China. In May 2015 the government launched a new high-tech surveillance project, Sharp Eyes, which uses newer technologies, such as facial recognition and cloud computing, to upgrade Skynet and extend video surveillance to the countryside.[63]

Crackdown on the Periphery

The party has always perceived China's peripheral regions, whether areas with large populations of ethnic minorities such as Tibet and Xinjiang or newly regained territories such as Hong Kong and Macau, as areas harboring separatists or dissidents who are supported by hostile external forces. In the post-Tiananmen era the party abandoned a more conciliatory approach in favor of a more repressive policy to maintain China's grip on these areas. However, as resistance to Chinese rule continued in spite of the tightened security measures, the party under Xi decided to escalate the repression to an unprecedented level.

Xinjiang, the northwestern province that was not formally incorporated into China until the late nineteenth century, quickly became the epicenter of conflict between its largest ethnic minority group, the Uighurs, and the Han Chinese. To be sure, political violence and separatism in the region had been on the rise after the end of the Cold War as resentment of Chinese rule grew among ethnic minority groups that sought more autonomy.[64] But Beijing was able to use both carrots (economic development) and sticks (the "war on terror") to maintain an uneasy peace in Xinjiang.[65] This fragile equilibrium collapsed on July 5, 2009, when violent clashes between ethnic Uighurs and Han Chinese erupted in Urumqi, the capital of Xinjiang, killing several hundred people. The violence persisted afterward despite heightened security measures.[66]

In response to the deteriorating conditions in Xinjiang, Xi opted for draconian measures to eradicate the so-called three evils—fundamentalism, separatism, and terrorism. He paid a personal visit to the region in May 2014, and in August 2016 he appointed Chen Quanguo, a hard-liner with extensive background in security, as Xinjiang's new party chief. Prior to his appointment in

Xinjiang, Chen had demonstrated, as party chief in Tibet from 2011 to 2016, an ability to pacify ethnic unrest. During his tenure in Tibet, he had introduced new security measures and largely succeeded in ending a wave of self-immolations by Tibetans protesting Chinese rule.[67] Xi's mandate for Chen in Xinjiang was to restore stability at all costs.

Consequently, with Xi's support, Chen put more than one million ordinary Uighurs and other ethnic minorities in concentration camps, euphemistically called "vocational training schools." Local officials had complete discretion to incarcerate Uighurs in these camps. The detainees were reportedly subject to brainwashing and routine abuse.[68] Simultaneously, the government adopted strict surveillance measures and restrictions on the lives of Uighurs.[69]

Tactically, the harsh security measures seemed to have accomplished Xi's goal of pacifying ethnic unrest in Xinjiang, judging by the near disappearance of reported acts of violence. Politically, however, China has paid dearly. Its persecution of the Uighurs, for which the West has imposed sanctions, has been labeled "genocide" by many Western countries. In terms of long-term consequences, the brutal treatment of the Uighurs will almost certainly foster more extremism and boost support for separatism in the future.

When China signed an agreement with the United Kingdom in 1984 on the return of Hong Kong to China in July 1997, Deng Xiaoping pledged that the British colony would retain its economic and social systems for fifty years and enjoy a "high degree of autonomy."[70] Subsequently, the NPC passed the Hong Kong "Basic Law," the city's mini-constitution, in April 1990, formalizing its autonomy and China's commitment to maintaining the economic and social systems of Hong Kong for fifty years.

But the Sino-British agreement on Hong Kong and the Basic Law left two critical issues unresolved. One was democratic self-rule in Hong Kong, and the other was a National Security Law that the city's legislature was supposed to adopt after 1997. On the first issue, China made a vague promise that gradually the city's chief executive and Legislative Council would be elected through universal suffrage. After 1997 Hong Kong's chief executive was elected by an "election committee" of 1,500 unelected individuals, most of them pro-Beijing. The city's seventy-seat Legislative Council was also elected largely undemocratically, with half of its members elected directly and the other half indirectly by "functional constituencies." On the second issue, Article 23 of the Basic Law requires that Hong Kong pass its own law on national security. As the article could easily result in a law restricting the city's civil rights and freedoms, it was seen as a persistent existential threat to the "one country, two systems" model.[71]

Yet, it would take nearly two decades before conflict over democracy and civil liberties between the CCP and the people of Hong Kong led to the death of the "one country, two systems" model. On the surface, China largely honored its part of the deal until the rise of Xi Jinping in 2012. The only significant foreshadowing of the eventual demise of the "one country, two systems" model were the mass protests against the city leadership's attempt to pass a National Security Law in 2003, which forced Hong Kong's pro-Beijing chief executive to abandon the plan. However, tensions over political rights, protection of civil rights, and identity were never far below the superficial calm.[72]

Shortly after Xi became CCP chief in late 2012, prodemocracy forces began to pressure Beijing more aggressively to honor its promise of universal suffrage. In March 2013 three academics called for a civil disobedience movement, "Occupy Central," the key demand of which was the replacement of Hong Kong's undemocratic electoral system with direct democratic elections. Instead of a positive response, the Chinese government issued a hard-line white paper on Hong Kong in June 2014 that flatly rejected the idea of instituting universal suffrage in the city. Most ominously, the white paper claimed that the central government has "comprehensive governing authority" over the city, a key concept that later helped legitimize Beijing's adoption of the 2020 National Security Law that effectively ended "one country, two systems" in Hong Kong.[73]

If Beijing expected this document to pacify the demands for democracy in Hong Kong, it achieved the opposite effect. From the end of September to mid-December 2014, tens of thousands of students launched what came to be known as the "Umbrella Movement"—a series of peaceful sit-ins in the busiest section of the central part of Hong Kong. Although the movement failed to force Beijing to back down, the outpouring of public support for the demonstrators and outrage against the use of excessive force by the police became a harbinger of the far larger confrontation between Hong Kong citizens and Beijing that would take place five years later.[74]

The display of defiance by Hong Kong's prodemocracy activists appeared to have hardened Xi's resolve. In July 2017, at the ceremony marking the twentieth anniversary of Hong Kong's return, Xi delivered a thinly veiled threat against the city's prodemocracy forces. He warned, "Any activities that harm national sovereignty and security, challenge the power of the central government and the authority of the Basic Law, and use Hong Kong to conduct infiltration and sabotage against the mainland . . . violate our bottom line and are absolutely not permitted."[75]

Two years later, Hong Kong's prodemocracy forces tested Xi's "bottom line" when they organized mass protests against proposed legislation on extraditing Hong Kong residents to the mainland for criminal prosecution. Launched in March 2019, these protests grew progressively larger and eventually resulted in violent confrontations with the police. On several occasions, an estimated one to two million protesters marched in the streets. Clashes between police and protesters paralyzed the city, Asia's premium commercial hub, for days. This round of protests, known as the "anti-extradition" movement, ended in January 2020 after Hong Kong was locked down due to the Covid-19 pandemic.[76]

The anti-extradition movement was apparently the last straw for Xi. In May 2020 the NPC passed a National Security Law for Hong Kong in a clear violation of both the technical provisions of the Basic Law (which stipulates that only the city's Legislative Council can pass such a law) and China's pledge to maintain Hong Kong's social and economic systems for fifty years. The law, which effectively guts the city's rule of law and deprives its citizens of their civil liberties, went into effect on July 1, 2020. Following implementation, Beijing dispatched its own security agents to the city as Hong Kong police, almost certainly under the direction of Beijing, arrested and charged protest organizers and civic leaders. Deng's much-vaunted "one country, two systems" model lasted a mere twenty-three years.[77]

Although Xi crushed the prodemocracy movement in Hong Kong, the costs for China, the CCP, and Xi himself were horrific. The United States terminated its preferential treatment for the city. The end of the rule of law in Hong Kong also fatally damaged the city's status as a center of commerce, resulting in the exodus of Western businesses and talent to other parts of Asia, mostly Singapore.[78] Internationally, China lost its credibility. The crackdown in Hong Kong, seen widely as unnecessary, excessive, and self-destructive, served only to reinforce the view that a powerful autocratic China cannot be trusted and must be confronted.

What Made the Return of Totalitarian Rule Possible

Few could have imagined the transformative changes Xi brought about almost single-handedly within a decade of rising to the top. The reversion to neo-Stalinist rule is all the more remarkable—and puzzling—given Xi's weak powerbase and the massive socioeconomic modernization China experienced in the post-Mao era. In all likelihood, Xi himself probably did not anticipate the relative ease with which he could dismantle the post-Tiananmen order and restore a regime bearing the essential characteristics of neo-Stalinism: personalistic rule, permanent purges, ruthless repression, and an expansionist foreign policy.

Xi could reconstruct a neo-Stalinist order against ostensibly poor odds primarily because the regime's totalitarian institutional framework had remained largely intact in spite of the post-Mao economic reforms and opening to the West. Indeed, even a cursory comparison between China in 1979 and China in 2012 shows that foundational institutions of totalitarianism remained essentially untouched by the country's "reform and opening." Most critically, the institutional pillar of totalitarianism—a Leninist party-state—was completely preserved. The CCP's closed and hierarchical organizational structure and procedures for leadership selection were not fundamentally different in 2012 from what they were in 1979. Despite attempts to separate the party from the state, the party remained deeply entrenched in and dominant over the state. Its organizational penetration of Chinese society, down to the neighborhood and village levels, had deepened and expanded rather than withering, allowing the party to retain its unrivaled capacities for social control and political mobilization.

Almost equally critical was the party's control of instruments of state violence without any constitutional or legal constraints. To be sure, the indiscriminate mass terror of the Mao era was replaced by selective repression. But the party had at its disposal the military, the secret police, and a vast surveillance apparatus to guard its political monopoly. When necessary, as demonstrated by the crackdown on the Tiananmen movement and the suppression of the Falungong spiritual group, the party could mobilize state violence to crush any challenges to its power. The revival of totalitarianism under Xi would not have been possible without a coercive apparatus that received massive state investments during the post-Tiananmen era.[79]

Although the post-Mao reforms eroded the regime's capacity to control the economy and its access to information, the party-state could easily reassert its control when necessary. Economically, the regime retained the "commanding heights" of the economy, such as the financial system, energy, transportation, and telecom services. It also monopolized ownership of land and wielded immense regulatory power. Aware of the threats posed by free flows of information, the party maintained strict control of the media and, when confronted by the internet, quickly adopted effective countermeasures to neutralize the information revolution.[80]

Prior to Xi's rise, three features of a classic totalitarian regime were missing: One was a domineering totalitarian leader. But that was largely a historical accident because the fragile balance of power at the top prevented the reemergence of a Stalinist or Maoist dictator. Also missing were the permanent purges, thanks to the collective leadership maintained by the same balance of power. The third missing feature was an official ideology legitimating party rule. Although the CCP never formally abandoned its Communist ideology, in reality the ideology atrophied due to the general worldwide failure of Communist regimes and Mao's disastrous rule. Economic performance became the party's real source of legitimacy, while pragmatism, not orthodox ideology, dictated policy.

Of these three missing features of classic totalitarianism, the first two could be easily revived, as demonstrated by Xi's record. Once the fragile balance of power ceased to exist, the party had no means to prevent a ruthless leader from restoring one-man rule and reviving permanent purges to terrorize the party. Reinvigorating the orthodox Communist ideology was, by comparison, a far more challenging undertaking, even for Xi, because it held little appeal to a party and a society thoroughly secularized by the socioeconomic changes and the post-Mao era contacts with the outside world.

Ironically, although Xi reversed Deng's policy of reform and opening, he owes much of his success to Deng's commitment to one-party rule and to his personal political interests. In saving the party from Mao's disastrous rule, Deng's consistent strategy was to change economic policy without endangering one-party rule. The most important of his "four cardinal principles" is the political supremacy of the party. For Deng, reform and opening were simply the means to save the CCP and to perpetuate its rule. Specifically, Deng left two political legacies that later greatly facilitated Xi's efforts to restore totalitarian rule. The first was his unwavering opposition to any political reform or to any ideological liberalization that might weaken party rule or expose its dark side. Deng's conservatism precluded a thorough reckoning of the disasters of the Maoist era or a liberalization that could lead to a stronger civil society or had the potential to resist any reversion to totalitarian rule. Most critically, Deng's purge of Hu Yaobang in 1987 and Zhao Ziyang in 1989 decimated the liberals in the party and decisively shifted the balance of power in favor of the hard-liners.

The second legacy was Deng's flawed reforms to preserve collective leadership and prevent the return of a Mao-like figure. The formal provisions on term limits, mandatory retirement, and rights of party members were intentionally left vague and impossible to enforce. For example, the only explicit term limit was that imposed on the state president, the least important of the three positions held by the regime's top leader (the other two being the general secretary and the chairman of the CMC). But as the party made it easy to change the constitution, this limit too could be abolished without much trouble, as Xi did in 2018. Deng himself set a bad example by violating the rules he tried to establish. He held on to power despite his advanced age and lack of formal titles. He made a mockery of the party's formal procedures by holding private meetings with senior leaders in his home rather than allowing the Politburo Standing Committee to act in its capacity as the party's top decision-making body. His most momentous decisions were made mostly by himself or in consultation with a small number of aging revolutionaries. Most important, although Deng paid lip-service to "democratic political life within the party," he made no attempt to establish inner-party democracy, depriving the party of a mechanism to hold its leaders accountable and to block the return of a Mao-like figure.

The survival of collective leadership and adherence to the procedures and norms of succession in the post-Deng era created the deceptive impression that Deng's reforms were effective and durable. Overlooked was the difficulty, if not the impossibility, of institutionalizing politics in an autocracy.[81] Indeed, the inherent flaws of Deng's reforms enabled Xi to amass the power of a totalitarian leader without any real opposition.

Peaking Xi?

Despite Xi's success in reviving totalitarian rule, signs that his neo-Stalinist agenda had run its course began to emerge toward the end of his second term. The initial pushback against him came from the United States in 2018 when Donald Trump launched a trade war against China. Although Trump was motivated less by grand geopolitical designs than by his personal political interests, the US-China trade war quickly led to a comprehensive deterioration of US-China relations that immediately escalated to a new cold war.

The Covid-19 pandemic that struck China in late December 2019 marked the beginning of the unraveling of Xi's neo-Stalinist agenda on the domestic front. Although the initial success of the Chinese government in containing the pandemic gave the party a political boost, the emergence of a more infectious viral variant in 2022 rendered Xi's zero-Covid strategy ineffective. Instead of abandoning this untenable approach, Xi stuck to it, most likely because he did not want to see an explosive rise in the number of infections and deaths ahead of the Twentieth Party Congress, scheduled for the fall of 2022 (which was to grant him a third term). Nationwide lockdowns resulted in a steep decline in economic activities and stoked public anger. By late November 2022, a month after the conclusion of the party congress, the Chinese public had had enough. After a fire killed ten people in their apartments under lockdown in Urumqi on November 24, thousands of young students and professionals spontaneously began demonstrating in more than a dozen cities, some even shouting "Xi Jinping, step down!"[82] Apparently shocked by this outburst of public anger, Xi relented and ordered an immediate end to zero-Covid, marking his first humiliating retreat from a demonstrably failed policy.[83]

But that may have been too late, as far as the Chinese economy was concerned. Instead of a robust recovery that failed to materialize after the end of zero-Covid, the economy struggled on all fronts, with an imploding real estate sector, slumping exports, falling investment, and high youth unemployment.[84] To be sure, most of the factors responsible for China's economic difficulties, such as high levels of debt, the gigantic real estate bubble, and deteriorating relations with the West, had preceded the pandemic. Nevertheless, these problems were exacerbated by Xi's zero-Covid policy. Its restrictions on international travel made normal business activities almost impossible, frequently disrupted supply chains, and led to the closure of many small businesses.

The persistent economic weaknesses may derail Xi's agenda of strengthening one-party rule at home and surpassing the United States as the world's largest economy. Dwindling financial resources could force him to curtail spending on his pet projects, such as military modernization, technological self-sufficiency, and "common prosperity," a plan to reduce socioeconomic inequality. Tighter budgets might also limit the party's ability to distribute resources to its favored interest groups, such as SOEs and key provinces. Protracted slow growth will result in stagnant standards of living and undermine the confidence of both the private sector and foreign investors in China's economic future. The performance legitimacy that has undergirded party rule since the Tiananmen crackdown will likely evaporate.

Judging by his response to China's economic difficulties, Xi seems to have no new ideas to sustain his neo-Stalinist project, except for placing national security at the top of the party's priorities. Instead of launching economic initiatives to rekindle growth, Xi has approved a series of measures, such as passage of a broad anti-espionage law and a campaign to catch foreign spies in 2023, succeeding only to further alienate Western investors and reinforce the pessimism of private entrepreneurs. Politically, Xi may benefit, at least in the short term, by underscoring the danger of hostile foreign forces and blaming Washington's economic cold war for China's problems. In the long run, however, the continuation of a security-centered survival strategy will make economic stagnation more likely, forcing Xi to depend even more on repression to keep the party—and himself—in power.

7

End of the Chinese Economic Miracle

THE DETERIORATION of the Chinese economy shortly after the country emerged from its Covid-19 lockdowns in December 2022 caught both Chinese leaders and outside observers by surprise. Weighed down by the collapse of the largest real estate bubble in history, heavily indebted local governments and SOEs, and geopolitical tensions, China struggled to regain the same rate of growth prior to the pandemic. But in retrospect, the end of the Chinese economic miracle in the Xi Jinping era was a foregone conclusion. The party's failure to implement more radical market-oriented reforms in the Hu Jintao era led to a gradual erosion of overall efficiency and diminished the country's growth prospects. As explained in chapters 3 and 4, stagnation was the logical outcome of a "trapped transition"—the progressive loss of the political incentives to pursue reform by a neo-authoritarian regime. When Xi Jinping succeeded in reviving China's dormant totalitarian institutions, the adoption of radical pro-market reforms to rejuvenate growth would be ideologically and politically impossible, thus spelling the end of the economic miracle.

Ideologically, Xi's brand of neo-Stalinist rule would further elevate the political supremacy of the party, resulting in the strengthening of the party-state's direct control of the economy and the extension of its hold on the private sector. Theoretically, a promising course of reform might exist on paper, as evidenced by sensible prescriptions well-known to Chinese leaders.[1] However, such economic reforms would be impracticable without accompanying political reforms. By the time Xi ascended to the top, powerful interests benefiting from the systemic inefficiencies of China's partially reformed economy—such as families of senior officials and their cronies in the business world, local government officials, state-owned enterprises and, most important, the party itself—would resist these reforms that threatened their power and privileges. It is worth repeating that these political forces were themselves the inevitable consequences of the inherent limitations of Dengist neo-authoritarianism. With favorable one-off structural factors, economic development under one-party rule might score impressive early results but would eventually lose steam and stagnate, as happened in the Xi era.

The Economy Xi Inherited

Growth started sputtering even before Xi assumed power in late 2012. Economic output recorded its last double-digit growth of 10.2 percent in 2010. In 2012 growth had slowed to 8.1 percent.[2] To be sure, sustaining double-digit growth for an economy of $8.5 trillion in 2012 would be no easy feat. Reversion to the mean—a fall in growth rates that brings the expansion of output to the historical average—is the law of economics that applies to China in the same way as it does to all economies.[3] However, China's apparent entry into a period of moderate growth, what its leaders preferred to call "the new normal," was accompanied by several economic abnormalities that compounded the challenges faced by the CCP in its attempts to sustain sufficient dynamism and turn China into a high-income economy.

Perhaps the most important economic anomaly—and a persistent constraint on the economy—was the structural imbalance that emerged in the post-Tiananmen period and remained uncorrected throughout the Hu Jintao era. Specifically, economic growth was excessively reliant on investment, a dependency that inevitably results in diminishing returns and overcapacity. If anything, this macroeconomic imbalance worsened under Hu. At the end of 2002, when Hu became party chief, investment accounted for about 38 percent of GDP. By 2012, when Xi succeeded Hu, investment had risen to 48 percent of GDP.[4] Although Hu was able to muddle through despite the growing macroeconomic imbalance, the odds that Xi would be able to do so during the period of "the new normal" appeared to be far less favorable. He did not enjoy many of the advantages of the Hu regime, such as relatively low levels of debt, a massive expansion of exports due to China's WTO entry, and healthy demographics, just to mention a few.

In addition to the worsening macroeconomic imbalances, another serious and potentially perilous obstacle confronting Xi was the rapidly rising level of debt following China's credit-fueled stimulus in response to the 2008 global financial crisis. Total outstanding credit to the nonfinancial sector stood at

192 percent of GDP at the end of 2012. By comparison, when Hu became party chief a decade earlier, the amount of debt was 142 percent of GDP. Under Xi, this ratio would grow even higher, reaching 297 percent of GDP by the end of 2022. Debt incurred by the state (mostly local governments) was 35 percent of GDP at the end of 2012 and would rise to 78 percent of GDP by 2022. At the end of 2012, the leverage of companies, mostly SOEs, was at 128 percent of GDP; ten years later it reached 158 percent of GDP.[5]

The housing bubble, the third economic challenge confronting Xi, was at an early stage in 2012. Residential housing had boomed under Hu. In 2003 about 2.6 billion square meters of floor space were under construction; by 2012, the figure was roughly four times that amount, at 9.86 billion square meters.[6]

The last major danger lurking on the horizon was the fraying of relations with China's main trading partners in the West as a result of the sustained high trade deficits. America's bilateral merchandise trade deficit with China ballooned from $124 billion in 2003 to $315 billion in 2012.[7] In the same period, the European Union's bilateral merchandise trade deficit with China nearly doubled, from $74 billion to $130 billion.[8] Even though bilateral trade imbalances do not necessarily mean that one of the parties has been harmed, persistently high deficit levels are often seen as evidence of unfair trade practices perpetuated by the party recording a surplus. In the case of Sino-American trade, high imbalances in China's favor were exploited successfully by Donald Trump to win the support of blue-collar workers in the US rust belt, igniting a US-China trade war in 2018.[9]

By 2012, most of the favorable structural and political factors that had earlier propelled double-digit growth had either dissipated or were weakening. The pool of cheap labor from the rural areas was declining, causing wages to rise rapidly. In the manufacturing sector, the average wage in 2012 was 2.3 times higher than it had been in 2002 in real terms.[10] The population was also aging. About 94 million people (7.3 percent of the population) were aged 65 or older in 2002. Ten years later, the country had 127 million people aged 65 or older (9.4 percent of the population). In 2021 over 200 million, or 14.2 percent of the population, would be aged 65 or older.[11] The lack of reform during the Hu period and the shift of resources to the real estate sector and to unproductive infrastructure due to the 2009 stimulus package caused a precipitous fall in productivity.[12]

This summary of the Chinese economy in late 2012 reveals serious risks, such as macroeconomic imbalances, high and growing levels of debt, an incipient housing bubble, and deteriorating ties with its major trading partners. Although the Chinese government put a positive spin on the slowing growth, claiming that the country had entered "the new normal" phase of development, these risks threatened to make the new normal anything but normal. Economic stagnation could easily result from the chronic lack of consumption-driven demand and the overreliance on one sector, i.e., housing, as a driver of growth. The high debt levels could trigger a financial crisis, and the sustained trade imbalances could ignite trade wars. Indeed, these economic difficulties would culminate, during Xi's third term, in a prolonged economic slump marked by high youth unemployment, a colossal real estate collapse, and deflation.

Unkept Promises

At the Third Plenum of the Eighteenth Central Committee in November 2013, Xi unveiled a sixty-point reform plan, apparently to establish his credentials as a reformer. Despite its title, "Decision of the Central Committee of the Communist Party of China on Some Major Issues Concerning Comprehensively Deepening the Reform," Xi's blueprint is notable for its contradictions and incompatible objectives.[13] Rhetorically, the decision seems to have made an ideological breakthrough by stating: "We must deepen economic system reform by centering on the decisive role of the market in allocating resources." Previously, the party had allowed the market to play only a role that was subordinate to that of the state. However, this ideological framing contradicts the decision's insistence that in China's economic system the state-owned sector is the main entity (*zhuti*), with economic actors of other ownership developing side by side. To underscore its determination to maintain the dominance of the state-owned sector, the decision states: "We must unswervingly consolidate and develop the public economy, persist in the dominant position of public ownership, give full play to the leading role of the state-owned sector, and continuously increase its vitality, controlling force and influence. We must unwaveringly encourage, support and guide the development of the nonpublic sector, and stimulate its dynamism and creativity." However convoluted, the ideological formulation in the decision leaves an unmistakable impression that the party was seeking to maintain an economic system based on state ownership, with nonstate economic entities playing a subordinate role.

Substantively, the decision consists of two separate packages of "reform." One package addresses the flaws in the economy (such as the state-owned enterprises, the fiscal system, the financial sector, and so forth) and the delivery of public services. The other package seeks institutional changes in state institutions (the military, the legal system, and the bureaucracy).

At first glance, the proposed package of economic reforms seems more radical than any of the previous reforms announced by the party in the post-Tiananmen era. For example, it proposes land reform that will benefit farmers, a fiscal reform that will raise local revenues and increase the provision of social services, price reform that will liberalize energy, utility, telecom, and transportation markets, an opening up of the financial sector to private firms, and taking rapid steps in the direction of interest and currency liberalization. Unfortunately, few of these reforms were implemented in subsequent years. If anything, the party reversed course and, instead of allowing the market to play a "decisive role," brought back the state at the expense of the private sector.[14]

The other package seeks to strengthen the party and its control over the state. The most notable proposals were the establishment of the CCP National Security Commission, the restructuring of the military, and tighter social controls (cybersecurity, censorship, and neighborhood-level surveillance through "grid management"). Unlike the unfulfilled economic reform promises, these measures were fully implemented during Xi's first term.

Xi abandoned his economic reform plan but adhered to his blueprint to strengthen the party-state for three probable reasons. The first is the fundamental incompatibility of a fully marketized economy with the supremacy of a Leninist regime, whereby any loss of control over economic activities carries an unacceptable risk of ceding political power to economic and social forces that might underwrite or become organized opposition. This is the same dilemma that had confronted Xi's predecessors. Like them, Xi simply could not square the circle and therefore had to forgo whatever ambitions he might have had to "comprehensively deepen" reform.

The second factor is the combination of practical difficulties and political resistance from actors and groups that had benefited from the status quo. Some reforms, such as financial sector reforms, currency liberalization, strengthening of the social safety net, and restructuring of central-local fiscal relations, would be complex and challenging in terms of technical knowledge, resource requirements, and political opposition. For example, expanding local fiscal revenue by levying a property tax would encounter strong resistance from urban residents.

The third explanation is that Xi, a hardcore Leninist, saw the task of shoring up the foundations of Leninist rule as far more important and urgent than injecting a new dose of dynamism into the economy. Politically, he would also benefit from measures to strengthen party control over the state and society because these steps would centralize his authority and grant him more power. Not surprisingly, the institutional changes proposed in the decision gave Xi more direct control over national security, cybersecurity, and any major policy changes after he assumed his new roles as head of the new commissions and the "small leading groups" overseeing these domains.

Supply-Side Reform

After abandoning his own package of economic reforms unveiled in November 2013, Xi opted for a set of more targeted measures at the end of 2015. Titled "supply-side reform," this program aims to address four major flaws in the Chinese economy: excess capacity, excess inventory, high debt leverage, and shortfalls in indigenous high-tech products. Conceived by his chief economic advisor, Vice Premier Liu He, supply-side reform was launched on November 10, 2015, and billed as an effort to increase the efficiency of the economy.[15] Even though Xi appears to have invested enormous political capital in this package, including inserting supply-side reform into the CCP charter in late 2017, the reforms are more tactical than structural and do not confront the most serious economic problem: the imbalance between investment and consumption. Excess capacity and high debt levels, however serious, are symptoms, not causes, of the structural flaws in an economy in which the state controls too much capital and invests it wastefully. Additionally, these reforms were implemented almost exclusively through administrative fiat, thus resulting in discrimination against the private sector.

Excess industrial capacity has been a chronic problem in China due to overinvestment by local governments seeking to expand their economic fiefdom. Local officials have additional political incentives to create large industrial firms under their control because they can then generate economic activities that will help improve their chances for promotion. Consequently, as most local government officials play this game, their decisions unavoidably lead to the construction of factories that supply more than the market demands, and the brutal price competition in sectors with excess production capacity leads to financial losses. Unlike in market economies where there are hard budget constraints (firms do not have unlimited access to funds), loss-making firms owned by local governments in China, free from such constraints, can count on the local authorities to fund their losses and keep them afloat. In the post-Mao era, industries producing consumer goods have become liberalized and dominated by private and foreign firms. Excess capacity in these industries is usually eliminated by the exit of uncompetitive firms. But because SOEs maintain a significant presence, or even dominance, in heavy industries, such as steel, nonferrous metals, cement, chemicals, and coal, SOE access to subsidies and bailouts makes it difficult to eliminate excess capacity.[16]

Xi's supply-side reform package set ambitious targets for reducing excess capacity in heavy industry. In the case of crude steel, the State Council announced in February 2016 that it was seeking to cut capacity by 100–150 million tons within five years (8–12 percent of total capacity).[17] Subsequently, the government painted a rosy picture of the progress of the reform, claiming it had removed more than 140 million tons of steel industry capacity between 2016 and September 2018.[18] But data from the National Bureau of Statistics show more modest progress. China's production capacity for crude steel was cut from 1.126 billion tons in 2015 to 1.085 billion tons in 2020. This means that, within five years, Xi's reform succeeded in cutting only 41 million tons of crude steel, much less than the target set in early 2016. Like steel, cement production capacity was reduced only marginally as well, from 3.442 billion tons to 3.397 billion tons (i.e., only 45 million tons, or 1.3 percent), during the same period.[19]

After the 2008 global financial crisis, China relied heavily on an expansion of the supply of credit through the financial system to sustain growth. Consequently, the level of debt in the nonfinancial sector grew rapidly. However, during the initial three years of Xi's first term, the party made no effort to slow down the borrowing. The average annual increase in credit to the nonfinancial sector was nearly 16 percent between 2013 and 2015, two percentage points more than that in 2009–2012, during which time credit growth had skyrocketed. By the end of 2015, credit to the nonfinancial sector stood at 239 percent of GDP, creating a potential financial crisis that would be a serious threat to the Chinese economy.[20] One unique feature of China's high levels of debt further exacerbated the risks of a financial crisis: heavy borrowing by local governments (mostly through local government financing vehicles).

The primary reason for the buildup of local debt was the 1994 fiscal reform that recentralized revenue without shifting expenditures from the localities to Beijing. In 1993, the year before fiscal recentralization, local governments received nearly 80 percent of total revenue. But after the reform, their share fell to about 50 percent. The share of public expenditures borne by local governments remained the same, however, at around 80 percent of all public expenditures. This created a huge structural deficit for local governments, equivalent to 30 percent of total public revenue. The structural shortfall of revenue means that local governments lacked funds to invest in infrastructure and other big-ticket items. Aside from seeking funding from Beijing, an unreliable solution, local governments grew increasingly dependent on revenues from land sales and borrowing to fund local infrastructure and, in the less wealthy areas, even to cover routine operational expenses.[21]

The magnitude of land-related revenues for local public finance can be seen in the following numbers. In 2020 land-related taxes, 2 trillion yuan, contributed roughly 20 percent of total local tax revenue. But proceeds from land sales were a whopping 8.4 trillion yuan, equivalent to 80 percent of total local tax revenue. Typically, local governments use the land under their control as collateral to borrow from the banks. This creates a huge risk because the land pledged as collateral is illiquid, and its value is difficult to determine. As the true value of the land critically depends on the real estate market, a deterioration of that market will impair the value of the collateral and inflict large losses on banks.[22]

As discussed earlier, local governments did not begin their borrowing binge until the Hu administration launched its credit-fueled stimulus package in 2008–2009. In subsequent years, the amount of debt owed by local governments exploded. Official data on local debt authorized by the central government report 15.4 trillion yuan at the end of 2014. However, local governments kept far more debt off the books. Estimates by economists suggest that the amount of off-the-books debt borrowed by local governments could have been 200–250 percent of the amount on the books. What this implies is that at the end of 2014, real local debt might have been 45–53 trillion yuan, or 70–82 percent of GDP. The deleveraging campaign does not appear to have lowered the leverage, as local governments reported total debt of 18.4 trillion yuan on their books at the end of 2018. Moreover, in subsequent years, local debt continued to grow. At the end of 2021, the officially declared amount of local debt was 30 trillion yuan, implying that real local debt might have been as high as 90–105 trillion yuan, or 80–93 percent of GDP.[23]

Of all the outstanding nonfinancial sector debt at the end of 2015, corporations, both state-owned and private, accounted for roughly two-thirds (about 108 trillion yuan), according to the Chinese central bank. Of this amount, roughly 40 percent was borrowed by local-government-owned SOEs (including many local government financing vehicles) that were typically smaller, less profitable, and more leveraged. Loans extended to SOEs in general, and to local SOEs in particular, are far riskier because these firms are less profitable than private firms. Perversely, due to their political influence and privileged positions in the economy, they also have greater access to credit, thus enabling them to borrow more.[24]

Like other so-called reforms during the Xi era, deleveraging—reducing the debt-to-asset ratios—was implemented by administrative fiat. Banks were ordered to call in loans regardless of their credit risks. Because private firms with weak political connections could not shield themselves from this campaign, the main burdens fell on the private sector. When their lenders demanded early payment, many private firms that had pledged their assets as collateral were forced either to sell (mostly to SOEs) or to declare bankruptcy.[25] Deleveraging also raised the borrowing costs for private firms due to the perception that they carried heightened credit risks.[26] One piece of evidence suggesting that the private sector bore the brunt of the deleveraging campaign is that the outstanding amount of debt borrowed by nonfinancial SOEs actually rose by 10 trillion yuan in the first two years after the launch of the deleveraging campaign in 2016.[27]

The party abruptly halted the deleveraging campaign in mid-2018 after the start of the US-China trade war. Chinese leaders apparently worried that they could not risk slower growth in the middle of the worst trade conflict in the post–Cold War era. The phrase "deleveraging" suddenly disappeared from official rhetoric and was soon replaced by a new phrase—"stabilizing leverage."[28]

Based on data from the Bank of International Settlements, China's debt level was rising, instead of declining, during the deleveraging campaign. At the end of 2015, credit to the nonfinancial sector stood at 239 percent of GDP. By the time Xi ended the campaign in July 2018, it was 260 percent of GDP. If we judge the success of deleveraging by the amount of the reduction in the growth of debt, then the deleveraging campaign can be considered a modest success because the debt grew at an annual rate of 8.4 percentage points of GDP during this period, compared with 15.6 percent during 2013–2015. In the four years after the official end of the deleveraging campaign, debt growth averaged 8.5 percentage points of GDP each year.[29] The singular achievement of deleveraging was a reduction in the growth of debt, not a reduction in the leverage itself. In spite of the slower growth of debt, however, China's high leverage continued to threaten the stability of its financial sector and deprive its leaders of policy options when the economy was confronted with prospects of stagnant growth and deflation, as was the case in mid-2023.

The Housing Bubble

In 2003 the government designated the real estate sector as a "pillar industry." In the following decade, the explosive expansion of the sector turned it into one of the main drivers of growth. In 2003 investment in the sector was only

TABLE 7.1. Investment in Real Estate, 2013–2023

Year	Amount (trillion yuan)	Change from Prior Year (%)
2013	8.22	18.8
2014	9.02	9.8
2015	9.09	0.7
2016	9.69	6.6
2017	10.34	6.7
2018	11.27	9.0
2019	12.36	9.6
2020	13.2	6.8
2021	13.76	4.3
2022	12.38	−10.0
2023	11.21	−9.5
Total	120.54	

Source: *ZGTJNJ 2024*, https://www.stats.gov.cn/sj/ndsj/.

1 trillion yuan. By 2012, the end of the Hu period, investment in the sector reached 7.18 trillion yuan.[30] During the Xi period, the growth of investment in the sector cooled off. In absolute terms, however, massive resources were nevertheless misallocated into the overbuilt sector. Cumulatively, between 2013 and 2023, real estate investment totaled 120 trillion yuan, almost equal to China's GDP in 2023 (table 7.1).

To make things worse, the booming sector led to a rapid increase in housing prices, prompting the government to take repeated measures to cool housing. Starting in 2005, the State Council issued a series of documents to control excess investment in the real estate sector and to restrict purchases so to dampen speculative behavior. These measures, however, had at best a marginal impact on containing the surging housing prices, especially in the largest and most prosperous cities, such as Shanghai, Beijing, and Shenzhen.[31]

Several factors made it difficult for the government to prevent a housing bubble. First, at the national level, the housing sector contributed close to one-third of annual GDP growth by the end of the 2010s.[32] Thus a drastic slowdown in the housing sector would hurt growth. Second, local governments depended on the housing sector for revenue. In addition to the taxes collected from real estate transactions, the income realized through the sale of land to developers and the credit obtained from banks using land as collateral constituted the principal sources of nontax revenue for local governments.

Therefore, the local governments had incentives to sustain the real estate boom as long as possible. Third, housing—in particular, housing in large cities—was perhaps the only profitable asset for Chinese savers. Capital controls made it impossible to invest abroad, while the volatile domestic stock market, dominated by the inefficient SOEs, delivered poor results. As a result, the overlapping interests of a growth-obsessed central government, revenue-hungry local authorities, aggressive real estate developers, and residents seeking better housing or higher investment returns fueled the housing bubble and kept it from crashing.[33]

In December 2016 Xi Jinping personally ordered the first serious effort to cool the housing sector when he declared that "housing is for living, not for speculation." This mantra instantly prompted the government to adopt tough regulations. In addition to limiting the number of housing units individuals or families could purchase, the crackdown included prohibitions against selling new units within two years after the initial purchase, higher interest rates on mortgages, a ban on the issuance of mortgages to purchasers who already owned two units, and an increase in the supply of low-cost rental housing.[34]

Despite implementation of these measures, the bubble in the housing sector grew bigger, albeit at a slower pace. The amount of investment in the real estate sector rose on average 8.4 percent per year between 2017 and 2019, 50 percent more than the annual average growth of 5.7 percent between 2014 and 2016, but nearly a third of the annual average increase in growth of 22.6 percent recorded between 2009 and 2013.[35] Instead of declining, the average price per square meter rose, from slightly under 7,500 yuan to 10,000 yuan, from 2016 to 2020.[36]

The ineffectiveness of the policies implemented after Xi's edict forced the government to double down in 2020, despite the economic downturn attributed to the Covid-19 pandemic. In August the government rolled out an unprecedented regulation, popularly known as the "three red lines," to force developers to reduce their leverage. Specifically, developers could increase their debt level by 15 percent if they met three criteria: a liability-to-asset ratio of less than 70 percent (excluding prepayments made by purchasers for unfinished housing units), net debt below total equity, and cash on hand equal to or exceeding 100 percent of short-term debt. If they met only two of the three criteria, they could increase their leverage by 10 percent. If they met only one of the three, they could raise their debt level by 5 percent. If they failed on all three measures, they could not raise their debt level. The government likely intended for this seemingly nuanced policy to achieve a soft landing in the housing bubble. However, the government did not anticipate the risks of contagion precipitated by the loss of access to credit by even a small number of highly indebted real estate developers. At the time of the policy announcement, about one-quarter of China's two hundred largest real estate firms met none of the three criteria and were facing the prospect of losing access to credit. Consequently, implementation of the policy precipitated a disorderly unwinding of China's real estate bubble that could not have been the original intention of policymakers.[37]

Unlike previous attempts, the "three red lines" perhaps worked too well, judging by the implosion of the real estate sector that was to follow. In 2021 investment in the sector grew only 4.3 percent, and sales measured in floor space rose only 1.9 percent. Ominously, the amount of land purchased by developers for potential projects, a leading indicator, fell 15.5 percent.[38] For the heavily indebted real estate developers, enforcement of the three red lines sounded a death knell. Evergrande, one of China's largest real estate developers that met none of the three criteria, was immediately pushed to the brink of insolvency. Saddled with nearly two trillion yuan of debt, Evergrande could not raise new debt to pay its bills. By August 2023, it filed for bankruptcy and its founder was placed under criminal investigation.[39] The unavoidable contagion triggered by Evergrande's default quickly plunged other large and equally indebted real estate developers into a liquidity crisis after they lost access to new financing.

The deflation of the real estate bubble accelerated in 2022 when investment in the sector fell 10 percent from the previous year. Sales measured by transactions dropped 27 percent.[40] In 2023 the real estate sector was in a meltdown. By September, two-thirds of the top fifty private real estate firms were in default of their dollar-denominated bonds.[41] Housing prices in major cities recorded a consistent decline despite the government's efforts to limit the fall in sale prices and the use of massaged data to conceal the extent of the decline in prices.[42] Compared with 2022, sales of homes by floor space fell 7.5 percent in the first nine months of 2023, while investment in the real estate sector declined by 9.5 percent for the whole year.[43]

The crash of the real estate sector in 2023–2024 dragged down the economy and forced the government to relax enforcement of the three red lines. To resuscitate the real estate sector, local governments scrapped the restrictions on purchasing homes, and banking regulators lowered the amount of down payment required to obtain mortgages.[44] However, the crisis in the real estate sector was so vast and deep that these modest measures did not make much of a difference. The housing sector is expected to be weak and to depress growth for years to come.[45]

The US-China Trade War

Sino-American trade tensions were simmering even before the trade war launched by Donald Trump in 2018. After China joined the WTO in December 2001, bilateral merchandise trade boomed. In 2001 the United States exported \$19 billion worth of goods to China and imported \$102 billion. By the time Trump won his surprise victory in 2016, the United States was exporting \$116 billion to China and importing \$462 billion from China.[46] During this period, a persistent high trade deficit, restricted market access in China, and violations of the intellectual property rights of US firms stoked tensions between Washington and Beijing. However, the high-level exchanges between China and the United States on trade yielded no meaningful outcomes. America's trade deficit with China remained stubbornly high, while charges of theft of intellectual property and of China's failure to honor its WTO commitments grew louder.

Disappointment over China's lack of action to address these concerns eroded corporate America's goodwill. Even more important, the combination of technological change and globalization resulted in the loss of millions of blue-collar manufacturing jobs in America's politically crucial rust belt, creating an opening for a populist like Trump to exploit resentment among these victims of globalization. During his presidential bid in 2016, Trump adroitly seized the trade issue, accusing China of "raping" America and engaging in the "greatest theft in the history of the world."[47]

After he entered the White House, Trump appointed a trade hawk, Robert Lighthizer, as his trade representative. In August 2017 Lighthizer initiated an investigation into China's violations of America's intellectual property rights. In early April of the following year, he produced a report finding China in violation of intellectual property rights. As a penalty, the report proposed levying 25 percent additional tariffs on \$50 billion of Chinese goods imported into the United States. China reacted by threatening to impose 25 percent tariffs on \$50 billion of American goods exported to China. Thus began the largest trade war in post–World War II history to that time.

As Xi responded to Trump's trade war with retaliatory tariffs on American goods, the United States and China engaged in a series of negotiations in an attempt to resolve their disputes, albeit without much success. A ray of hope for an ending to the trade war emerged in early 2019 when it appeared that China might accept an American proposal that would force major changes in its trading practices. But the CCP Politburo Standing Committee rejected the proposal, a development that prompted an infuriated Trump to escalate the trade war.[48] Subsequently, Trump extended tariffs of between 10 and 25 percent on nearly all Chinese imports to the United States. But in January 2020 the two countries signed the so-called Phase One Deal that withheld planned further tariff increases on $160 billion worth of Chinese imports, cut tariffs from 15 to 7.5 percent on $120 billion of Chinese goods, but maintained the 25 percent tariff on $250 billion worth of Chinese imports. In return, China pledged to increase its purchases of American exports and services by at least $200 billion over the next two years. Although Trump touted the deal as a "win," China did not buy the promised extra American goods and services in 2020 and 2021.[49]

By the time Trump left office in January 2021, the trade war had placed additional cumulative tariffs on $550 billion of Chinese imports, while China had retaliated with cumulative punitive tariffs on $185 billion worth of American products. After Joe Biden entered the White House, he kept Trump's tariffs in place, both because reducing or removing them would cost him dearly in a country in which protrade policies were no longer popular and because the ongoing deterioration in US-China relations made such a concession difficult.[50]

Despite the ferocity of the trade war, its immediate economic impact was modest. China's GDP growth was 7.3 percent in 2017; it fell to 6.4 percent in 2018 and to 6.1 percent in 2019.[51] US GDP growth rose from 2.2 in 2017 to 2.9 percent in 2018, but it fell to 2.2 percent in 2019.[52] Most of the costs of the trade war—higher prices of China-made consumer goods due to the additional tariffs—were borne by American consumers.[53]

Judging by trade and investment flows, the trade war appears to have had only a minor impact on China. To be sure, China's exports to the United States in 2018 and 2019 fell significantly as the result of higher tariffs (table 7.2). The Covid-19 pandemic, which caused disruptions, further depressed Chinese exports to the United States in 2020. But in 2021 and 2022, Chinese exports to the United States recovered to the level prior to the trade war. The effects of "decoupling" became more pronounced starting in 2023, when Chinese exports to the United States fell to $427 billion, a decline of 20 percent from 2022.

TABLE 7.2. Trade in Goods with China (in billion USD)

Year	Imports from United States	Exports to United States	Surplus
2016	116	462	347
2017	130	505	375
2018	120	539	418
2019	106	449	343
2020	125	432	308
2021	151	504	352
2022	154	536	383
2023	147	427	279

Source: US Census Bureau, https://www.census.gov/foreign-trade/balance/c5700.html.

TABLE 7.3. Chinese Foreign Trade in Goods (in trillion USD)

Year	Exports	Imports	Balance (USD, billions)
2017	2.263	1.844	419
2018	2.487	2.136	351
2019	2.499	2.078	421
2020	2.590	2.066	524
2021	3.316	2.679	637
2022	3.544	2.707	837
2023	3.379	2.557	822

Sources: *ZGTJNJ 2022*, https://www.stats.gov.cn/sj/ndsj/2022/indexch.htm; *ZGTJNJ 2024*, https://www.stats.gov.cn/sj/ndsj/2024/indexch.htm.

China's overall foreign trade was not initially affected by the trade war. Exports grew moderately between 2018 and 2020 and exploded between 2021 and 2022, likely reflecting China's central role in the global supply chains. Overall trade in 2023 held steady if measured in RMB but declined 5 percent in dollar terms, reflecting the depreciation of the Chinese currency (table 7.3)

In the immediate aftermath, foreign direct investment in China was more negatively affected by the trade war. In 2017 China recorded $181 billion in FDI. This amount fell to $135 billion in 2018 and $138 billion in 2019. It recovered close to the pre–trade-war level in 2021 ($173 billion) and 2022 ($189 billion).[54]

Despite the modest negative impact of the trade war on the Chinese economy in the short term, the US-China trade war marked the beginning of a "decoupling" of the Chinese economy from that of the United States and, to a lesser extent, from the economies of America's allies. On its own, the trade war raised the costs of Chinese goods in the United States, thus incentivizing manufacturers to relocate their manufacturing facilities to other countries, particularly to facilities in Southeast Asia, to avoid the additional tariffs. However, the trade war was not the sole trigger of the decoupling between the two economies. The outbreak of the Covid-19 pandemic in 2020 added another reason for the West to reduce its reliance on China. The pandemic inflicted massive disruptions on the global supply chains concentrated in China.[55] For companies accustomed to counting on dependable deliveries from China, the disruptions caused by the lockdowns threatened normal operations.

Russia's invasion of Ukraine in February 2022 probably provided the most powerful incentive for Western manufacturers to accelerate relocation of their supply chains from China. After the war began, the West imposed unprecedented economic sanctions on Russia, freezing its assets and choking its access to Western imports and financial systems. In retaliation, Russia seized the assets of Western companies in Russia. The geopolitical risks of doing business with China rose exponentially overnight, mainly because of the prospect of a war between mainland China and Taiwan, which Beijing considers a breakaway province (in 1949, the defeated Chinese Nationalists withdrew to Taiwan, then part of China). A war across the Taiwan Strait would likely be far more economically devastating if the United States were to intervene to defend Taiwan. As China is the world's largest manufacturing economy and is far more integrated with the global economy than is Russia, fears of a catastrophic war involving mainland China, Taiwan, and potentially the United States immediately became an irresistible motivator for companies to move out of China or to source supplies from other countries.

To make matters worse, US-China relations continued to spiral downward after Joe Biden entered the White House. Even though on the surface Biden's strategy of containment did not advocate full-fledged economic decoupling, in practice the widespread perception in the business community that geopolitical tensions between the two countries were here to stay and could escalate out of control led to a repricing of the risks of doing business with or in China. Relations between Beijing and Brussels also fell victim to Russia's war against Ukraine. The Chinese-EU relationship had faced severe strains due to clashes over trade and human rights even before the war. Nevertheless, in the realm of security, China was eager to ensure the strategic neutrality of the EU in the Sino-American rivalry, and the EU was initially reluctant to take sides.

When Vladimir Putin ordered the invasion of Ukraine, less than three weeks after he signed a joint declaration with Xi announcing a "no-limit friendship," the EU's relationship with China took a fateful turn. The largest and most violent war in Europe since World War II rendered the EU's efforts to maintain strategic neutrality in the Sino-American rivalry untenable. In the meantime, Washington's unflinching support for Ukraine in resisting Russian aggression revealed to the EU not only its dependence on American power but also the value of an alliance with the United States that no amount of trade with China could match. Consequently, the EU took initial steps to reduce its economic ties with China. Some of its member states adopted investment restrictions and export controls targeting China even though the EU leadership preferred a less jarring phrase, "derisking," as label for its policy.[56]

Trade and investment data for 2023 may offer a glimpse into the trend of decoupling between China and the West. Although several factors, such as rising interest rates in the United States, the resultant economic weaknesses in the West, and China's disappointing economic growth and historically high exports in 2022, likely muddy the picture in 2023, the amount of utilized FDI in 2023 was $163.2 billion, $13.9 billion less than the previous year. While overall exports held steady in 2023, Chinese exports to the United States fell far more dramatically. Between January and September 2023, China exported about $90 billion less goods to the United States than it did in the previous year, indicating an acceleration of the bilateral "decoupling."[57] In all likelihood, the full negative effects of the trade war on China's exports and inbound FDI will play out over an extended period. As Trump launches another trade war following his return to the White House in 2025, Chinese exports could suffer another devastating blow.

The short-term negative impact of the US-China trade war on the Chinese economy might be moderate, as shown by trade and investment data. But the prospect of an economic "decoupling" between the United States and China has led to the most profound change in economic policy and orientation since the post-Mao era. When Deng launched reform and opening in 1979, integration with the capitalist economies in the West, most critically the development of trade and investment ties with the United States, the world's largest and technologically most advanced economy, was a strategic priority. In the four decades that followed Deng's January 1979 historic visit to Washington, China's impressive growth record was made possible, in large part, by its broad and dense economic ties with the West, in particular the United States.

The free fall of Sino-American relations in the aftermath of the trade war threatened the viability of China's development strategy that focused on economic integration with the West. By early 2020, US-China decoupling was moving ahead at full steam, threatening not only hundreds of billions of dollars in bilateral merchandise trade but also Chinese access to advanced American technologies. During the first trade war, the Trump administration simultaneously began to impose a series of sanctions on Chinese technology companies by banning them from purchasing high-end semiconductors made in the United States or made with American technologies. Following the escalation of the trade war in May 2019, the United States put China's telecom giant Huawei, a global leader in 5G technology, on the so-called Entity List, thereby requiring that American firms planning to supply Huawei must first obtain a license from the Commerce Department, with the presumption that such applications would be denied.[58]

By spring 2020, the bottom of US-China relations fell out as Trump, increasingly worried about the damage of the raging Covid-19 pandemic on his reelection bid, gave the hawks in his administration carte blanche to punish China, the source of the virus. The collapsing US-China relations in general, and the decoupling between the two countries in particular, prompted Chinese leaders to draft a new economic strategy for a changed world.

In May 2020 Xi articulated the "dual circulation" strategy, a central concept in China's development approach for a world of great power rivalry and economic fragmentation. According to official media, the strategy of dual circulation was first proposed at a meeting of the Politburo Standing Committee on May 13, 2020. Shortly thereafter, Xi began to personally promote this idea in his public speeches. The Politburo formally endorsed the concept at the end of July 2020.[59]

The concept of dual circulation was translated into policy in November 2020, when the Fifth Plenum of the Central Committee approved the Fourteenth Five-Year Plan and proposed the development goals for 2021–2035. The "Proposal of the CCP Central Committee on Formulating the Fourteenth Five-Year Plan for National Economic and Social Development and the Long-Term Goals for 2035" explicitly puts forth a new development strategy centered on domestic demand and technological self-reliance.[60]

Based on authoritative statements by Xi himself as well as by his chief economic adviser, Vice Premier Liu He, the party's new development strategy was crafted in response to America's policy of containing China's rise through economic decoupling and the tech war. In his speech to the Fifth Plenum, Xi warned: "In recent years, along with the changes in the global political and economic environment, the upsurge in deglobalization and the unilateralism and protectionism acts by certain countries, the traditional global circulation has been notably weakened." He went on to urge that efforts be made "to root China's development inside the country and rely more on the domestic market to achieve economic growth."[61]

Both Xi and Liu offered upbeat assessments of the feasibility of dual circulation by listing China's size advantage: a middle-income country with 1.4 billion people and a market with the largest growth potential in the world. This huge market will be able to generate sufficient domestic demand to sustain growth in the future in spite of an unfriendly external environment because consumption will rise and producers will increase efficiency through the adoption of modern technology and improvements in supply chains.[62]

As a framework document, the proposal lists key objectives. The section on generating new sources of domestic demand refers to upgrading and increasing household consumption and providing more social services. However, the document does not include new policies that might actually raise household income to increase or upgrade consumption. Investment would retain its role as a key driver of growth as the proposal offers a long list of major infrastructure projects to be built in the coming years.

In addition to reducing reliance on external demand, the proposal also calls for greater resilience and security of supply chains and technological self-sufficiency. Reflecting his awareness of China's vulnerability to Western technological sanctions, Xi set the goal of resilience of supply chains in April 2020 when he addressed the Central Finance Small Group, the party's top economic decision-making body. He urged, "In order to ensure our industrial security and national security, we must strive to build self-reliant, controllable, secure, and dependable production and supply chains. We must seek to have at least one alternative source for critical products and supplies." In a veiled but obvious reference to a potential conflict with the United States, Xi stated that he believed that more resilient and secure supply chains centered domestically would help China increase its national security and allow it to "maintain normal economic activities under extreme conditions."[63]

The proposals of the Fifth Plenum add more details to Xi's concept of economic security. Judging by the space devoted to technological self-sufficiency, it is evident that the party views this as an overriding priority. Section III of the proposals contain specific ambitious programs designed to enable China to develop indigenous capabilities and overcome the West's technological containment. These include formulation of a comprehensive plan that would mobilize the resources of the entire nation to achieve new scientific and technological progress, in particular in emerging areas such as artificial intelligence (AI), quantum computing, semiconductors, and life sciences. Also mentioned are new large national research projects, talent recruitment programs, and incentives for innovation by domestic entities.[64]

Even though Xi tried to strike a balance between development and security, his speech to the plenum implies that security should override development. According to Xi, it will be wise to "overestimate difficulties [and] deepen our thinking about risks," implying that in devising a development strategy, China must give more weight to potential security risks.[65] The proposal duly reflects Xi's broadened definition of security risks by declaring that China "must maintain its ability to secure and control critical industries, infrastructure, strategic resources, and major scientific and technological areas."[66]

On the surface, Xi's vision of dual circulation does not entail severing ties with the global economy. But it is clear that dual circulation would consist primarily of "great domestic circulation" based on reliable domestic demand and secure sources of technology.[67] In the years following issuance of this landmark document, the party implemented several measures to turn Xi's vision into reality. The bulk of efforts in 2021–2023 were on building a domestic semiconductor supply chain to overcome US-led efforts to cut off China's access to advanced chips.

In September 2023 China launched a new $40 billion state-backed fund to invest in the semiconductor industry. This was on top of the nearly $48 billion the government had raised between 2014 and 2019 for the China Integrated Circuit Industry Investment Fund (ICF), commonly known as the "Big Fund."[68] Although establishment of the Big Fund in 2014 long preceded the US-China tech war, Beijing's additional investment in September 2023 was definitely a direct response to America's escalating export controls to cripple China's semiconductor sector, in particular the package of measures the Biden administration unveiled in October 2022 that sought to block Chinese access to high-end chips and the equipment capable of producing them.

Despite Xi's repeated invocation of the dire need for greater economic security, aside from increasing R&D there were few effective measures the party could undertake in the short term. Although China stepped up efforts to reduce its reliance on the US dollar by denominating more trade in renminbi, its use of the dollar was unlikely to fall dramatically simply because there were no alternatives in the foreseeable future for China to settle trade and manage its huge foreign exchange reserves.[69] Food self-sufficiency, another prized security goal Xi has emphasized repeatedly, is also unlikely to be achieved in the near term because China does not have enough arable land, and its food self-sufficiency ratio was only 66 percent as of 2020.[70]

But Chinese leaders are unlikely to be deterred by the challenge of building up an economic fortress. The costs of such an undertaking will be staggering. "Forced import substitution" in the case of advance technologies will make China reallocate resources to economic activities for which it lacks a comparative advantage. Achieving food self-sufficiency by producing more grains domestically at the expense of higher-value cash crops will reduce income from agriculture. Shifting supplies away from the United States and its allies will cut competition and increase costs. Chinese manufacturers that rely excessively on the domestic market will not be competitive with their global peers. Regardless of the culpability of the US-China decoupling and tech war, the end result of China's response—a security-focused development strategy—will be less economic efficiency and lower growth for the long term. For the party and Xi, this seems a price worth paying if the alternative will place China at the mercy of a hostile West that sees a powerful China as an existential threat.

Reversion to Statism

The CCP's schizophrenic attitude toward the private sector is well-known. On the one hand, the party's imperative of sustaining performance legitimacy dictates a pragmatic approach to the private sector, the largest contributor to economic output. On the other hand, political distrust of private entrepreneurs, lingering ideological hostility to capitalism, and entrenched regime interests to preserve a large state sector motivate the party to discriminate against the private sector regardless of the loss of efficiency.[71] In practice, such discrimination manifests itself in regulatory barriers restricting the entry of private firms into strategic sectors (such as finance, energy, and telecom), favorable access to credit and subsidies for SOEs, and harassment and mistreatment of private firms by local authorities that see them as easy prey.[72] In spite of government discrimination, however, private firms thrived in the post-Tiananmen era, as evidenced by their growing share of GDP, urban employment, and exports.[73]

Complaints that "the state advances and the private retreats" (*guojin mintui*) became more frequent toward the end of the Hu Jintao era, prompted mostly by the government's massive stimulus package implemented in 2009 to sustain growth following the global financial crisis. As the state sector was the primary beneficiary of the package, which consisted of four trillion yuan in fiscal spending and an infusion of bank credit several times that amount, the government's response elicited concerns that party policy toward the private sector was being reversed. Additionally, the government encouraged giant SOEs to acquire other (usually struggling) SOEs and even well-established private firms.[74]

In the post-Tiananmen era, the state had always maintained an extensive presence in the economy, but the pivot back to statism at the expense of the private sector became more pronounced after 2009.[75] However, like the shift toward a more assertive foreign policy and a regressive domestic agenda, *guojin mintui* on the eve of Xi's rise to power lacked an ideologically coherent program and was notable for the absence of a high-profile crackdown on iconic private firms or well-known private entrepreneurs. All this would change under Xi.

Before his ascent to the top, Xi had said or done few things that revealed his views of the private sector. His three-and-one-half-year stint as party chief of Zhejiang province (November 2002 to March 2007) may bolster his image as a probusiness official, but his record in Zhejiang contains no evidence of major initiatives that supported the private sector. As an astute politician, Xi was careful to avoid close ties with wealthy private entrepreneurs. Although his extended family members had reportedly amassed large fortunes through questionable business deals, Xi and his immediate family are not known to have been implicated in corruption.[76]

Only after he became party chief did Xi reveal what he really thought about the relationship between the state and the private sector. His rhetoric grew more unabashedly supportive of the state sector after he quietly abandoned the reform blueprint unveiled with great fanfare in November 2013. In October 2016 he emphasized that SOEs are "an important material and political basis for socialism with Chinese characteristics and an important pillar and reliable force for the CCP's governance of the country," and that the party will "firmly and unwaveringly make SOEs stronger, bigger, and better."[77]

In terms of policy, however, the party did not adopt one single major policy package to roll back the private sector. Early on, Xi launched a campaign to force private and foreign-invested companies to establish party organizations as a means of asserting political control.[78] Later, policies that favored the state sector over the private sector were rolled out in a piecemeal fashion until Xi ordered a more drastic crackdown on the private sector that began in late 2020. The first prong of Xi's economic strategy to preserve the state sector as the "dominant entity" was the 2015 unveiling of "Made in China 2025." Although China had proposed similar industrial policy packages with aspirational goals in the past, "Made in China 2025," a ten-year, state-led industrial strategy to establish China's global dominance in the high-tech manufacturing industry and to reduce its dependence on foreign technology, was far more ambitious and controversial.[79] China's main trading partners in the West saw it as an undisguised effort by China to displace the West as the global technological leader. The plan stipulated that China would attain 70 percent self-sufficiency in high-tech industries by 2025 and would achieve a leading position in global markets by 2049, the centennial of the People's Republic of China.[80] In addition to the worrisome security implications, "Made in China 2025" also involved massive government subsidies and protectionist measures that were bound to conflict with the West's economic interests. At home, it would funnel huge resources to the state sector, which was tasked with realizing the ambitious goals.

Another step the party undertook to bolster SOEs was to make them even bigger, a trend that had started under Hu. Giant SOEs directly under the control of the central government acquired small and poor-performing ones, ostensibly to increase the economies of scale. During Xi's first term, SASAC engineered some of the largest mergers of SOEs in history, such as the combination of CSR Corporation and CNR Corporation, two manufacturers of locomotives and rolling stock in 2015, as well as several others. Based on data provided by SASAC, such mergers did make the centrally controlled SOEs bigger, as measured by their assets. But their efficiency actually declined, and their debt-to-asset ratio rose.[81]

The government's direct intervention in the stock market in 2015 is another example of the revival of statism under Xi. Starting in June 2014, China's stock markets began a bull run. Investor exuberance, fueled in part by the official media, drove the main index on the Shanghai Stock Exchange up more than 150 percent within the year. When the bubble began to burst in mid-June 2015, the top leadership viewed the slide in stock prices as a negative reflection of its economic stewardship and ordered that the "national team"—mainly state-owned financial entities—pour trillions of yuan into the market to support the prices. This intervention failed miserably. In addition to the waste of huge amounts of money, the government-orchestrated rescue did not stop the crash. By the time the market stabilized in March 2016, the Shanghai index was down 45 percent from its peak.[82] Although this was not the first time the Chinese state had intervened to prevent stock prices from collapsing, it had never before engineered such a broad, costly, and ultimately doomed effort.

In addition to channeling resources to the state sector, the government also implemented policies that systematically hurt the private sector. An early indication of policies that were less friendly to private entrepreneurs was the dramatic reduction in loans to the private sector by state-owned banks. In 2013 about 57 percent of all loans flowed to nonfinancial private firms. But this trend was reversed in 2014, when only 34 percent of such loans went to nonfinancial private firms. By 2015, only a trickle of credit—19 percent—was made available to nonfinancial firms. When the government launched its "deleveraging" campaign in 2016, private firms were hit especially hard. In that year, their share of credit collapsed to 11 percent.[83]

Private firms were easy targets during the deleveraging campaign between 2016 and mid-2018 because, in spite of their efficiency, they had costly and unstable access to credit. As state-owned banks require collateral from private firms and fear responsibility if their loans to private firms go sour, private firms must primarily rely on the shadow banking system (trust companies and wealth management firms) to borrow short-term loans at higher interest rates. Consequently, when the government required that the entire financial system reduce its leverage, the supply of credit to private firms fell because the state-owned banks could call back loans to shrink their balance sheets, whereas the shadow banking system, which indirectly also relied on the formal banking system for funding, was forced to cut credit to private firms.[84]

The negative impact of deleveraging on the private sector can be seen in the slower growth of the number of private firms and their employment, and, more important, the relative decline of the private sector as an investor in the domestic economy. In the three years (2013–2015) prior to the deleveraging campaign, the number of private firms and their employment numbers had grown, on average, 20.6 percent and 11.9 percent, respectively. During the three years of deleveraging (2016–2018), the corresponding numbers were 18.1 percent and 10.1 percent, respectively, indicating the slower growth of the private sector.[85]

Investment data during this period paint an even clearer picture of the retreat of the private sector under Xi. In 2016 and 2017, the height of the deleveraging campaign, private sector investment in fixed assets grew only 2.8 and 5.2 percent, respectively. By comparison, investment by SOEs rose 18.7 and 10.1 percent, respectively, providing evidence that the deleveraging campaign was not having a negative impact on SOEs.[86] Overall, the private sector's investment did not recover in the wake of the campaign. Official data show that private investment in fixed assets peaked at 58.9 percent of the total in 2014. In 2016, the first year of the deleveraging campaign, it fell to 56.3 percent. By 2019, the year before the pandemic, it accounted for 56.8 percent of total fixed asset investment.[87]

If major economic policies, such as "Made in China 2025" and the deleveraging campaign, hurt the private sector indirectly, the crackdown on the private sector that occurred in 2021 was fully motivated by political concerns. Prior to the Xi era, the party did not implement policies that would be seen as blatantly hostile to the private sector, even though the government consistently favored the SOEs. All this would change during Xi's second term.

Xi's first shot signaling a major shift in the party's policy was the abrupt suspension of the Initial Public Offering (IPO) of a private firm, the Ant Group, on November 3, 2020 (the IPO was later cancelled). The Ant Group, a fintech company affiliated with the e-commerce giant Alibaba, was on course to raise a record $37 billion by listing its shares in Hong Kong and Shanghai. But on the eve of the IPO, Xi reportedly ordered that Chinese regulators scuttle the Ant Group's listing.[88] One factor that allegedly drove Xi to intervene personally was the discovery that families of several senior retired officials were early investors in the group and would have reaped small fortunes if the IPO had gone ahead.[89]

The real reason appears to be Xi's fears that the private sector could erode the party's control of a vital economic sector—the financial system. At a Politburo seminar on the digital economy on October 18, 2020, shortly before his intervention, Xi gave a speech emphasizing the need to "prevent the expansion of platform monopolies (such as Alibaba) and the disorderly expansion of capital."[90] In retrospect, cancellation of the Ant Group IPO is not an isolated incident but rather the beginning of a concerted crackdown directed by Xi to rein in "the disorderly expansion of capital."

The campaign quickly claimed most of China's high-tech firms, in particular its e-commerce platform companies. After abandoning the IPO of the Ant Group, Alibaba was fined a record eighteen billion yuan in April 2021 for breaking antitrust regulations. Well-known tech giants, such as Tencent, Meituan, Baidu, Didi, JD.com, and others, were later ordered to pay huge fines for alleged violations of the antimonopoly law and data security regulations.[91] But compared with those private firms providing after-school coaching services, these tech firms were far luckier. Xi's crackdown on the platform economy diminished their status and precipitated a plunge in their stock prices that destroyed $1.1 trillion in market value within two years.[92] But they remained in business.

By comparison, the after-school coaching industry, which had generated $100 billion in revenue annually, was completely wiped out after the government announced a nationwide ban on July 21, 2023. This crackdown, again allegedly carried out at the direction of Xi, was supposedly motivated by the government's desire to make the education playing field more equal. Because of fierce competition for slots in high-quality middle schools and prestigious universities, Chinese parents sent their children to after-school tutoring programs in hopes that they would then perform better on exams. Xi likely saw this industry as perpetuating inequality since only the well-off could afford the extra costs. However, his drastic solution—banning the entire industry as part of a program to reduce the students' academic burdens and their families' expenses for after-school tutoring—merely addressed the symptom of the problem but failed to deal with its root causes, that is, the inadequate supply of high-quality education and a culture obsessed with exams.[93]

This crackdown backfired disastrously. The draconian ban on an entire privately run industry was unprecedented in the post-Mao era. Overnight it destroyed a large number of private businesses and made hundreds of thousands of people working in the industry jobless. Most important, the crackdown was a wake-up call to private entrepreneurs that their property rights were totally insecure under CCP rule. The crackdown failed to achieve its objective as it merely drove the industry underground, raising the costs for parents and making access to after-school coaching even more unequal than before the crackdown.[94]

The Covid Pandemic

When the Covid-19 pandemic first surfaced in Wuhan in December 2019, the Chinese economy was already in a precarious state. The housing bubble was on the verge of its inevitable burst. Overall levels of debt were at record highs, limiting the government's ability to use credit-fueled investment to prop up growth. Although the economy managed to expand by 6.4 percent in 2019, this was 25 percent less than growth in 2012, the year Xi ascended to the top.[95] But even this moderate rate of growth would be beyond reach in the wake of the pandemic. A combination of adverse factors after the spread of the Covid-19 pandemic was responsible for the economy's lackluster performance. The most obvious reason was the direct economic cost of the pandemic as lockdowns inflicted lasting economic damage. Ill-advised government policies—an inflexible zero-Covid policy and refusal to stimulate the economy with fiscal spending—caused needless pain throughout the period of the pandemic.

Unlike Western countries that provided substantial Covid relief to businesses and ordinary people immediately after the pandemic struck, Beijing offered no material relief either to businesses or to individuals. At least seven million small private businesses went bust in 2020 and 2021.[96] To be fair, zero-Covid—the party's immediate response to the pandemic—was probably the correct policy in the early days of the pandemic, and it did succeed in containing the virus quickly and restoring most economic activities by the middle of 2020. However, when a more contagious variant—omicron—emerged at the end of 2021, zero-Covid proved to be both ineffective and prohibitively costly. Although nearly all countries gave up zero-Covid when omicron morphed into the dominant strain, China doubled down in 2022. It enforced population-wide tests and imposed lengthy lockdowns on entire cities. In September 2022, for example, more than 300 million people in over seventy cities were under full or partial lockdown.[97]

Shanghai, the country's largest city with a population of over twenty-two million under lockdown from March to May in 2022, became China's most prominent victim of the zero-Covid policy. The primary reason for the party's continuation of this policy even after its ineffectiveness became abundantly clear is almost certainly Xi's own personal political interest. The strongman was seeking a norm-busting third term as CCP chief at the Twentieth Party Congress scheduled for the fall of 2022. Worried that an uncontrollable outbreak of infections ahead of the congress would dent his image and mar an important political event designed to establish his open-ended rule, Xi had compelling incentives to demand that local party officials continue to enforce zero-Covid regardless of the costs. This argument is supported by the fact that Xi decided to abandon the policy suddenly at the end of November—one month after the conclusion of the Twentieth Party Congress. Although the spread of antilockdown protests likely made Xi act sooner than he had originally planned, zero-Covid was no longer critical to him after the congress duly handed him a third term and allowed him to pack the Politburo with loyalists.[98]

The damage caused by Xi's zero-Covid policy is both measurable and incalculable at the same time. Despite the party's claim that this strategy kept China's Covid-related fatalities among the lowest in the world, researchers estimate that as many as 1.87 million excess deaths in China occurred among individuals thirty years and older during the first two months after the end of its zero-Covid policy.[99] This is more than the total number of deaths (1.158 million) attributed to Covid-19 in the United States as of December 2023 (China has a population more than four times that of the United States).[100] Due to disruptions caused by the zero-Covid lockdowns, the Chinese economy grew only 2.9 percent in 2022, marking the slowest growth in the post-Mao era and well below the official target of 5.5 percent. The invisible damage to the policy includes the loss of confidence among private entrepreneurs and foreign investors in CCP competence. The party's headstrong insistence on zero-Covid despite its ineffectiveness and mounting economic toll is a painful reminder that the narrow political interests of the Chinese regime and its personalistic ruler will always outweigh economic considerations. The one-two punch of Russia's invasion of Ukraine and the nationwide economic disruptions attributed to Xi's zero-Covid policy likely accelerated foreign investors' plans to diversify their supply chains away from China so as to reduce exposure to potential geopolitical black swan events. For domestic private entrepreneurs, the party's behavior during the pandemic reinforced a desire to seek safe havens outside of China for their assets and themselves. About twenty-five thousand "high-net-worth" Chinese reportedly emigrated in 2022 and 2023.[101]

After it abandoned the zero-Covid policy in December 2022, the party hoped that the economy would bounce back. But despite an initial robust recovery in early 2023, growth stalled as the real estate crisis deepened. Given its size, the burst of the real estate bubble was obviously the most important factor leading to China's economic underperformance in 2023. In addition to registering lower than expected growth in 2023, the Chinese economy continued to struggle in 2024, weighed down by deflation, exodus of foreign firms, escalating trade tensions, and further deterioration in the collapsing real estate sector.

Summary

In retrospect, the end of the Chinese "economic miracle," which coincided with the Covid pandemic, is largely due to the many policy failures that preceded Xi's rise. Topping the list is the failure to undertake genuine reforms to correct macroeconomic imbalances. Such reforms would have entailed increasing real household income by providing more social services and protection. But because the party during the Hu era made at most modest progress in increasing social spending, the macroeconomic imbalances remained uncorrected, and thus they continued unabated into the Xi era.

The party created an unprecedented credit bubble that began in 2009 and reached a dangerous magnitude by 2023, as described earlier in this chapter. Even though Xi implemented a deleveraging campaign in 2016, it achieved only modest results and had to be abandoned in mid-2018 in response to the US-China trade war. Consequently, the bubble grew so big that, when zero-Covid ended in December 2022, another major infusion of credit was not feasible as it would have raised the level of debt even higher and elevated the risks of a financial crisis.

Similarly, the party relied too heavily on the real estate sector to drive growth during the early part of Xi's first term, as shown by the double-digit increase of investment in real estate from 2013 to 2015.[102] Even after Xi grew concerned about the excessively high housing prices and ordered measures to cool down the sector in 2016, the party was unable to prevent a further expansion of the housing bubble. When the government finally ordered a crackdown in the summer of 2020, not only was the timing inauspicious (in the middle of the pandemic), but the cure also turned out to be too harsh. Instead of a soft landing, the crackdown precipitated a crash.

In addition to these policy mistakes, the Xi regime was less fortunate than its predecessors because most of the favorable structural factors that had earlier produced the Chinese economic miracle had either disappeared or become less favorable. The year that Xi ascended to the top, 2012, is likely to be remembered as China's "Lewis Turning Point"—an exhaustion in the supply of rural surplus labor.[103] Rising labor costs made China less competitive in low-end manufacturing, and Chinese society was beginning to age rapidly, increasing healthcare and pension expenditures. Because the Hu regime did not privatize the inefficient SOEs or push through meaningful reforms to improve the overall efficiency of the economy, productivity growth was stalling, and it would completely collapse under Xi.

China's external environment became less favorable at the end of the Hu era mostly because of the country's increasing assertiveness in international affairs and Beijing's resistance to addressing the concerns of its Western trading partners about unfair trading practices. After Xi implemented an even more aggressive foreign policy during his first term, it became increasingly difficult for the West to sustain its decades-long policy of engagement. But it was Donald Trump's trade war in 2018 that marked the beginning of the end of China's economic integration with the West. As the Sino-American relationship turned progressively adversarial, the commercial relationship unraveled quickly. The trade war would escalate and morph into an economic cold war covering technology transfers and investments. However reluctant they were initially, after the Russian invasion of Ukraine in early 2022 America's allies in Europe and Japan fell in line and implemented measures to restrict the flow of technology to China and to actively pursue "derisking," or to reduce substantially their economic linkages with China. If globalization helped create the Chinese economic miracle, the reversal of globalization, which is certain to accelerate during the second Trump administration, will unavoidably weaken the Chinese economy and darken its prospects.

8

From Engagement to a New Cold War

AS IS THE case with its domestic political developments, China's relations with the outside world, in particular the West, went through three distinct phases in the post-Mao period. Chinese power, the overall geopolitical environment, and the ideological values and leadership skills of the top leadership shaped Beijing's foreign policy and its ties with the West during each phase. Despite the substantive differences in Chinese foreign policy and its relations with the West in these three phases, the underlying logic of path dependence connects all of them. The prospects of engagement and even full integration with the West were the brightest in the 1980s when the possibility of a more open and free China was the greatest. Such prospects dimmed but did not disappear completely in the post-Tiananmen era, because of both the effectiveness of China's strategic restraint and the West's optimistic bet on globalization. But engagement became untenable once totalitarian rule was revived under Xi Jinping, as China started asserting its power and directly challenging the US-led order.

The first phase, from 1979 to June 1989, was the "golden age" of relations between China and the West. Devastated by three decades of economic mismanagement and political chaos under Maoist rule, in 1979 China was an impoverished nation that posed no real military threat to the West. Geopolitically, both China and the West saw the Soviet Union as the primary security threat. Ideologically, Deng Xiaoping's pro-market reforms gained enthusiastic support in the West because his efforts represented a decisive break with communism. Despite Deng's avowed adherence to one-party rule, his regime presented an enticing opportunity to change China for the better and thus was worth a strategic bet.

A consummate pragmatist, Deng radically reoriented Chinese foreign policy to place it in the service of domestic economic development. By skillfully leveraging China's favorable geopolitical position, he cultivated friendly and economically beneficial ties with the United States and Japan, the two countries whose support would be indispensable to his "reform and opening." Although Deng's foreign policy would tie China's economic destiny to the West, he had no intention of becoming part of the West-led system. He viewed integration as the sole viable tactic for ensuring the party's survival and for restoring China to its place in the world. Steeped in geopolitical realism, Deng was convinced that only national strength could guarantee Chinese security and CCP rule. However, he believed that at the end of the Maoist era, China was not strong enough to safeguard either objective. If China succeeded in modernizing with the help of the West, in his view, the growth of Chinese power over time would improve the country's geopolitical position. Even though he was not explicitly thinking of confronting the West, Deng's grand strategy of building up strength with Western support and not being part of the West would sow seeds of conflict decades later, after his grand strategy had actually achieved its objective.

The crushing of the prodemocracy movement in June 1989 and the collapse of the Soviet Union in December 1991 fundamentally redefined Beijing's relations with the West and necessitated substantial adjustments to Chinese foreign policy. During the post-Tiananmen era, the two critical factors—China's status as a strategic partner of the West in an anti-Soviet common cause and muted ideological distaste for CCP autocratic rule—disappeared. The Tiananmen crackdown revealed the ideological chasm between China and the West, and it would make Chinese human rights a key issue for the West. Practically overnight, the end of the Cold War in 1991 downgraded China's geopolitical importance to the West.

The West's sanctions against China following the Tiananmen crackdown and its triumph over the Soviet Union directly gave rise to a grim view of the emerging West-led world order in Beijing. If a bipolar world order in the 1980s served Chinese interests by allowing China ample space to maneuver between two opposing camps, a unipolar world order under American dominance was decidedly not in Chinese interests. It was in the early 1990s that Deng began to explicitly and consistently express opposition to the West-led order and to voice China's desire to change it. However, as China was too weak to challenge the post–Cold War order for most of the post-1989 era, its grand strategy was to avoid a self-defeating clash with the West, buy time, and build up strength to better protect its national interests.

Despite incipient worries about growing Chinese power and constant tensions over its human rights record, the West adopted a policy of engagement with strategic hedging. Under this policy, economic and diplomatic engagement with China continued, with the implicit goal of integrating China into the post–Cold War order and becoming a stakeholder that would share the benefits of an inclusive order. At the same time, the United States would maintain a robust military presence and security alliances along China's periphery as insurance policies.

Jiang Zemin implemented Deng's strategy effectively. Ironically, however, the very success of the policy, especially in gaining the time and space necessary to amass national power, also made conflict more likely. As China's growing clout boosted its leaders' confidence and ambitions, Deng's dictum on strategic caution gradually lost its power of restraint. The initial, albeit subtle, break with the post-Tiananmen foreign policy of strategic caution occurred under the leadership of Hu Jintao in the wake of the 2008 global financial crisis. Convinced that China could find the right balance between strategic caution and strategic activism, Hu and his colleagues embarked on a new course to probe the soft spots in the West-led order and test its response to Chinese actions.

Although the initial abandonment of strategic caution occurred in the waning years of the Hu era, the rise of Xi Jinping at the end of 2012 marked a decisive break with China's post-Tiananmen grand strategy. To be sure, Deng's ultimate objectives of strategic caution—safeguarding one-party rule and restoring China's status as a great power—did not differ from those of Xi. But Xi misjudged Chinese strength, set overly ambitious objectives, embraced excessively risky and confrontational tactics, and underestimated the US resolve and response.

Inspired mostly by domestic political considerations, the trade war Donald Trump launched in early 2018 quickly triggered a cascade of actions and reactions that in short order led to a complete rupture of Sino-American relations. As the confrontation between the two countries escalated, Xi made the fateful strategic decision to align with Russia to counter American power. But Russia's invasion of Ukraine in February 2022 drove the European nations, most of which probably would have preferred neutrality in the Sino-US conflict, into the arms of the United States.

The outcome has been a full-fledged new cold war (NCW). Ideologically, China is aligned with the major autocratic regimes, such as Russia and Iran, which share its opposition to the US-led order that threatens Chinese regime security and its vital security interests. Economically, China and the West have begun a costly and complex process of severing the trade, technological, and financial ties that had been forged during the prior four decades of engagement. Militarily, the United States and China have accelerated preparations for a direct conflict in the Taiwan Strait and the South China Sea.

Birth of Engagement

When Mao died in September 1976, the dictator bequeathed to China a relatively favorable external environment following the Sino-American rapprochement that he and Richard Nixon had engineered in 1971–1972.[1] By the time of his death, China and the United States were quasi-allies in their common cause against the Soviet Union. Beijing had reclaimed Chinese membership in the United Nations and held a veto-wielding permanent seat on its Security Council. China had also restored diplomatic relations with most Western countries. Although the Cold War would not end for another decade and a half, by the mid-1970s the cold war between China and the West was effectively over. For a country isolated from the capitalist world for nearly three decades, friendly relations with the economically dominant West was a precondition for its reintegration into the global economy and economic modernization.

After Deng became de facto paramount leader in December 1978 and launched his "reform and opening," China's external environment would improve even more dramatically. The tensions between the Soviet Union and the West escalated after the former invaded Afghanistan at the end of 1979. Because Deng embarked on a path toward capitalism, the West had additional incentives to cultivate ties with China. The economic potential of a market of nearly one billion people was too enticing to ignore, despite China's low level of development. Ideologically, Deng's "reform and opening" was worth supporting because it represented a great leap forward from Mao's totalitarianism and could lead to more personal freedoms and even political openness.

Besides these favorable factors, Deng's positive assessment of China's external environment and near-total influence over foreign policy reinforced his determination to seize this historic opportunity to advance his agenda of "opening." In January 1980 he articulated the essence of his strategy of "biding your time and building your strength," even though he did not use these exact words in a talk to senior leaders. "Of all our tasks," Deng said, "modernization is . . . the essential condition for solving both our domestic and our external problems. . . . The role we play in international affairs is determined by the extent of our economic growth. If our country becomes more developed and prosperous, we will be in a position to play a greater role in international affairs. . . . In the final analysis, the return of Taiwan . . . depends on our running our affairs at home well."[2]

However effusive he might have sounded about the importance of opening, Deng did not envision China becoming part of the West-led international order. He saw this order as something China could exploit profitably, but he said nothing about accepting the values and rules embodied in it. Indeed, Deng's opening was transactional and restricted primarily to economic relations. From his perspective, China would take advantage of the economic benefits of the West-led order but would remain independent of it in all other aspects.

For Deng's "developmental diplomacy" to succeed, he needed first to dramatically improve ties with the United States and Japan, the world's two largest economies, which could provide China with more access to capital, technology, and markets than any other country.[3] Gaining the support of the United States as part of Deng's "reform and opening" was critical because the US stance on China could also influence the position of its allies. In the case of Japan, its geographic proximity to China made it an even more promising trading partner and investor than the United States. Therefore, Deng took personal charge of these two vital diplomatic tasks in 1978, even before he effectively became paramount leader in December of that year.

Although the visit by Richard Nixon in February 1972 initiated the US-China strategic rapprochement, disagreement over the Taiwan issue prevented the two countries from normalizing diplomatic relations. The United States was seeking a form of normalization with the People's Republic of China without derecognizing the Republic of China (ROC), a position Beijing emphatically rejected. Washington and Beijing were essentially deadlocked over the Taiwan issue until late 1978, when President Jimmy Carter signaled that the United States could meet China's three conditions: severing official ties with the ROC, withdrawing US troops from Taiwan, and abrogating the US-ROC mutual defense treaty. At the most critical stage in the Sino-American normalization talks in mid-December 1978, Deng personally participated in the negotiations and made a key concession by tacitly agreeing to continued US arms sales to Taiwan despite his vocal opposition.[4] On December 16 the United States and China released a joint communiqué announcing the normalization of diplomatic relations.[5]

To be sure, the United States and China did not resolve their fundamental differences over the status of Taiwan, but the "one China policy" that the

United States formulated and later modified largely struck the right balance between reassuring Beijing and deterring reunification through military means. The Taiwan issue would become more complicated and more volatile in the 1990s after pro-independence political forces gained greater influence on the island, but in the 1980s China and the United States managed their differences over Taiwan skillfully and cooperatively.

When the ink on the Sino-American communiqué normalizing relations was barely dry, Deng embarked on a weeklong historic visit to the United States at the end of January 1979 to cement the Sino-American partnership. In addition to specific agreements signed during his trip, Deng succeeded in winning over both the American political establishment and the American public with his style of straight talk and friendly gestures (including donning a cowboy hat during a rodeo in Houston).[6]

Normalization of Sino-American relations in general, and Deng's successful visit to the United States in 1979 in particular, ushered in a golden era of relations between the two countries. Prior to normalization, their commercial relations were negligible, with two-way trade in 1978 totaling $1.1 billion.[7] But by 1989 bilateral trade had risen to nearly $17 billion.[8] The rapid expansion of trade was made possible because the United States granted China "most-favored-nation" (MFN) trade status following the "Agreement on Trade Relations between the United States of America and the People's Republic of China," which was signed in July 1979 and became effective on February 1, 1980. (China's MFN status was subject to annual renewal by the US president.)[9]

Cooperation in science and technology also blossomed after the January 31, 1979, signing of the US-China Agreement on Scientific and Technological Cooperation. Based on the agreement's framework, the two countries reached a series of separate deals covering specific areas, such as agriculture, civilian nuclear energy, and aerospace. The United States also significantly relaxed export controls and even allowed the export of defensive military technologies to China.[10] Regular high-level exchanges further solidified the Sino-American partnership in the 1980s. Top American leaders paid frequent visits to China. In April 1984 President Ronald Reagan visited China after hosting Premier Zhao Ziyang three months earlier. George H. W. Bush made China a stop on his trip to East Asia in February 1989, shortly after becoming president. Frequent cabinet-level exchanges also took place between the two countries.[11]

China's relationship with Japan experienced rapid improvement during the same period. On October 22, 1978, Deng began a weeklong visit to Japan—the first visit by a top Chinese leader since 1949.[12] Just as he would do a few months later in the United States, Deng won over Japanese political elites, business leaders, and the public alike with his straight talk, friendly demeanor, and diplomatic skills. He studiously avoided or downplayed the territorial dispute over the Senkaku/Diaoyu Islands, which both Japan and China claim.[13] In December 1979 Prime Minister Masayoshi Ohira of Japan visited Beijing and announced a five-year loan program, totaling 370 billion yen ($1.5 billion), to help fund the building of several major projects in China. In addition, Ohira offered preferential tariff treatment on Chinese goods, a grant to build a hospital in Beijing, and other technical assistance.[14] In subsequent years, Japan's Official Development Assistance (ODA) program would channel valuable resources into China's economic development at a time when the country was desperately in need of foreign capital. Between 1979 and 2005, the amount of development assistance provided by Japan in concessional loans, grant aid, and technical assistance totaled 3.4 trillion yen (over $10 billion), more than that of any other country in the world.[15] Japanese FDI in China in the 1980s reached $3.2 billion, accounting for about 15 percent of total FDI received by China, and second only to the amount of FDI from Hong Kong.[16]

Diplomatic ties blossomed even more than Sino-Japanese commercial relations in the wake of Deng's visit. During his December 1979 trip to Beijing, Prime Minister Ohira signed a Sino-Japanese cultural exchange agreement. In March 1980 the first meeting of a regular Sino-Japanese diplomatic dialogue was held in Tokyo. Two months later, Chinese Premier Hua Guofeng visited Japan and signed a Sino-Japanese agreement on cooperation in science and technology. Sino-Japanese relations reached a new high following the visit by Hu Yaobang, then CCP general secretary, to Japan in November 1983. One of the highlights of Hu's visit was an agreement with Prime Minister Yasuhiro Nakasone to form the Sino-Japanese Friendship Committee for the 21st Century, an organization whose sole mission was to improve bilateral relations.[17] The warming of Sino-Japanese relations also led to an increase in people-to-people exchanges. During his visit to Japan in late 1983, Hu invited three thousand Japanese youths to spend a week in China the following year (the visit took place in September 1984). In March 1985 a delegation of two hundred Chinese young people, headed by future Chinese leader Hu Jintao, visited Japan at the invitation of the Japanese government.[18]

Reintegration into the international community was another foreign policy goal in the 1980s. During the Maoist era, self-isolation had led to the exclusion of China from nearly all key international organizations. In 1977 China was a member of only twenty-one international organizations.[19] This would change immediately after Deng became paramount leader. In 1979 China would join most of the UN-affiliated international organizations, such as UNDP, UNICEF, UNHCR, and WEP, and in the 1980s it would become a member of the rest, such as FO and ILO.[20] China also joined a large number of international nongovernmental organizations.[21]

For a leadership laser-focused on economic development, membership in international economic institutions promised to deliver immense benefits. In April 1980 China became a member of the International Monetary Fund (IMF) and the World Bank. Six years later, it joined the Asian Development Bank and also applied to join the General Agreement on Tariffs and Trade (GATT), the predecessor of the World Trade Organization. Of these international financial institutions, the World Bank was the source of the most valuable assistance to China in the 1980s. Besides lending close to $7 billion to China during the entire decade, the World Bank's technical expertise in economic development and reform helped Chinese technocrats craft more effective policies.[22]

Another of Deng's priorities was to send a large number of Chinese students abroad for higher education and advanced training. The country's higher education system, devastated during the Cultural Revolution, was unable to produce the scientists and engineers China urgently needed for economic development. Among top Chinese leaders, Deng was the most enthusiastic advocate for broadening educational exchanges with the West.[23] Western educational institutions and foundations, in particular those in the United States, offered generous funding to Chinese students as most Chinese students could not afford the tuition and living expenses in the West. The number of Chinese students grew rapidly. At the end of the Maoist era, few Chinese students were studying abroad. But by 1988, the United States alone was hosting more than twenty-eight thousand Chinese students and scholars.[24] This trickle would grow into a flood in later years as China opened its doors wider and well-to-do Chinese could afford to send their children abroad to study at their own expense. Official Chinese data show that about eight million Chinese students and researchers studied in more than 160 countries between 1979 and 2021.[25] The benefits to China's economic modernization generated by this infusion of human capital are incalculable.

Crafting a New Grand Strategy

In the 1980s Deng accomplished most of his priority foreign policy objectives. The normalization of relations with the United States opened access to American capital and technology as well as the US market. Washington's embrace of

Deng's "reform and opening" encouraged its allies to adopt similar friendly policies toward Beijing. A relationship of quasi-alliance between the United States and China was also forged during this decade, resulting in frequent high-level visits and close cooperation in national security, education, science and technology, and commerce. China's relationship with its most important Asian neighbor, Japan, reached an unprecedented level of warmth and delivered rich economic benefits to Deng's modernization program. In the rest of Asia, with the exception of Vietnam, China could boast friendly, or vastly improved, ties. Most remarkably, China and the Soviet Union, its primary geopolitical adversary since the late 1960s, had reached a rapprochement. Beginning in late 1982, both Moscow and Beijing began to explore a path forward to lower tensions. The initial pace was slow, but when Mikhail Gorbachev became Soviet leader in March 1985, he immediately expressed greater openness to repairing Soviet-Chinese ties, and he later followed up with a series of unilateral concessions that Beijing positively received.[26] The event marking full normalization of bilateral state relations was Gorbachev's summit with Deng, held in Beijing on May 16, 1989.

This "golden era" was cut short on June 4, 1989, when Deng ordered the PLA to crush the prodemocracy movement in Tiananmen Square. Just as the Tiananmen crackdown irrevocably altered China's domestic political trajectory in the post-Mao era, it had a comparable impact on relations with the West, and it exposed the previously somewhat hidden but unbridgeable ideological chasm between China's Leninist regime and the Western democracies that would become a major source of friction in the post-Tiananmen era. Before the tanks of the PLA rolled into Tiananmen Square, China's human rights record was a troubling, but not dominant, issue for the West. Confronting the existential security threat of the Soviet Union took precedence. Additionally, largely due to the policies of liberal reformers like Hu Yaobang and Zhao Ziyang, China's human rights conditions were improving substantially in the 1980s, despite periodic but short-lived conservative backlashes in the ideological arena.

But all this changed after June 4, 1989. Although Deng was directly responsible for the Tiananmen crackdown, the paramount leader himself was infuriated by the sanctions imposed by the United States and its allies, and his attitude toward the West underwent a profound change. Prior to the Tiananmen crackdown, Deng consistently emphasized the West's indispensable role in Chinese economic modernization, and he downplayed its potential ideological threat to CCP rule. But after June 4, Deng saw the West as an implacable ideological adversary. The phrase "peaceful evolution," party shorthand for the West's plot to subvert the Chinese regime through economic and political engagement, never appeared in any of his speeches prior to June 1989. Indeed, it was seldom used in official publications. A search of China National Knowledge Infrastructure (CNKI) shows that the phrase appeared only twelve times between January 1, 1979, and April 20, 1989 (the Tiananmen protests began on April 15). But it ominously resurfaced in Deng's speech in September 1989.[27] Apparently to underscore Deng's warning, the compilers of his *Selected Works* titled a conversation between Deng and a visiting foreign leader in November 1989 "We Must Adhere to Socialism and Prevent Peaceful Evolution Towards Capitalism."[28] (The frequency of the appearance of the term "peaceful evolution" rose dramatically after June 4. A search of this phrase on CNKI shows that it appeared 2,889 times in official journals between June 5, 1989, and December 1, 1999.)

If anything, by late 1989, as the Soviet bloc was teetering on a complete meltdown, Deng had grounds to suspect that China would be the next target of the NCW. Indeed, he openly sounded the warning of an NCW shortly after the fall of the Berlin War in November 1989: "It seems that one Cold War has come to an end," Deng warned, "but that two others have already begun: One is being waged against all countries of the South and the Third World, and the other against socialism. The Western countries . . . want to bring about the peaceful evolution of the socialist countries."[29]

However, despite his dim view of the West's intentions and the danger of "peaceful evolution," Deng remained convinced that a major new war was unlikely and believed that China needed to gain as much time as possible to make itself stronger. To be sure, he saw the post–Cold War international order, centering on American unipolarity ("hegemonism and great power politics" in Chinese official rhetoric), as fundamentally unjust, hence something that had to be changed. But he was also realistic enough to know that China lacked the power to make such a change happen, and any attempt to do so would be against Chinese interests.[30]

In a series of speeches to top party leaders between late 1989 and the end of 1990, Deng spelled out the core tenets of a new grand strategy for the post–Cold War era. China's long-term strategic mission and objective would include "opposing hegemonism and power politics" and "working to establish a new international political order and a new international economic order."[31] At the same time, despite the upheaval in some socialist countries, Deng still saw the possibility of China doubling its GNP in real terms for the second time, according to plan.[32] In September 1989 he coined three phrases, consisting of twelve Chinese characters that would become the guiding principle of Chinese foreign policy in the post-Tiananmen era. Translated as "Observe the situation coolly, hold our ground, and act calmly," this policy was cautious, reactive, and centered on self-preservation. In December 1990 Deng added another element: "Make a contribution."[33]

Deng was making it crystal clear that the goal of this risk-averse foreign policy was to gain time to build up strength, as summarized by the phrase *taoguang yanhui* (hiding your brightness and building up strength), which Deng invoked in April 1992. The aging leader, who had just returned from his history-bending southern tour, told his staff, "We will become a more significant political power if only we *taoguang yanhui* for a few years. The weight of China's voice on the global stage will be different."[34] A consummate realist, Deng knew that a successful strategy of *taoguang yanhui* would nevertheless instill anxiety about Chinese power in the West. The best response Deng prescribed was not open confrontation but rather maintaining cooperation, accompanied, at the same time, by vigilance. Despite the West's suspicions or nefarious design for China, Deng urged his successors to avoid conflict. "We should keep them as friends but also have a clear understanding of what they are doing."[35]

Although Deng presciently laid out the core principles of a foreign policy for the post–Cold War era two years prior to the fall of the Soviet Union, the formal dissolution of the world's erstwhile superpower on December 25, 1991, nevertheless demoralized and worried the Chinese leadership. Ideologically, the fall of the first Communist state, which had inspired the CCP, was yet another confirmation, after the collapse of the Soviet satellites in Eastern Europe in late 1989, that communism had been a complete failure. Geopolitically, China's position drastically worsened overnight. The favorable external environment of the 1980s became history. Conflict over security issues that had largely been frozen but not resolved, such as the status and future of Taiwan and Chinese territorial and maritime disputes with its neighbors, would become far more prominent and, like human rights issues, constitute a major source of tensions between China and the United States in the post–Cold War decades. As its capabilities grew, China's long-term intentions would soon become a top concern of both the United States and its allies. Deng's premonitions about the dynamic of a classical security dilemma would come true, albeit probably later than he had expected. Growing Chinese power did raise the specter of the rise of another Communist behemoth when America's neocons gained power in the administration of George W. Bush in 2001, but their strategic blunder of invading Iraq in 2003 would give China fifteen more years—until Donald Trump launched the 2018 trade war that formally ended the era of engagement between China and the United States.

It is not an exaggeration to say that the seeds of the NCW between China and the West that had been sown even before the Cold War was completely over. Given the ideological chasm and clashing visions of the international order, Deng had made it clear that China would never give up its autonomy as a "socialist country" in international affairs. Speaking to several leading members of the Central Committee shortly after the Tiananmen crackdown, Deng vowed: "The Western imperialists are trying to make all socialist countries abandon the socialist road, to bring them in the end under the rule of international monopoly capital. . . . We have to take a clear-cut stand against this adverse current. Because if we did not uphold socialism we would eventually become, at best, a dependency of other countries."[36] Deng might not have been aware of his tone at the time, but he was sounding a lot more like Chen Yun. More seriously, Deng's pledge that China would never become part of the West-dominated international system foreshadowed not only future Chinese leaders' resistance to full integration as encouraged by the West through engagement but also the likely clash with this order after China gains sufficient power.

Biding Time and Building Strength

Deng may have laid down the broad foreign policy principles for his successors, but translating them into policy was still a challenge in a unipolar world. With a GDP that was about 7.5 percent that of the United States in dollar terms (1992), China was a much weaker power, and it was highly vulnerable to hostile American actions.[37] Geopolitically, the "China card" was no longer valuable.[38] Ideologically, America's view of China darkened following the Tiananmen crackdown. Bilateral conflict over human rights became a major source of tensions in the 1990s. When Bill Clinton was running for the White House in 1992, he accused his opponent, then-president George H. W. Bush, of "coddling with dictators," and he later pledged to link China's MFN trade status to its human rights record (a policy he had to reverse in 1994).[39]

Most ominously for the post-Deng leadership, powerful groups in the United States, encompassing labor and human rights advocates on the left and national security hawks and the religious right at the other end of the ideological spectrum, all viewed China as an enemy that had to be confronted before it grew too powerful.[40] Influential media figures as well as some academics eloquently made the case for containing China. A common thread ran through their warnings about China: The United States and China have irreconcilable ideological differences and clashing geopolitical interests, and should China gain enough power, conflict between the two countries will become inevitable.[41]

Such calls for a preemptive containment strategy may seem prescient in hindsight, but they did not become American policy in the 1990s, most likely because there was no broad-based support for an offensive policy against a country whose rapid rise was hardly guaranteed. Indeed, few in Washington, or in China itself, foresaw the supercharged growth of Chinese power in the subsequent two decades that would turn Beijing into a near-peer rival. Those advocating an alternative strategy could also muster powerful counterarguments. Among other things, critics of a preemptive containment strategy pointed to the near certainty of an otherwise avoidable dangerous clash between the United States and China, the lack of support from allies in the event of such a conflict, and the weakness of Chinese power and an exaggeration of its threat to American interests in East Asia.[42] The framework of such an alternative strategy has since been given various labels, such as "conditional engagement" or "strategic hedging." Its essence is a finely balanced strategy mixing deterrence and engagement. Specifically, instead of hard containment, Washington would place greater emphasis on economic and diplomatic engagement with Beijing through expansion of trade and investment and high-level exchanges. However, to hedge against potential Chinese threats to American interests in East Asia, the United States would maintain and strengthen its alliance networks, continue forward military deployment, and impose restrictions on transfers of advanced technologies (such as semiconductors) to China.[43] The evolution of this strategy took some time and did not garner sufficient political support in Washington until bilateral relations were stabilized with Jiang Zemin's 1997 state visit to the United States.[44]

To the post-Deng leaders, America's "strategic hedging" was preferable to full-fledged containment. But at the same time, they were not blind to its components that smacked of "containment." In a foreign policy speech in 1993, Jiang Zemin laid out the dilemma China faced in dealing with the United States. On the one hand, he pointed out that "peaceful evolution" remained the long-term goal of "some Americans" who did not want to see a stronger reunified China and would continue to pressure China on human rights, trade, and Taiwan. On the other hand, the United States was the world's most powerful country, an important export market, and a source of capital and technology for China. The best strategy was to be "both combative and conciliatory, . . . improving relations between China and the U.S. . . . to put our relations on a more stable course."[45]

Even after Sino-American relations had fully stabilized in 1998 after a rocky period, Jiang made a similar warning in a speech. He said there are people in America whose "underlying goal is . . . to change China's socialist system and eventually incorporate China into the Western capitalist system. This is a long and complex struggle."[46] In the face of this challenge, the best counterstrategy was "to use a two-pronged approach against their two-sided policy." America's "two sides" here obviously refer to engagement (one side) and containment (the other side). China's counterstrategy in response, according to Jiang, was both to "cooperate" (one side) and "confront" (the other side) by "adhering to principles without losing flexibility."[47]

To be sure, this pragmatic strategy was designed to avoid a frontal collision from a position of structural vulnerability with the world's sole superpower in the post–Cold War era. By the 1990s, China had grown significantly dependent on access to the US market and American technologies, and a sudden rupture of ties with the United States could derail economic modernization.[48] However difficult it might have been for Jiang and his colleagues to endure what they saw as bullying acts of "American hegemonism," the harsh reality of a lopsided balance of power unfavorable to China counseled prudence and patience.[49] In the same speech, Jiang made it clear that Beijing desired a multipolar world and a new "just and equitable new international political and economic order."[50] It was a refrain that Chinese leaders would invoke repeatedly, even at the risk of antagonizing the United States, the architect and primary defender of the order that China viewed as unjust and unreasonable. Nevertheless, Jiang emphasized that China had to act with calm and avoid taking the lead to confront the United States and its allies. Repeating Deng's dictum of *taoguang yanhui*, he added three additional strategic principles: *shoulian fengmang* (exercise restraint), *baocun ziji* (preserve ourselves), and *xutu fazhan* (develop gradually).[51] In essence, Jiang was prescribing Deng's strategy of buying time and avoiding conflict to cope with American dominance in the post–Cold War era.

Reorienting Security Strategy

In the 1980s Deng's assessment that a great power war was unlikely led to a cut of one million PLA soldiers and the starving of the military of funding and investments. But the party's prioritization of butter over guns created its own problems, such as corruption in the military as the PLA was allowed to operate for-profit businesses to generate off-the-books income (a practice the party ended in 1998).[52] In the 1990s China also began to implement a sustained program of modernizing its outdated military. The impetus was not a sudden change in its assessment of the likelihood of a world war. In fact, during his tenure in office, Jiang Zemin consistently maintained that the external environment was favorable and a new world war was unlikely.[53] Instead, the initial direct trigger for Chinese military modernization in the post–Cold War era was the awesome demonstration of America's high-tech military during the first Gulf War of 1990–1991, when a US-led coalition routed the Iraqi army. Jiang personally attended three seminars on the Gulf War in June 1991, and thereafter he gave a series of speeches on military strategy and technology that underscored the need to increase defense "appropriately" and to develop indigenous defense technologies.[54] After intense deliberations, the Central Military Commission formulated a new defense doctrine in 1993 that emphasized "winning local wars under modern technological conditions."[55] Implementation of this doctrine would drive military modernization during the following two decades.

The task of building a high-tech military force gained greater urgency after the ascendance of pro-independence political forces in Taiwan in the mid-1990s. Chinese leaders realized that they required credible military options to deter both Taiwanese independence and potential American military intervention. Starting in the mid-1990s, China's military modernization program focused largely on possible Taiwan contingencies, thus unleashing the dynamics of an escalating security dilemma with the United States and its East Asian ally, Japan, in the subsequent two decades.[56]

Based on official data, defense spending began its sustained rise in 1991 (see table 8.1). In nominal terms, China's military budget quadrupled between 1990 and 2000, or doubled after adjusting for inflation.[57] Buoyed by the fast-growing economy, China accelerated investments in its military capabilities in the 2000s, with defense spending in real terms rising at an average of 12.5 percent per annum, significantly higher than the 7.8 percent per annum in the 1990s.[58] By 2012, China's defense budget would reach $157 billion, second only to America's $684 billion.[59] Whether official data truly reflect China's defense budget is hotly debated. Highly reputable research organizations and scholars have arrived at different estimates, most of which are higher than the official Chinese data.[60] What is not in dispute, however, is that within two decades, Chinese military modernization achieved a level of progress few had anticipated. By the end of the post-Tiananmen era, the PLA had been transformed

TABLE 8.1. Official Defense Budget, 1990–2000

Year	Amount (billion yuan)
1990	29.0
1991	33.0
1992	37.8
1993	42.6
1994	55.1
1995	63.7
1996	72.0
1997	81.4
1998	93.5
1999	107.6
2000	120.8

Source: ZGTJNJ 2004, 293.

into a technologically advanced fighting force due to imports of advanced Russian weapons systems, such as Sukhoi jetfighters, *Sovremennyy*-class destroyers, supersonic antiship missiles, and indigenously produced high-tech weapons. As China's focus was on developing anti-access/area denial (A2/AD) capabilities to deter potential US intervention in a war with Taiwan, improvements in the Chinese navy and air force were especially rapid and significant.[61]

Accompanying military modernization was a comprehensive reorientation of China's security and foreign policies to improve relations with its neighbors, in particular Russia and the Southeast Asian countries. As Chinese leaders reevaluated potential security threats, it became obvious that maritime threats, mainly Taiwan-related contingencies, had supplanted any danger of a land invasion from the former Soviet Union during the Cold War.[62] Accordingly, China took dramatic steps to elevate ties with Russia in the immediate wake of the Cold War. The two countries reached an agreement on their eastern border in 1991 and a similar agreement on their western border three years later. In 1996 Jiang Zemin and President Boris Yeltsin announced establishment of a "strategic partnership." Bilateral defense cooperation greatly expanded the transfer of advanced weapons to China. Although the Sino-Russian "strategic partnership" at that time had serious limits, it vastly improved China's security situation in the north, allowing it to focus on its east and south maritime flanks.[63] Beijing and Moscow would upgrade their defense cooperation in 2001 when, based on a Chinese initiative, they became the main sponsors of the Shanghai Cooperation Organization (SCO), which initially consisted of China, Russia, Kazakhstan, Kyrgyzstan, and Tajikistan but would later grow to include also India, Iran, Pakistan, and Uzbekistan, turning it into a regional multilateral security forum.[64]

China made significant strides in Southeast Asia as well. In 1991 China normalized relations with Vietnam, which it had invaded in 1979. The two countries also signed an agreement demarcating their land borders in 1999. Throughout the 1990s, Beijing launched a charm offensive to reassure the Southeast Asian nations of its benign intentions. Its activities included more frequent visits to the region by top Chinese leaders and expansion of trade and cultural exchanges. Although China's seizure of the disputed Mischief Reef in 1995 momentarily damaged Beijing's credibility, its subsequent restraint calmed tensions. During the Asian financial crisis of 1997–1998, China raised its standing considerably in Southeast Asia by coming to the aid of Thailand, one of the hardest-hit countries, while Washington chose to take a pass.[65]

Elsewhere in Asia, Chinese progress was more mixed. Relations with India warmed with exchange of visits by top leaders and a steady increase in trade, but negotiations over their long-disputed border made little progress and their geopolitical rivalries continued, albeit in a more subdued form.[66] In Northeast Asia, China's greatest gain was the rapid development of ties with South Korea, with which China had established diplomatic relations in 1992. But ties with Japan deteriorated further in the 1990s as the result of disputes over sovereignty of the Senkaku/Diaoyu Islands (an issue Chinese leaders had wisely shelved in the 1980s), history, Chinese military modernization, and Taiwan.[67]

Confronting the Taiwan Challenge

Except for the US-China dispute over arms sales, Taiwan did not present much of a foreign policy challenge to the mainland in the 1980s. Militarily, China lacked the capabilities to reunify with the island, to which the Nationalists (Kuomintang, KMT) retreated after losing the civil war to the Communists in 1949. Deng's top priority—economic modernization in a peaceful external environment—relegated reunification to the back burner. The government of the Republic of China (Taiwan's official name), then dominated by KMT elders, was not seeking de jure independence even as it began to liberalize the island's political system and open the door to political forces with a strong Taiwanese identity. Above all, stable and cooperative Sino-American relations throughout the decade bolstered mutual trust and restraint.

All this would change in the post–Cold War era. To be sure, relations between the mainland and Taiwan initially appeared to be headed for a breakthrough. In 1992 the PRC and ROC reached a critical formula, the so-called 92 Consensus, that basically papered over their differences over the definition of "one China." The 92 Consensus allowed each side to interpret or define its own meaning of one China while ostensibly accepting the concept of "one China."[68] As China insisted on acceptance of its "one-China principle" as a precondition for dialogue across the Taiwan Strait, the 92 Consensus allowed Beijing and Taipei to explore a new modus vivendi despite the vast gulf existing between them. By the early 1990s, the mainland had also become an important trading partner and investment destination for Taiwan business. Taiwan's direct investments in China totaled $3.9 billion by 1994 and two-way trade in goods reached $16.3 billion, with Taiwan recording a large surplus of nearly $12 billion.[69]

In spite of their growing commercial ties, however, cross-strait relations would undergo a radical change beginning in 1995. As the democratization process accelerated on the island of Taiwan in the late 1980s, especially after establishment of Taiwan's Democratic Progressive Party (DPP), which openly advocated independence, the political landscape experienced a dramatic transformation. Lee Teng-hui, the first native Taiwanese to hold the presidency of the ROC, who had assumed office after Chiang Ching-kuo died in January 1988, initially displayed an openness to dialogue with Beijing, as evidenced by the 92 Consensus. But Lee's mainland policy took a 180-degree turn in 1995 when he became a champion of Taiwanese sovereignty and identity—a change that not only prompted Beijing to label him a separatist but also led to a series of crises in cross-strait relations.

The first crisis, now called the "Third Taiwan Strait Crisis," began when Taiwan supporters in the United States successfully pressured the administration of Bill Clinton to issue an unprecedented visa to President Lee so he could travel to the United States and deliver the alumni reunion speech at his alma mater, Cornell University. In his speech, titled "Always in My Heart," Lee made remarks that mainland Chinese leaders saw as an open challenge to Beijing. In response, Beijing ordered the PLA to conduct a series of military exercises in the summer of 1995 that would culminate in the largest military drill in the Taiwan Strait in March 1996, around the time of the first popular presidential election held on the island that delivered to Lee a landslide victory. China's military intimidation against Taiwan, which included firing missiles close to the island, prompted US intervention. Clinton dispatched two carrier battle groups to the waters around Taiwan. Although the crisis ended without incident, this would be a powerful motivator for China to accelerate its military modernization and acquire capabilities to deal with future Taiwan-related contingencies.[70]

But the 1995–1996 crisis was merely the beginning of more than a decade of escalating tensions. Lee continued to contest Beijing's claim of sovereignty over Taiwan. In July 1999 he publicly redefined the nature of cross-strait relations as "special state-to-state" relations, directly challenging Beijing's "one-China principle." Fortunately, even though Lee's rhetoric of "state-to-state" relations nearly touched China's red line, he did not take any legal action, such as amending the constitution or changing the national flag, to formalize his "two-state theory." China reacted angrily and issued threats, but it took no military actions, most likely because it did not want to derail its negotiations with the United States on WTO entry or precipitate a new confrontation with Washington right after the accidental NATO bombing of the Chinese Embassy in Belgrade in May of that year.

Tensions with Taiwan persisted after the election of Chen Shui-bian of the DPP as president in 2000. The rise of the DPP represented a sea change in Taiwan's political landscape, brought about by the island's transition to democracy and growth of a distinct Taiwanese identity separate from that of China. Fortunately for China, US-China relations stabilized after 9/11. As a result, the Chen government did not move further than Lee had in redefining cross-strait relations—except for an unsuccessful attempt to pass a referendum on Taiwan's self-defense and dialogue with the mainland (Chen had to water down the language due to American pressure).[71] Although cross-strait relations stabilized after the KMT recaptured the presidency in 2008, the island's status and future would become a central point of contention between China and the United States. Even prior to the Xi Jinping era, as the rise of Taiwanese identity greatly dimmed prospects of peaceful reunification, Chinese leaders grew increasingly aware that only strong military capabilities could deter Taiwan and its foreign (mainly American) supporters from "acting rashly," as described by Jiang Zemin in summarizing the accomplishments of the PLA in the 1990s.[72] With Taiwan assuming China's foremost national security priority and driving its military modernization program, the dynamics for exacerbating the US-China security dilemma ensued. The capabilities China was seeking to make its military options more credible would also erode America's unstated but nevertheless clear deterrence against this very option, thus triggering countermeasures. If the United States did not have to seriously worry about China's military strength in the early 1990s, this was no longer the case by the end of the post-Tiananmen era.

Embracing Globalization

A novel challenge that Deng did not anticipate but that Jiang Zemin had to confront was globalization—the rapid expansion of trade and investment flows across borders unleashed by the end of the Cold War. As geopolitical barriers fell and economic reforms in China and India accelerated in the 1990s, previously closed markets opened up, and a huge pool of workers in the developing countries became available for companies searching for low-cost labor.[73] As noted by Jiang in a speech on foreign policy in 1998, for China, globalization represented both opportunities and challenges. Because the West possessed advantages in capital, technology, talent, finance, and nearly all other domains of globalization, it was poised to be the greatest beneficiary. According to Jiang, the developing countries, on the whole, would be disadvantaged; China could gain from globalization by acquiring more foreign capital, advanced technologies, and access to markets, even though it lacked overall economic competitiveness and it was the West that had made the rules of globalization and controlled international financial institutions. As no country could be immune from globalization, Jiang argued, China had to adapt to its trends and actively participate in international economic cooperation and competition. The overall strategic framework Jiang laid out in his 1998 speech was to be "clearly aware of the risks that economic globalization brings, maintain our independence and initiative, increase our level of vigilance, and become better able to fend off and defuse risks in order to effectively safeguard our country's economic security."[74]

This strategy to maximize the upsides of economic globalization and mitigate its risks guided China's international economic policy during the post-Tiananmen period. On the one hand, China aggressively courted international capital and technology and vigorously competed for market share in manufactured goods, leveraging the cost advantage of its immense labor force and unrivaled economies of scale. The most important step it took was to secure accession to the WTO in 2001. On the other hand, China also maintained protectionist measures and implemented an industrial policy to limit foreign competition in its domestic market and to overcome its disadvantages in more technology-intensive or emerging sectors, such as renewable energy.[75]

Judging by the colossal gains of Chinese exports, the strategy laid out by Jiang was an unqualified success. In the year before its formal accession to the WTO on December 11, 2001, China's total merchandise exports totaled $266 billion, and it had a trade surplus of $22.5 billion. In 2012, the end of the post-Tiananmen period, China was exporting $2.04 trillion in goods and reporting a trade surplus of $230 billion.[76] Paradoxically, however, the success of China's strategy of both embracing and safeguarding against globalization at the same time would damage trade ties with its Western partners, which likely did not anticipate the surge in Chinese exports after its accession to the WTO. At the same time, Chinese protectionism and industrial policies frustrated Western partners' efforts to gain access to its growing domestic markets and to compete with China on a level playing field. Although it would take two more decades for the West to start "decoupling" from China, the source of the breakdown was created by the successful, self-interested, but ultimately unsustainable strategy that Chinese leaders adopted in response to globalization.

End of Hide-and-Bide

Chinese foreign policy during the Jiang era was not without its moments of scares. In particular, Sino-American relations were severely tested by a series of crises, such as the Taiwan crisis of 1995–1996, the accidental NATO bombing of the Chinese Embassy in Belgrade in May 1999, and the midair collision of a Chinese jetfighter and a US reconnaissance plane in April 2001. Fortunately, in each case restraint and diplomacy enabled both sides to defuse tensions. If there was one pivotal moment when China's grand strategy of *taoguang yanghui* was seriously imperiled, it was the election of George W. Bush in 2000, which was accompanied by entry into the US administration of national security hawks who had grown increasingly alarmed by the sustained growth of Chinese power in the 1990s. Chinese GDP measured in US dollars had risen from 7.5 percent of US GDP in 1992 to nearly 12 percent in 2000.[77] Although the size of the Chinese economy was still a fraction of that of the American economy and smaller than the economies of Japan, Germany, and the United Kingdom, China was obviously catching up at a rapid pace. It should have come as no surprise that the Bush administration would designate China not as a "strategic partner" but as a "strategic competitor."[78] Indeed, in the early months of the Bush administration, and particularly after the plane collision in 2001, Washington adopted a hard-line China policy, especially on the most sensitive issue of Taiwan (by allowing President Chen Shui-bian, leader of Taiwan's pro-independence DPP, to make an unprecedented, high-profile "transit visit" to New York).

Had 9/11 not occurred, it is highly likely that Sino-American relations would have continued their downward spiral, precipitating the full-fledged confrontation that was to occur two decades later. But the terrorist attacks on September 11, 2001, changed the course of history. Bush's global war on terror immediately refocused America's strategic attention from China, a traditional strategic competitor, to a nonstate terrorist network, Al-Qaeda, and the war in Afghanistan that the United States launched less than a month after 9/11. Tensions between Beijing and Washington quickly subsided in the wake of 9/11. The Bush administration committed a much worse strategic blunder in March 2003 when it invaded Iraq on false pretenses, plunging the United States into a quagmire and extending China's strategic window of opportunity.[79]

When Hu Jintao took over from Jiang at the end of 2002, he inherited perhaps China's most favorable external environment of the post–Cold War era. Nevertheless, even with a distracted hegemon, Hu faced two new challenges that had not existed under Jiang. The first challenge was to counter the "China threat theory" that was gaining credence as a result of the rise of Chinese power during the Jiang period. This would require strategic reassurances through rhetoric and action. But at the same time, efforts to ease fears of China by its Asian neighbors, the United States, and its Western allies were likely made less credible by the measures China took to protect its expanding overseas interests, hence the second challenge. The new geopolitical reality, created in no small part by the very success of Deng's strategy of prioritizing domestic development and avoiding conflict with the West, meant that it would become increasingly difficult to adhere to *taoguang yanghui*. As Hu pointed out in a 2006 foreign policy speech, "the more developmental success" that China achieved, the more likely it would "encounter challenges of external resistance and risks," especially at a time when its overseas economic interests and emerging new opportunities demanded a more activist foreign policy.[80]

To assuage fears of a rising China, Hu relied mainly on a rhetorical campaign emphasizing China's peaceful intentions. The "peaceful rise" narrative, energetically promoted by one of Hu's advisers in 2003, sought to project a benign image and to dispel any fears that the growth of Chinese power would lead to conflict and war. However, judging by the lukewarm, if not skeptical, foreign reaction to the "peaceful rise" rhetoric, this initiative apparently failed. Even worse, Hu Jintao did not appear to have gained enough political support within the party for using the phrase "peaceful rise" to frame the party's strategic reassurance efforts. Officially, the party preferred "peaceful development," thus incorporating it in Hu's speeches and official documents as a standard declaration of strategic intentions. The campaign to promote the "peaceful rise" rhetoric quickly fizzled out.[81]

Hu's record in handling the second challenge was mixed. He highlighted the new strategic dilemma in a speech on foreign policy in August 2003. Unlike Jiang, who continued to reiterate Deng's dictum of *taoguang yanghui* when speaking on foreign policy, Hu highlighted the challenge of balancing *taoguang yanghui* and *yousuo zuowei* (making a contribution), a secondary guiding foreign policy principle that Deng had added in December 1990.[82] Although Hu declared that China would adhere to Deng's caution against foreign entanglements, circumstances had changed and foreign policy decisions needed to be tailored to specific circumstances.[83]

In terms of actual Chinese policy, the subtle revision of *taoguang yanghui* as revealed in Hu's speech in 2003, did not have an immediate impact. During his first term (2002–2007), Chinese foreign policy essentially followed the path laid out by Deng in 1990. This period saw marked improvement and stability in Sino-American relations. In August 2003, China sponsored the "six-party talks," including the United States, Japan, and South Korea, to seek a diplomatic solution to North Korea's development of nuclear weapons. (The talks yielded no results.) China's relations with most of its neighbors remained friendly. Ties with Europe warmed to such an extent that, in 2005, the European Union was mulling over lifting the arms embargo against China that it had imposed after the Tiananmen crackdown in 1989. (The idea was abandoned in face of fierce American opposition.)[84]

Chinese restraint during this period was likely the result of a combination of factors. Most importantly, this was because Jiang retained enormous influence through his proxies on the PSC and because Hu Jintao, in addition to his risk-averse personality, lacked foreign policy experience and political heft to "make a contribution." Tensions with Taiwan remained high because the pro-independence DPP controlled the presidency until 2008, when the more mainland friendly KMT returned to power. An assertive foreign policy would have been ill-advised when China needed all the international goodwill it could get to isolate Taiwan. Despite waging two costly wars, in Iraq and Afghanistan, and risking a long-term quagmire, there were no signs of an imminent American decline. Instead, the epic real estate bubble in the United States produced a booming economy.

But things changed dramatically after 2008. China's successful hosting of the Summer Olympics in Beijing in August of that year delivered a powerful psychological boost to the Chinese leadership and symbolically marked the arrival of China as a great power on the global stage. Even more importantly, the GFC that began the spring of 2008 and culminated in the collapse of the giant American investment bank Lehman Brothers in September of that year threatened to plunge the United States and its key European allies into the worst financial crisis since the Great Depression. Chinese leaders' confidence was further bolstered by the stellar performance of the Chinese economy after they rolled out a huge credit-fueled stimulus package at the end of 2008.

It was in this context that Hu Jintao signaled the most consequential change of direction in Chinese foreign policy in the post-Tiananmen era.[85] In a speech to Chinese ambassadors in July 2009, Hu unveiled a new foreign policy principle of *jianchi taoguang yanghui, jiji yousuo zuowei*—continuing to keep a low profile and actively making a contribution. The addition of "actively" is no mere wordplay. As Hu elaborated, it was necessary to maintain a low profile and avoid conflict as China remained a developing country despite its recent progress. However, its growing external interests, rising "comprehensive national power," and international status required that it also take greater initiatives in foreign affairs and "actively push the development of the international political and economic order in a more just and reasonable direction." However, a more active foreign policy, Hu clarified, did not mean that China would bear any global responsibilities beyond its capabilities, despite Westerners calling on Beijing to become a "responsible stakeholder," thereby implying that China would become more active only to further its national interests.[86]

Although Hu's version of foreign policy activism lacked the ambition, aggressiveness, and strategic coherence of the policy adopted by Xi Jinping after 2012, it marked the beginning of the end of Deng's strategy of "keeping a low profile." In practice, the shift was most pronounced in the expansion of Chinese external economic footprint through investment, loans, and aid, the projection of Chinese "soft power" through the establishment of Chinese language schools (the Confucius Institutes) and media outlets tasked with improving the country's image, and confrontational tactics in asserting Chinese maritime claims in the South China Sea and over the Senkaku Islands.

Chinese foreign aid measured in concessional and nonconcessional loans averaged $7.6 billion between 2000 and 2008, but in the last four years of Hu's tenure (2009–2012), it averaged more than five times that, at $38.2 billion a year.[87] In early 2009 China established a special $7.25 billion program to expand its overseas propaganda activities. Consequently, the presence of official Chinese media organizations, such as China Central Television, Xinhua, and *Global Times*, gained much higher visibility outside of China.[88] Beijing also began to press its maritime claims more confrontationally. After a Chinese fishing crawler collided with two Japanese Coast Guard patrol boats in the waters near the disputed Senkaku/Diaoyu Islands in September 2010, Beijing chose to escalate, instead of defusing, the tensions with Tokyo. It also overreacted to Japan's plan to "nationalize" the same disputed islands (to prevent an ultra-nationalist from purchasing them), triggering the worst crisis in Sino-Japanese relations in the post-Mao period.[89] In the South China Sea, China began harassing US naval vessels that were conducting freedom of navigation operations in China-claimed waters, and, in both 2009 and 2010, it imposed a unilateral three-month moratorium on fishing in the disputed areas that were also claimed by Vietnam.[90]

Such muscle-flexing immediately alarmed some strategic analysts. In a prescient essay, initially published online in 2009, Li-tai Xue was the first to warn that China's hubris would inevitably lead to confrontation with the United States.[91] Indeed, China's newfound activism actually had a perverse effect, discrediting Beijing's pledge of "peaceful development" and pushing its worried neighbors into the arms of Washington.[92] It did not take long for the United States to seize this opportunity and begin to reassess its approach to Beijing. In November 2011 Secretary of State Hillary Clinton announced a new strategy, "Pivot to Asia," which would redirect American diplomatic, military, and economic resources to the region to counter China's growing influence.[93]

China's own pivot to "actively make a contribution," starting in Hu Jintao's second term, and America's response shortly thereafter would mark the beginning of the fraying of engagement between the two countries. To be sure, the collapse of relations would have to wait until Donald Trump and his China hawks launched their trade war in early 2018. But like the neo-authoritarian political order and the Chinese economic miracle at the end of the Hu Jintao era, the writing was clearly on the wall for a foreign policy that had served the party well—perhaps a bit too well for its own good—in the post-Tiananmen era.

A New Cold War

Xi Jinping took huge and risky steps to exploit what he deemed to be unprecedented opportunities immediately after he ascended to top leader at the end of 2012. Notably, Hu Jintao at least had attempted to strike a delicate balance between strategic caution and assertiveness. He used *taoguang yanhui* in his foreign policy speeches to underscore the importance of strategic caution. Xi, however, did not even attempt to strike this balance. Indeed, if the invocation of *taoguang yanhui* is to be used as a rhetorical marker of strategic caution, it did not appear even once in Xi's many published speeches on foreign policy.

Instead, Xi characterized his early foreign policy moves as "proactive planning, striving for progress and gains" (*zhudong mohua, nuli jinqu*), as he put it in his speech at the party work conference on foreign policy in November 2014. The backdrop of his shift toward a more proactive foreign policy was the opportunity created by favorable changes in the world, which he characterized as "a world in which the international system and the international order are undergoing profound adjustments and . . . the international balance of power is undergoing profound changes and moving in a direction favorable to peace and development."[94] Less than two years later, Xi was apparently pleased with this shift. Rephrasing it as "seizing opportunities and taking initiatives" (*zhuazhu jiyu, zhudong zuowei*), as he told the Politburo in September 2016, he cited a series of strategic initiatives, such as the Belt and Road Initiative (BRI), the Asian Infrastructure Investment Bank, and other efforts to promote "reform of unfair and unreasonable arrangements in the global governance system." These bold actions were justified because "as the relative international balance of power changes and global challenges rise, strengthening global governance and promoting reform of the system of global governance is an irresistible trend."[95]

Although the phrase "the East is rising and the West is declining" (*dongsheng xijiang*) cannot be found in any of his published speeches, Xi appeared convinced that the balance of power had evolved in favor of those countries or forces seeking a fundamental restructuring of the West-led political and economic order. He spelled out his analysis comprehensively at a January 2016 seminar for provincial leaders and ministers. Describing "unprecedented positive changes in the balance of power in the world," Xi listed the "rise of emerging markets and developing countries, the trends of multi-polarity and democratization of international relations, and emerging signs of changes in the West-led global governance system, . . . the rapid rise of China's weight in the global economy and governance, and China's entry into a more balanced period in opening to the outside world" (which implied that China no longer needed the outside world as much as it used to). However, Xi did not allow his upbeat assessment of favorable global trends to ignore the challenges and obstacles. He cautioned that "the West's economic, technological, political, and military superiorities have yet to change."[96]

In addition to his reassessment of the changing balance of power, Xi was also motivated by his ideological antipathy toward the West and his grim view of

America's security role in Asia, which China had consistently regarded as an instrument of containment. Perhaps the most explicit expression of Xi's ideological opposition to the West-led order can be found in his March 2013 speech in Moscow. "No country or group of countries can dominate world affairs single-handedly," Xi told his audience. There has been "an apparent upsurge of . . . rising hegemonism, power politics and neo-interventionism are gaining some momentum. . . . [the West] cannot live in the twenty-first century while thinking in the old fashion, lingering in the age of colonial expansion or with the zero-sum mentality of the Cold War. . . . Only the people can best tell if the development path they have chosen for their country suits or not."[97]

Like his predecessors, Xi accused unnamed "hostile forces at home and abroad" of attempting to bring about regime change in China. But he went beyond the boilerplate language of blaming the West for causing chaos through its interventionism. "Since the end of the Cold War," he said in a December 2015 speech, "some countries have been turned into a total mess because of the encouragement of Western values . . . some splintered, some engulfed in the flames of war, and some in persistent chaos. . . . If we use Western values to evaluate our development . . . the consequences are unthinkable. In the end, we either have to follow [the West] step by step or become objects of verbal abuse."[98]

While neither Jiang Zemin nor Hu Jintao made public their opposition to the role played by the United States in Asian security, Xi broke the taboo in May 2014 when he spoke at a high-profile regional security forum held in Shanghai. Without naming the United States, Xi declared, "In the final analysis, let the people of Asia run the affairs of Asia, solve the problems of Asia and uphold the security of Asia."[99] Although he did not invoke "Asia for Asians," the phrase used by Japan in the 1930s, the implicit meaning of this statement came too close for Washington's comfort.

Strategic Initiatives to Remake the World Order

Xi's assessment of favorable global trends, in particular the rapid gains in Chinese power relative to that of the United States, was not delusional thinking. The Chinese economy was growing, on average, 9 percent per year between 2009 and 2013. By comparison, US growth during the same period averaged only 1.14 percent, largely due to the lingering effects of the global financial crisis. The euro area recorded, on average, negative growth of 0.3 percent per annum, and the Japanese economy barely grew during this period.[100] What likely encouraged Xi the most was the size of the Chinese economy relative to that of the United States. When Hu told his colleagues to strike a balance between caution and activism in 2009, China's GDP was one-third that of the United States in dollar terms. By 2012, China's GDP had risen to $8.53 trillion, about half of America's $16.25 trillion. Under his watch, the gap would close further: when the US-China trade war broke out in 2018, Chinese economic output would reach $13.89 trillion, or 68 percent of America's $20.53 trillion.[101] In terms of purchasing power, China reached parity with the United States in 2016, and it surpassed the United States as the world's largest economy in 2017.[102]

Militarily, even after President Barack Obama withdrew all American forces from Iraq in 2011, the United States was still bogged down in Afghanistan. The two wars had cost Washington trillions of dollars. The Pentagon has reported that it had spent $1.7 trillion on military operations in the Middle East and Afghanistan in the two decades following 9/11.[103] Nongovernmental analysts estimate that the Afghanistan war alone drained $2.3 trillion from American coffers between 2001 and 2022.[104]

The erosion of American power not only threatened the durability of the US-led order but also encouraged its geopolitical rivals, such as Russia, to exploit those opportunities that a more disorderly world might offer. As for Xi, Russia's pivot away from the West since 2007, when Vladimir Putin delivered a bellicose speech denouncing the West at the Munich Security Conference, probably presented a historic opportunity to promote the shift from a unipolar world to a multipolar would—a goal shared by Beijing and Moscow.[105]

Although Xi's unveiling of the BRI in September 2013 is commonly regarded as one of China's most consequential steps signaling a decisive break with Deng's dictum of *taoguang yanhui*, his selection of Moscow as the destination for his first foreign trip after assuming the presidency in March 2013 probably represented an even more important change in Chinese post-Tiananmen foreign policy. As Moscow drifted farther away from the West, the forging of a close partnership with Vladimir Putin promised to instantly strengthen Xi's hand in dealing with the United States. Indeed, Xi's bet on Putin yielded quick dividends: After Russia seized Crimea and instigated a proxy war in eastern Ukraine in 2014, Moscow became firmly anchored inside Beijing's orbit, as reflected by the frequent summits, expansion of defense cooperation, and near-quadrupling of trade between 2012 and 2023.[106]

Immediately after his outreach to Putin, Xi launched a series of strategic initiatives at dizzying speed. The $1 trillion One-Belt, One-Road (later renamed the Belt and Road Initiative, or BRI) was launched in late 2013 to finance infrastructure such as ports, railways, highways, and power plants throughout the world. Although the intent, merits, and feasibility of this ambitious venture have since been hotly debated, the only uncontroversial fact about it is that the BRI represents China's most expensive effort ever to increase its global influence through economic means.[107] To establish a financing vehicle, in November 2014 Xi announced the Silk Road Fund, which was to be launched with $40 billion from Chinese state-owned financial entities.

As a direct but subtle challenge to the West-led World Bank and International Monetary Fund, China set up the Asian Infrastructure Investment Bank in 2016, a Shanghai-based new multilateral international financial institution, with China as the largest shareholder. China also embraced the idea of a new development bank, initially proposed by India at a summit of the BRICS (Brazil, Russia, India, China, and South Africa) in March 2012. This bank, named the New Development Bank and headquartered in Shanghai, was formally launched in July 2014. China and the other BRICS each held a 20 percent share of the bank, which had initial authorized capital of $100 billion.[108]

In addition to flexing China's financial muscle to promote a new multipolar global economic order, Xi began to test the boundaries of the American security order in East Asia. The first step he took was the announcement of the East China Sea Air Defense Identification Zone (ADIZ), in November 2013. Many countries, including the United States and Japan, have set up such zones, which require aircraft entering airspace within them to identify themselves and report their course and destination to air traffic control authorities. But China's new ADIZ was seen as provocative because it covers the airspace over the disputed Senkaku/Diaoyu Islands.[109]

An even more aggressive step taken by Xi was his decision to begin building large artificial islands on the reefs controlled by China in the South China Sea in December 2013. This gray zone move was designed to simultaneously accomplish several strategic objectives: By solidifying physical control of these areas contested by the Philippines and Vietnam, China hoped to strengthen its claims of sovereignty over most of the South China Sea without engaging in war. Since the Philippines and Vietnam are too weak to push back, China could also, theoretically at least, take additional gray zone steps, such as enforcing its maritime regulations on ships and aircraft transiting the waters and the airspace over the South China Sea, to assert its claims.

An implicit but equally important strategic goal is to test US credibility as defender of the security order in East Asia. Although the United States has maintained neutrality in the maritime disputes in the South China Sea, a coercive move such as building large artificial islands would directly challenge the US role as provider of security in East Asia. A confrontation with China over its artificial islands could potentially escalate into a great power conflict. But acquiescing to Chinese aggression in this instance risked undermining the region's confidence in America's resolve when challenged by a great power.[110] On the surface, it appears that it was Xi who took the strategic initiative to build the artificial islands. In all likelihood, this option must have been weighed seriously, if not approved, by the prior top leadership because the logistics for constructing these large artificial islands, such as building specialized ships for dredging and acquiring special materials, would have required years of planning and preparation. In this sense, Xi merely pulled the proverbial trigger of a loaded gun.

The fateful initiatives Xi took immediately after his rise—in combination with his turn toward neo-Stalinist rule domestically—fundamentally altered the nature of the relationship between China and the West, in particular the United States, triggering a series of reactions that would later escalate into a new cold war.[111]

How Engagement Ended in a New Cold War

The backlash against China's turn toward an assertive foreign policy that started in 2009 was initially muted. Under President Barack Obama, in response the United States began to implement its "pivot to Asia" policy centered on two pillars: strengthening military deterrence and creating a new free trade zone—the Trans-Pacific Partnership (TPP)—that would include most of China's neighbors but exclude China. Although the pace of reorienting the US defense posture toward East Asia was relatively slow, Washington's leadership of a new free trade agreement bore fruit quickly. Trade ministers from twelve countries inked the deal in October 2015.[112]

Despite warnings from seasoned observers that US-China relations were on the brink of collapse, the NCW did not formally start until the arrival of Donald Trump in the White House in January 2017.[113] Judging by the formal designation of China as a "revisionist power" seeking to "displace the United States in the Indo-Pacific region," the US "National Security Strategy" released in December 2017 signaled a fundamental shift in US policy toward China.[114] Although Trump is credited with ending America's decades-long policy of engagement with China, his initial motivation was probably not geopolitical. A trade protectionist pandering to crucial battleground state workers who blamed China for losses of manufacturing jobs, the former real estate tycoon immediately withdrew the United States from the TPP and, one year later, launched a trade war with China. Xi's retaliation led to Trump escalating that war and, in May 2019, imposing sanctions on Chinese tech companies—most important, Huawei, the national telecom champion.

US-China relations went into a free fall after the outbreak of Covid-19 in early 2020.[115] Worried about the potential damage to his reelection bid, Trump blamed—and punished—China for unleashing the deadly virus. He ordered the closure of the Chinese consulate in Houston and expelled its diplomats (China retaliated by shutting down America's consulate in Chengdu). The victory of Joe Biden in November 2020 did not end the downward spiral. If anything, the US-China cold war entered a new and more complex phase. Unlike the erratic Trump administration, Biden's foreign policy team crafted a more sophisticated containment strategy. As spelled out by the key players on Biden's national security team, the new China policy rested on four pillars: building up economic capacities at home to strengthen US competitiveness, contesting Chinese power in all domains, strengthening alliances, and establishing safeguards to avoid a calamitous conflict.[116]

To counter the United States, Xi decided to elevate China's strategic partnership with Russia in the belief that the overall geopolitical interests of Moscow and Beijing—fear and resentment of US power—were identical. But a few weeks after Xi and Putin announced their "no-limit friendship" in Beijing in early February 2022, Russia invaded its neighbor, Ukraine, launching the largest and bloodiest war on continental Europe since the end of World War II. Europe saw China as Russia's accomplice and began to adopt a more hawkish China policy, closely aligned with that of the United States.

Speaking to the delegates at the annual session of the Chinese People's Political Consultative Conference on March 6, 2023, Xi acknowledged the obvious. Although he avoided the term "cold war," he formally accused the United States of leading its allies to implement "all-round containment, encirclement, and suppression of China."[117] He did not bother to explain what had caused this NCW. It is highly unlikely that he would have attributed his own actions as a possible cause of the hostile and dangerous Sino-US confrontation—a great power conflict expected to last for decades and to make his dream of the "great rejuvenation of the Chinese nation" an unachievable goal.

Conclusion

THIS ACCOUNT of political and economic developments in post-Mao China explores the factors that likely have prevented the country from moving in the direction of becoming a more open, liberal, and democratic society. Instead, they have facilitated the revival of totalitarian rule in spite of more than four decades of sustained rapid economic development. In the 1980s the CCP leadership agreed that the Maoism that had impoverished the country, traumatized the party, and discredited the Communist ideology should be brought to an end. But the leadership was deeply divided about reforming the country's economic and political systems. Pragmatic Leninists represented by Deng Xiaoping and hardcore conservatives led by Chen Yun clashed over the direction and scope of economic reforms. Deng aggressively pushed market-oriented reforms and integration with the capitalist West because he believed that this strategy would deliver favorable economic outcomes and ensure the survival of the party and the rise of China as a great power. In contrast, Chen and his followers resisted such reforms and sought to repair and restore the command economy as a safer strategy to salvage the party. Nevertheless, despite their differences over economic policy, these two groups that dominated the elite political scene in the 1980s shared an identical objective of preserving the party's political monopoly. A third group of leaders were liberal reformers who sought both economic and political liberalization. But due to their political weakness, their success critically depended on support from Deng.

When Deng needed the liberals to advance his economic agenda, this coalition could overcome the resistance of the hard-liners and make progress in implementing market reforms. But the political reform agenda promoted by the liberals was anathema to both the pragmatic Leninists and the hardcore conservatives. Whenever the top leadership confronted the issue of political liberalization in the 1980s, Deng not only would form an ad hoc coalition with the hard-liners but also would take the lead in opposing liberalization. The combination of Deng's staunch antiliberal stance and the power of the other hard-liners thus precluded any meaningful political reform. Consequently, Maoism as a set of policies and practices might have ended, but the underlying totalitarian institutions that had made it possible and potentially revivable were preserved.

The crackdown on the prodemocracy protests in June 1989 resulted in a complete purge of the liberal reformers represented by Zhao Ziyang and their replacement by politically conservative technocrats. Although Deng's "reform and opening" appeared all but dead immediately after the crackdown, paradoxically the collapse of the Soviet Union in December 1991 enabled Deng to rally a thoroughly demoralized party behind his neo-authoritarian developmentalism as the only feasible survival strategy in a world in which liberal capitalist democracies had won a decisive victory over communism.

During the post-Tiananmen neo-authoritarian period (1992–2012), the party under the leadership of Jiang Zemin and Hu Jintao put Deng's vision into practice, largely through experimentation and adaption. With the party solidly behind the neo-authoritarian developmental consensus, Chinese leaders were able to implement more radical economic reforms, maintain domestic stability through a mix of performance legitimacy, nationalism, soft repression, and co-optation, and pursue a cautious foreign policy to stabilize ties with the West—China's most important external source of capital, demand, and technology. A fragile balance of power, produced mainly by accidental factors (the transfer of power from the revolutionary titans to relatively weak leaders in the 1990s), sustained a collective leadership. Although socioeconomic modernization produced some forces that challenged party power, such as the information revolution, social unrest, and the growing civil society, the regime had no difficulty containing these emerging threats.

But the post-Tiananmen order began to crack even before the rise of Xi Jinping. During the second half of Hu Jintao's rule (2007–2012), the economy started losing momentum. The lack of deeper reform during Hu's first term (2003–2007) resulted in a less dynamic economy. Only a massive injection of credit into the economy, which in turn inflated a colossal real estate bubble, kept the economy on track. At the same time, a succession struggle began to intensify, triggering a new round of elite conflicts that ended with the most sordid scandal in post-Mao history and installed an unknown princeling who was thought to be a "safe" choice to take over from Hu Jintao. On the foreign policy front, Chinese leaders, bolstered by the rapid change in the relative balance of power between China and the West due to the global financial crisis and America's "forever wars" in the Middle East and Afghanistan, more aggressively pursued China's global interests.

The waning of neo-authoritarian developmentalism toward the end of the Hu Jintao era should not have made the return of totalitarian rule inevitable. The regime conceivably could have muddled through in the same way as Hu had during his decade in power. But the combination of accidental and institutional factors would produce a great leap backward few had seen coming. Specifically, the choice of Xi Jinping as Hu Jintao's successor was an accident—a disastrous mistake made by those who had selected him almost certainly in full ignorance of his ambition and ruthlessness. Until he became the party chief of Shanghai in March 2007, Xi had been a plausible but not inevitable successor to Hu. His eventual selection as the party's future leader in November 2007 was the outcome of a power struggle between two unrelated factions.

But once he gained the top position in November 2012, there were few obstacles preventing him from amassing power and reinstituting totalitarianism. The rules on collective leadership that Deng had established were too weak to stop Xi. Furthermore, Xi's weaponization of anticorruption prosecution gave him terrifying leverage over any rivals daring to challenge his power. Meanwhile, well-preserved totalitarian institutions, in particular the Leninist party-state and the regime's total control of the means of violence, enabled him to reimpose tight organizational discipline on the party and to reestablish the rule of fear over society. In all likelihood, Xi might not have anticipated the ease with which he could, almost single-handedly, dismantle the post-Tiananmen order and restore personalistic rule. In retrospect, he probably underappreciates how much he owes his rise and subsequent success to Deng Xiaoping and his policies.

Limitations of Deng Xiaoping and Dengism

Our examination of party politics in the 1980s and the long-term consequences of Deng Xiaoping's policies raises questions both about Deng's political leadership and about the limitations of Deng's neo-authoritarian developmentalism. To be sure, it is unreasonable to expect Deng, a veteran of the Chinese revolution emotionally committed to the preservation of the CCP, to have acted like a liberal democrat. Additionally, Deng's personal contribution to Chinese economic modernization is beyond dispute because of his outsized role in launching "reform and opening" in 1979. But in retrospect, Deng was also a flawed leader with a distorted vision of modernization. His shortcomings as a political leader severely limited what he could achieve during the 1980s and, even more important, created conditions for a reversal of many of the policies he had crafted to achieve economic modernization.

Ideologically, Deng's visceral hostility to liberal democracy unavoidably undercut his effectiveness in pushing through his economic reform agenda and led to the purge of those liberal leaders who had been indispensable to the success of his reforms. After he dismissed Hu Yaobang in January 1987, Deng was unable to restore the momentum of his economic reforms. His decision to order the military to crush the prodemocracy protests in June 1989 and his purge of Zhao Ziyang, the liberal party chief who had been instrumental in launching Deng's economic reform agenda, not only tarnished his own personal legacy but also deprived him of the only remaining partner at the top of the regime who could have helped advance his "reform and opening." In fact, Deng's modernization project was all but dead in the immediate aftermath of the Tiananmen crackdown in June 1989. But he managed to breathe new life into it after the fall of the Soviet Union in December 1991 so shocked and demoralized the hard-liners that they reluctantly rallied behind his neo-authoritarian survival strategy.

Deng's neo-authoritarian developmentalism—unreserved embrace of capitalism and globalization as a means of economic modernization under one-party rule—initially achieved spectacular results in the post-Tiananmen era. But over time, the flaws in this strategy became visible. The logic of the partial reform trap reduced the incentives for the post-Deng leadership to adopt more politically difficult economic reforms, while the hybrid economy bred voracious crony capitalism and fueled rising social tensions.

The pervasive corruption and the stalled reforms created favorable conditions for the return of a strongman leader who could capitalize on both popular dissatisfaction and the festering rot within the regime to reestablish political dominance. Had Deng erected solid institutional and political guardrails in the 1980s to prevent the future return of a Mao-like figure, Xi Jinping likely would have encountered greater obstacles in his attempts to restore totalitarianism.

The truth is that the steps Deng took in the 1980s were only partial and, in the end, ineffective in enforcing the party's own rules against lifetime tenure, the concentration of power in one man, and the revival of a personality cult. Technically, the rules on term limits, collective leadership, and a personality cult that Deng had stipulated in the early 1980s were vague and unenforceable. Due to his antipathy toward democracy, he did not allow any political forces to exist outside the party, thus making the party (specifically its top leaders) the sole enforcer of its rules. When power was evenly distributed among the top leaders and their factions, as it had been between 1992 and 2012, these rules could be enforced. But when this fragile balance of power disappeared after the rise of Xi in late 2012, the edifice of collective leadership collapsed like a house of cards.

Given the systematic reversal of Deng's foreign and domestic policies under Xi's rule, it is tempting to conclude that Xi's regime represents a fundamental break with Deng's regime. This assessment is true when it comes to the differences in tactics and the key strategic assumptions (such as the main source of threats to the party's survival and the balance of geopolitical power). Xi, a dogmatic Leninist, is the opposite of Deng, who was a pragmatic Leninist. But if we look at what these two leaders have in common, perhaps we will find that the discontinuities are superficial and the continuities between the two are fundamental. Both are hardcore Leninists who regard preservation of the party's monopoly of power as the overriding objective of their rule. They achieved this objective regardless of the costs: Deng would order a brutal suppression of the peaceful protests and would purge the leaders who did the most to help him launch his "reform and opening," while Xi would resort to totalitarian practices to neutralize all threats, real or imagined, to party rule. Both have a strong ideological antipathy to liberal democracy; both believe that only hard power can protect China from Western domination; both see the liberal West as an existential threat to one-party rule; and both regard the US-led international order as illegitimate and unjust. The answer to why Xi would adopt policies and tactics that Deng almost certainly would not have approved must be sought in their respective calculations of Chinese power and the costs of a given course of action. Deng had a far more realistic and astute assessment of Chinese power and a better understanding of the costs of his policies. In contrast, Xi has demonstrated a tendency to overestimate Chinese power and to underestimate the costs of his policies.

An Inevitable New Cold War?

The NCW between China and the United States that began toward the end of the 2010s and escalated after Russia's invasion of Ukraine in 2022 has plunged the world into another dark era of great power confrontation and has resurrected the specter of war between nuclear-armed adversaries. Future historians will undoubtedly debate the causes of the NCW. Our account of China's political and economic developments in the post-Mao era reaches a more nuanced conclusion regarding whether the NCW was inevitable. On the one hand, the odds of integrating China into a West-led international order were evidently poor because Chinese leaders themselves consistently viewed this order as illegitimate and unjust. The nature of the one-party regime also meant that it would be nearly impossible to fully integrate a CCP-ruled China into the West-dominated international order due to the ideological incompatibility between autocracy and democracy. Finally, the enormous power China had acquired in the post-Mao era thoroughly disrupted the military balance, commerce, and international governance. Even if China were a democracy, it would likely pursue self-interested policies that conflict with those of the West on many issues, as we have seen in the cases of India, Brazil, and South Africa.

Although the rise of China as a superpower would almost certainly result in unprecedented geopolitical and economic disruptions, it would be an exaggeration to say that China's arrival as the world's new superpower would trigger a NCW. Human agency—specifically individual leaders and their policies—also played a critical role in starting the NCW. Most crucially, Xi Jinping's aggressive foreign policy made the West's engagement with China untenable. Had a different Chinese leader succeeded Hu Jintao, the country's foreign policy might have continued to be assertive, but it unlikely would have been as reckless, risky, and confrontational as the foreign policy adopted by Xi during his first term. On the side of the West, the rise of America's far-right populist leader Donald Trump and the trade war he launched also helped set off a new cold war. Had Hillary Clinton won the US presidential election in 2016, Washington would almost certainly have adopted a tougher China policy, but a precipitous descent into an NCW would have been much less likely as her administration would most probably have pursued a more incremental policy of strategic competition, leaving room for de-escalation and compromise. Furthermore, Trump's escalation of confrontation with China in 2020 after the outbreak of the Covid-19 pandemic created a new political reality and virtually eliminated any possibility of building a new foundation for US-China relations to reverse the course of a new cold war.

The End of the China Dream

Immediately after he became CCP chief in November 2012, Xi Jinping revived the decade-old party slogan "the great rejuvenation of the Chinese nation" and relabeled it as the "China dream." Although he has frequently invoked the "China dream" in his speeches, he has never precisely defined its meaning.[1]

Judging by his post-2012 policies to realize his vision, it is reasonable to conclude that Xi's dream is to turn a CCP-led China into a global superpower on an equal footing with the United States. His record in fulfilling this dream after more than a decade in power, however, shows that he is failing more than he is succeeding. Despite his political ruthlessness and his success in amassing power and making himself the most powerful ruler since Mao Zedong, Xi's policies have put his "China dream" into serious long-term jeopardy. At home, he has all but ensured a destabilizing succession struggle after he departs from the political scene. His personalistic rule has made policymaking both overcentralized and prone to costly errors (as revealed most prominently in the case of his zero-Covid policy in 2022). The revival of the permanent purge is terrorizing the party and most likely traumatizing and alienating those elites who do not have any direct personal connections to Xi or to his faction. Similarly, his crackdown on the private sector has estranged and disillusioned China's private entrepreneurs, the group the party had previously courted. Economically, stagnation looms on the horizon. With the bursting of the real estate bubble, the record-high debt burden, and the demographic catastrophe for which the CCP's "one-child policy" is largely responsible, in the foreseeable future the Chinese economy will be struggling to regain its former dynamism. The decoupling of trade and investment from the West, a process initiated by the United States but later reinforced by Xi's agenda of securitizing the Chinese economy, will significantly hurt China's economic development as the country loses access to Western markets, capital, and advanced technology. Geopolitically, the NCW has sparked an open-ended and dangerous confrontation between China and the United States, endangering not only China's national security but also the CCP's own survival.

Few should lament that Xi's version of a "China dream" will not be fulfilled. The tragedy brought about by the return to totalitarian rule and the outbreak of the new cold war under his rule is that the real China dream—an economically prosperous and politically liberal and open China—will be beyond the reach of its people for at least another generation.

ACKNOWLEDGMENTS

THE BROKEN China Dream is a brief account of political and economic developments in post-Mao China. It is also a compressed intellectual journey of its author. China opened its door to the outside world when I was a college student in Shanghai. The US-China engagement that began with the normalization of relations in 1979 made it possible for me to come to the United States and study political science. My first book, *From Reform to Revolution: The Demise of Communism in China and the Soviet Union* (1994), was an optimistic assessment of Deng Xiaoping's reform. Its key theoretical assumption, based on the modernization theory, was that capitalist economic development could undermine the power of the Chinese Communist Party and create favorable conditions for a potential democratic transition. But as I gained greater intellectual maturity and a deeper understanding of the predatory nature of autocracy, I came to realize that Deng's neo-authoritarian developmentalism would be a dead end. This intellectual awakening inspired my second book, *China's Trapped Transition: The Limits of Developmental Autocracy* (2006). Published ahead of its time, this book laid out the logic of a "trapped transition," arguing that the CCP would lose incentives to pursue fundamental economic reforms and preside over a stagnating economy in the foreseeable future. My third book, *China's Crony Capitalism: The Dynamics of Regime Decay* (2016), details the pathologies of neo-authoritarian rule in the post-Tiananmen era. *The Broken China Dream* thus represents a synthesis of my research on post-Mao China over the last three decades.

I am deeply indebted to many colleagues in writing this book. Bridget Flannery-McCoy and Eric Crahan at Princeton University Press first planted the idea for this book in 2020 and provided invaluable advice and encouragement. A grant from the Smith Richardson Foundation enabled me to take a sabbatical to write the first draft in 2022–2023. I am especially grateful to the support of Marin Strmecki and Allan Song of the foundation for their enthusiasm for the project. I want to thank Hilary Appel for giving me a book subvention grant from the Keck Center for International and Strategic Studies at Claremont McKenna College. Nancy Hearst proofread and polished the manuscript with unrivaled editing skills.

Andy Walder, Guoguang Wu, and Patricia Thornton read the drafts of the book and offered helpful guidance. I also benefited from the constructive comments of two anonymous readers. Celine Wang, my able and diligent research assistant, deserves the credit for checking and standardizing the notes.

This book is dedicated to Larry Diamond, a dear friend and generous mentor who has been a source of intellectual inspiration for more than three decades.

NOTES

Introduction

1. Agnes Chang et al., "What Happened to Hu Jintao," *New York Times*, October 27, 2022, https://www.nytimes.com/interactive/2022/10/27/world/asia/hu-jintao-congress-videos.html.

2. Zhong Yuhao, "中纪委公布十八大以来被查的中央委员、中央候补委员人数" [The Central Commission for Discipline Inspection announces the number of Central Committee members and alternate members who have been investigated since the Eighteenth National Party Congress], *The Paper*, October 17, 2022, https://m.thepaper.cn/newsDetail_forward_20332452.

3. Calculated from data in the *Statistical Yearbook of China 2013* (Beijing: Zhongguo tongji chubanshe, 2014), https://www.stats.gov.cn/sj/ndsj/.

4. World Bank, "GDP per Capita, PPP (current international $)—China," https://data.worldbank.org/indicator/NY.GDP.PCAP.PP.CD?locations=CN.

5. *Statistical Yearbook of China 2013*.

6. *Statistical Yearbook of China 1995* (Beijing: Zhongguo tongji chubanshe, 1996), 588; *Statistical Yearbook of China 2013*.

7. Calculated from *Statistical Yearbook of China 2013*; *Statistical Yearbook of China 1995*, 537.

8. Seymour Martin Lipset, "Some Social Requisites of Democracy: Economic Development and Political Legitimacy," *American Political Science Review* 53, no. 1 (1959): 69–105; Robert A. Dahl, *Polyarchy: Participation and Opposition* (New Haven, CT: Yale University Press, 1971).

9. Barbara Geddes, "What Causes Democratization," in *The Oxford Handbook of Political Science*, ed. Robert Goodin (New York: Oxford University Press, 2013), 593–615.

10. Guillermo O'Donnell and Philippe C. Schmitter, *Transitions from Authoritarian Rule: Tentative Conclusions About Uncertain Democracies* (Baltimore: Johns Hopkins University Press, 1986); Samuel P. Huntington, *The Third Wave: Democratization in the Late Twentieth Century* (Norman: University of Oklahoma Press, 1991); Stephan Haggard and Robert R. Kaufman, *Dictators and Democrats: Masses, Elites, and Regime Change* (Princeton, NJ: Princeton University Press, 2016), 142–72.

11. Adam Przeworski and Fernando Limongi, "Modernization: Theories and Facts," *World Politics* 49, no. 2 (1997): 155–83.

12. 邓小平 [Deng Xiaoping], "坚持四项基本原则" [Maintain the four cardinal principles], in 邓小平文选第二卷 [Selected works of Deng Xiaoping, vol. 2] (Beijing: People's Press, 1994), 164–65.

13. Wu Guoguang, 趙紫陽與政治改革 [Zhao Ziyang and political reform] (Hong Kong: Taipingyang shiji yanjiusuo, 1997).

14. Bruce J. Dickson, *The Dictator's Dilemma: The Chinese Communist Party's Strategy for Survival* (New York: Oxford University Press, 2016); David L. Shambaugh, *China's Communist*

Party: Atrophy and Adaptation (Berkeley: University of California Press, and Washington, DC: Woodrow Wilson Center Press, 2008); Dimitar D. Gueorguiev, *Retrofitting Leninism: Participation Without Democracy in China* (New York: Oxford University Press, 2021).

15. Suisheng Zhao, *A Nation-State by Construction: Dynamics of Modern Chinese Nationalism* (Stanford, CA: Stanford University Press, 2004); Zheng Wang, *Never Forget National Humiliation: Historical Memory in Chinese Politics and Foreign Relations* (New York: Columbia University Press, 2012).

16. Jie Chen and Bruce J. Dickson, *Allies of the State: China's Private Entrepreneurs and Democratic Change* (Cambridge, MA: Harvard University Press, 2010).

17. Yuhua Wang and Carl Minzner, "The Rise of the Chinese Security State," *China Quarterly*, no. 222 (2015): 339–59; Minxin Pei, *The Sentinel State: Surveillance and the Survival of Dictatorship in China* (Cambridge, MA: Harvard University Press, 2024).

18. Carl Friedrich and Zbigniew Brzezinski, "The General Characteristics of Totalitarian Dictatorship," in *Comparative Government: A Reader*, ed. Jean Blondel (London: Macmillan Education, 1969), 187–99; Juan J. Linz, *Totalitarian and Authoritarian Regimes* (Boulder, CO: Lynne Rienner, 2000).

19. Ivo Banac, ed., *Eastern Europe in Revolution* (Ithaca, NY: Cornell University Press, 1992); Archie Brown, *The Rise and Fall of Communism* (New York: Ecco, 2011).

20. Vladislav M. Zubok, *Collapse: The Fall of the Soviet Union* (New Haven, CT: Yale University Press, 2021); Michael A. McFaul, *Russia's Unfinished Revolution: Political Change from Gorbachev to Putin* (Ithaca, NY: Cornell University Press, 2002).

21. Martin K. Dimitrov, ed. *Why Communism Did Not Collapse: Understanding Authoritarian Regime Resilience in Asia and Europe* (New York: Cambridge University Press, 2013).

22. Jeffrey Sachs and Wing Thye Woo, "Structural Factors in the Economic Reforms of China, Eastern Europe, and the Former Soviet Union," *Economic Policy* 9, no. 18 (1994): 101–45.

23. Yingyi Qian and Chenggang Xu, "The M-Form Hierarchy and China's Economic Reform," *European Economic Review* 37, no. 2–3 (1993): 541–48; Xueguang Zhou, *The Logic of Governance in China: An Organizational Approach* (New York: Cambridge University Press, 2022).

24. Xin Yuan and Yuan Gao, "Demographic Transition and Economic Miracles in China: An Analysis Based on Demographic Perspective," *International Journal of Economic Policy Studies* 14, no. 1 (2020): 25–45.

25. Ezra F. Vogel, *The Four Little Dragons: The Spread of Industrialization in East Asia* (Cambridge, MA: Harvard University Press, 1991).

26. Andrew G. Walder, "Bending the Arc of Chinese History: The Cultural Revolution's Paradoxical Legacy," *China Quarterly*, no. 227 (2016): 613–31.

27. Steven Levitsky and Lucan Way, *Revolution and Dictatorship: The Violent Origins of Durable Authoritarianism* (Princeton, NJ: Princeton University Press, 2022).

28. Adam Tooze, *The Wages of Destruction: The Making and Breaking of the Nazi Economy* (New York: Penguin, 2008); Carl J. Friedrich and Zbigniew K. Brzezinski, *Totalitarian Dictatorship and Autocracy* (Cambridge, MA: Harvard University Press, 1956).

29. Timothy Brook and B. Michael Frolic, eds., *Civil Society in China* (London: Routledge, 2015).

30. Mancur Olson, "Dictatorship, Democracy, and Development," *American Political Science Review* 87, no. 3 (1993): 567–76; Daron Acemoglu et al., "Institutions as the Fundamental Cause of Long-Run Growth," in *Handbook of Economic Growth: Volume 1A*, ed. Steven N. Durlauf and Philippe Aghion (Elsevier, 2005), 385–472.

31. Joel S. Hellman, "Winners Take All: The Politics of Partial Reform in Post-Communist Transitions," *World Politics* 50, no. 2 (1998): 203–34; Victor Shih, "Partial Reform Equilibrium, Chinese Style: Political Incentives and Reform Stagnation in Chinese Financial Policies," *Comparative Political Studies* 40, no. 10 (2007): 1238–62.

32. Minxin Pei, *China's Crony Capitalism: The Dynamics of Regime Decay* (Cambridge, MA: Harvard University Press, 2016); Andrew Wedeman, "The Dynamics and Trajectory of Corruption in Contemporary China," *China Review* 22, no. 2 (2022): 21–48.

33. "Neo-authoritarianism" here refers to a unique variety of autocracy that seeks to accelerate economic development under authoritarian rule. Historically, South Korea, Taiwan, Singapore, and Chile under Pinochet are classical examples of this type of regime. Deng Xiaoping's vision of economic modernization is, in essence, neo-authoritarian. "Neo-Stalinism" can be defined as a form of totalitarianism that adopts the institutional and political practices characteristic of Stalinist Soviet Union, such as the dominance of an individual dictator, a cult of personality, the use of purges to terrorize the party, conformity to an official ideology, and strict social control. This form of totalitarianism differs from Maoist mass totalitarianism in the dictator's preferred instrument of terror. Neo-Stalinist regimes rely on the coercive apparatus of the state to maintain the rule of fear while Maoist regimes prefer the mobilization of the masses to carry out terror campaigns.

Chapter 1. The Decisive Decade

1. Andres Onate, "Hua Kuo-Feng and the Arrest of the Gang of Four," *China Quarterly*, no. 75 (1978): 540–65.

2. Leng Rong and Wang Zuoling, eds., 邓小平年谱 (1975–1997) [Deng Xiaoping chronology (1975–1997)] (Beijing: Zhongyang wenxian chubanshe, 2004), 156–57; Ezra Vogel, *Deng Xiaoping and the Transformation of China* (Cambridge, MA: Belknap Press of Harvard University Press, 2011), 190–200.

3. Roderick MacFarquhar, "The Succession to Mao and the End of Maoism," in *The Politics of China: Sixty Years of the People's Republic of China*, 3rd ed., ed. Roderick MacFarquhar (New York: Cambridge University Press, 2011), 246–336.

4. Robert L. Suettinger, *The Conscience of the Party: Hu Yaobang, China's Communist Reformer* (Cambridge, MA: Harvard University Press, 2024).

5. Michael Schoenhals, "The 1978 Truth Criterion Controversy," *China Quarterly*, no. 126 (1991): 243–68.

6. David L. Shambaugh, *The Making of a Premier: Zhao Ziyang's Provincial Career* (London: Routledge, 2019).

7. Yang Jisheng, 中国改革年代的政治斗争 [Political struggles in China's reform era] (Hong Kong: Excellent Culture Press, 2004), 11–14.

8. Zhao Ziyang, 改革历程 [The course of reform] (Hong Kong: New Century, 2009), 241.

9. Yang Jisheng, 中国改革年代的政治斗争, 16–17.

10. Deng Xiaoping, "On the Reform of the System of Party and State Leadership," August 18, 1980, in *Selected Works of Deng Xiaoping* (1975–1982) (Beijing: Foreign Languages Press, 1984), 302–25.

11. Deng Xiaoping, 323.

12. Deng Xiaoping, 324.

13. "关于党内政治生活的若干准则" [Some guidelines on political life within the party], 人民网 [People's daily online], February 29, 1980, http://dangjian.people.com.cn/GB/136058/427510/428086/428088/428312/index.html.

14. Melanie Manion, *Retirement of Revolutionaries in China: Public Policies, Social Norms, Private Interests* (Princeton, NJ: Princeton University Press, 1993).

15. 中共中央关于建立老干部退休制度的决定 (1982年2月20日) [Decision of the Central Committee of the Chinese Communist Party on establishing a retirement system for veteran cadres (February 20, 1982)], http://cpc.people.com.cn/BIG5/64162/71380/71387/71591/4854975.html.

16. 中国人大制度理论研究会,"彭真在主持起草 1982 宪法的那些日子里" [The days when Peng Zhen presided over the drafting of the 1982 constitution], 中国人大网 [China National People's Congress network], June 3, 2016, http://www.npc.gov.cn/zgrdw/npc/bmzz/llyjh/2016-06/03/content_1990992.htm.

17. Yang Jisheng, 中国改革年代的政治斗争, 343.

18. Zhao Ziyang, 改革历程, 190–91.

19. Douglass North and Barry R. Weingast, "Constitutions and Commitment: The Evolution of Institutions Governing Public Choice in Seventeenth-Century England," *Journal of Economic History* 49, no. 4 (1989): 803–32.

20. Zhao Ziyang, 改革历程, 99; David Bachman, "Differing Visions of China's Post-Mao Economy: The Ideas of Chen Yun, Deng Xiaoping, and Zhao Ziyang," *Asian Survey* 26, no. 3 (1986): 292–321.

21. Zhu Jiamu, ed., 陈云年谱(下) [Chen Yun chronology] [Beijing: Zhongyang wenxian chubanshe, 2000), 316; Leng and Wang, 邓小平年谱, 948.

22. Zhao Ziyang, 改革历程, 119, 136–38.

23. Zhu Jiamu, 陈云年谱 (下), 309. Chen made this analogy in November 1982.

24. Yang Jisheng, 中国改革年代的政治斗争, 193–95; Leng and Wang, 邓小平年谱, 1006.

25. Zhu Jiamu, 陈云年谱 (下), 238–39, 262–65, 288–90.

26. Zhao Ziyang, 改革历程, 110–11, 119.

27. Leng and Wang, 邓小平年谱, 516; Yang Jisheng, 中国改革年代的政治斗争, 236–38.

28. Leng and Wang, 邓小平年谱, 954, 963.

29. Leng and Wang, 1008.

30. Zhao Ziyang, 改革历程, 102.

31. Zhu Jiamu, 陈云年谱 (下), 263–64, 290, 340.

32. Zhu Jiamu, 339.

33. Zhao Ziyang, 改革历程, 110.

34. Yang Jisheng, 中国改革年代的政治斗争, 341–42.

35. Donald Clarke, "Legislating for a Market Economy in China," *China Quarterly*, no. 191 (2007): 567–85.

36. Pitman Potter et al., eds., *Domestic Law Reforms in Post-Mao China* (Armonk, NY: M. E. Sharpe, 1994).

37. Kenneth Lieberthal and David M. Lampton, eds., *Bureaucracy, Politics, and Decision Making in Post-Mao China* (Berkeley: University of California Press, 1992); Donald Clarke, "The Execution of Civil Judgments in China," *China Quarterly*, no. 141 (1995): 65–81.

38. Stanely Lubman, *Bird in a Cage: Legal Reform in China After Mao* (Stanford, CA: Stanford University Press, 1999).

39. Murray Scot Tanner, *The Politics of Lawmaking in Post-Mao China: Institutions, Processes, and Democratic Prospects* (New York: Oxford University Press, 1999).

40. Zhao Ziyang, 改革历程, 243–44.

41. Deng Xiaoping, "Remarks on the Domestic Economic Situation," June 10, 1986, in *Selected Works of Deng Xiaoping* (1975–1982), 163; 邓小平文选, 第三卷 (Beijing: Renmin chubanshe, 1993), 160.

42. Zhao Ziyang, 改革历程, 236–37.

43. Zhao Ziyang, 243–44, 251–52.

44. Zhao Ziyang, 237–39.

45. Wu Guoguang, 赵紫阳与政治改革 [Zhao Ziyang and political reform] (Taipei: Yuanjing chuban shiye gongsi, 1997); Wu Wei, 中国80年代政治改革的台前幕后 [Behind the scenes of China's political reforms in the 1980s] (Hong Kong: New Century, 2013). The two best books on how Zhao led this project of political reform are by two participants.

46. Wu Wei, 中国80年代政治改革的台前幕后.

47. Wu Wei.

48. Wu Wei, "邓小平谈不要照搬三权分立" [Deng Xiaoping discusses not blindly copying the separation of powers], 纽约时报中文网 [New York Times Chinese website], July 7, 2014, https://cn.nytimes.com/china/20140707/cc07wuwei19/.

49. Wu Wei, "邓小平就是中国最大的实际" [Deng Xiaoping epitomizes the practical side of China], 纽约时报中文网 [New York Times Chinese website], July 14, 2014, https://cn.nytimes.com/china/20140714/cc14wuwei20/.

50. Wu Wei, "政改总体设想艰难过关" [The overall political reform plan faces formidable challenges], 纽约时报中文网 [New York Times Chinese website], July 21, 2014, https://cn.nytimes.com/china/20140721/cc21wuwei/.

51. Wu Wei, "邓小平谈不要照搬三权分立"; Wu Wei, "邓小平就是中国最大的实际."

52. Wu Wei, "选举制度改革：十三大后的探索" (Exploration into the reform of the electoral system after the Thirteenth Party Congress), 纽约时报中文网 [New York Times Chinese website], September 15, 2014, https://cn.nytimes.com/china/20140915/cc15wuwei29/.

53. Wu Wei, "十三大后的党政分开改革" [Reform of separation of the functions of party and government after the Thirteenth National Congress], 纽约时报中文网 [New York Times Chinese website], September 30, 2014, https://cn.nytimes.com/china/20140930/cc30wuwei31/.

54. Wu Wei.

55. Michael S. Duke, *Blooming and Contending: Chinese Literature in the Post-Mao Era* (Bloomington: Indiana University Press, 1985).

56. 周杨 [Zhou Yang], "关于马克思主义的几个理论问题的探讨" [Exploring several theoretical issues of Marxism], 人民日报 [People's daily], March 16, 1983, https://www.sxlib.org.cn/dfzy/rwk/bqzmkjwwrw/zy/qwts/zywlx/201707/t20170719_837392.html; Bill Brugger, "Alienation Revisited," *Australian Journal of Chinese Affairs* 12 (1984): 143–51.

57. Jing Wang, *High Culture Fever: Politics, Aesthetics, and Ideology in Deng's China* (Berkeley: University of California Press, 1996); Xudong Zhang, "On Some Motifs in the Chinese 'Cultural Fever' of the Late 1980s: Social Change, Ideology, and Theory," *Social Text* 39 (1994): 129–56.

58. Alice de Jong, "The Demise of the Dragon: Backgrounds to the Chinese Film 'River Elegy,'" *China Information* 4, no. 3 (1989): 28–43.

59. Jilin Xu, Geremie R. Barmé, and Gloria Davies, "The Fate of an Enlightenment: Twenty Years in the Chinese Intellectual Sphere (1978–98)," in *Chinese Intellectuals Between State and Market*, ed. Edward X. Gu and Merle Goldman (London: RoutledgeCurzon, 2004), 183–203.

60. Dingxin Zhao, "Decline of Political Control in Chinese Universities and the Rise of the 1989 Chinese Student Movement," *Sociological Perspectives* 40, no. 2 (1997): 159–82.

61. Yang Jisheng, 中国改革年代的政治斗争.

62. Richard Baum, *Burying Mao: Chinese Politics in the Age of Deng Xiaoping* (Princeton, NJ: Princeton University Press, 1994), 71–75, 80–83.

63. 邓小平 [Deng Xiaoping], "贯彻调整方针，保证安定团结" [Implement policies of adjustment, safeguard stability and unity], in邓小平文选第二卷 [Selected works of Deng Xiaoping, vol. 2], 354–74.

64. "中共中央关于当前报刊新闻广播宣传方针的决定" [CCP Center's decision on propaganda policy for print and broadcast media], http://www.71.cn/2011/0930/632663.shtml.

65. 邓小平 [Deng Xiaoping], "关于思想战线上的问题的讲话" (Speech on problems on the ideological front," in邓小平文选第二卷 [Selected Works of Deng Xiaoping, vol. 2], 389–93.

66. Lin Mu, "胡耀邦抵制专制主义" [Hu Yaobang resists authoritarianism], in 人民心中的胡耀邦 [Hu Yaobang in the people's hearts], ed. Su Shaozhi, Chen Yizi, and Gao Wenqian (Hong Kong, Mingjing chubanshe, 2006), 126–28.

67. Yang Jisheng, 中国改革年代的政治斗争, 256–75; Lin Mu, "胡耀邦抵制专制主义," 128–31.

68. Leng and Wang, 邓小平年谱, 939–40.

69. Zhao Ziyang, 改革历程, 164; Thomas Gold, "'Just in Time!': China Battles Spiritual Pollution on the Eve of 1984," *Asian Survey* 24, no. 9 (1984): 947–74.

70. Zhao Ziyang, 改革历程, 164; Li Rui, "胡耀邦去世前的谈话" [A conversation with Hu Yaobang before his death], in人民心中的胡耀邦, 35.

71. Ligang Song, "State-owned Enterprise Reform in China: Past, Present and Prospects," in *China's 40 Years of Reform and Development 1978–2018*, ed. Ross Garnaut, Ligang Song, and Cai Fang (Canberra: ANU Press, 2018), 345–69.

72. You Ji, "Zhao Ziyang and the Politics of Inflation," *Australian Journal of Chinese Affairs*, no. 25 (1991): 69–91.

73. "雷宇: 从副省级高官到普通百姓" [Lei Yu: From a deputy provincial official to an ordinary citizen], 南方周末 [Southern weekend], February 2, 2008. https://www.infzm.com/contents/9736.

74. Richard Baum, "The Road to Tiananmen," in *The Politics of China: Sixty Years of the People's Republic of China*, ed. Roderick MacFarquhar, 3rd ed. (New York: Cambridge University Press, 2011), 396–98.

75. Yang Jisheng, 中国改革年代的政治斗争, 149–50, 166.

76. Zhu Houze, "胡耀邦的全面改革主张" [Hu Yaobang's comprehensive reform initiatives], 炎黄春秋 [China through the ages], no. 9 (2010): 1–5; Suettinger, *The Conscience of the Party*, 272–316.

77. Chen Weiren, "胡耀邦与西藏" [Hu Yaobang and Tibet], in人民心中的胡耀邦, 166–84.

78. Su, Chen, and Gao, 人民心中的胡耀邦, 26.

79. Zhao Ziyang, 改革历程, 161–62.

80. Zhao Ziyang, 162.

81. Zhao Ziyang, 163–64.

82. Zhao Ziyang, 163–74; Baum, *Burying Mao*, 391–94.

83. Zhao Ziyang, 改革历程, 163.

84. Yang Jisheng, 中国改革年代的政治斗争, 356–58; Richard Baum, "Deng Liqun and the Struggle Against 'Bourgeois Liberalization,' 1979–1993," *China Information* 9, no. 4 (1995): 1–35.

85. Wu Wei, "邓小平与 '5•13讲话'" [Deng Xiaoping and the "5·13 Speech"], 炎黄春秋 [China through the ages], no. 3 (2015): 4–9.

86. Zhao Ziyang, 改革历程, 189; Yang Jisheng, 中国改革年代的政治斗争, 360–61.

87. Zhao Ziyang, 改革历程, 120. According to Zhao, Chen was not in poor health and had no reason except to show his displeasure for leaving the stage.

88. Zhao Ziyang, 220–21.

89. Zhao Ziyang, 230–33.

90. Zhao Ziyang, 24–25, 38–39, 52–54.

91. Yang Su, *Deadly Decision in Beijing* (New York: Cambridge University Press, 2023).

92. Zhao Ziyang, 改革历程, 241.

93. Samuel Huntington, *The Third Wave: Democratization in the Late Twentieth Century* (Norman: University of Oklahoma Press, 1993), 124–41.

94. Zhao Yuezhi, *Media, Market, and Democracy in China: Between the Party Line and the Bottom Line* (Urbana: University of Illinois Press, 1998).

Chapter 2. Reform and Growth in the 1980s

1. Lorean Brandt and Thomas G. Rawski, eds., *China's Great Economic Transformation* (New York: Cambridge University Press, 2008).

2. Wu Jinglian, "中国经济改革三十年历程的制度思考" [Institutional reflections on the thirty years of China's economic reforms], in 中国经济 50 人看三十年：回顾与分析 [Fifty

perspectives on China's economy over thirty years: Review and analysis], ed. Wu Jinglian et al. (Beijing: Zhonghua jingji chubanshe, 2008), 4.

3. Deng Xiaoping, "Some Comments on Economic Work," October 4, 1979, https://www.marxists.org/reference/archive/deng-xiaoping/1979/82.htm.

4. Deng Xiaoping, "We Can Develop a Market Economy Under Socialism," November 26, 1979, https://www.marxists.org/reference/archive/deng-xiaoping/1979/152.htm.

5. Justin Yifu Lin and Zhiqiang Liu, "Fiscal Decentralization and Economic Growth in China," *Economic Development and Cultural Change* 49, no. 1 (2000): 1–21; Christine Wong, "Central–Local Relations in an Era of Fiscal Decline: The Paradox of Fiscal Decentralization in Post-Mao China," *China Quarterly*, no. 128 (1991): 691–715.

6. Sebastian Heilmann, "From Local Experiments to National Policy: The Origins of China's Distinctive Policy Process," *China Journal*, no. 59 (2008): 1–30.

7. Lawrence Lau et al., "Reform Without Losers: An Interpretation of China's Dual-Track Approach to Transition," *Journal of Political Economy* 108, no. 1 (2000): 120–43.

8. Wu Xiang, 中国农村改革实录 [Record of China's rural reform] (Hangzhou: Zhejiang renmin chubanshe, 2001); Daniel Kelliher, *Peasant Power in China: The Era of Rural Reform, 1979–1989* (New Haven, CT: Yale University Press, 1992); David Zweig, *Freeing China's Farmers: Rural Restructuring in the Reform Era* (Armonk, NY: M. E. Sharpe, 1997).

9. Wu Jinglian, "中国经济改革三十年历程的制度思考," 4.

10. Lin Chonggeng "中国改革开放过程中的对外思想开放" [China's opening of the mind to the outside world in the process of reform and opening], in 中国经济50人看三十年, ed. Wu Jinglian, 20–40.

11. Wu Jinglian, "中国经济改革三十年历程的制度思考," 9–11; Lin Chonggeng, "中国改革开放过程中的对外思想开放," 20–40; for an excellent account of the influence of Western and Eastern European economists on China's reform, see Julian Gewirtz, *Unlikely Partners: Chinese Reformers, Western Economists, and the Making of Global China* (Cambridge, MA: Harvard University Press, 2017).

12. 中国统计年鉴 *1995* [China statistical yearbook 1995] (hereafter cited as *ZGTJNJ 1995*) (Beijing: Zhongguo tongji chubanshe, 1996), 26, 59.

13. Shukai Zhao, *The Politics of Peasants* (Singapore: Springer, 2017); David Shambaugh, *The Making of a Premier: Zhao Ziyang's Provincial Career* (Boulder, CO: Westview, 1984); Kate Xiao Zhou, *How the Farmers Changed China: Power of the People* (Boulder, CO: Westview, 1996); Zhao Ziyang, 改革历程 [The course of reform] (Hong Kong: New Century, 2009), 136.

14. Deng Xiaoping, "On Questions of Rural Policy," May 31, 1980, in *Selected Works of Deng Xiaoping (1975–1982)* (Beijing: Foreign Languages Press, 1984), 297–99.

15. Zhao Ziyang, 改革历程, 137–38.

16. Yang Jisheng, 中国改革年代的政治斗争 [Political struggles in China's reform era] (Hong Kong: Excellent Culture Press, 2004), 231.

17. Yasheng Huang, "How Did China Take Off?," *Journal of Economic Perspectives* 26, no. 4 (2012): 147–70.

18. *ZGTJNJ 1995*, 32.

19. Justin Yifu Lin, "Rural Reforms and Agricultural Growth in China," *American Economic Review* 82, no. 1 (1992): 34–51; Guanzhong James Wen, "Total Factor Productivity Change in China's Farming Sector: 1952–1989," *Economic Development and Cultural Change* 42, no. 1 (1993): 1–41.

20. *ZGTJNJ 1995*, 233, 279.

21. Deng Xiaoping, "Our Magnificent Goal and Basic Policies," October 6, 1984, in *Selected Works of Deng Xiaoping, vol. 3 (1982–1992)* (Beijing: Foreign Languages Press, 1994), 85–87.

22. Hongyi Chen, *The Institutional Transition of China's Township and Village Enterprises: Market Liberalization, Contractual Form Innovation, and Privatization* (London: Routledge,

2018); Louis Putterman, "On the Past and Future of China's Township and Village-Owned Enterprises," *World Development* 25, no. 10 (1997): 1639–55.

23. Jean Oi, "Fiscal Reform and the Economic Foundations of Local State Corporatism in China," *World Politics* 45, no. 1 (1992): 99–126.

24. Enrico Perotti et al., "State-Owned Versus Township and Village Enterprises in China," *Comparative Economic Studies* 41, no. 2 (1999): 151–79; Jeffrey Nugent et al., "Competition, Incentives, and Productivity in Chinese Township and Village Enterprises," *Pacific Economic Review* 4, no. 2 (1999): 91–113; David Zweig, "Internationalizing China's Countryside: The Political Economy of Exports from Rural Industry," *China Quarterly*, no. 128 (1991): 716–41.

25. Yasheng Huang, *Capitalism with Chinese Characteristics: Entrepreneurship and the State* (New York: Cambridge University Press, 2008); Kellee Tsai, *Back-Alley Banking: Private Entrepreneurs in China* (Ithaca, NY: Cornell University Press, 2004).

26. Chen, *Institutional Transition.*

27. Deng Xiaoping, "We Shall Speed Up Reform," June 12, 1987, in *Selected Works of Deng Xiaoping*, 3:236.

28. Huang, "How Did China Take Off?," 155–57.

29. Zhang Houyi and Ming Lizhi, 中国私营企业发展报告 1978–1998 [Report on the development of private enterprises in China 1978–1998] (Beijing: Shehui kexue wenxian chubanshe, 1999); Victor Nee and Frank W. Young, "Peasant Entrepreneurs in China's Second Economy: An Institutional Analysis," *Economic Development and Cultural Change* 39, no. 2 (1991): 293–310.

30. Zhang Houyi, "私营企业主阶层在我国社会结构中的地位" [The position of private business owners in the social structure of our country], 中国社会科学 [China social sciences], no. 6 (1994): 101.

31. *ZGTJNJ 1990* (Beijing: Zhongguo tongji chubanshe, 1991), 33, 641.

32. Nora Wang, "Deng Xiaoping: The Years in France," *China Quarterly*, no. 92 (1982): 698–705.

33. Leng Rong and Wang Zuoling, eds., 邓小平年谱上册 (1975–1997) [Deng Xiaoping chronology (1975–1997)] (Beijing: Zhongyang wenxian chubanshe, 2004), 512.

34. Leng and Wang, 254–87.

35. Deng Xiaoping, "Some Comments on Economic Work," October 4, 1979, https://www.marxists.org/reference/archive/deng-xiaoping/1979/82.htm.

36. Deng Xiaoping, "We Can Develop a Market Economy Under Socialism," November 26, 1979, https://www.marxists.org/reference/archive/deng-xiaoping/1979/152.htm.

37. Deng Xiaoping, "Our Magnificent Goal and Basic Policies," October 6, 1984, in *Selected Works of Deng Xiaoping*, 3:86.

38. China passed an interim enterprise bankruptcy law in 1986. A semifunctioning capital market did not emerge until the 1990s with the establishment of stock exchanges and the reorganization of the banking system.

39. Leng and Wang, 邓小平年谱上册, 519–20.

40. Leng and Wang, 525.

41. 全国人民代表大会 [National People's Congress], "中华人民共和国中外合资经营企业法" [Law of the People's Republic of China on Chinese-foreign equity joint ventures], July 8, 1979, https://law.pkulaw.com/falv/44fe519756440da6bdfb.html.

42. Leng and Wang, 邓小平年谱上册, 529; Margaret Pearson, *Joint Ventures in the People's Republic of China* (Princeton, NJ: Princeton University Press, 1992).

43. "中华人民共和国外资企业法" [Law of the People's Republic of China on foreign-funded enterprises], http://tfs.mofcom.gov.cn/article/ba/bl/201101/20110107349307.shtml.

44. 中华人民共和国商务部 [Ministry of Commerce of the People's Republic of China], "中华人民共和国外资企业法实施细则" [Implementation regulations of the People's Republic

of China on foreign-funded enterprises], December 12, 1990, http://wzs.mofcom.gov.cn/article/n/200208/20020800037017.shtml.

45. The provisions of this law resemble the joint-venture law issued in 1979, but the contributions of joint-venture partners could include noncash items. "中华人民共和国中外合作经营企业法" [Law of the People's Republic of China on Sino-foreign contractual joint ventures], http://www.npc.gov.cn/zgrdw/npc/xinwen/2017-11/28/content_2032723.htm.

46. Hooshang Amirahmadi and Weiping Wu, "Export Processing Zones in Asia," *Asian Survey* 35, no. 9 (1995): 828–49.

47. Leng and Wang, 邓小平年谱上册, 510.

48. Clyde Stoltenberg, "China's Special Economic Zones: Their Development and Prospects," *Asian Survey* 24, no. 6 (1984): 642–43; "国务院关于厦门经济特区实施方案的批复" [State Council approval of the implementation plan for Xiamen Special Economic Zone], June 29, 1985, http://www.gov.cn/xxgk/pub/govpublic/mrlm/201309/t20130929_66434.html.

49. George Crane, *The Political Economy of China's Economic Zones* (Armonk, NY: M. E. Sharpe, 1989); Wei Ge, "Special Economic Zones and the Opening of the Chinese Economy: Some Lessons for Economic Liberalization," *World Development* 27, no. 7 (1999): 1267–85.

50. 第五届全国人民代表大会常务委员会 [Standing Committee of the Fifth National People's Congress], "广东省经济特区条例" [Regulations on the special economic zones in Guangdong province], August 26, 1980, http://www.zhxz.gov.cn/xxgk/fggw/dfxfg/content/post_1448488.html.

51. Guo Shiping and Chen Hongbo, "深圳特区与其他特区经济发展状况的比较研究" [Comparative study of the economic development in Shenzhen Special Economic Zone and other special economic zones], 特区经济 [Special economic zone economy], no. 2 (1995): 47–49; *ZGTJNJ 1990*, 653.

52. Guo and Chen, "深圳特区与其他特区经济发展状况的比较研究," 49; *ZGTJNJ 1990*, 641.

53. Yue-man Yeung et al., "China's Special Economic Zones at 30," *Eurasian Geography and Economics* 50, no. 2 (2009): 222–40.

54. Guo and Chen, "深圳特区与其他特区经济发展状况的比较研究," 47.

55. Zhao Ziyang, 改革历程, 141–49; Fuh-Wen Tzeng, "The Political Economy of China's Coastal Development Strategy: A Preliminary Analysis," *Asian Survey* 31, no. 3 (1991): 270–84.

56. Nicholas Lardy, *Foreign Trade and Economic Reform in China* (New York: Cambridge University Press, 1991), 1–15; Peter Harrold, "China: Foreign Trade Reform: Now for the Hard Part," *Oxford Review of Economic Policy* 11, no. 4 (1995): 134; Changjun Yue and Ping Hua, "Does Comparative Advantage Explain Export Patterns in China?" *China Economic Review* 13, no. 2–3 (2002): 276–96.

57. *ZGTJNJ 1990*, 33, 641.

58. Harrold, "China: Foreign Trade Reform," 135.

59. Weijian Shan, "Reforms of China's Foreign Trade System: Experiences and Prospects," *China Economic Review* 1, no. 1 (1989): 35–38; Nicholas R. Lardy, *Integrating China into the Global Economy* (Washington DC: Brookings, 2002), 29.

60. Shan, "Reforms of China's Foreign Trade System," 38–39; Nai-Ruenn Chen and Jeffrey Lee, *China's Economy, and Foreign Trade 1981–85* (Washington, DC: US Department of Commerce, 1984).

61. Shan, "Reforms of China's Foreign Trade System," 39–44; Lardy, *Foreign Trade and Economic Reform*, 41; Yang Sujin, "论中国外贸体制的改革," *Modern China Studies*, no. 2 (1997), https://www.modernchinastudies.org/us/issues/past-issues/57-mcs-1997-issue-2/401-2011-12-29-17-45-11.html.

62. Shan, "Reforms of China's Foreign Trade System," 43–45; Harrold, "China: Foreign Trade Reform," 136–38; Lardy, *Foreign Trade and Economic Reform*, 46–69.

63. Shuanglin Lin, "Foreign Trade and China's Economic Development: A Time-Series Analysis," *Journal of Economic Development* 25, no. 1 (2000): 148.

64. *ZGTJNJ 1990*, 33, 641.

65. Lin Yifu and Li Yongjun, "对外贸易与经济增长关系的再考察" [Reexamination of the relationship between foreign trade and economic growth], 国际贸易 [International trade], no. 9 (2001): 23–27.

66. Douglas Zhihua Zeng, *How Do Special Economic Zones and Industrial Clusters Drive China's Rapid Development?* (Washington, DC: World Bank, 2011); Françoise Lemoine and Deniz Ünal-Kesenci, "Assembly Trade and Technology Transfer: The Case of China," *World Development* 32, no. 5 (2004): 829–50; Qiao Yu, "Capital Investment, International Trade and Economic Growth in China: Evidence in the 1980–1990s," *China Economic Review* 9, no. 1 (1998): 73–84.

67. Harrold, "China: Foreign Trade Reform," 138–39.

68. Andrew Walder, "China's Private Sector," in *China's Domestic Private Firms*, ed. Anne Tsui et al. (London: Routledge, 2006), 311–26.

69. Barry Naughton, *Growing Out of the Plan: Chinese Economic Reform, 1978–1993* (New York: Cambridge University Press, 1995).

70. Zhao Ziyang, 改革历程, 122–24.

71. Nicholas Lardy, "Private Sector Development," in *China's 40 Years of Reform and Development, 1978–2018*, ed. Ross Garnaut et al. (Canberra: ANU Press, 2018), 330.

72. *ZGTJNJ 1990*, 414.

73. Wu Jinglian, 当代中国经济改革 [Economic reforms in contemporary China] (Shanghai: Yuanjing chubanshe, 2003), 66–68; Lau et al., "Reform Without Losers," 120–43.

74. Wu Jinglian, 当代中国经济改革, 66–68.

75. Zhao Ziyang, 改革历程, 122–24.

76. 国务院 [State Council], "关于城镇非农业个体经济若干政策性规定" [Several policy provisions on nonagricultural individually operated economic activities in urban areas], July 7, 1981, http://www.reformdata.org/1981/0707/6330.shtml.

77. "中华人民共和国宪法" [Constitution of the People's Republic of China], https://www.elegislation.gov.hk/hk/A1%21en-sc.assist.pdf.

78. "当前农村经济政策的若干问题" [Several issues regarding current rural economic policies], January 2, 1983, https://finance.sina.cn/sa/2010-02-01/detail-ikftssan9543782.d.html; 国务院关于农民个人或联户购置机动车船和拖拉机经营运输业的若干规定 [State Council regulations on farmers' individual or joint purchases of motor vehicles, boats, and tractors to operate in transportation businesses], February 27, 1984, https://www.flfgk.com/detail/8e66166d9c7e0a57577c1fd2f51a02f1.html.

79. Yang Jisheng, 中国改革年代的政治斗争, 240–43; Keith Forster, "The 1982 Campaign Against Economic Crime in China," *Australian Journal of Chinese Affairs*, no. 14 (1985): 1–19.

80. "中国改革先锋项南'晋江假药案'蒙冤下台" [Chinese reform pioneer Xiang Nan, falsely implicated in the "Jinjiang fake drug case," steps down from office], September 4, 2008, http://phtv.ifeng.com/program/tfzg/200809/0904_2950_764236.shtml.

81. Leng and Wang, 邓小平年谱下册, 1008.

82. The language of the amendment replaces *geti jingji* with *siying jingji*. No other provisions were changed. "中华人民共和国宪法修正案" [Amendments to the Constitution of the People's Republic of China], 1988, https://www.elegislation.gov.hk/hk/A2%21zh-Hant-HK.assist.pdf.

83. "中华人民共和国私营企业暂行条例" [Interim regulations of the People's Republic of China on private enterprises], https://www.gov.cn/gongbao/shuju/1988/gwyb198815.pdf.

84. Zhang Houyi, "又一支异军突起" [Another new force emerges], in Zhang and Ming, 中国私营企业发展报告, 16, 42.

85. *ZGTGNJ 1990*, 400. In 1978 all TVEs were collectives, but most of the newly created TVEs were private.

86. *ZGTGNJ 1990*, 20, 401. "Total social output," a Chinese accounting method used in the 1980s, was about 45 percent of GDP.

87. Yanjie Bian and Zhangxin Zhang, "Explaining China's Emerging Private Economy," in *China's Domestic Private Firms*, ed. Anne Tsui et al., 25–39; David Wank, "Bureaucratic Patronage and Private Business: Changing Networks of Power in Urban China," in *The Waning of the Communist State: Economic Origins of Political Decline in China and Hungary*, ed. Andrew G. Walder (Berkeley: University of California Press, 1995), 153–83.

88. Zhang Houyi, "又一支异军突起," 15.

89. Anne Tsui et al., "Explaining the Growth and Development of the Chinese Domestic Private Sector," in *China's Domestic Private Firms*, ed. Tsui et al., 9; Zhang Houyi, "又一支异军突起," 51–53.

90. David Daokui Li, "A Survey of Economics Literature on China's Nonstate Enterprises," in *China's Domestic Private Firms*, ed. Tsui et al., 128–46.

91. Zhang Houyi, "又一支异军突起," 51.

92. Huang, "How Did China Take Off?" 154.

93. Zhang Houyi, "私营企业主阶层在我国社会结构中的地位," 101–2.

94. *ZGTJNJ 1990*, 29, 115.

95. David Granick, "The Industrial Environment in China and the CMEA Countries," in *China's Industrial Reform*, ed. Gene Tidrick and Chen Jiyuan (Washington, DC: World Bank, 1987), 103–31.

96. Wu Jinglian, 当代中国经济改革, 133–36; Janos Kornai, "The Soft Budget Constraint," *Kyklos* 39, no. 1 (1986): 3–30.

97. Xiaoyuan Dong and Louis Putterman, "Soft Budget Constraints, Social Burdens, and Labor Redundancy in China's State Industry," *Journal of Comparative Economics* 31, no. 1 (2003): 110–33; Justin Yifu Lin et al., "Competition, Policy Burdens, and State-Owned Enterprise Reform," *American Economic Review* 88, no. 2 (1998): 422–27.

98. Bernard Chavance and Charles Hauss, *The Transformation of Communist Systems: Economic Reform Since the 1950s* (Boulder, CO: Westview, 1994).

99. Naughton, *Growing Out of the Plan*, 97–109; Ma Jiantang, "三十年巨变：国有企业改革进程简要回顾与评述" [Thirty years of profound changes: A brief review and commentary on the reform process of state-owned enterprises], in 中国经济50人看三十年, ed. Wu Jinglian, 349–58.

100. "关于扩大国营工业企业经营管理自主权的若干规定" [Several provisions on expanding the operational autonomy and management of state-owned industrial enterprises], http://www.reformdata.org/1979/0713/5879.shtml.

101. Ma Jiantang, "三十年巨变：国有企业改革进程简要回顾与评述," 350.

102. Wu Jinglian, 当代中国经济改革, 142; Ligang Song, "State-Owned Enterprise Reform in China," in Garnaut et al., *China's 40 Years of Reform and Development*, 347.

103. Wu Jinglian and Liu Jirui, 论竞争性市场体制 [On the competitive market system] (Beijing: Zhongxin chubanshe, 2017), 118.

104. Wu Jinglian, 当代中国经济改革, 156; Ma Jiantang, "三十年巨变," 350–51.

105. "国务院体制改革办公室关于实行工业生产经济责任制若干问题的意见" [Opinions of the State Council Institutional Reform Office on several issues regarding implementation of the system of industrial production and economic responsibility], October 29, 1981, http://www.reformdata.org/1981/1029/5884.shtml.

106. "全民所有制工业企业承包经营责任制暂行条例" [Interim regulations on the contract management responsibility system for industrial enterprises owned by the whole people], https://www.gov.cn/gongbao/content/2011/content_1860724.htm.

107. Wu Jinglian, 当代中国经济改革, 140.

108. Ma Jiantang, "三十年巨变," 350–51.

109. Wu Jinglian, 当代中国经济改革, 139–40; Ma Jiantang, "三十年巨变," 351–52.

110. Gary Jefferson and Thomas Rawski, "Enterprise Reform in Chinese Industry," *Journal of Economic Perspectives* 8, no. 2 (1994): 47–70; William Byrd, *Chinese Industrial Firms Under Reform* (Oxford: Oxford University Press, 1992).

111. Wu Jinglian, 当代中国经济改革; Ma Jiantang, "三十年巨变": Wing Thye Woo et al., "How Successful Has Chinese Enterprise Reform Been? Pitfalls in Opposite Biases and Focus," *Journal of Comparative Economics* 18, no. 3 (1994): 410–37.

112. Weiye Li and Louis Putterman, "Reforming China's SOEs: An Overview," *Comparative Economic Studies*, no. 50 (2008): 353–80.

113. Zhao Ziyang, 改革历程, 124.

114. Zhang Jun, "China's Price Liberalization and Market Reform: A Historical Perspective," in Garnaut et al., *China's 40 Years of Reform and Development*, 215–33.

115. Edward Lazear, *Economic Transition in Eastern Europe and Russia: Realities of Reform* (Stanford, CA: Hoover Press, 1995).

116. Zhang Weiying, "双轨制与价格改革" [The dual-track system and price reform], in 中国经济50人看三十年, ed. Wu Jinglian, 582–99.

117. "国务院关于进一步扩大国营工业企业自主权的暂行规定" [Interim provisions of the State Council on further expanding the autonomy of state-owned industrial enterprises], 广东省人民政府 [Guangdong People's Government], August 21, 1984, http://www.gd.gov.cn/zwgk/gongbao/1984/10/content/post_3354361.html.

118. Lau et al., "Reform Without Losers," 120–43; Gang Fan, "Incremental Changes and Dual-Track Transition: Understanding the Case of China," *Economic Policy* 9, no. 19 (1994): 100–22.

119. Jinglian Wu and Zhao Renwei, "The Dual Pricing System in China's Industry," *Journal of Comparative Economics* 11, no. 3 (1987): 309–18; Anthony Koo and Norman Obst, "Dual-Track and Mandatory Quota in China's Price Reform," *Comparative Economic Studies*, no. 37 (1995): 1–17.

120. Leong Liew, "Rent-Seeking and the Two-Track Price System in China," *Public Choice* 77, no. 2 (1993): 359–75; Wu and Zhao, "The Dual Pricing System."

121. Naughton, *Growing Out of the Plan*, 220–27.

122. *ZGTJNJ 1990*, 34, 250, 49, 250, 42, 414.

123. *ZGTJNJ 1990*, 641, 653.

124. Zhao Ziyang, 改革历程, 124.

125. Nicholas Lardy, *The State Strikes Back: The End of Economic Reform in China?* (Washington, DC: Peterson Institute for International Economics, 2019).

Chapter 3. Building Neo-Authoritarianism, 1992–2002

1. Yang Jisheng, 中国改革年代的政治斗争 [Political struggles in China's reform era] (Hong Kong: Excellent Culture Press, 2004).

2. Barry Naughton, *Growing Out of the Plan: Chinese Economic Reform, 1978–1993* (New York: Cambridge University Press, 1995).

3. 中国统计年鉴*1995* [China statistical yearbook] [hereafter cited as *ZGTJNJ 1995*] (Beijing: Zhongguo tongji chubanshe, 1996), 32.

4. *ZGTJNJ 1995*, 365.

5. Julian Gewirtz, *Unlikely Partners: Chinese Reformers, Western Economists, and the Making of Global China* (Cambridge, MA: Harvard University Press, 2017), 282; Joseph Fewsmith, "Reaction, Resurgence, and Succession: Chinese Politics Since Tiananmen," in *The Politics of China: Sixty Years of the People's Republic of China*, ed. Roderick MacFarquhar (New York: Cambridge University Press, 2011), 3rd ed., 479–81; Richard Baum, *Burying Mao: Chinese Politics in the Age of Deng Xiaoping* (Princeton, NJ: Princeton University Press, 1994), 326–28.

6. Stanley Rosen, "The Effect of Post-4 June Re-education Campaigns on Chinese Students," *China Quarterly*, no. 134 (1993): 310–34.

7. Baum, *Burying Mao*, 315–16; Hong Shi, "China's Political Development After Tiananmen," *Asian Survey* 30, no. 12 (1990): 1206–17.

8. Yang Jisheng, 中国改革年代的政治斗争, 477; Baum, *Burying Mao*, 333–37.

9. Tony Saich, *From Rebel to Ruler: One Hundred Years of the Chinese Communist Party* (Cambridge, MA: Harvard University Press, 2021), 311–16.

10. David Shambaugh, "China in 1990: The Year of Damage Control," *Asian Survey* 31, no. 1 (1991): 49.

11. Fewsmith, "Reaction, Resurgence, and Succession," 482–92.

12. Leng Rong and Wang Zuoling, eds., 邓小平年谱下册 (1975–1997) [Deng Xiaoping chronology (1975–1997)] (Beijing: Zhongyang wenxian chubanshe, 2004), 1325–28.

13. Gerald Segal, "China and the Disintegration of the Soviet Union," *Asian Survey* 32, no. 9 (1992): 848–68.

14. John Garver, "The Chinese Communist Party and the Collapse of Soviet Communism," *China Quarterly*, no. 133 (1993): 15–16.

15. "Review Your Experience and Use Professionally Trained People," August 20, 1991, in *Selected Works of Deng Xiaoping, vol. 3 (1982–1992)* (Beijing: Foreign Languages Press, 1994), 357.

16. Elizabeth Perry, "China in 1992: An Experiment in Neo-Authoritarianism," *Asian Survey* 33, no. 1 (1993): 12–21; Barry Sautman, "Sirens of the Strongman: Neo-Authoritarianism in Recent Chinese Political Theory," *The China Quarterly*, no. 129 (1992): 72–102.

17. Leng and Wang, 邓小平年谱下册, 1341–46.

18. Baum, *Burying Mao*, 341–68; Suisheng Zhao, "Deng Xiaoping's Southern Tour," *Asian Survey* 33, no. 8 (1993): 739–56; *ZGTJNJ 1995*, 32.

19. Deng Xiaoping, "邓小平原汁原味的南方讲话" [The original Deng Xiaoping southern speech], https://finance.sina.com.cn/roll/2024-08-23/doc-inckqshv8372587.shtml. The official version of Deng's talks can be found in *Selected Works of Deng Xiaoping, vol. 3 (1982–1992)*, 358–70.

20. Deng Xiaoping, "邓小平原汁原味的南方讲话"; Chris Buckley, "Vows of Change in China Belie Private Warning," *New York Times*, February 14, 2013, https://www.nytimes.com/2013/02/15/world/asia/vowing-reform-chinas-leader-xi-jinping-airs-other-message-in-private.html.

21. Yang Jisheng, 中国改革年代的政治斗争, 496; Ezra Vogel, *Deng Xiaoping and the Transformation of China* (Cambridge, MA: Belknap Press of Harvard University Press, 2011), 679.

22. Zhu Jiamu and Liu Shukai, eds., 陈云年谱 （下） [Chen Yun chronology, vol. 3] (Beijing: Zhongyang wenxian chubanshe, 2000), 440–52.

23. James Miles, *The Legacy of Tiananmen: China in Disarray* (Ann Arbor: University of Michigan Press, 1996).

24. World Bank, "GDP per Capita, PPP (Current International $)—China," World Bank Open Data, https://data.worldbank.org/indicator/NY.GDP.PCAP.PP.CD?locations=CN.

25. Jie Chen et al., "The Level and Sources of Popular Support for China's Current Political Regime," *Communist and Post-Communist Studies* 30, no. 1 (1997): 45–64.

26. Zhu and Liu, 陈云年谱 (下), 442–48. Chronology of Chen's activities shows he was politically inactive and spent many months "resting."

27. Xiaowei Zang, "The Fourteenth Central Committee of the CCP," *Asian Survey* 33, no. 8 (1993): 787–803.

28. Richard Ewing, "Hu Jintao: The Making of a Chinese General Secretary," *China Quarterly*, no. 173 (2003): 17–34.

29. Yang Jisheng, 中国改革年代的政治斗争, 589. Zhao relayed information about this conversation with Deng to journalist Yang Jisheng on October 29, 1996, when Yang was interviewing Zhao at his residence.

30. Other influential advocates were Wu Jiaxiang, a junior researcher on Zhao Ziyang's political reform task force, and Xiao Gongqin, a Shanghai-based historian. Liu Jun and Li Lin, eds., 新权威主义: 对改革理论纲领的论争 [New authoritarianism: Debates on theoretical reform programs] (Beijing: Beijing jingji xueyuan chubanshe, 1989); Mark Petracca and Mong Xiong, "The Concept of Chinese Neo-Authoritarianism: An Exploration and Democratic Critique," *Asian Survey* 30, no. 11 (1990): 1099–1117.

31. Ezra Vogel, *The Four Little Dragons: The Spread of Industrialization in East Asia* (Cambridge, MA: Harvard University Press, 1991); Frederic Deyo, ed., *The Political Economy of the New Asian Industrialism* (Ithaca, NY: Cornell University Press, 1987); World Bank, *The East Asian Miracle: Economic Growth and Public Policy* (New York: Oxford University Press, 1993).

32. Jialin Zhang, *China's Response to the Downfall of Communism in Eastern Europe and the Soviet Union* (Stanford, CA: Hoover Institution Press, 1994); David Shambaugh, *The Chinese Communist Party: Atrophy and Adaptation* (Berkeley: University of California Press, 2008).

33. Guan Guihai and Luan Jinghe, eds., "苏联解体对当代中国政治的影响" [The impact of the collapse of the Soviet Union on contemporary Chinese politics], in 中俄关系的历史与现实 [Sino-Russian relations: History and reality] (Beijing: Shehui kexue wenxian chubanshe, 2009), 551–58.

34. Leng and Wang, 邓小平年谱下册, 1323.

35. Bruce J. Dickson, "The Survival Strategy of the Chinese Communist Party," *Washington Quarterly* 39, no. 4 (2016): 27–44.

36. Zhang Lifan, "邓力群之殇与党国理论界的黄昏" [The tragedy of Deng Liqun and the twilight of party-state theoretical circles], *New York Times* (Chinese ed.), February 20, 2015, https://cn.nytimes.com/china/20150220/tc20dengliqun/.

37. "中共中央关于建立社会主义市场经济体制若干问题的决定" [Resolution of the CCP Central Committee on several questions on establishing institutions of a socialist market economy], 中华人民共和国中央人民政府 [Central Government of the People's Republic of China], October 21, 2003, http://www.gov.cn/test/2008-08/13/content_1071062.htm.

38. "关于党内政治生活的若干准则" [Some guidelines on political life in the party], 人民网 [People's daily online], February 29, 1980, http://dangjian.people.com.cn/GB/136058/427510/428086/428088/428312/index.html.

39. "党政领导干部选拔任用工作条例; 中国共产党纪律处分条例（试行）" [Trial regulations on the selection and appointment of party and government leading cadres; regulations on Chinese Communist Party disciplinary punishments], 中共中央办公厅法规局 [Regulations Bureau of the General Office of the Central Committee], "国共产党党内法规体系" [Regulations on Chinese Communist Party discipline and sanctions], 中华人民共和国中央人民政府 [Central Government of the People's Republic of China], July 2021, http://www.gov.cn/xinwen/2021-08/06/content_5629962.htm.

40. Pierre Landry, *Decentralized Authoritarianism in China: The Control of Local Elites in the Post-Mao Era* (New York: Cambridge University Press, 2008); Joseph Fewsmith, *Elite Politics in Contemporary China* (London: Routledge, 2015); Jiangnan Zhu, "Why Are Offices for Sale in China? A Case Study of the Office-Selling Chain in Heilongjiang Province," *Asian Survey* 48, no. 4 (2008): 558–79.

41. Victor Shih et al., "Getting Ahead in the Communist Party: Explaining the Advancement of Central Committee Members in China," *American Political Science Review* 106, no. 1 (2012): 166–87.

42. Andrew Walder, "Rebellion of the Cadres: The 1967 Implosion of the Chinese Party-State," *China Journal*, no. 75 (2016): 102–20.

43. Zengke He, "Corruption and Anti-Corruption in Reform China," *Communist and Post-Communist Studies* 33, no. 2 (2000): 243–70.

44. Central Commission for Discipline Inspection, "中央纪委关于处分违犯党纪的党员批准权限的具体规定" [Specific provisions on approval authority for punishing party members

who violate party discipline], 法律法规库 [Library of laws and regulations], July 6, 1983, https://www.flfgk.com/detail/6a986a4bda844c5aa686b0117132a192.html.

45. Bo Zhiyue, *China's Elite Politics: Political Transition and Power Balancing* (Singapore: World Scientific, 2007).

46. "李瑞环告别政协退出政坛" [Li Ruihuan bids farewell to the CPPCC and retires from politics], VOA (Chinese), March 5, 2003, https://www.voachinese.com/a/a-21-a-2003-03-05-22-1-63435732/1002079.html.

47. Andrew Nathan, "China's Resilient Authoritarianism," *Journal of Democracy* 14, no. 1 (2003): 6–17; Frederick Teiwes, "Normal Politics with Chinese Characteristics," *China Journal*, no. 45 (2001): 69–82.

48. Joseph Fewsmith, *Rethinking Chinese Politics* (New York: Cambridge University Press, 2021).

49. Leng and Wang, 邓小平年谱下册, 1280.

50. State Education Commission, 《中小学加强中国近代现代史及国情教育的总体纲要》(初稿) [General Outline of Strengthening Education on Modern History and National Conditions in Primary and Secondary Schools (first draft)] (Beijing: People's Education Press, 1991); "关于充分运用文物进行爱国主义和革命传统教育的通知" [Notice on the full use of cultural relics for education on patriotism and the revolutionary tradition], 法律法规库 [Library of laws and regulations], August 28, 1991, https://www.flfgk.com/detail/5e117729ee28e77bb8e8e9790241fe55.html.

51. State Council, 爱国主义教育实施纲要 [Outline on implementation of patriotic education], 国务院公报 [State Council gazette], September 20, 1990, http://www.gov.cn/gongbao/shuju/1994/gwyb199420.pdf.

52. Suisheng Zhao, "A State-Led Nationalism: The Patriotic Education Campaign in Post-Tiananmen China," *Communist and Post-Communist Studies* 31, no. 3 (1998): 287–302.

53. Wang Dehua and Li Yali, "新形势下高校爱国主义教育的实践与启示" [Practice and enlightenment of patriotic education in colleges and universities under the new situation], 思想理论教育 [Ideological and theoretical education], no. 3 (1994): 45–48; Political and Education Department, Yunnan Provincial Education Commission, "高扬主旋律 用多种载体 营造大氛围" [Highlighting the main melody and using a variety of carriers to create a grand atmosphere], 思想理论教育 [Ideological and theoretical education], no. 4 (1995): 8–10.

54. Zheng Wang, "National Humiliation, History Education, and the Politics of Historical Memory: Patriotic Education Campaign in China," *International Studies Quarterly* 52, no. 4 (2008): 783–806.

55. Zhu Xinjun, "大力加强高校爱国主义教育" [Vigorously strengthen patriotic education in colleges and universities], 高等教育 [Higher education], no. 1 (1996): 10–13.

56. Xu Suping, "高校爱国主义教育的重点内容" [Key contents of patriotic education in colleges and universities], 安徽大学学报 [Journal of Anhui University], no. 3 (1995): 76–77.

57. Zheng Wang, *Never Forget National Humiliation: Historical Memory in Chinese Politics and Foreign Relations* (New York: Columbia University Press, 2014).

58. Andrew Scobell, "Show of Force: Chinese Soldiers, Statesmen, and the 1995–1996 Taiwan Strait Crisis," *Political Science Quarterly* 115, no. 2 (2000): 227–46.

59. Peter Hays Gries, "Tears of Rage: Chinese Nationalist Reactions to the Belgrade Embassy Bombing," *China Journal*, no. 46 (2001): 25–43.

60. Peter Hays Gries, *China's New Nationalism: Pride, Politics, and Diplomacy* (Berkeley: University of California Press, 2004); Suisheng Zhao, *A Nation-State by Construction: Dynamics of Modern Chinese Nationalism* (Stanford, CA: Stanford University Press, 2004).

61. Yuhua Wang and Carl Minzner, "The Rise of the Chinese Security State," *China Quarterly*, no. 222 (2015): 339–59.

62. "中共中央关于维护社会稳定加强政法工作的通知" [Notice of the Central Committee on maintaining social stability and strengthening political and legal work], 中国改革信息库 [China reform information database], April 2, 1990, http://www.reformdata.org/1990/0402/4106.shtml.

63. "中共中央、国务院关于加强社会治安综合治理的决定" [Decision of the Central Committee and State Council on strengthening comprehensive management of public security], 中国改革信息库 [China reform information database], February 19, 1991, http://www.reformdata.org/1991/0219/4159.shtml.

64. 公检法支出财务统计资料, *1991–1995* [Financial statistics on expenditures by the Public Security Bureau, 1991–1995] (Nanjing: Jiangsu keji chubanshe, 1991), 166, 169; *ZGTJNJ 2003* [China statistical yearbook 2003] (Beijing: Zhongguo tongji chubanshe, 2004), 292.

65. 1987–1997 中国法律年鉴（珍藏版）[1987–1997 China legal yearbook (collector's edition)] (Beijing: Zhongguo falü nianjianshe, 1998), 778; Shen Xiaohong et al., "基层公安机关警力配置现状与思考" [The current situation and reflections on allocation of the police force in grassroots public security organs], 江西警察学院学报 [Journal of Jiangxi Public Security College], no. 4 (July 2010): 107. No official data on the size of the police force nationwide in the 1990s or early 2000s are available.

66. 湖北公安志 [Hubei public security chronicle] (N.p.: Hubei gong'an ting, 2010), 259; 浙江通志: 公安志 [Zhejiang general chronicle: Public security chronicle] (Hangzhou: Zhejiang renmin chubanshe, 2018), 63.

67. 玉溪市年鉴 1990 [Yuxi City yearbook, 1990] (Yuxi: Yuxishi difangzhi bangongting, 1990), 301; Tai Ming Cheung, "Guarding China's Domestic Front Line: The People's Armed Police and China's Stability," *China Quarterly*, no. 146 (1996): 525–47.

68. 建国以来公安工作大事要览 [Overview of major events in public security work since the founding of the People's Republic of China] (Beijing: Qunzhong chubanshe, 2003), 820, 917, 932, 1084–85, 1132, 1141.

69. 陕西省志: 公安志 [Shaanxi provincial chronicle: Public security chronicle] (Xi'an: Shaanxi renmin chubanshe, 2011), 554–58.

70. 建国以来公安工作大事要览, 880.

71. 建国以来公安工作大事要览, 988, 1073–74, 1227.

72. Denny Roy, "Singapore, China, and the 'Soft Authoritarian' Challenge," *Asian Survey* 34, no. 3 (1994): 231–42; Edwin Winckler, "Institutionalization and Participation on Taiwan: From Hard to Soft Authoritarianism?," *China Quarterly*, no. 99 (1984): 481–99.

73. Kevin O'Brien and Yanhua Deng, "Preventing Protest One Person at a Time: Psychological Coercion and Relational Repression in China," *China Review* 17, no. 2 (2017): 179–201; Lynette Ong, "'Thugs-for-Hire': Subcontracting of State Coercion and State Capacity in China," *Perspectives on Politics* 16, no. 3 (2018): 680–95; Rory Truex, "Focal Points, Dissident Calendars, and Preemptive Repression," *Journal of Conflict Resolution* 63, no. 4 (2019): 1032–52.

74. Ware Fong, "Depoliticization, Politicization, and Criminalization: How China Has Been Handling Political Prisoners Since 1980s," *Journal of Chinese Political Science* 24, no. 2 (2019): 315–39; Michael Sullivan, "Development and Political Repression: China's Human Rights Policy Since 1989," *Bulletin of Concerned Asian Scholars* 27, no. 4 (1995): 24–39.

75. James Tong, *Revenge of the Forbidden City: The Suppression of the Falungong in China, 1999–2005* (New York: Oxford University Press, 2009).

76. Xiao Sa, "论党的阶级基础与群众基础" [On the party's class and mass foundations], 云南省社会科学院 [Yunnan Academy of Social Sciences], November 3, 2010, http://www.sky.yn.gov.cn/ztzl/yq30zn/zgwj/zxyjs/637351293615183996.

77. 大专及以上 (college-level education and higher) refers to a three-year college education or higher. Central Organization Department, "中国共产党党内统计资料汇编 (1921–2010)" [Compilation of statistical data on the Communist Party of China (1921–2010)] (Beijing: Dangjian duwu chubanshe, 2011), 48–49.

78. "关于加强党的建设几个重大问题的决定" [Decision of the Central Committee of the Communist Party of China on several major issues concerning strengthening party building], 中共中国人民大学委员会党校 [Party Committee of the Party School of People's University], June 11, 2016, http://dangxiao.ruc.edu.cn/llxx/llqy/hygb/99cb834ed166416e8391a58b8d3da4f3.htm.

79. Xiaowei Zang, "University Education, Party Seniority, and Elite Recruitment in China," *Social Science Research* 30, no. 1 (2001): 62–75; Guihua Xie and Yangyang Zhang, "Seeking Out the Party: A Study of the Communist Party of China's Membership Recruitment Among Chinese College Students," *Chinese Journal of Sociology* 3, no. 1 (2017): 98–134.

80. "中共中央组织部、中共教育部党组、共青团中央关于加强和改进在大学生中发展党员工作和大学生党支部建设的意见" [Opinions of the Organization Department, the party group of the Ministry of Education, and the Central Committee of the CYL on strengthening and improving the development of party members among college students and the construction of party branches among college students], 中华人民共和国自然资源部 [Ministry of Natural Resources of the People's Republic of China], May 24, 2016, https://m.mnr.gov.cn/zt/dj/jgdj/ztjy/lxyz/d/201812/t20181203_2371769.html.

81. Ma Xueling and Xiao Yuanyuan, "青春与信仰 聚焦中国大学生党员群体" [Youth and faith focus on Chinese university student party members], 中国新闻网 [China News Network], June 28, 2011, https://www.chinanews.com.cn/gn/2011/06-28/3142241.shtml.

82. Xiaojun Yan, "Engineering Stability: Authoritarian Political Control Over University Students in Post-Deng China," *China Quarterly*, no. 218 (2014): 493–513.

83. 中共中央组织部, 中国共产党党内统计资料汇编 *(1921–2010)*, 48–51.

84. Xiao Sa, "论党的阶级基础与群众基础."

85. Zhou Yingfeng, "我国目前有党员8260.2万名 基层党组织402.7万个" [Our country currently has 82.602 million party members and 4.027 million grassroots party organizations], 新华社 [New China News Agency], June 30, 2012, http://www.gov.cn/jrzg/2012-06/30/content_2174072.htm. Official data for 2021 reported that 53 percent of party members had a college-level education or higher, but they did not disclose the share of workers and peasants. "党员9671.2万名 基层党组织493.6万个" [There are 96.712 million party members and 4.936 million grassroots party organizations], 新华社 [New China News Agency], June 29, 2022, http://www.gov.cn/xinwen/2022-06/29/content_5698405.htm.

86. "江泽民在庆祝中共成立80周年大会上的讲话" [Jiang Zemin's speech at the conference celebrating the 80th anniversary of the founding of the Communist Party of China], 中国新闻网 [China News Network], July 2, 2001, https://www.chinanews.com.cn/2001-07-02/26/101847.html.

87. 中国私营企业发展报告 2002 [China private enterprise development report 2002] (Beijing: Shehui kexue wenxian chubanshe, 2003), 4–5; *ZGTJNJ 2004* (Beijing: Zhongguo tongji chubanshe, 2005), 53.

88. 中国私营企业发展报告 2002, 31.

89. 中国私营企业发展报告 2002, 31.

90. Central Organization Department, 2008年中国共产党党内统计公报 [2008 internal-party statistical bulletin of the Communist Party of China], 复旦大学党委组织部 [Organization Department of the Party Committee of Fudan University], July 1, 2009, https://zzb.fudan.edu.cn/62/10/c2623a25104/page.htm.

91. Bruce Dickson, *Red Capitalists in China: The Party, Private Entrepreneurs, and Prospects for Political Change* (New York: Cambridge University Press, 2003); Jie Chen and Bruce Dickson, *Allies of the State: China's Private Entrepreneurs and Democratic Change* (Cambridge, MA: Harvard University Press, 2010).

92. Xiaojun Yan, "Regime Inclusion and the Resilience of Authoritarianism: The Local People's Political Consultative Conference in Post-Mao Chinese Politics," *China Journal*, no. 66 (2011): 53–75; Yue Hou, *The Private Sector in Public Office: Selective Property Rights in China* (New York: Cambridge University Press, 2019).

93. *ZGTJNJ 1995*, 61.

94. Ben Hillman and Gray Tuttle, eds., *Ethnic Conflict and Protest in Tibet and Xinjiang: Unrest in China's West* (New York: Columbia University Press, 2016); James Tong, "Anatomy of Regime Repression in China: Timing, Enforcement Institutions, and Target Selection in Banning the Falungong, July 1999," *Asian Survey* 42, no. 6 (2002): 795–820; Feng Chen, "Industrial Restructuring and Workers' Resistance in China," *Modern China* 29, no. 2 (2003): 237–62.

95. Pitman Potter, "The Chinese Legal System: Continuing Commitment to the Primacy of State Power," *China Quarterly*, no. 159 (1999): 673–83; Stanley Lubman, *Bird in a Cage: Legal Reform in China After Mao* (Stanford, CA: Stanford University Press, 1999); Randall Peerenboom, *China's Long March Toward Rule of Law* (New York: Cambridge University Press, 2002).

96. Robert Pastor and Qingshan Tan, "The Meaning of China's Village Elections," *China Quarterly*, no. 162 (2000): 490–512; Kevin O'Brien and Rongbin Han, "Path to Democracy? Assessing Village Elections in China," *Journal of Contemporary China* 18, no. 60 (2009): 359–78; Joseph Fewsmith, *The Logic and Limits of Political Reform in China* (New York: Cambridge University Press, 2013).

97. Andrew Wedeman, "Anticorruption Campaigns and the Intensification of Corruption in China," *Journal of Contemporary China* 14, no. 42 (2005): 93–116; Ting Gong, "Dangerous Collusion: Corruption as a Collective Venture in Contemporary China," *Communist and Post-Communist Studies* 35, no. 1 (2002): 85–103; Jiangnan Zhu, "Why are Offices for Sale in China? A Case Study of the Office-Selling Chain in Heilongjiang Province," *Asian Survey* 48, no. 4 (2008): 558–79.

98. Shawn Shieh, "The Rise of Collective Corruption in China: The Xiamen Smuggling Case," *Journal of Contemporary China* 14, no. 42 (2005): 67–91.

99. Murray Scot Tanner, "China Rethinks Unrest," *Washington Quarterly* 27, no. 3 (2004): 137–56.

100. Jianrong Yu, "Social Conflict in Rural China," *China Security* 3, no. 2 (2007): 2–17; Christian Goebel, "Social Unrest in China: A Bird's-Eye View," in *Handbook of Protest and Resistance in China*, ed. Teresa Wright (Cheltenham, UK: Edward Elgar, 2019), 27–45.

101. Joel Hellman, "Winners Take All: The Politics of Partial Reform in Postcommunist Transitions," *World Politics* 50, no. 2 (1998): 203–34.

102. Minxin Pei, *China's Trapped Transition: The Limits of Developmental Autocracy* (Cambridge, MA: Harvard University Press, 2006).

Chapter 4. Stagnation in the Hu Jintao Era

1. Of the nine members, at least four—Huang Ju, Wu Bangguo, Zeng Qinghong, and Jia Qingling—were Jiang's close associates.

2. *ZGTJNJ 2003*, 67.

3. World Bank, https://data.worldbank.org/indicator/SI.POV.GINI?locations=CN.

4. World Bank, "Out-of-Pocket Health Expenditure (% of Current Health Expenditure)," 2023, https://data.worldbank.org/indicator/SH.XPD.OOPC.CH.ZS. The world average, according to the World Bank, was 19.3 percent in 2020. I cannot find data on the world average in 2002, so I use data for 2020.

5. Data for 1990 and 1994 calculated from data in *ZGTJNJ 1995*, 692, and *ZGTJNJ 2005*, e-book; data for 1998–2002 obtained from *ZGTJNJ 2005*, e-book.

6. Jonathan Schwartz and R. Gregory Evans, "Causes of Effective Policy Implementation: China's Public Health Response to SARS," *Journal of Contemporary China* 16, no. 51 (2007): 195–213; Yanzhong Huang, *Governing Health in Contemporary China* (London: Routledge, 2013), 82–111.

7. Hu Jintao, "把促进经济社会协调发展摆到更加突出的位置" [Put promotion of coordinated economic and social development in a more prominent position], in 胡锦涛文选第二卷 [Selected works of Hu Jintao, vol. 2] (Beijing: Renmin chubanshe, 2016), 65–77.

8. Hu Jintao, "构建社会主义和谐社会" [Building a socialist harmonious society], in 胡锦涛文选第二卷, 273–99.

9. *ZGTJNJ 2006, 2007*, https://www.stats.gov.cn/sj/ndsj/.

10. Wusheng Yu and Hans G. Jensen, "China's Agricultural Policy Transition: Impacts of Recent Reforms and Future Scenarios," *Journal of Agricultural Economics* 61, no. 2 (2010): 343–68.

11. Xiaxin Wang and Yan Shen, "The Effect of China's Agricultural Tax Abolition on Rural Families' Incomes and Production," *China Economic Review*, no. 29 (2014): 185–99; Jianrong Yu, "Social Conflict in Rural China," *China Security* 3, no. 2 (2007): 2–17.

12. Keith Hand, "Using Law for a Righteous Purpose: The Sun Zhigang Incident and Evolving Forms of Citizen Action in the People's Republic of China," *Columbia Journal of Transnational Law*, no. 45 (2006): 114–95.

13. *ZGTJNJ 2014*, e-book.

14. Ling Li et al., "Chinese Healthcare Reform: A Shift Toward Social Development," *Modern China* 38, no. 6 (2012): 630–45.

15. *ZGTJNJ 2008*, e-book, https://www.stats.gov.cn/sj/ndsj/.

16. Pierre Landry et al., "Does Performance Matter? Evaluating Political Selection Along the Chinese Administrative Ladder," *Comparative Political Studies* 51, no. 8 (2018): 1074–1105.

17. Andrew G. Walder, "China's Extreme Inequality: The Structural Legacies of State Socialism," *China Journal* 90, no. 1 (2023): 1–26.

18. Murray Scot Tanner, "China Rethinks Unrest," *Washington Quarterly* 27, no. 3 (2004): 137–56.

19. Liu Neng, "当代中国的群体性事件" [Mass incidents in contemporary China], 江苏行政学院学报 [Journal of Jiangsu Administration Institute], no. 56 (2011): 54–55.

20. Xi Chen, *Social Protest and Contentious Authoritarianism in China* (New York: Cambridge University Press, 2012), 38; Feng Chen, "Subsistence Crises, Managerial Corruption and Labour Protests in China," *China Journal*, no. 44 (2000): 41–63.

21. Yanqi Tong and Shaohua Lei, *Social Protest in Contemporary China, 2003–2010: Transitional Pains and Regime Legitimacy* (London: Routledge, 2013), 50.

22. Christian Goebel and Lynette Ong, "Social Unrest in China," Europe China Research and Academic Network (ECRAN), 2012.

23. Ji Li, "Suing the Leviathan: An Empirical Analysis of the Changing Rate of Administrative Litigation in China," *Journal of Empirical Legal Studies* 10, no. 4 (2013): 815–46.

24. Kevin O'Brien and Lianjiang Li, *Rightful Resistance in Rural China* (New York: Cambridge University Press, 2006).

25. Goebel and Ong, "Social Unrest in China"; Tong and Lei, *Social Protest in Contemporary China, 2003–2010*.

26. Yongshun Cai, *Collective Resistance in China: Why Popular Protests Succeed or Fail* (Stanford, CA: Stanford University Press, 2020).

27. "中共中央关于进一步加强和改进公安工作的决定" [Decision of the Central Committee of the Communist Party of China on further strengthening and improving public security work], 中国改革信息库 [Reformdata.org], November 18, 2003, http://www.reformdata.org/2003/1118/4921.shtml.

28. *ZGTJNJ 2003*, 292; *ZGTJNJ 2005, 2008, 2013*, e-book.

29. "'金盾工程'一期建设基本完成 利用信息破案占两成" [The first phase of the "Golden Shield Project" is basically completed, and 20 percent of the cases have been solved using information], 中国政府门户网站 [Central People's Government], November 30, 2005, https://www.gov.cn/gzdt/2005-11/30/content_113209.htm; Ministry of Public Security, 建国以来公安工作大事要览 [An overview of major events in public security work since the founding of the People's Republic] (Beijing: Qunzhong chubanshe, 2003), 1227.

30. Rogier Greemers, "Cyber China: Upgrading Propaganda, Public Opinion Work and Social Management for the Twenty-First Century," *Journal of Contemporary China* 26, no. 103

(2017): 85–100; Wen-Hsuan Tsai, "How 'Networked Authoritarianism' Was Operationalized in China," *Journal of Contemporary China* 25, no. 101 (2016): 731–44.

31. Margaret E. Roberts, *Censored: Distraction and Diversion Inside China's Great Firewall* (Princeton, NJ: Princeton University Press, 2018); Gary King et al., "How the Chinese Government Fabricates Social Media Posts for Strategic Distraction, Not Engaged Argument," *American Political Science Review* 111, no. 3 (2017): 484–501.

32. Rebecca MacKinnon, "Liberation Technology: China's 'Networked Authoritarianism,'" *Journal of Democracy* 22, no. 2 (2011): 32–46; "Clinton's Words on China," *New York Times*, March 9, 2000, https://www.nytimes.com/2000/03/09/world/clinton-s-words-on-china-trade-is-the-smart-thing.html.

33. Ministry of Public Security, "关于开展城市报警与监控技术系统建设的意见" [Opinions on carrying out the construction of urban alarm and monitoring systems], August 25, 2005, http://www.e-gov.org.cn/article-82800.html. The full document referenced here is not publicly available.

34. Ministry of Public Security, "关于印发《关于深入开展城市报警与监控系统应用工作的意见》的通知 公科信 (2010) 30号" [Notice on issuance of the "Opinions on in-depth development of the application of urban alarm and monitoring systems (2010) no. 30]; Huang Haijun, "新平安城市建设需要什么?" [What is needed to build a new safe city?], 中国安防 [China Security], no. 3 (2013): 71–74.

35. "维稳办走上前台" [The Stability Maintenance Office comes to the front], 双周 [Biweekly], no. 8 (2009): 44–46.

36. Seymour Martin Lipset, "Some Social Requisites of Democracy: Economic Development and Political Legitimacy," *American Political Science Review* 53, no. 1 (1959): 69–105; Michael Ross, "Does Oil Hinder Democracy?," *World Politics* 53, no. 3 (2001): 325–61.

37. Samuel Huntington, *The Third Wave: Democratization in the Late Twentieth Century* (Norman: University of Oklahoma Press, 1993); Guillermo O'Donnell and Philippe Schmitter, *Transitions from Authoritarian Rule: Tentative Conclusions About Uncertain Democracies* (Baltimore, MD: Johns Hopkins University Press, 1986).

38. Biao Teng, "The Rights Defense Movement in China," *Chinese Law & Government* 46, no. 5–6 (2013): 4–12.

39. Eva Pils, *China's Human Rights Lawyers: Advocacy and Resistance* (London: Routledge, 2014); Hualing Fu and Richard Cullen, "Weiquan (Rights Protection) Lawyering in an Authoritarian State: Building a Culture of Public-Interest Lawyering," *China Journal*, no. 59 (2008): 111–27.

40. Teng Biao, "中国维权运动的起起落落| 观点" [The rise and fall of the rights protection movement], 自由亚洲电台 [Radio Free Asia], April 22, 2019, https://www.rfa.org/mandarin/duomeiti/guandian/gd-04222019111314.html.

41. Zheng Enchong, "郑恩宠：人权律师已成中共的政敌" [Human rights lawyers have become political opponents of the CCP], *Duli Zhongwen bihui* [Independent Chinese PEN Center], July 26, 2015, https://www.chinesepen.org/blog/archives/31846.

42. Teng Biao, "中国维权运动的历史和现状" [The history and current situation of China's human rights movement], 滕彪独立博客 [Teng Biao's independent blog], August 30, 2020, https://tengbiao.wordpress.com/2020/08/30/中国维权运动的历史和现状/.

43. "CNNIC统计报告：中国网民数量半年激增1330万" [CNNIC statistical report: The number of Chinese internet users surged by 13.3 million in half a year], 中国新闻网 [China News Network], January 16, 2003, http://www.chinanews.com.cn/n/2003-01-16/26/264408.html; Zhang Xinxin, "我国网民规模达到5.64亿" [The number of internet users in China reaches 564 million], 人民网 [People's daily online], January 15, 2013, http://finance.people.com.cn/n/2013/0115/c1004-20210588.html.

44. Miao Ning et al., "Estimation of Incidence of Viral Hepatitis B and Analysis on Case Characteristics in China, 2013–2020," *Chinese Journal of Epidemiology* 42, no. 9 (2021): 1527–31.

45. "乙肝歧视第一案" [First case of hepatitis-B discrimination], 北京青年报 [Beijing Youth Daily], December 20, 2003, https://news.sohu.com/2003/12/20/67/news217166762.shtml;

"乙肝歧视第一案波澜再起 芜湖市人事局提出上诉" [The first hepatitis-B discrimination case resurfaces, Wuhu City Personnel Bureau files appeal], 中国新闻网 [China News Network], April 18, 2004, http://www.chinanews.com.cn/n/2004-04-18/26/426799.html.

46. "2008年曝光的三聚氰胺毒奶事件造成中国超过30万幼儿中毒, 至少6名幼儿死亡" [The 2008 melamine-tainted milk incident poisoned more than 300,000 children and at least six children died], BBC News (Chinese), November 24, 2009, https://www.bbc.com/zhongwen/simp/china/2009/11/091124_china_melamine.

47. "质检总局: 全国液态奶三聚氰胺专项监督检查结果" [General Administration of Quality Supervision, Inspection, and Quarantine: Results of national special supervision and inspection of melamine in milk], 中央政府门户网站 [Central government portal], September 19, 2018, https://www.gov.cn/jrzg/2008-09/19/content_1099280.htm.

48. "山西黑砖窑案新进展" [New progress in Shanxi black brick kiln case], 中国新闻网 [China News Network], April 3, 2008, https://www.chinanews.com.cn/sh/news/2008/04-03/1211156.shtm.

49. "中国艾滋病维权人士田喜被正式起诉" [Chinese AIDS activist Tian Xi is formally charged], DW [Made for minds], July 9, 2010, https://www.dw.com/zh/中国艾滋病维权人士田喜被正式起诉/a-5981223.

50. Sophia Woodman, "Law, Translation, and Voice: Transformation of a struggle for Social Justice in a Chinese Village," *Critical Asian Studies* 43, no. 2 (2011): 185–210.

51. "上千油老板陷入涉案金逾50亿的陕北油田案" [Thousands of oil bosses trapped in northern Shaanxi oilfield involving more than 5 billion yuan], 民营经济报 [Private economic news], November 11, 2004, http://finance.sina.com.cn/leadership/jygl/20041111/13401148289.shtml.

52. "民营企业家孙大午被从轻发落" [Private entrepreneur Sun Dawu is given a lighter sentence], 中国青年报 [China youth news], October 31, 2003, http://zqb.cyol.com/.

53. Xu Zhiyong, "公盟" [Open constitution initiative], *Duli Zhongwen bihui* [Independent Chinese PEN Center], February 25, 2020, https://www.chinesepen.org/blog/archives/143930.

54. Andrew Wedeman, *Double Paradox: Rapid Growth and Rising Corruption in China* (Ithaca, NY: Cornell University Press, 2012).

55. Transparency International, "Corruption Perception Index," https://www.transparency.org/en/cpi/2022. Transparency International began to publish its Corruption Perception Index in 1995.

56. Inflation data obtained from *ZGTJNJ 2013*.

57. Andrew Wedeman, "The Dynamics and Trajectory of Corruption in Contemporary China," *China Review* 22, no. 2 (2022): 21–48.

58. Andrew G. Walder, "Elite Opportunity in Transitional Economies," *American Sociological Review* 68, no. 6 (2003): 899–916; Minxin Pei, *China's Crony Capitalism: Dynamics of Regime Decay* (Cambridge, MA: Harvard University Press, 2016).

59. Yuen Yuen Ang, *China's Gilded Age: The Paradox of Economic Boom and Vast Corruption* (New York: Cambridge University Press, 2020).

60. *ZGTJNJ 2003*, 469; *ZGTJNJ 2013*, e-book.

61. Jiangnan Zhu, "The Shadow of the Skyscrapers: Real Estate Corruption in China," *Journal of Contemporary China* 21, no. 74 (2012): 243–60.

62. "近20年17名省交通厅长被查" [Seventeen provincial transportation directors have been investigated in the past 20 years], 人民网 [People's daily online], October 17, 2014, http://politics.people.com.cn/n/2014/1017/c1001-25854895-12.html.

63. Jia Chunwang, "最高人民检察院工作报告" [Work report of the Supreme People's Procuratorate], 中华人民共和国最高人民检察院 [Supreme People's Procuratorate of the People's Republic], March 10, 2008, https://www.spp.gov.cn/spp/gzbg/201208/t20120820_2495.shtml.

64. Lant Pritchett and Daniel Kaufmann, "Civil Liberties, Democracy, and the Performance of Government Projects," *Finance and Development*, no. 35 (1998): 26–29.

65. Fenfei Li and Jinting Deng, "The Limits of the Arbitrariness in Anticorruption by China's Local Party Discipline Inspection Committees," *Journal of Contemporary China* 25, no. 97 (2016): 75–90.

66. Andrew Wedeman, "Anticorruption Campaigns and the Intensification of Corruption in China," *Journal of Contemporary China* 14, no. 42 (2005): 93–116.

67. Wedeman, *Double Paradox*; Ang, *China's Gilded Age.*

68. Susan Rose-Ackerman and Bonnie Palifka, *Corruption and Government: Causes, Consequences, and Reform* (New York: Cambridge University Press, 2016); Pranab Bardhan, "Corruption and Development: A Review of Issues," *Journal of Economic Literature* 35, no. 3 (1997): 1320–46.

69. Tony Saich, *From Rebel to Ruler: One Hundred Years of the Chinese Communist Party* (Cambridge, MA: Harvard University Press, 2021), 378; Willy Wo-Lap Lam, *Chinese Politics in the Era of Xi Jinping* (London: Routledge, 2015), 57–58.

70. Cheng Li, "Was the Shanghai Gang Shanghaied? The Fall of Chen Liangyu and the Survival of Jiang Zemin's Faction," *China Leadership Monitor*, no. 20 (2007): 1–17, https://www.hoover.org/sites/default/files/uploads/documents/clm20cl.pdf.

71. Lam, *Chinese Politics in the Era of Xi Jinping*, 44–51.

72. "中国共产主义青年团第十九次全国代表大会在京开幕" [Nineteenth National Congress of the CYL opens in Beijing], June 19, 2023, http://www.news.cn/politics/leaders/2023-06/19/c_1129706114.htm.

73. Jérôme Doyon, *Rejuvenating Communism: The Communist Youth League as a Political Promotion Channel in Post-Mao China* (New York: Columbia University Press, 2017).

74. David M. Lampton, *Following the Leader: Ruling China, from Deng Xiaoping to Xi Jinping* (Berkeley: University of California Press, 2014).

75. Alice Miller, "The Politburo Standing Committee Under Hu Jintao," *China Leadership Monitor*, no. 35 (2011): 1–9, https://www.hoover.org/sites/default/files/uploads/documents/CLM35AM.pdf.

76. Ouyang Yanqin and Luo Jieqi, "令计划被查 仕途逆转早有时" [If Ling Jihua's plan is investigated, his career will be reversed sooner rather than later], 财新 [Caixin], December 23, 2014, https://china.caixin.com/2014-12-23/100766806.html.

77. Zhiyue Bo and Gang Chen, *Bo Xilai and the Chongqing Model* (Singapore: East Asia Institute, National University of Singapore, 2009).

78. Pin Ho and Wenguang Huang, *A Death in the Lucky Holiday Hotel: Murder, Money, and an Epic Power Struggle in China* (New York: PublicAffairs, 2013).

79. Chun Han Wong, *Party of One: The Rise of Xi Jinping and China's Superpower Future* (New York: Avid Reader Press, 2023), 53.

80. James Hollyer and Leonard Wantchekon, "Corruption and Ideology in Autocracies," *Journal of Law, Economics, and Organization* 31, no. 3 (2015): 499–533; Milan Svolik, *The Politics of Authoritarian Rule* (New York: Cambridge University Press, 2012).

81. Joel Hellman, "Winners Take All: The Politics of Partial Reform in Postcommunist Transitions," *World Politics* 50, no. 2 (1998): 203–34; Minxin Pei, *China's Trapped Transition: The Limits of Developmental Autocracy* (Cambridge, MA: Harvard University Press, 2006).

82. Susan Shirk, *Overreach: How China Derailed Its Peaceful Rise* (New York: Oxford University Press, 2022).

Chapter 5. China's Economic Miracle

1. Yasheng Huang, "Debating China's Economic Growth: The Beijing Consensus or The Washington Consensus," *Academy of Management Perspectives* 24, no. 2 (2010): 31–47; Scott Kennedy, "The Myth of the Beijing Consensus," *Journal of Contemporary China* 19, no. 65 (2010): 461–77.

2. World Bank, "GDP (current US$)—China," https://data.worldbank.org/indicator/NY.GDP.MKTP.CD?locations=CN.

3. Alessandro Nicita and Carlos Razo, "The Rise of a Trade Titan," UNCTAD, April 27, 2021, https://unctad.org/news/china-rise-trade-titan.

4. Dani Rodrik, "What's So Special About China's Exports?," *China and World Economy* 14, no. 5 (2006): 1–19.

5. *ZGTJNJ 2013*, e-book, https://www.stats.gov.cn/sj/ndsj/.

6. *ZGTJNJ 2013*, e-book.

7. *ZGTJNJ 2013*, e-book.

8. World Bank, "GDP Per Capita, PPP (current international $)—China," https://data.worldbank.org/indicator/NY.GDP.PCAP.PP.CD?locations=CN.

9. World Bank and the Development Research Center of the State Council of the PRC, *Four Decades of Poverty Reduction in China: Drivers, Insights for the World, and the Way Ahead* (Washington, DC: World Bank, 2022), 6.

10. *ZGTJNJ 1995* (Beijing: Zhongguo tongji chubanshe, 1996), 375.

11. "中共中央关于建立社会主义市场经济体制若干问题的决定 (中发[1993]13号)" [Resolution on several questions on the construction of a socialist market economic system (Guofa [1993], no. 13)], 中国共产党第十四届中央委员会第三次全体会议1993年11月14日通过 [Adopted at the Third Plenary Session of the 14th Central Committee of the Communist Party of China on November 14, 1993], https://www.waizi.org.cn/law/3442.html.

12. Yi Gang, "改革开放三十年来人民币汇率体制的演变" [Evolution of the RMB exchange rate system during the thirty years of reform and opening], 金融四十人论坛 [Finance forty forum], December 1, 2018, http://www.cf40.com/news_detail/678.html.

13. Shu-Ki Tsang, "Towards Full Convertibility? China's Foreign Exchange Reforms," *China Information* 9, no. 1 (1994): 1–41.

14. *ZGTJNJ 1995*, 537, 574.

15. *ZGTJNJ 2003* (Beijing: Zhongguo tongji chubanshe, 2004), 287.

16. Christine P. W. Wong, "Central–Local Relations in an Era of Fiscal Decline: The Paradox of Fiscal Decentralization in Post-Mao China," *China Quarterly*, no. 128 (1991): 691–715.

17. *ZGTJNJ 2003*, 282–83.

18. *ZGTJNJ 2003*, 287.

19. Le-Yin Zhang, "Chinese Central-Provincial Fiscal Relationships, Budgetary Decline and the Impact of the 1994 Fiscal Reform: An Evaluation," *China Quarterly*, no. 157 (1999): 115–41; Ran Tao et al., "Land Leasing and Local Public Finance in China's Regional Development: Evidence from Prefecture-level Cities," *Urban Studies* 47, no. 10 (2010): 2217–36.

20. *ZGTJNJ 2010* (Beijing: Zhongguo tongji chubanshe, 2011), 307.

21. Adam Liu, Jean Oi, and Yi Zhang, "China's Local Government Debt: The Grand Bargain," *China Journal*, no. 87 (2022): 40–71.

22. State Council, "关于金融体制改革的决定 (国发[1993]91号)" [Decision on the reform of the financial system (Guofa [1993]), no. 91)], 中国改革信息库 [China reform information database], December 25, 1993, http://www.reformdata.org/1993/1225/23288.shtml.

23. Stephen Bell, *The Rise of the People's Bank of China: The Politics of Institutional Change* (Cambridge, MA: Harvard University Press, 2013).

24. Nicholas Lardy, *China's Unfinished Economic Revolution* (Washington, DC: Brookings, 1998), 59–127; Wendy Dobson and Anil K. Kashyap, "The Contradiction in China's Gradualist Banking Reforms," *Brookings Papers on Economic Activity*, no. 2 (2006): 103–62.

25. Ross Garnaut et al., *Private Enterprise in China* (Canberra: ANU Press, 2012), 54–55.

26. Yunling Chen, Ming Liu, and Jun Su, "Greasing the Wheels of Bank Lending: Evidence from Private Firms in China," *Journal of Banking and Finance* 37, no. 7 (2013): 2533–45.

27. *ZGTJNJ 2013*, e-book.

28. "中共中央关于建立社会主义市场经济体制若干问题的决定."

29. Lardy, *China's Unfinished Economic Revolution*, 21–58.

30. Nicholas R. Lardy, *Markets Over Mao: The Rise of Private Business in China* (Washington, DC: Peterson Institute for International Economics, 2014), 48–58; Barry Naughton, "The State Asset Commission: A Powerful New Government Body," *China Leadership Monitor*, no. 8 (2003): 1–10, https://www.hoover.org/sites/default/files/uploads/documents/clm8_bn.pdf.

31. Lardy, *Markets Over Mao*, 11–41.

32. X. L. Ding, "The Illicit Asset Stripping of Chinese State Firms," *China Journal*, no. 43 (2000): 1–28.

33. *ZGTJNJ 1998* (Beijing: Zhongguo tongji chubanshe, 1999), 431–32; *ZGTJNJ 1999, 2000*, e-book; *ZGTJNJ 2003* (Beijing: Zhongguo tongji chubanshe, 2004), 460.

34. Feng Chen, "Subsistence Crises, Managerial Corruption and Labour Protests in China," *China Journal*, no. 44 (2000): 41–63; Fulong Wu, "Urban Poverty and Marginalization Under Market Transition: The Case of Chinese Cities," *International Journal of Urban and Regional Research* 28, no. 2 (2004): 401–23.

35. Feng Chen "Industrial Restructuring and Workers' Resistance in China," *Modern China* 29, no. 2 (2003): 237–62.

36. Kenneth Rogoff and Yuanchen Yang, "Peak China Housing," National Bureau of Economic Research, Working Paper no. 27697 (2020).

37. Chong-En Bai, Jiangyong Lu, and Zhigang Tao, "How Does Privatization Work in China?," *Journal of Comparative Economics* 37, no. 3 (2009): 453–70; Jean Oi, "Patterns of Corporate Restructuring in China: Political Constraints on Privatization," *China Journal*, no. 53 (2005): 115–36.

38. He Li, "Debating China's Economic Reform: New Leftists vs. Liberals," *Journal of Chinese Political Science*, no. 15 (2010): 1–23.

39. Cheryl Long, Jing Zhang, and Jin Yang, "Uncovering Asset Stripping During China's Privatization," *Economics of Transition and Institutional Change* 29, no. 4 (2021): 652.

40. Hongbin Li and Scott Rozelle, "Saving or Stripping Rural Industry: An Analysis of Privatization and Efficiency in China," *Agricultural Economics* 23, no. 3 (2000): 251.

41. Hongyi Chen, *The Institutional Transition of China's Township and Village Enterprises: Market Liberalization, Contractual Form Innovation and Privatization* (Brookfield, VT: Ashgate, 2000).

42. *ZGTJNJ 2003*, 134.

43. *ZGTJNJ 1995*, 375; *ZGTJNJ 2013*, e-book.

44. *ZGTJNJ 1995*, 375; calculated from the data in tables 14–1 and 14–6. *ZGTJNJ 2012*, e-book, https://www.stats.gov.cn/sj/ndsj/.

45. *ZGTJNJ 1995*, 554.

46. Richard Hu and Weijie Chen, *Global Shanghai Remade: The Rise of Pudong New Area* (London: Routledge, 2020).

47. Guangdong Provincial Planning Commission, "省计委关于下放外商直接投资项目审批权限意见的通知 ([1992]36号)" [Notice on the decentralization of approval authority for foreign direct investment projects (1992) no. 36], 广东省人民政府 [Guangdong Province People's Government], May 16, 1992, http://www.gd.gov.cn/zwgk/gongbao/1992/5/content/post_3356383.html.

48. "指导外商投资方向暂行规定" [Interim regulations to guide the direction of foreign investment], June 20, 1995, 法律法规库 [Laws and regulations library], https://www.flfgk.com/detail/961475ca38c91a2de22a3bdf277d2db1.html.

49. Chunlai Chen, "The Liberalisation of FDI Policies and the Impacts of FDI on China's Economic Development," in *China's 40 Years of Reform and Development 1978–2018*, ed. Ross Garnaut, Ligang Song, and Cai Fang (Canberra: ANU Press, 2018), 598.

50. Nicholas R. Lardy, *China in the World Economy* (Washington, DC: Institute for International Economics, 1994), 63–71.

51. Calculated from *ZGTJNJ 1995*, 114.

52. Yi Huang, Liugang Sheng, Gewei Wang, "How Did Rising Labor Costs Erode China's Global Advantage?," *Journal of Economic Behavior & Organization*, no. 183 (2021): 632–53.

53. Min Ye, *Diasporas and Foreign Direct Investment in China and India* (New York: Cambridge University Press, 2014).

54. Calculated from data in *ZGTJNJ 1998* (Beijing: Zhongguo tongji chubanshe, 1999), 639; *ZGTJNJ 1999, 2000, 2001*, e-book, https://www.stats.gov.cn/sj/ndsj/; *ZGTJNJ 2003*, 672; *ZGTJNJ 2005, 2007*, e-book, https://www.stats.gov.cn/sj/ndsj/.

55. Geng Xiao, "People's Republic of China's Round-Tripping FDI: Scale, Causes and Implications," ADB Institute Discussion Paper, no. 7 (July 2004), https://www.adb.org/sites/default/files/publication/156758/adbi-dp7.pdf.

56. Yasheng Huang, *Selling China: Foreign Direct Investment During the Reform Era* (New York: Cambridge University Press, 2003).

57. *ZGTJNJ 1998*, 142; *ZGTJNJ 2013*, e-book.

58. Ziliang Deng, *Foreign Direct Investment in China: Spillover Effects on Domestic Enterprises* (London: Routledge, 2012); Cheryl Xiaoning Long and Galina Hale, *Foreign Direct Investment in China: Winners and Losers* (Singapore: World Scientific, 2012), 49–67.

59. *ZGTJNJ 1995*, 552–553; *ZGTJNJ 2013*, e-book.

60. Robert Koopman, Zhi Wang, and Shang-Jin Wei, "How Much of Chinese Exports Is Really Made in China? Assessing Domestic Value-Added When Processing Trade Is Pervasive," National Bureau of Economic Research, Working Paper 14109, (2008); Bawoo Kim, "What Has China Learned from Processing Trade?," *Journal of Economic Structures* 6, no. 1 (2017): 11; Chen, "The Liberalisation of FDI Policies," 607.

61. State Council, 国务院关于进一步深化对外贸易体制改革的决定, 国发 (1994) 4号 [Decision on further deepening the reform of the foreign trade system, Guofa (1994) no. 4], 人民政府 [Central Government of the People's Republic of China], January 11, 1994, https://www.gov.cn/zhengce/content/2010-11/15/content_1429.htm.

62. Nicholas Lardy, "Is China a Closed Economy?," Brookings Institution, February 24, 2000, https://www.brookings.edu/articles/is-china-a-closed-economy/.

63. Sheng Bin and Wei Fang, "新中国对外贸易发展70年" [Seventy years of foreign trade development in new China], 财贸经济 [Finance and trade economics] 40, no. 10 (2019): 38, http://cmjj.ajcass.org/UploadFile/Issue/dqwwyicc.pdf.

64. "2012年中国对外贸易发展情况" (Development of China's foreign trade in 2012), 中华人民共和国商务部 [PRC Ministry of Commerce], April 28, 2013, http://zhs.mofcom.gov.cn/article/Nocategory/201304/20130400107790.shtml.

65. Xiang Bo, ed., "Private Firms Lead China's Imports, Exports for First Time," Xinhua, January 14, 2020, http://www.xinhuanet.com/english/2020-01/14/c_138704308.htm.

66. Congressional Research Service, "China's Currency Policy: An Analysis of the Economic Issues," July 22, 2013, https://crsreports.congress.gov/product/pdf/RS/RS21625/70#.

67. Carlos Razo, "Evolution of the World's 25 Top Trading Nations," UNCTAD, April 6, 2021, https://unctad.org/topic/trade-analysis/chart-10-may-2021.

68. Hui Feng, *The Politics of China's Accession to the World Trade Organization* (London: Routledge, 2006); Nicholas Lardy, *Integrating China into the Global Economy* (Washington, DC: Brookings Institution Press, 2001).

69. Robert Lighthizer, *No Trade Is Free: Changing Course, Taking on China, and Helping America's Workers* (New York: Broadside Books, 2023); John Mearsheimer, "The Inevitable Rivalry: America, China, and the Tragedy of Great-Power Politics," *Foreign Affairs* 100, no. 6 (November–December 2021): 48–58.

70. Henry Gao, Damian Raess, and Ka Zeng, eds., *China and the WTO: A Twenty-Year Assessment* (New York: Cambridge University Press, 2023).

71. *ZGTJNJ 2012*, e-book.

72. *ZGTJNJ 2012*, e-book.

73. Loren Brandt et al., "WTO Accession and Performance of Chinese Manufacturing Firms," *American Economic Review* 107, no. 9 (2017): 2784–20; Zhiming Zhang, Xin Zhang, and Riming Cui, "Research on the Effects of WTO Accession on China's Economic Growth: Path Analysis and Empirical Study," *Journal of Chinese Economic and Foreign Trade Studies* 6, no. 2 (2013): 70–84.

74. Bilge Erten and Jessica Leight, "Exporting Out of Agriculture: The Impact of WTO Accession on Structural Transformation in China," *Review of Economics and Statistics* 103, no. 2 (2021): 364–80.

75. Steve Ching et al., "Economic Benefits of Globalization: The Impact of Entry to the WTO on China's Growth," *Pacific Economic Review* 16, no. 3 (2011): 285–301; Chinese GDP growth data are obtained from *ZGTJNJ 2008* (Beijing: Zhongguo tongji chubanshe, 2009), 40.

76. Yeling Tan, "How the WTO Changed China: The Mixed Legacy of Economic Engagement," *Foreign Affairs* 100, no. 2 (2021): 90–102.

77. Congressional Research Service, "China-U.S. Trade Issues Updated," July 30, 2018, 50–53.

78. David Autor et al., "Importing Political Polarization? The Electoral Consequences of Rising Trade Exposure," *American Economic Review* 110, no. 10 (2020): 3139–83.

79. David Bloom and Jeffrey Williamson, "Demographic Transitions and Economic Miracles in Emerging Asia," *World Bank Economic Review* 12, no. 3 (1998): 419–55; Andrew Mason and Tomoko Kinugasa, "East Asian Economic Development: Two Demographic Dividends," *Journal of Asian Economics* 19, no. 5–6 (2008): 389–99.

80. Cai Fang, Ross Garnaut, and Ligang Song, "How Reform Captured China's Demographic Dividend," in Garnaut et al., *China's 40 Years of Reform and Development: 1978–2018*, 8–10.

81. Mason and Kinugasa, "East Asian Economic Development."

82. *ZGTJNJ 1990* (Beijing: Zhongguo tongji chubanshe, 1991), 90.

83. *ZGTJNJ 1995*, 61.

84. Fang Cai and Dewen Wang, "China's Demographic Transition: Implications for Growth," in *The China Boom and Its Discontents*, ed. Ross Garnaut and Ligang Song (Canberra: Asia Pacific Press, 2005), 34–52; Haifeng Zhang, Hongliang Zhang, and Junsen Zhang, "Demographic Age Structure and Economic Development: Evidence from Chinese Provinces," *Journal of Comparative Economics* 43, no. 1 (2015): 170–85.

85. National Bureau of Statistics, 2013 年全国农民工监测调查报告 [2013 National migrant workers monitoring survey report], 中央政府门户网站 [Central government portal], May 12, 2014, https://www.gov.cn/xinwen/2014-05/12/content_2677889.htm.

86. Xiaodong Zhu, "Understanding China's Growth: Past, Present, and Future," *Journal of Economic Perspectives* 26, no. 4 (2012): 103–24.

87. Fang Cai, "How Has the Chinese Economy Capitalised on the Demographic Dividend During the Reform Period?" in Garnaut et al., *China's 40 Years of Reform and Development: 1978–2018*, 235–55; Fang, Garnaut, and Song, "How Reform Captured China's Demographic Dividend," 8–10.

88. Fang Cai, "Haste Makes Waste: Policy Options Facing China After Reaching the Lewis Turning Point," *China and World Economy* 23, no. 1 (2015): 1–20.

89. *ZGTJNJ 2013*, e-book.

90. World Bank, *The East Asian Miracle: Economic Growth and Public Policy* (New York: Oxford University Press, 1993).

91. Alwyn Young, "The Tyranny of Numbers: Confronting the Statistical Realities of the East Asian Growth Experience," *Quarterly Journal of Economics* 110, no. 3 (1995): 641–80; Paul Krugman, "The Myth of Asia's Miracle," *Foreign Affairs* 73, no. 6 (1994): 62–78.

92. Loren Brandt and Xiaodong Zhu, "Accounting for China's Growth," *IZA Discussion Paper*, no. 4764 (2010), https://www.iza.org/publications/dp/4764/accounting-for-chinas-growth.

93. Barry Bosworth and Susan Collins, "Accounting for Growth: Comparing China and India," *Journal of Economic Perspectives* 22, no. 1 (2008): 45–66; Dwight H. Perkins and Thomas G. Rawski, "Forecasting China's Economic Growth to 2025," in *China's Great Economic Transformation*, ed. Loren Brandt and Thomas Rawski (New York: Cambridge University Press, 2010), 839.

94. World Bank, https://databank.worldbank.org/source/world-development-indicators#.

95. *ZGTJNJ 2013*, e-book.

96. Aart Kraay, "Household Saving in China," *World Bank Economic Review* 14, no. 3 (2000): 545–70.

97. Franco Modigliani and Shi Larry Cao, "The Chinese Saving Puzzle and the Life-Cycle Hypothesis," *Journal of Economic Literature* 42, no. 1 (2004): 145–70.

98. Marcos Chamon, Kai Liu, and Eswar Prasad, "Income Uncertainty and Household Savings in China," National Bureau of Economic Research, Working Paper 16565, (December 2010).

99. Longmei Zhang et al., "China's High Savings: Drivers, Prospects, and Policies," International Monetary Fund, Working Paper WP18/277, (2018).

100. Edward Gleaser et al., "A Real Estate Boom with Chinese Characteristics," *Journal of Economic Perspectives* 31, no. 1 (2017): 93–116; Zhenya Liu and Shixuan Wang, "Decoding Chinese Stock Market Returns: Three-State Hidden Semi-Markov Model," *Pacific-Basin Finance Journal*, no. 44 (2017): 127–49.

101. "温家宝：中国具备继续保持经济平稳较快发展的条件" [Wen Jiabao: China has the conditions to continue to maintain stable and rapid economic development], 中央政府门户网站 [Central government portal], March 16, 2007, https://www.gov.cn/wszb/zhibo20070316b/content_552718.htm.

102. Wen Jiabao, "2013年国务院政府工作报告" [2013 government work report], 中央政府门户网站 [Central government portal], March 19, 2013, https://www.gov.cn/test/2013-03/19/content_2357136.htm.

103. *ZGTJNJ 2021*, e-book.

104. Nicholas Lardy, *Sustaining China's Economic Growth After the Global Financial Crisis* (Washington, DC: Peterson Institute for International Economics, 2012), 47.

105. *ZGTJNJ 2013*, e-book.

106. Tian Zhu, *Catching Up to America: Culture, Institutions, and the Rise of China* (New York: Cambridge University Press, 2021), 102; Dominik Peschel and Wenyu Liu, "The Long-Term Growth Prospects of the People's Republic of China," Asian Development Bank Institute, East Asia Working Paper, no. 54 (2022): 27.

107. Loren Brandt et al., "China's Productivity Slowdown and Future Growth Potential," World Bank, Policy Research Paper no. 9298 (2020): 15–16.

108. Guo-liang Yang, Hirofumi Fukuyama, and Yao-yao Song, "Estimating Capacity Utilization of Chinese Manufacturing Industries," *Socio-Economic Planning Sciences*, no. 67 (2019): 94–110; Qing Yang et al., "The Drivers of Coal Overcapacity in China: An Empirical Study Based on the Quantitative Decomposition," *Resources, Conservation and Recycling*, no. 141 (2019): 123–32.

109. Brandt et al., "China's Productivity Slowdown," 12–13; Lardy, *Markets Over Mao*, 34, 97.

110. Shang-Jin Wei, Zhuan Xie, and Xiaobo Zhang, "From 'Made in China' to 'Innovated in China': Necessity, Prospect, and Challenges," *Journal of Economic Perspectives* 31, no. 1 (2017): 56–57.

111. Harry X. Wu, "Sustainability of China's Growth Model: A Productivity Perspective," *China and World Economy* 24, no. 5 (2016): 51.

112. Xie Wei and Zhang, "From 'Made in China' to 'Innovated in China,'" 57.

113. *ZGTJNJ 2008*, 57, 708.

114. Margot Schüler and Yun Schüler-Zhou, "China's Economic Policy in the Time of the Global Financial Crisis: Which Way Out?," *Journal of Current Chinese Affairs* 38, no. 3 (2009): 165–81.

115. Nicholas Borst, "China's Credit Boom: New Risks Require New Reforms," *Policy Brief 2013–24* (Washington, DC: Peterson Institute for International Economics, 2013), 5.

116. *ZGTJNJ 2011*, *ZGTJNJ 2021*, e-book.

117. *ZGTJNJ 2011*, e-book.

118. Lardy, *Sustaining China's Economic Growth After the Global Financial Crisis*, 5; Yan Liang, "China and the Global Financial Crisis: Assessing the Impacts and Policy Response," *China and World Economy* 18, no. 3 (2010): 56–72; Shaun Breslin, "Paradigm(s) Shifting? Responding to the Global Financial Crisis," in *The Consequences of the Global Financial Crisis The Rhetoric of Reform and Regulation*, ed. Wyn Grant and Graham K. Wilson (New York: Oxford University Press, 2012), 226–46.

119. Bank of International Settlements, "Credit to the Non-Financial Sector," https://www.bis.org/statistics/totcredit.htm.

120. Borst, "China's Credit Boom."

121. Sally Chen and Joong Shik Kang, "Credit Booms—Is China Different?," International Monetary Fund, Working Paper 18/2 (2018): 5–6.

122. Brandt et al., "China's Productivity Slowdown,"17.

123. *ZGTJNJ*, various years, e-book.

124. Yasheng Huang, *Capitalism with Chinese Characteristics: Entrepreneurship and the State* (New York: Cambridge University Press, 2008).

125. World Bank and Development Research Center of the State Council of China, *China 2030: Building a Modern, Harmonious, and Creative Society* (Washington, DC: World Bank, 2013).

Chapter 6. Revival of Totalitarianism Under Xi Jinping

1. Guillermo O'Donnell and Philippe C. Schmitter, *Transitions from Authoritarian Rule: Tentative Conclusions About Uncertain Democracies* (Baltimore: Johns Hopkins University Press, 1986), 1–14; Samuel P. Huntington, *The Third Wave: Democratization in the Late Twentieth Century* (Norman: University of Oklahoma Press, 1991), 121–40.

2. Hu Jintao, 胡锦涛在中国共产党第十八次全国代表大会上的报告 [Hu Jintao's report to the Eigthteenth Party Congress], 中央政府门户网站 [Central government portal], November 17, 2012, https://www.gov.cn/ldhd/2012-11/17/content_2268826_2.htm.

3. "Vows of Change in China Belie Private Warning," *New York Times*, February 14, 2013, https://www.nytimes.com/2013/02/15/world/asia/vowing-reform-chinas-leader-xi-jinping-airs-other-message-in-private.html.

4. Xu Jingyue and Huo Xiaoguang, "习近平：毫不动摇坚持和发展中国特色社会主义" [Xi Jinping: Unswervingly uphold and develop socialism with Chinese characteristics], 中央政府门户网站 [Central government portal], January 5, 2013, https://www.gov.cn/ldhd/2013-01/05/content_2305247.htm.

5. "习近平：关于坚持和发展中国特色社会主义的几个问题" [Xi Jinping: Several issues regarding upholding and developing socialism with Chinese characteristics], 中国共产党新闻网 (Central government portal), April 1, 2019, http://dangjian.people.com.cn/n1/2019/0401/c117092-31006792.html.

6. "习近平：关于坚持和发展中国特色社会主义的几个问题."

7. Alfred Chan, *Xi Jinping: Political Career, Governance, and Leadership, 1953–2018* (New York: Oxford University Press), 301–4.

8. Roy Medvedev, *Let History Judge: The Origins and Consequences of Stalinism* (New York: Columbia University Press, 1989); Andrew Walder, "Actually Existing Maoism," *Australian Journal of Chinese Affairs*, no. 18 (1987): 155–66.

9. Willy Wo-Lap Lam, *Chinese Politics in the Era of Xi Jinping: Renaissance, Reform, or Retrogression?* (London: Routledge, 2015), 24–25.

10. Chris Buckley, "China Takes Aim at Western Ideas," *New York Times*, August 19, 2013, https://www.nytimes.com/2013/08/20/world/asia/chinas-new-leadership-takes-hard-line-in-secret-memo.html.

11. Chris Buckley, "Crackdown on Bloggers Is Mounted by China," *New York Times*, September 10, 2013, https://www.nytimes.com/2013/09/11/world/asia/china-cracks-down-on-online-opinion-makers.html.

12. Tony Lee, "Pernicious Custom? Corruption, Culture, and the Efficacy of Anti-Corruption Campaigning in China," *Crime, Law and Social Change*, no. 70 (2018): 349–61; Andrew Wedeman, "Anticorruption Campaigns and the Intensification of Corruption in China," *Journal of Contemporary China* 14, no. 42 (2005): 93–116.

13. "中国共产党章程" [Constitution of the Communist Party of China], 共产党员网 [Communist Party network], October 22, 2022, https://www.12371.cn/special/zggcdzc/zggcdzcqw/. The party amended its charter several times in the post-Mao era. But the provisions on investigations and penalties for officials who violate party discipline remain unchanged.

14. Xuezhi Guo, "Controlling Corruption in the Party: China's Central Discipline Inspection Commission," *China Quarterly*, no. 219 (2014): 597–624.

15. Ling Li, "Politics of Anticorruption in China: Paradigm Change of the Party's Disciplinary Regime 2012–2017," *Journal of Contemporary China* 28, no. 115 (2019): 47–63; Andrew Wedeman, "Xi Jinping's Tiger Hunt: Anti-Corruption Campaign or Factional Purge?," *Modern China Studies* 24, no. 2 (2017): 35–94.

16. "2022年，至少32名中管干部落马" [At least thirty-two cadres will be dismissed in 2022], 中国新闻周刊 [China news weekly], January 23, 2023, https://www.inewsweek.cn/politics/2023-01-03/17329.shtml.

17. "2023伏虎收官" [Tigers captured in 2023], 财新 [Caixin], December 31, 2023, https://china.caixin.com/2023-12-31/102151756.html; "2024公布被处分中管干部增至60人," [The published number of punished centrally supervised cadres rose to 60 in 2024], 财新 [Caixin], December 16, 2024, https://china.caixin.com/2024-12-16/102268377.html.

18. "中共中央, 中共中央决定给予周永康开除党籍处分 移送司法机关" [Central Committee of the Communist Party of China decides to expel Zhou Yongkang from the party and transfer him to the judicial authorities], 中央政府门户网站 [Central government portal], December 6, 2014, https://www.gov.cn/govweb/xinwen/2014-12/06/content_2787500.htm; "周永康一审被判处无期徒刑" [Zhou Yongkang is sentenced to life imprisonment in the first instance], Xinhuashe, June 11, 2015, http://www.xinhuanet.com/politics/2015-06/11/c_1115590304.htm.

19. "十八大以来已有45名军老虎落马" [Since the Eighteenth Party Congress, 45 military tigers have been dismissed], 北京青年报 [Beijing youth daily], November 14, 2015, https://news.qingdaonews.com/zonghe/2015-11/14/content_11354144.htm.

20. Ding Miao, "中共十八大后落马'军虎'增至75人" [The number of "military tigers" dismissed after the Eighteenth Party Congress increases to 75], 财新 [Caixin], October 29, 2019, https://datanews.caixin.com/m/2019-10-29/101476521.html.

21. Kainan Gao and Margaret Pearson, "The Role of Political Networks in Anti-corruption Investigations," *China Review* 22, no. 2 (2022): 81–111.

22. CCP Central Commission for Discipline Inspection, "中共中央纪律检查委员会向党的第十五次全国代表大会的工作报告" [Work report of the CCP Central Commission for Discipline Inspection to the Fifteenth Party Congress] , 共产党员网 [Communist Party member network], September 9, 1997, https://news.12371.cn/2017/09/21/ARTI1505963461358568.shtml; CCP Central Commission for Discipline Inspection, "中央纪委向党的十六大的工作报告" [Work report of the Central Commission for Discipline Inspection to the Sixteenth Party Congress], 中央纪委监察部网站 [Central Commission for Discipline Inspection and Ministry

of Supervision website], November 14, 2002, https://www.ccdi.gov.cn/xxgk/hyzl/201307/t20130726_114134.html; CCP Central Commission for Discipline Inspection, "十八届中央纪律检查委员会向中国共产党第十九次全国代表大会的工作报告" [Work report of the Eighteenth Central Commission for Discipline Inspection to the Nineteenth Party Congress], 中华人民共和国驻乌拉圭东岸共和国大使馆 [Embassy of the PRC in the Eastern Republic of Uruguay], October 24, 2017, http://uy.china-embassy.gov.cn/ztbd/shijiuda/201710/t20171031_4691291.htm.

23. Zhong Yuhao, "中纪委公布十八大以来被查的中央委员、中央候补委员人数" [Central Commission for Discipline Inspection announces the number of Central Committee members and alternate members who have been investigated since the Eighteenth Party Congress], 澎湃新闻 [The paper], October 17, 2022, https://m.thepaper.cn/newsDetail_forward_20332452. The data for 1992–2012 were obtained by examining the backgrounds of the disgraced high-ranking officials.

24. Sheena Chestnut Greitens, "The Saohei Campaign, Protection Umbrellas, and China's Changing Political-Legal Apparatus," *China Leadership Monitor*, no. 65 (2020), https://www.prcleader.org/post/the-saohei-campaign-protection-umbrellas-and-china-s-changing-political-legal-apparatus.

25. "公安部原党委委员副部长孙力军严重违纪违法被开除党籍和公职" [Sun Lijun, former member of the Party Committee and vice minister of the Ministry of Public Security, is expelled from the party and public office for serious violations of discipline and the law], Xinhuashe, September 30, 2021, http://www.news.cn/politics/2021-09/30/c_1127922308.htm.

26. "已有几十位政法委书记落马" [Dozens of secretaries of political and legal committees have been dismissed], 网易 [NetEase], July 23, 2022, https://www.163.com/dy/article/HCVH8QM405435FFX.html.

27. "陈一新：全国第一批政法队伍教育整顿取得'四个阶段性成效'" [Chen Yixin: The rectification of the first batch of political and legal teams has achieved "four stages of results"], 中国政府法制信息网 [China government legal network], June 10, 2021, http://www.moj.gov.cn/pub/sfbgw/gwxw/xwyw/ywzfyw/202106/t20210610_427220.html.

28. "八项规定" [Eight provisions], 中国共产党新闻网 [CPC news], http://dangjian.people.com.cn/GB/399416/399420/399445/index.html.

29. "中国共产党纪律处分条例 (2003)" (Disciplinary punishment regulations of the Chinese Communist Party (2003)), 中国科学院理论物理研究所 (Institute of Theoretical Physics, Chinese Academy of Sciences), January 24, 2004, http://www.itp.cas.cn/djykxwh/llxx/dnfg/202011/t20201124_5777782.html.

"中国共产党纪律处分条例 (2015)" [Disciplinary punishment regulations of the Chinese Communist Party (2015)], 国家能源局 [National Energy Administration], October 26, 2015, http://www.nea.gov.cn/2015-10/26/c_134749716.htm.

30. "中华人民共和国监察法" [Supervision law of the People's Republic of China], 中华人民共和国中央人民政府 [People's government of the PRC], March 26, 2018, https://www.gov.cn/xinwen/2018-03/26/content_5277463.htm.

31. Minxin Pei, "How Not to Fight Corruption: Lessons from China," *Daedalus* 147, no. 3 (2018): 216–30.

32. Xuezhi Guo, *The Politics of the Core Leader in China: Culture, Institution, Legitimacy, and Power* (New York: Cambridge University Press, 2019); Alice Miller, "Core Leaders, Authoritative Persons, and Reform Pushback," *China Leadership Monitor*, no. 50 (2016): 1–12, https://www.hoover.org/publications/china-leadership-monitor/summer-2016-issue-50.

33. "中国共产党第十八届中央委员会第六次全体会议公报" [Communiqué of the Sixth Plenary Session of the 18th CCP Central Committee], 共产党员网 [Communist Party member network], October 27, 2016, https://news.12371.cn/2016/10/27/ARTI1477566918346559.shtml.

34. Elizabeth Economy, "China's Imperial President: Xi Jinping Tightens His Grip," *Foreign Affairs* 93, no. 6 (2014): 80–91; Wen-Hsuan Tsai and Wang Zhou, "Integrated Fragmentation and the Role of Leading Small Groups in Chinese Politics," *China Journal*, no. 82 (2019): 1–22.

35. "中共中央政治局召开会议" [Politburo of the CCP Central Committee holds a meeting], Xinhuashe, October 27, 2017, http://www.xinhuanet.com/politics/19cpcnc/2017-10/27/c_1121868508.htm.

36. "中国共产党第十一届中央委员会, 关于党内政治生活的若干准则" [Eleventh CCP Central Committee, several guidelines on inner-party political life], 共产党员网 [Communist Party member network], February 29, 1980, https://news.12371.cn/2015/03/11/ARTI1426059362559711.shtml.

37. "中国共产党第十八届中央委员会, 关于新形势下党内 政治生活的若干准则" [Eighteenth CCP Central Committee, some guidelines for political life within the party under the new situation], 共产党员网 [Communist Party member network], October 27, 2016, https://news.12371.cn/2016/11/02/ARTI1478091665764299.shtml.

38. "中共中央关于党的百年奋斗重大成就和历史经验的决议" [Resolution of the CCP Central Committee on the party's major achievements and historical experience during its centenary of struggle], 中华人民共和国中央人民政府 [PRC Central People's Government], November 11, 2021, http://www.gov.cn/zhengce/2021-11/16/content_5651269.htm.

39. "中华人民共和国宪法修正案" [Amendments to the PRC Constitution], 中国人大网 [National People's Congress network], March 11, 2018, http://www.npc.gov.cn/zgrdw/npc/xinwen/2018-03/12/content_2049190.htm.

40. "Document 9: A ChinaFile Translation," November 8, 2013, https://www.chinafile.com/document-9-chinafile-translation.

41. Xi Jinping, "把宣传思想工作做得更好" [Advance publicity and theoretical work], in 谈治国理政 [The governance of China] (Beijing: Foreign Languages Press, 2014), 153–57.

42. "31位省（市区）党委宣传部长畅谈学习总书记8·19重要讲话" [31 propaganda heads of provincial (municipal) party committees talk about studying the important speech by the general secretary on August 19], 中国共产党新闻网 [Chinese Communist news network], August 30, 2013, http://theory.people.com.cn/n/2013/0830/c83855-22748014.html.

43. "打击网络谣言幕后：有关部门曾发文严防扩大化" [Behind the scenes of cracking down on internet rumors: Relevant departments issue a document to strictly prevent their expansion], 新浪 [Sina], September 6, 2013, http://news.sina.com.cn/c/sd/2013-09-06/021028143964.shtml.

44. 最高人民法院 [Supreme People's Court] and 最高人民检察院 [Supreme People's Procuratorate], "关于办理利用信息网络实施诽谤等刑事案件适用法律若干问题的解释" [Interpretation of several issues concerning the application of laws in the handling of criminal cases such as defamation using information networks], 检察日 [Procuratorate daily], September 10, 2013, https://www.spp.gov.cn/spp/zdgz/201309/t20130910_62417.shtml.

45. Mary Gallagher and Blake Miller, "Who Not What: The Logic of China's Information Control Strategy," *China Quarterly*, no. 248 (2021): 1011–36.

46. Rogier Greemers, "Cyber China: Upgrading Propaganda, Public Opinion Work and Social Management for the Twenty-First Century," *Journal of Contemporary China* 26, no. 103 (2017): 85–100.

47. "中华人民共和国网络安全法" [Cybersecurity law of the PRC], 中华人民共和国中央人民政府 [Central People's Government of the PRC], November 7, 2016, https://www.gov.cn/xinwen/2016-11/07/content_5129723.htm.

48. Eva Pils, "The Party's Turn to Public Repression: An Analysis of the '709' Crackdown on Human Rights Lawyers in China," *China Law and Society Review* 3, no. 1 (2018): 1–48.

49. Tom Mitchell, "China Crackdown on Labour Activism Bolstered by Court Ruling," *Financial Times*, April 15, 2014, https://www.ft.com/content/aa194620-c46d-11e3-8dd4-00144feabdc0; Michael Forsythe and Chris Buckley, "China Arrests at Least 3 Workers' Rights Leaders Amid Rising Unrest," *New York Times*, December 6, 2015, https://www.nytimes.com/2015/12/06/world/asia/china-arrests-at-least-3-workers-rights-leaders-amid-rising-unrest.html.

50. Ben Westcott and Yong Xiong, "Young Marxists Are Going Missing in China After Protesting for Workers," CNN, November 14, 2018, https://www.cnn.com/2018/11/13/asia/china-student-marxist-missing-intl/index.html.

51. Ivan Franceschini and Elisa Nesossi, "State Repression of Chinese Labor NGOs: A Chilling Effect?," *China Journal*, no. 80 (2018): 111–29.

52. Han Zhu and Lu Jun, "The Crackdown on Rights-Advocacy NGOs in Xi's China: Politicizing the Law and Legalizing the Repression," *Journal of Contemporary China* 31, no. 136 (2022): 518–38.

53. John Ruwitch, "China Professor Says Sacked for Criticizing President and Not Recanting," Reuters, December 10, 2013, https://www.reuters.com/article/us-china-professor/china-professor-says-sacked-for-criticizing-president-and-not-recanting-idUSBRE9BA04W20131211.

54. He Haiwei, "被学生举报的中国大学教授后来怎么了" [What happened to the Chinese university professor who was reported on by his students?], *New York Times* (Chinese edition), November 13, 2019, https://cn.nytimes.com/china/20191113/china-informer-professor/; "这些年受处分的大学老师" [The university professors who have been punished over the years], *China Digital Times*, October 14, 2020, https://chinadigitaltimes.net/chinese/657214.html.

55. Ben Westcott and Nectar Gan, "Chinese Academic Who Criticized Leader Xi Jinping Allegedly Fired from Top University," CNN, July 14, 2020, https://www.cnn.com/2020/07/14/asia/xu-zhangrun-arrested-fired-tsinghua-intl-hnk/index.html.

56. Gu Ting, "原贵州大学教授杨绍政被以"煽颠罪"判刑四年半" [Former Guizhou University professor Yang Shaozheng is sentenced to four and a half years in prison for "inciting subversion"], RFA, August 31, 2023, https://www.rfa.org/mandarin/yataibaodao/renquanfazhi/gt2-08312023024136.html.

57. Xiaojun Yan, "Engineering Stability: Authoritarian Political Control Over University Students in Post-Deng China," *China Quarterly*, no. 218 (2014): 493–513; Javier C. Hernández, "Professors, Beware. In China, Student Spies Might Be Watching," *New York Times*, November 1, 2019, https://www.nytimes.com/2019/11/01/world/asia/china-student-informers.html.

58. "中华人民共和国教育部, 新时代高校教师职业行为十项准则" [Ministry of Education: Ten codes of professional conduct for college teachers in the new era], 中华人民共和国教育部 [PRC Ministry of Education], November 14, 2018, http://www.moe.gov.cn/srcsite/A10/s7002/201811/t20181115_354921.html.

59. "中共中央, 中华人民共和国境外非政府组织境内活动管理法" [CCP Central Committee, law of the PRC on the administration of domestic activities by overseas nongovernmental organizations], 中国人大网 [National People's Congress network], November 28, 2017, http://www.npc.gov.cn/zgrdw/npc/xinwen/2017-11/28/content_2032719.htm.

60. "Clampdown in China Restricts 7,000 Foreign Organizations," *New York Times*, April 28, 2016, https://www.nytimes.com/2016/04/29/world/asia/china-foreign-ngo-law.html; "China Law Puts Foreign NGOs Under Tighter Control," *Financial Times*, April 22, 2018, https://www.ft.com/content/a61994da-3ec1-11e8-b7e0-52972418fec4.

61. CCP 18th Central Committee, "十八届三中全会全面深化改革若干重大问题决定" [The Third Plenary Session of the Eighteenth CCP Central Committee decides to comprehensively deepen reforms on several major issues], 中华人民共和国中央人民政府 [Central People's Government], November 15, 2013, https://www.gov.cn/jrzg/2013-11/15/content_2528179.htm.

62. State Council, "社会信用体系建设规划纲要 (2014–2020年)" [Construction planning outline of the social credit system (2014–2020)], 中华人民共和国中央人民政府 [Central

People's Government], June 14, 2014, http://www.gov.cn/zhengce/content/2014-06/27/content_8913.htm.

63. Josh Chin and Liza Lin, *Surveillance State: Inside China's Quest to Launch a New Era of Social Control* (NY: St. Martins, 2022); Minxin Pei, "Grid Management: China's Latest Institutional Tool of Social Control," *China Leadership Monitor*, no. 67 (2021), https://www.prcleader.org/post/grid-management-china-s-latest-institutional-tool-of-social-control; Fan Liang et al., "Constructing a Data-Driven Society: China's Social Credit System as a State Surveillance Infrastructure," *Policy & Internet* 10, no. 4 (2018): 415–53.

64. Colin Mackerras, "Xinjiang at the Turn of the Century: The Causes of Separatism," *Central Asian Survey* 20, no. 3 (2001): 289–303; James Millward, *Violent Separatism in Xinjiang: A Critical Assessment* (Washington, DC: East-West Center, 2004).

65. Nicolas Becquelin, "Staged Development in Xinjiang," *China Quarterly*, no. 178 (2004): 358–78; Michael Clarke, "China's 'War on Terror' in Xinjiang: Human Security and the Causes of Violent Uighur Separatism," *Terrorism and Political Violence* 20, no. 2 (2008): 271–301.

66. Chien-peng Chung, "China's Uyghur Problem After the 2009 Urumqi Riot: Repression, Recompense, Readiness, Resistance," *Journal of Policing, Intelligence and Counter Terrorism* 13, no. 2 (2018): 185–201.

67. Adrian Zenz and James Leibold, "Chen Quanguo: The Strongman Behind Beijing's Securitization Strategy in Tibet and Xinjiang," *China Brief* 17, no. 12 (2017): 16–24, https://jamestown.org/program/chen-quanguo-the-strongman-behind-beijings-securitization-strategy-in-tibet-and-xinjiang/.

68. Michael Clarke, ed., *The Xinjiang Emergency: Exploring the Causes and Consequences of China's Mass Detention of Uyghurs* (Manchester, UK: Manchester University Press, 2022).

69. James Leibold, "Surveillance in China's Xinjiang Region: Ethnic Sorting, Coercion, and Inducement," *Journal of Contemporary China* 29, no. 121 (2020): 46–60.

70. "中华人民共和国政府和大不列颠及北爱尔兰联合王国政府关于香港问题的联合声明" [Joint statement of the government of the PRC and the government of the United Kingdom of Great Britain and Northern Ireland on the question of Hong Kong], 中华人民共和国香港特别行政区政府政制及内地事务局 [Constitutional and Mainland Affairs Bureau, government of the Hong Kong Special Administrative Region], December 19, 1984, https://www.cmab.gov.hk/gb/issues/jd2.htm.

71. "中华人民共和国香港特别行政区基本法" [Basic Law of the Hong Kong Special Administrative Region of the PRC], 中国政府门户网站 [Chinese government portal], April 4, 1990, https://www.gov.cn/test/2005-07/29/content_18298.htm.

72. Ho-fung Hung, *City on the Edge: Hong Kong under Chinese Rule* (New York: Cambridge University Press, 2022); Brian Fong, "One Country, Two Nationalisms: Center-Periphery Relations Between Mainland China and Hong Kong, 1997–2016," *Modern China* 43, no. 5 (2017): 523–56; Ming Sing, ed., *Politics and Government in Hong Kong: Crisis Under Chinese Sovereignty* (London: Routledge, 2008).

73. "'一国两制'在香港特别行政区的实践白皮书" [White paper on the practice of "one country, two systems" in the Hong Kong Special Administrative Region], 国务院新闻办公室 [State Council Information Office], June 10, 2014, http://www.scio.gov.cn/ztk/dtzt/2014/31039/31042/Document/1372893/1372893.htm.

74. Stephan Ortmann, "The Umbrella Movement and Hong Kong's Protracted Democratization Process," *Asian Affairs* 46, no. 1 (2015): 32–50.

75. Xi Jinping, "在庆祝香港回归祖国20周年大会暨香港特别行政区第五届政府就职典礼上的讲话" [Speech at the celebration of the twentieth anniversary of Hong Kong's return to the motherland and the inauguration ceremony of the fifth government of the Hong Kong Special Administrative Region], Xinhuashe [New China News Agency], July 1, 2017, http://www.xinhuanet.com//politics/2017-07/01/c_1121247124.htm.

76. Martin Purbrick, "A Report of the 2019 Hong Kong Protests," *Asian Affairs* 50, no. 4 (2019): 465–87.

77. Michael Davis, *Freedom Undone: The Assault on Liberal Values and Institutions in Hong Kong* (New York: Columbia University Press, 2024).

78. Kimberly Lim and Su-Lin Tan, "Hong Kong's Talent Exodus to Singapore: Can It Be Reversed and Is 'A New Wave of Expats' Inbound?," *South China Morning Post*, February 4, 2023, https://www.scmp.com/week-asia/people/article/3209048/hong-kongs-talent-exodus-singapore-can-it-be-reversed-and-new-wave-expats-inbound.

79. Yuhua Wang and Carl Minzner, "The Rise of the Chinese Security State," *China Quarterly*, no. 222 (2015): 339–59.

80. Margaret Roberts, *Censored: Distraction and Diversion Inside China's Great Firewall* (Princeton, NJ: Princeton University Press, 2018).

81. Joseph Fewsmith, *Rethinking Chinese Politics* (New York: Cambridge University Press, 2021).

82. Lily Kuo, "Rare Protests Against China's 'Zero Covid' Policy Erupt Across Country," *Washington Post*, November 27, 2022, https://www.washingtonpost.com/world/2022/11/27/china-covid-lockdown-protest-xinjiang/.

83. Minxin Pei, "The Sudden End of Zero-Covid: An Investigation," *China Leadership Monitor*, no. 75 (2023), https://www.prcleader.org/post/the-sudden-end-of-zero-covid-an-investigation.

84. Gerard DiPippo, "China's Economy After Covid-19," *China Leadership Monitor*, no. 76 (2023), https://www.prcleader.org/post/china-s-economy-after-covid-19.

Chapter 7. End of the Chinese Economic Miracle

1. The World Bank and the Development Research Center of the State Council, *China 2030: Building a Modern, Harmonious, and Creative Society* (Washington, DC: World Bank, 2013).

2. *ZGTJNJ 2013* (Beijing: Zhongguo tongji chubanshe, 2013), https://www.stats.gov.cn/sj/ndsj/2013/indexch.htm.

3. Lant Pritchett and Lawrence Summers, "Asiaphoria Meets Regression to the Mean," *The Digest* (National Bureau for Economic Research), no. 3 (March 2015), https://www.nber.org/digest/mar15/asiaphoria-meets-regression-mean.

4. *ZGTJNJ 2013*.

5. Bank of International Settlements, https://www.bis.org/statistics/totcredit.htm.

6. *ZGTJNJ 2004* (Beijing: Zhongguo tongji chubanshe, 2004), https://www.stats.gov.cn/sj/ndsj/yb2004-c/indexch.htm; *ZGTJNJ 2013*.

7. U.S. Census Bureau, "Trade in Goods with China," https://www.census.gov/foreign-trade/balance/c5700.html#2003.

8. World Integrated Trade Solution, "European Union Trade Balance, Exports and Imports by Country 2003," https://wits.worldbank.org/CountryProfile/en/Country/EUN/Year/2003/TradeFlow/EXPIMP/Partner/by-country; data for 2012 are converted from Euros. Eurostat, "China-EU—International Trade in Goods Statistics," February 2023, https://ec.europa.eu/eurostat/statistics-explained/index.php?title=China-EU_-_international_trade_in_goods_statistics#:~:text=Between%20January%202021%20and%20December,EU%20countries%20increased%20by%2028.8%20%25.

9. David Autor et al., "Importing Political Polarization? The Electoral Consequences of Rising Trade Exposure," *American Economic Review* 110, no. 10 (2020): 3139–83.

10. *ZGTJNJ 2003* (Beijing: Zhongguo tongji chubanshe, 2003), 154; *ZGTJNJ 2013*.

11. *ZGTJNJ 2022*.

12. Shang-Jin Wei, Zhuan Xie, and Xiaobo Zhang, "From 'Made in China' to 'Innovated in China': Necessity, Prospect, and Challenges," *Journal of Economic Perspectives* 31, no. 1 (2017): 56–57; Harry Wu, "Sustainability of China's Growth Model: A Productivity Perspective," *China and World Economy* 24, no. 5 (2016): 51.

13. "中共中央关于全面深化改革若干重大问题的决定" [Decision of the CCP Central Committee on some major issues concerning comprehensively deepening the reform], 中国经济网 [China economic net], November 18, 2013, http://www.ce.cn/xwzx/gnsz/szyw/201311/18/t20131118_1767104.shtml.

14. Nicholas Lardy, *The State Strikes Back: The End of Economic Reform in China?* (Washington, DC: Peterson Institute for International Economics, 2019).

15. Liu Qiong, "习近平主持召开中央财经领导小组第十一次会议" [Xi Jinping presides over the 11th meeting of the Central Financial and Economic Leading Group], 新华网 [New China News Agency], November 10, 2015, https://www.xinhuanet.com/politics/2015-11/10/c_1117099915.htm.

16. Yongmei Liang, Minjie Dong, and Qizi Zhang, "China's Industrial Capacity Utilization: Sectoral Comparison, Regional Differences and Determinants," *China Economist* (Beijing) 11, no. 2 (2016): 109–25; Wing Thye Woo, "China's Soft Budget Constraint on the Demand-Side Undermines Its Supply-Side Structural Reforms," *China Economic Review*, no. 57 (2019): 101–11.

17. "国务院关于钢铁行业化解过剩产能实现脱困发展的意见" [Opinions of the State Council on resolving excess production capacity and achieving development out of the difficulties in the steel industry], 中华人民共和国中央人民政府 [Central People's Government], February 4, 2016, https://www.gov.cn/zhengce/content/2016-02/04/content_5039353.htm.

18. Huang Hanquan, "'八字方针'为供给侧结构性改革定向指航" [The "eight-character policy" guides the supply-side structural reform], 中华人民共和国中央人民政府 [Central People's Government], December 28, 2018, https://www.gov.cn/zhengce/2018-12/28/content_5352861.htm.

19. *ZGTJNJ 2016* (Beijing: Zhongguo tongji chubanshe, 2016), https://www.stats.gov.cn/sj/ndsj/2016/indexch.htm ; *ZGTJNJ 2021* (Beijing: Zhongguo tongji chubanshe, 2021), https://www.stats.gov.cn/sj/ndsj/2021/indexch.htm.

20. Bank of International Settlements, https://www.bis.org/statistics/totcredit.htm.

21. Ouyang Hui and Ye Dongyan, "地方债狂奔" [Local debt is running wild], 中国改革 [China reform], no. 1 (2019), https://cnreform.caixin.com/2019-01-18/101371282.html/; Zhiwu Chen, "China's Dangerous Debt," *Foreign Affairs* 94, no. 3 (2015): 13–18.

22. Zhao Wei and Hou Qiannan, "地方财政土地依赖困局待解" [The fiscal dilemma of local land dependence must be solved], 中国改革 [China reform], no. 6 (2022), https://cnreform.caixin.com/2022-11-03/101959785.html; Chen, "China's Dangerous Debt."

23. Yu Hairong and Wang Xiaoxia, "地方启动去杠杆" [Local authorities initiate deleveraging], 财新周刊 [Caixin weekly], no. 10 (2018), https://weekly.caixin.com/2018-03-09/101219173.html; Xing Yun, "地方举债天花板" [Local debt ceiling], 财新周刊 [Caixin weekly], no. 35 (2015), https://weekly.caixin.com/2015-09-04/100846422.html; Zhou Xuan et al., "地方化债如何共克时限" [How to jointly overcome the time limit for local debt], 财新周刊 [Caixin weekly], no. 11 (2019), https://weekly.caixin.com/2019-03-23/101395961.html; Cheng Siwei and Wang Juanjuan, "地方隐形债务化解分步走" [Gradual steps to resolve local invisible debt], 财新周刊 [Caixin weekly], no. 47 (2021), https://weekly.caixin.com/2021-12-04/101813651.html ; *ZGTJNJ 2022*.

24. Wu Hong Yuran and Zhang Yuzhe, "去杠杆加速" [Deleveraging accelerates], 财新周刊 [Caixin weekly], no. 40 (2016), https://topics.caixin.com/qugangganjiasudu/; *ZGTJNJ 2016*; Terrence Chan, Eunice Tan, and Christine Ip, "China's SOEs Are Stuck in a Debt Trap," S&P

Global Ratings, September 20, 2022, https://www.spglobal.com/_assets/documents/ratings/research/global-debt-leverage-1.pdf.

25. Chen Changhua, "去杠杆任重道远" [Deleveraging has a long way to go], 财新周刊 [Caixin weekly], no. 1 (2020), https://weekly.caixin.com/2020-01-03/101500944.html.

26. Gao Shanwen, "去杠杆之争" [The debate over deleveraging], 金融四十人论坛 [Finance forty forum], July 5, 2018, http://www.cf40.com/news_detail/8074.html.

27. At the end of 2017, nonfinancial SOEs faced 118.5 trillion yuan in outstanding debt, compared with 108 trillion yuan at the end of 2015. Margit Molnar and Jiangyuan Lu, "State-Owned Firms Behind China's Corporate Debt," OECD Economics Department, Working Paper no. 1536 (2019): 16.

28. Wu Hong Yuran and Wu Xiaomeng, "去杠杆变稳杠杆之后" [After deleveraging and stabilizing leverage], 财新周刊 [Caixin weekly], no. 8 (2019), https://weekly.caixin.com/2019-03-02/101386270.html.

29. Bank of International Settlements, https://www.bis.org/statistics/totcredit.htm.

30. *ZGTJNJ 2013* (Beijing: Zhongguo tongji chubanshe, 2013), https://www.stats.gov.cn/sj/ndsj/2013/indexch.htm.

31. Jie Yunliang, "起底历次房地产调控" [Investigating the history of real estate regulation], 民生证券 [Minsheng securities], March 15, 2021, https://pdf.dfcfw.com/pdf/H3_AP202103151472037194_1.pdf?1615839137000.pdf.

32. Kenneth Rogoff and Yuanchen Yang, "Peak China Housing," National Bureau of Economic Research, Working Paper 27697, (August 2020); Edward Glaeser et al., "A Real Estate Boom with Chinese Characteristics," *Journal of Economic Perspectives* 31, no. 1 (2017): 93–116.

33. Simon Zhao et al., "How Big Is China's Real Estate Bubble and Why Hasn't It Burst Yet?," *Land Use Policy*, no. 64 (2017): 153–62.

34. "背景资料：中国政府2017年出台的房地产主要政策一览" [Background: Overview of the main real estate policies introduced by the Chinese government in 2017], Reuters, September 13, 2017, https://www.reuters.com/article/idUSL4S1LU3F1/.

35. *ZGTJNJ 2020*.

36. Arendse Huld, "What's Going on in China's Property Market?," *China Briefing*, January 14, 2022, https://www.china-briefing.com/news/explainer-whats-going-on-in-chinas-property-market/.

37. Wu Hong Yuran and Wang Jing, "房企降杠杆开始" [Real estate companies begin to reduce leverage], 财新周刊 [Caixin weekly], no. 37 (2020), https://weekly.caixin.com/2020-09-19/101607114.html.

38. *ZGTJNJ 2024*, https://www.stats.gov.cn/sj/ndsj/; Li Fang, "统计局：2021年全国商品房销售额181930亿元，增长4.8%" [Bureau of Statistics: National commercial housing sales in 2021 will be 18.193 billion yuan, an increase of 4.8%], 中国经济网 [China economic net], January 17, 2022, http://www.ce.cn/cysc/fdc/fc/202201/17/t20220117_37263309.shtml.

39. Clare Jim and Samuel Shen, "Embattled Evergrande Warns of Growing Default Risks as Pressures Mount," Reuters, September 14, 2021, https://www.reuters.com/business/china-evergrande-warns-further-property-sales-drop-liquidity-crunch-2021-09-14/.

40. "国家统计局：2022年全国房地产开发投资同比下降10%" [National Bureau of Statistics: National real estate development investment will drop by 10% year-on-year in 2022], 上海证券报 [Shanghai securities news], January 17, 2023, https://news.cnstock.com/news,bwkx-202301-5007276.htm.

41. "Debt Crisis Threatens to Engulf China's Surviving Developers," Bloomberg, September 5, 2023, https://www.bloomberg.com/news/articles/2023-09-04/debt-crisis-threatens-to-engulf-china-s-surviving-developers.

42. "China's Bursting Housing Bubble Is Doing More Damage than Official Data Suggest," Bloomberg, August 17, 2018, https://fortune.com/2023/08/17/china-home-sales-worse-than-official-data-real-estate-crisis/.

43. Liangping Gao and Ryan Woo, "China's Falling Property Sales, Investment Weigh on Recovery," Reuters, October 17, 2023, https://www.reuters.com/world/china/chinas-falling-property-sales-investment-weigh-recovery-2023-10-18/; *ZGTJNJ 2024*, https://www.stats.gov.cn/sj/ndsj/.

44. "China's Easing of 'Three Red Lines' Loan Rules for Property Sector Won't Have Immediate Impact on Struggling Developers, Analysts Say," *South China Morning Post*, January 7, 2022, https://www.scmp.com/business/china-business/article/3162592/chinas-easing-three-red-lines-loan-rules-property-sector; "8城全面取消限购 9月以来已有超30省市优化楼市政策" [Eight cities have completely canceled purchase restrictions. Since September, more than 30 provinces and cities have optimized property market policies], 澎湃新闻 [The paper], September 12, 2023, https://news.cctv.com/2023/09/12/ARTINFfRaO8Sn8Daysc4ql3s230912.shtml.

45. "China's Property Sector Set to Be Persistently Weak for Years, Goldman Sachs Says," Reuters, June 12, 2023, https://www.reuters.com/world/china/chinas-property-sector-set-be-persistently-weak-years-goldman-2023-06-12/.

46. US Census Bureau, "Trade in Goods with China," https://www.census.gov/foreign-trade/balance/c5700.html#2016.

47. Nick Gass, "Trump: 'We Can't Continue to Allow China to Rape Our Country,'" *Politico*, May 2, 2016, https://www.politico.com/blogs/2016-gop-primary-live-updates-and-results/2016/05/trump-china-rape-america-222689.

48. Bob Davis and Lingling Wei, *Superpower Showdown: How the Battle Between Trump and Xi Threatens a New Cold War* (New York: Harper Business, 2020).

49. Chad Bown, "China Bought None of the Extra $200 Billion of US Exports in Trump's Trade Deal," Peterson Institute for International Economics, July 19, 2022, https://www.piie.com/blogs/realtime-economics/china-bought-none-extra-200-billion-us-exports-trumps-trade-deal.

50. For a chronology of the trade war, visit https://www.china-briefing.com/news/the-us-china-trade-war-a-timeline/.

51. *ZGTJNJ 2022.*

52. World Bank, "GDP Growth (Annual %)—United States," https://data.worldbank.org/indicator/NY.GDP.MKTP.KD.ZG?locations=US.

53. Bablo Fajgelbaum and Amit Khandelwal, "The Economic Impacts of the US–China Trade War," *Annual Review of Economics*, no. 14 (2022): 205–28.

54. *ZGTJNJ 2022.*

55. Sanjoy Kumar Paul, Md. Abdul Moktadir, and Kamrul Ahsan, "Key Supply Chain Strategies for the Post-COVID-19 Era: Implications for Resilience and Sustainability," *International Journal of Logistics Management* 34, no. 4 (2023): 1165–87.

56. Janne Leino, "Walking on Eggshells: The Twin Transition and Europe's Quest to De-Risk from China," *European View* 22, no.1 (2023), https://doi.org/10.1177/17816858231206010.

57. *ZJTJNJ 2024*, https://www.stats.gov.cn/sj/ndsj/2024/indexch.htm; US Census Bureau, "Trade in Goods with China," https://www.census.gov/foreign-trade/balance/c5700.html.

58. Noah Barkin, "Export Controls and the US-China Tech War," MERICS China Monitor, no. 18 (2020), https://merics.org/sites/default/files/2020-04/merics_ChinaMonitor_US-CH-EU-Export%20Controls_en_final.pdf.

59. Xu Weibing, "如何理解'国内大循环'国内国际双循环" [How to understand 'domestic circulation' and domestic-international dual circulation], 中国经济时报 [China economic times], August 13, 2020, https://www.sohu.com/a/412838402_115495; Wang Zihui,"看习近平这几次重要讲话，弄懂'大循环'双循环'" [Read these important articles by Xi Jinping to understand "domestic circulation" and domestic-international dual circulation], 新华网 [New China News Agency], September 5, 2020, http://www.xinhuanet.com/politics/xxjxs/2020-09/05/c_1126455277.htm.

60. "中共中央关于制定国民经济和社会发展第十四个五年规划和二〇三五年远景目标的建议" [Proposal of the CCP Central Committee on formulating the 14th Five-Year Plan for National Economic and Social Development and the long-term goals for 2035], 中华人民共和国中央人民政府 [Central People's Government], October 29, 2020, https://www.gov.cn/zhengce/2020-11/03/content_5556991.htm.

61. Xi Jinping, "关于'中共中央关于制定国民经济和社会发展第十四个五年规划和二〇三五年远景目标的建议'的说明" [Explanation of the "Proposal of the Central Committee on Formulating the 14th Five-Year Plan for National Economic and Social Development and Long-term Goals for 2035"], 中华人民共和国中央人民政府 [Central People's Government of the PRC], November 3, 2020, http://www.gov.cn/xinwen/2020-11/03/content_5556997.htm.

62. Xi Jinping, "关于'中共中央关于制定国民经济和社会发展第十四个五年规划和二〇三五年远景目的建议'的说明"; Liu He, "加快构建以国内大循环为主体、国内国际双循环相互促进的新发展格局" [Accelerate the establishment of a new development pattern with domestic circulation as the main focus and mutually reinforcing dual circulation of domestic and international markets], 人民日报 [People's daily], November 25, 2020, 6, http://www.xinhuanet.com/politics/2020-11/25/c_1126785254.htm.

63. Xi Jinping, "国家中长期经济社会发展战略若干重大问题" [Several major issues in the national medium and long-term economic and social development strategy], 新华网 [New China News Agency], October 31, 2020, http://www.xinhuanet.com/politics/leaders/2020-10/31/c_1126681658.htm.

64. "中共中央关于制定国民经济和社会发展第十四个五年规划和二〇三五年远景目标的建议."

65. Xi Jinping, "关于《中共中央关于制定国民经济和社会发展第十四个五年规划和二〇三五年远景目的建议》的说明."

66. "中共中央关于制定国民经济和社会发展第十四个五年规划和二〇三五年远景目标的建议."

67. Alicia García-Herrero, "What Is Behind China's Dual Circulation Strategy," *China Leadership Monitor*, no. 69 (2021), https://www.prcleader.org/post/what-is-behind-china-s-dual-circulation-strategy.

68. Julie Zhu et al., "China to Launch $40 Billion State Fund to Boost Chip Industry," Reuters, September 5, 2023, https://www.reuters.com/technology/china-launch-new-40-bln-state-fund-boost-chip-industry-sources-say-2023-09-05/.

69. "China Is Trying to Protect Its Economy from Western Pressure," *Economist*, May 26, 2022, https://www.economist.com/briefing/2022/05/26/china-is-trying-to-protect-its-economy-from-western-pressure.

70. Asim Anand, "China's Quest for Food Security Is Bound to Be a Long Drawn Saga," S&P Global Community Insights, https://www.spglobal.com/commodityinsights/en/market-insights/blogs/agriculture/080923-chinas-quest-for-food-security-is-bound-to-be-a-long-drawn-saga.

71. Jun Du, Xiaoxuan Liu, and Ying Zhou. "State Advances and Private Sector Retreats? Evidence of Aggregate Productivity Decomposition in China," *China Economic Review*, no. 31 (2014): 459–74.

72. Di Guo et al., "Political Economy of Private Firms in China," *Journal of Comparative Economics* 42, no. 2 (2014): 286–303.

73. Nicholas Lardy, *Markets Over Mao: The Rise of Private Business in China* (Washington, DC: Peterson Institute for International Economics, 2014).

74. "陈志武：国进民退的五大后果" [Chen Zhiwu: Five major consequences of the country advancing and the people retreating], November 30, 2009, https://www.aisixiang.com/data/31019.html.

75. Sarah Eaton, *The Advance of the State in Contemporary China: State-market Relations in the Reform Era* (New York: Cambridge University Press, 2016).

76. "Xi Jinping Millionaire Relations Reveal Elite Chinese Fortunes," Bloomberg, June 29, 2012, https://www.bloomberg.com/news/articles/2012-06-29/xi-jinping-millionaire-relations-reveal-fortunes-of-elite.

77. Yang Anqi, "习近平在全国国有企业党的建设工作会议上的讲话" [Xi Jinping's speech at the National Conference on Party Building in State-owned Enterprises], 中国经济网 [China economic net], November 18, 2013, https://www.12371.cn/special/xjpgqdjjh/.

78. Daniel Koss, "Party Building as Institutional Bricolage: Asserting Authority at the Business Frontier," *China Quarterly* 248, no. S1 (2021): 222–43.

79. Derek Levine, "Made in China 2025," *Journal of Strategic Security* 13, no. 3 (2020): 1–16; Max Zenglein and Anna Holzmann, "Evolving Made in China 2025," MERICS Papers on China, no. 8 (July 2019), https://merics.org/en/report/evolving-made-china-2025.

80. "国务院关于印发'中国制造2025'的通知," 国发 (2015)28号 [Notice of the State Council on issuing "Made in China 2025"], *Guofa* (2015) no. 28.

81. Lardy, *The State Strikes Back*, 86–89.

82. Fanhua Zeng, Wei-Chiao Huang, and James Hueng, "On Chinese Government's Stock Market Rescue Efforts in 2015," *Modern Economy* 7, no. 4 (2016): 411–18.

83. Nicholas Lardy, "China's Private Firms Continue to Struggle," Peterson Institute for International Economics, June 14, 2019, https://www.piie.com/blogs/china-economic-watch/chinas-private-firms-continue-struggle.

84. Shi Lingling and Wang Mengmo, "中国民企融资环境报告：2020" [China private enterprise financing environment report: 2020], 中国智库网 [China think tank network], May 16, 2020, https://www.chinathinktanks.org.cn/content/detail/id/uspibe76.

85. *ZGTJNJ*, various years, e-book, https://www.stats.gov.cn/sj/ndsj/.

86. Liu Guishi, "民间投资增速为何逐月放缓?" [Why is the growth rate of private investment slowing down month by month?], 经济观察网 [Economic observer network], November 8, 2022, https://finance.sina.cn/china/gncj/2022-11-08/detail-imqqsmrp5389469.d.html?vt=4&cid=76729&node_id=76729.

87. *ZGTJNJ 2022*, e-book, https://www.stats.gov.cn/sj/ndsj/2022/indexch.htm.

88. Jing Yang and Lingling Wei, "China's President Xi Jinping Personally Scuttled Jack Ma's Ant IPO," *Wall Street Journal*, November 12, 2020, https://www.wsj.com/articles/china-president-xi-jinping-halted-jack-ma-ant-ipo-11605203556.

89. Lingling Wei, "China Blocked Jack Ma's Ant IPO After Investigation Revealed Likely Beneficiaries," *Wall Street Journal*, February 16, 2021, https://www.wsj.com/articles/china-blocked-jack-mas-ant-ipo-after-an-investigation-revealed-who-stood-to-gain-11613491292.

90. Zhao Wenhan, "习近平在中共中央政治局第三十四次集体学习时强调 把握数字经济发展趋势和规律 推动我国数字经济健康发展" [At the 34th collective study session of the CCP Politburo Xi Jinping emphasizes that we should grasp the development trends and laws of the digital economy and promote the healthy development of our country's digital economy], 新华网 [New China News Agency], October 19, 2021, http://www.news.cn/2021-10/19/c_1127973979.htm.

91. Sandra Colino, "The Case Against Alibaba in China and Its Wider Policy Repercussions," *Journal of Antitrust Enforcement* 10, no. 1 (2022): 217–29.

92. "Beijing's Regulatory Crackdown Wipes $1.1 Trillion off Chinese Big Tech," Reuters, July 12, 2023, https://www.reuters.com/technology/beijings-regulatory-crackdown-wipes-11-trln-off-chinese-big-tech-2023-07-12/.

93. Haiyan Qian, Allan Walker, and Shuangye Chen, "The 'Double-Reduction' Education Policy in China: Three Prevailing Narratives," *Journal of Education Policy*, June 12, 2023, doi.org/10.1080/02680939.2023.2222381.

94. "China's $100 Billion Tutoring Ban Backfires, Spawning Black Market," Bloomberg, July 23, 2023, https://www.bloomberg.com/news/articles/2023-07-20/china-s-tutoring-crackdown-sends-kids-to-underground-test-prep.

95. *ZGTJNJ 2020*.

96. "半月谈：疫情下百万家店铺倒闭" [Bimonthly talk: Millions of stores close down during the epidemic], 澎湃新闻 [The paper], March 2, 2021, https://m.thepaper.cn/kuaibao_detail.jsp?contid=11517690&from=kuaibao ; "森林聊创业: '400万企业倒闭后'" [Talk on entrepreneurship: "After 4 million businesses failed"], 今日头条, May 6, 2022, https://www.toutiao.com/article/7094639845871501838/?wid=1702345628351.

97. Nectar Gan and Shawn Deng, "Chinese Cities Rush to Lockdown in Show of Loyalty to Xi's 'Zero-Covid' Strategy," CNN, September 5, 2022, https://www.cnn.com/2022/09/05/china/china-covid-lockdown-74-cities-intl-hnk/index.html.

98. Minxin Pei, "The Sudden End of Zero-Covid: An Investigation," *China Leadership Monitor*, no. 75 (2022), https://www.prcleader.org/post/the-sudden-end-of-zero-covid-an-investigation.

99. Hong Xiao et al., "Excess All-Cause Mortality in China After Ending the Zero COVID Policy," *JAMA Network Open* 6, no. 8 (2023), https://jamanetwork.com/journals/jamanetworkopen/fullarticle/2808734.

100. "COVID Data Tracker," CDC, https://covid.cdc.gov/covid-data-tracker/#datatracker-home.

101. Charmaine Jacob, "China to See the World's Biggest Millionaire Exodus This Year, New Study Shows," CNBC, June 15, 2023, https://www.cnbc.com/2023/06/15/china-to-see-the-worlds-biggest-millionaire-exodus-this-year-study-shows-.html.

102. *ZGTJNJ 2020*.

103. Yiping Huang and Fang Cai, eds., *Debating the Lewis Turning Point in China* (New York: Routledge, 2016).

Chapter 8. From Engagement to a New Cold War

1. Andrew Walder, "Bending the Arc of Chinese History: The Cultural Revolution's Paradoxical Legacy," *China Quarterly*, no. 227 (2016): 613–31.

2. "The Present Situation and the Tasks Before Us," January 16, 1980, *Selected Works of Deng Xiaoping (1975–1982)*, 225.

3. Suisheng Zhao, *The Dragon Roars Back: Transformational Leaders and Dynamics of Chinese Foreign Policy* (Stanford, CA: Stanford University Press, 2023), 50–55.

4. Patrick Tyler, "The (Ab)normalization of U.S.-Chinese Relations," *Foreign Affairs* 78, no. 5 (1999): 93–122.

5. 邓小平年谱 上册 [Deng Xiaoping chronology, vol. 1] (Beijing: Central Party Literature Publishing House, 2004), 313–14, 452–53.

6. Ezra Vogel, *Deng Xiaoping and the Transformation of China* (Cambridge, MA: Harvard University Press, 2011), 333–48.

7. Tu Xinquan, Lü Yue, and Li Siqi, 70年来的中美经贸关系 [Sino-American Economic and Trade Relations since 1970] (Beijing: 对外经济贸易大学中国, WTO研究院, 2019), 3.

8. US Census Bureau, "Trade in Goods with China, 1989," https://www.census.gov/foreign-trade/balance/c5700.html#1989.

9. "Most-Favored-Nation Status of the People's Republic of China," CRS Report for Congress, July 25, 2001, https://www.everycrsreport.com/files/20010725_RL30225_4f01c5c4b2d3e63f78fd6bf059bfb534fc7cc3e6.pdf.

10. Jing-dong Yuan, "The Politics of the Strategic Triangle: The US, COCOM, and Export Controls on China, 1979–1989," *Journal of Northeast Asian Studies* 14, no. 1 (1995): 47–79; Larry Wortzel, "U.S. Technology Transfer Policies and the Modernization of China's Armed Forces," *Asian Survey* 27, no. 6 (1987): 615–37.

11. Harry Harding, *A Fragile Relationship: The United States and China Since 1972* (Washington, DC: Brookings Institution, 1992).

12. Deng Xiaoping, 邓小平年谱上册, 368.

13. Deng Xiaoping, 411–12.

14. Shinkichi Eto, "Recent Developments in Sino-Japanese Relations," *Asian Survey* 20, no. 7 (1980): 726–43.

15. Reinhard Drifte, "The Ending of Japan's ODA Loan Programme to China—All's Well That Ends Well?," *Asia-Pacific Review* 13, no. 1 (2006): 94–117.

16. Wang Mingyuan, "中曾根康弘、胡耀邦与80年代中日关系蜜月期" [Nakasone, Hu Yaobang and the honeymoon period of Sino-Japanese relations in the 1980s], 财新网 [Caixin], November 3, 2019. https://opinion.caixin.com/m/2019-12-03/101490078.html.

17. Wang Mingyuan.

18. Ye Jia and Sun Wei, "部分中国青年代表团成员与日本友人在东京联欢" [Members of the Chinese Youth Delegation partying with Japanese friends in Tokyo], Xinhua, May 8, 2008, https://www.gov.cn/jrzg/2008-05/08/content_964285.htm.

19. Yanzhong Huang et al., "China's Approach to Global Governance," Council on Foreign Relations, https://www.cfr.org/china-global-governance/.

20. United Nations, "The United Nations in China," https://china.un.org/en/about/about-the-un.

21. Samuel Kim, "International Organizations in Chinese Foreign Policy," *Annals of the American Academy of Political and Social Science* 519, no. 1 (1992): 140–57.

22. Gene Tidrick et al., *China: An Evaluation of World Bank Assistance* (Washington, DC: World Bank, 2005), 7; Pieter Bottelier, "China and the World Bank: How a Partnership Was Built," *Journal of Contemporary China* 16, no. 51 (2007): 239–58.

23. Cheng Li, ed., *Bridging Minds Across the Pacific: US–China Educational Exchanges, 1978–2003* (Lanham, MD: Lexington Books, 2005).

24. Eric Fish, "End of an Era? A History of Chinese Students in America," China Project, May 12, 2020. https://thechinaproject.com/2020/05/12/end-of-an-era-a-history-of-chinese-students-in-america/#.

25. Dong Jing, "2023中国留学白皮书在京发布" [The 2023 White Paper on Chinese students studying abroad released in Beijing], *China Daily*, March 18, 2023. https://cn.chinadaily.com.cn/a/202303/18/WS641564e2a3102ada8b2342fd.html.

26. John Garver, "The 'New Type' of Sino-Soviet Relations," *Asian Survey* 29, no. 12 (1989): 1136–52.

27. "We Are Confident That We Can Handle China's Affairs Well," September 16, 1989, in *Selected Works of Deng Xiaoping, Volume 3 (1982–1992)*, 315–16.

28. "We Must Adhere to Socialism and Present Peaceful Evolution Towards Capitalism," November 23, 1989, in *Selected Works of Deng Xiaoping, Volume 3 (1982–1992)*, 333–34.

29. "We Must Adhere to Socialism," 333.

30. "Seize the Opportunity to Develop the Economy," December 24, 1990, in *Selected Works of Deng Xiaoping, Volume 3 (1982–1992)*, 350.

31. "The International Situation and Economic Problems," March 3, 1990, in *Selected Works of Deng Xiaoping, Volume 3 (1982–1992)*, 341.

32. "With Stable Policies of Reform and Opening to the Outside World, China Can Have Great Hopes for the Future," September 4, 1989, in *Selected Works of Deng Xiaoping, Volume 3 (1982–1992)*, 310.

33. "With Stable Policies of Reform and Opening," 311; "Seize the Opportunity to Develop the Economy," December 24, 1990, in *Selected Works of Deng Xiaoping, Volume 3 (1982–1992)*, 350. The first twelve Chinese characters are 冷静观察，稳住阵脚，and 沉着应付. Deng later added 有所作为.

34. Deng Xiaoping, 邓小平年谱 下册, 1346.

35. Deng Xiaoping, "With Stable Policies of Reform and Opening to the Outside World, China Can Have Great Hopes for the Future," September 4, 1989, in *Selected Works of Deng Xiaoping, Volume 3*, 310.

36. Deng Xiaoping, "Urgent Trasks of China's Third Generation of Collective Leadership," June 16, 1989, in *Selected Works of Deng Xiaoping, Volume 3 (1982–1992)*, 311.

37. World Bank, "GDP (current US$)—China, United States," https://data.worldbank.org/indicator/NY.GDP.MKTP.CD?locations=CN-US.

38. Roger Sullivan, "Discarding the China Card," *Foreign Policy*, no. 86 (1992): 3–23.

39. Edward Walsh, "Clinton Indicts Bush's World Leadership," *Washington Post*, October 2, 1992, https://www.washingtonpost.com/archive/politics/1992/10/02/clinton-indicts-bushs-world-leadership/a68703ae-1982-4396-ab19-547994b82aaa/; John Broder and Staff Writers, "Clinton Reverses His Policy," *Los Angeles Times*, May 27, 1994. https://www.latimes.com/archives/la-xpm-1994-05-27-mn-62877-story.html.

40. Denny Roy, "The 'China Threat' Issue: Major Arguments," *Asian Survey* 36, no. 8 (1996): 758–71.

41. Gideon Rachman, "Containing China," *Washington Quarterly* 19, no. 1 (1996): 126–39; Denny Roy "Hegemon on the Horizon? China's Threat to East Asian Security," *International Security* 19, no. 1 (1994): 149–68; Richard Bernstein and Ross Munro, *The Coming Conflict with China* (New York: Knopf, 1997).

42. Scott Kennedy and Michael O'Hanlon, "Time to Shift Gears on China Policy," *Journal of East Asian Affairs* 10, no. 1 (1996): 45–73; Ezra Vogel, *Living with China: U.S.-China Relations in the Twenty-First Century* (New York: Norton, 1997); Michael Gallagher, "China's Illusory Threat to the South China Sea," *International Security* 19, no. 1 (1994): 169–94.

43. Bates Gill, "Limited Engagement," *Foreign Affairs* 78, no. 4 (1999): 65–76.

44. Robert L. Suettinger, *Beyond Tiananmen: The Politics of US-China Relations 1989–2000* (Washington, DC: Brookings Institution Press, 2003).

45. Jiang Zemin, "Our Diplomatic Work Must Unswervingly Safeguard the Highest Interests of the State and the Nation," July 12, 1993, in *Selected Works of Jiang Zemin*, vol. 1 (Beijing: Foreign Languages Press, 2010), 303–4.

46. Jiang Zemin, "The Present International Situation and Our Diplomatic Work," August 28, 1998, in *Selected Works of Jiang Zemin*, vol. 11 (Beijing: Foreign Languages Press, 2012), 193.

47. Jiang Zemin, 199.

48. Xiaoxiong Yi, "China's U.S. Policy Conundrum in the 1990s: Balancing Autonomy and Interdependence," *Asian Survey* 34, no. 8 (1994): 675–91.

49. David Lampton, *Same Bed, Different Dreams: Managing U.S.-China Relations, 1989–2000* (Berkeley: University of California Press, 2001).

50. Jiang Zemin, "The Present International Situation and Our Diplomatic Work," 193.

51. Jiang Zemin, 197.

52. Tai Ming Cheung, "Disarmament and Development in China: The Relationship Between National Defense and Economic Development," *Asian Survey* 28, no. 7 (1988): 757–74; Thomas Bickford "The Business Operations of the Chinese People's Liberation Army," *Problems of Post-Communism* 46, no. 6 (1999): 28–36.

53. Jiang Zemin, "Our Diplomatic Work Must Unswervingly Safeguard the Highest Interests of the State and the Nation," July 12, 1993, in *Selected Works of Jiang Zemin*, vol. 1, 302.

54. Jiang Zemin, "Concerning Our Military Strategic Principle and Issues of Defense Technology," June 8, 15, and 25, 1991, in *Selected Works of Jiang Zemin*, vol. 1, 142–50.

55. Jiang Zemin, "Respond to the Challenges of World Military Development in a Spirit of Reform and Innovation," December 14, 1996, in *Selected Works of Jiang Zemin*, vol. 1, 592.

56. Anthony Cordesman and Martin Kleiber, *Chinese Military Modernization: Force Development and Strategic Capabilities* (Washington, DC: CSIS Press, 2007); Thomas Christensen, "China, the US-Japan Alliance, and the Security Dilemma in East Asia," *International Security* 23, no. 4 (1999): 49–80.

57. *Statistical Yearbook of China 2004* (Beijing: 中国统计出版社, 2004), 323.

58. Anthony Cordesman and Joseph Kendall, "Chinese Strategy and Military Modernization," Center for Strategic and International Studies, Policy File 2007, 127.

59. Cordesman and Kendall, 135.

60. Shaoguang Wang, "Estimating China's Defence Expenditure: Some Evidence from Chinese Sources," *China Quarterly*, no. 147 (1996): 889–911; Richard A. Bitzinger, "Just the Facts, Ma'am: The Challenge of Analysing and Assessing Chinese Military Expenditures," *China Quarterly*, no. 173 (2003): 164–75.

61. Evan Medeiros et al., *A New Direction for China's Defense Industry* (Santa Monica, CA: Rand Corporation, 2005); Richard Bitzinger, "Modernising China's Military, 1997–2012," *China Perspectives*, no. 4 (2011): 7–15.

62. Qimao Chen, "New Approaches in China's Foreign Policy: The Post–Cold War Era," *Asian Survey* 33, no. 3 (1993): 237–51.

63. Gilbert Rozman, "Sino-Russian Relations in the 1990s: A Balance Sheet," *Post-Soviet Affairs* 14, no. 2 (1998): 93–113; Rajan Menon, "The Limits of Chinese–Russian Partnership," *Survival* 51, no. 3 (2009): 99–130.

64. Jing-dong Yuan, "China's Role in Establishing and Building the Shanghai Cooperation Organization (SCO)," *Journal of Contemporary China* 19, no. 67 (2010): 855–69.

65. Johannes Schmidt, "China's Soft Power Diplomacy in Southeast Asia," *Copenhagen Journal of Asian Studies* 26, no. 1 (2008): 22–49.

66. Amna Khokhar, "Sino-Indian Relations: Implications for Pakistan," *Strategic Studies* 30, no. 3/4 (2010): 73–84.

67. Michael Yahuda, *Sino-Japanese Relations After the Cold War: Two Tigers Sharing a Mountain* (London: Routledge, 2013).

68. Yu-Jie Chen, "'One China' Contention in China–Taiwan Relations: Law, Politics and Identity," *China Quarterly*, no. 252 (2022): 1025–44.

69. *Statistical Yearbook of China 1995* (Beijing: 中国统计出版社, 1995), 543, 555.

70. Robert Ross, "The 1995–96 Taiwan Strait Confrontation: Coercion, Credibility, and the Use of Force," *International Security* 25, no. 2 (2000): 87–123.

71. Kerry Dumbaugh, "Taiwan in 2004: Elections, Referenda, and Other Democratic Challenges," CRS Report for Congress, January 10, 2005. https://apps.dtic.mil/sti/pdfs/ADA462920.pdf.

72. Jiang Zemin, "Review and Summary of the Central Military Commission's Work Over the Last Ten Years," November 24, 1999, in *Selected Works of Jiang Zemin*, vol. 11, 465.

73. Martin Wolf, *Why Globalization Works* (New Haven, CT: Yale University Press, 2004).

74. Jiang Zemin, "The Present International Situation and Our Diplomatic Work," August 28, 1998, 197.

75. Yeling Tan, *Disaggregating China, Inc.: State Strategies in the Liberal Economic Order* (Ithaca, NY: Cornell University Press, 2021).

76. *Statistical Yearbook of China 2013*, https://www.stats.gov.cn/sj/ndsj/2013/indexch.htm.

77. World Bank, "GDP (current US$)—China, United States," https://data.worldbank.org/indicator/NY.GDP.MKTP.CD?locations=CN-US.

78. Richard Baum, "From 'Strategic Partners' to 'Strategic Competitors': George W. Bush and the Politics of U.S. China Policy," *Journal of East Asian Studies* 1, no. 2 (2001): 191–220.

79. David Lampton, "The Stealth Normalization of US-China Relations," *National Interest*, no. 73 (2003): 37–48.

80. "Guoji xingshi he waishi gongzuo" [The international situation and foreign affairs work], August 21, 2006, in Hu Jintao, 胡锦涛文选第二卷 [Selected works of Hu Jintao vol. 2] (Beijing: People's Publishing House, 2016), 510.

81. Robert L. Suettinger, "The Rise and Descent of 'Peaceful Rise,'" *China Leadership Monitor* 12, no. 2 (2004): 1–10.

82. "Seize the Opportunity to Develop the Economy," December 24, 1990, in *Selected Works of Deng Xiaoping, Volume 3 (1982–1992)*, 350.

83. Hu Jintao, 胡锦涛文选第二卷, 97–98.

84. Stephen Blank, "The End of the Six-Party Talks," *Strategic Insights* 6, no. 1 (2007): 1–16; Tomasz Grosse, "Geoeconomic Relations Between the EU and China: The Lessons from the EU Weapon Embargo and from Galileo," *Geopolitics* 19, no. 1 (2014): 40–65.

85. Rush Doshi, "Hu's to Blame for China's Foreign Assertiveness?," in *Global China: Assessing China's Growing Role in the World*, ed. Tarun Chhabra et al. (Washington DC: Brookings Institution Press, 2021), 25–32.

86. Hu Jintao, 胡锦涛文选第三卷, 236–38; Robert Zoellick, "Whither China: From Membership to Responsibility," US Department of State, September 21, 2005, https://2001-2009.state.gov/s/d/former/zoellick/rem/53682.htm.

87. Minxin Pei, "China in Xi's 'New Era': A Play for Global Leadership," *Journal of Democracy* 29, no. 2 (2018): 39.

88. Anne-Marie Brady, "Authoritarianism Goes Global (II): China's Foreign Propaganda Machine," *Journal of Democracy* 26, no. 4 (2015): 51–59.

89. Sanaa Hafeez, "The Senkaku/Diaoyu Islands Crises of 2004, 2010, and 2012: A Study of Japanese-Chinese Crisis Management," *Asia-Pacific Review* 22, no. 1 (2015): 73–99.

90. Carlyle Thayer, "The United States and Chinese Assertiveness in the South China Sea," *Security Challenges* 6, no. 2 (2010): 69–84.

91. Xue Litai, 盛世危言：远观中国大战略 [Warnings in times of prosperity: Long-term perspectives on Chinese grand strategy] (Shanghai: 东方出版社, 2014).

92. Thomas Christensen, "The Advantages of an Assertive China: Responding to Beijing's Abrasive Diplomacy," *Foreign Affairs* 90, no. 2 (2011): 54–67.

93. Hillary Clinton, "America's Pacific Century," *Foreign Policy*, no. 189 (2011): 56–63.

94. Xi Jinping, "中国必须有自己特色的大国外交" [China must have its unique great power diplomacy], in 习近平著作选读第一卷 (Beijing: 人民出版社, 2023), 317–20.

95. Li Jinqiu, "习近平：提高我国参与全球治理的能力" [Xi Jinping: Increase our country's capacity to participate in global governance], 新华社 [New China News Agency], September 24, 2019, http://cn.chinadiplomacy.org.cn/2019-09/24/content_75240337.shtml.

96. Xi Jinping, "深入理解新发展理念" [Deepening understanding of new concepts of development], in 习近平著作选读第一卷, 437–39.

97. Xi Jinping, "Follow the Trend of the Times and Promote Global Peace and Development," March 23, 2013, in Xi Jinping, *The Governance of China* (Beijing: Foreign Languages Press, 2014), 298–99.

98. Xi Jinping, "在全国党校工作会议上的讲话" [Speech at the National Conference on Party Schools], 求是 [Qiushi], May 1, 2016, http://www.xinhuanet.com/politics/2016-05/01/c_128951529.htm.

99. Xi Jinping, "New Approach for Asian Security Cooperation," May 21, 2014, in Xi Jinping, *The Governance of China*, 392.

100. World Bank, "GDP Growth (Annual %)—Euro Area, United States, Japan, China," https://data.worldbank.org/indicator/NY.GDP.MKTP.KD.ZG?locations=XC-US-JP-CN.

101. World Bank, "GDP (Current US$)—China, United States," https://data.worldbank.org/indicator/NY.GDP.MKTP.CD?locations=CN-US.

102. World Bank, "GDP, PPP (Current International $)—China, United States," https://data.worldbank.org/indicator/NY.GDP.MKTP.PP.CD?locations=CN-US.

103. Mackenzie Eaglen, "Estimating the Costs of 20 Years in Afghanistan," American Enterprise Institute, August 28, 2021, https://www.aei.org/op-eds/estimating-the-costs-of-20-years-in-afghanistan/.

104. Watson Institute of International and Public Affairs, "Costs of War,"Brown University, August 2021, https://watson.brown.edu/costsofwar/figures/2021/human-and-budgetary-costs-date-us-war-afghanistan-2001-2022.

105. Dmitri Trenin, "Russia Reborn: Reimagining Moscow's Foreign Policy," *Foreign Affairs* 88, no. 6 (2009): 64–78.

106. Elizabeth Wishnick, "Sino-Russian Consolidation at a Time of Geopolitical Rivalry," *China Leadership Monitor*, no. 63 (2020), https://www.prcleader.org/post/sino-russian-consolidation-at-a-time-of-geopolitical-rivalry; "China-Russia 2023 Trade Value Hits Record High of $240 bln," Reuters, January 12, 2024, https://www.reuters.com/markets/china-russia-2023-trade-value-hits-record-high-240-bln-chinese-customs-2024-01-12/.

107. Nadège Rolland, "China's 'Belt and Road Initiative': Underwhelming or Game-Changer?," *Washington Quarterly* 40, no. 1 (2017): 127–42.

108. Alice De Jonge, "Perspectives on the Emerging Role of the Asian Infrastructure Investment Bank," *International Affairs* 93, no. 5 (2017): 1061–84; Sergio Suchodolski and Julien Demeulemeester, "The BRICS Coming of Age and the New Development Bank," *Global Policy* 9, no. 4 (2018): 578–85.

109. Ian Rinehart and Bart Elias, "China's Air Defense Identification Zone (ADIZ)," Congressional Research Service, January 30, 2015. https://china.usc.edu/sites/default/files/article/attachments/crs-2015-china-air-defense-identification-zone.pdf.

110. Congressional Research Service, "U.S.-China Strategic Competition in South and East China Seas: Background and Issues for Congress," February 5, 2024, https://sgp.fas.org/crs/row/R42784.pdf.

111. Evan Medeiros, "Explaining and Understanding Competition in US-China Relations," in *Cold Rivals: The New Era of US-China Strategic Competition*, ed. Evan Medeiros (Washington, DC: Georgetown University Press, 2023), 25–45.

112. David Shambaugh, "Assessing the US 'Pivot' to Asia," *Strategic Studies Quarterly* 7, no. 2 (2013): 10–19; Michael J. Green and Matthew P. Goodman, "After TPP: The Geopolitics of Asia and the Pacific," *Washington Quarterly* 38, no. 4 (2015): 19–34.

113. James Steinberg and Michael O'Hanlon, "Keep Hope Alive: How to Prevent U.S.-Chinese Relations from Blowing Up," *Foreign Affairs* 93, no. 4 (2014): 107–17.

114. White House, "National Security Strategy of the United States of America," December 2017, https://trumpwhitehouse.archives.gov/wp-content/uploads/2017/12/NSS-Final-12-18-2017-0905.pdf.

115. Bonnie Glaser and Kelly Flaherty, "US-China Relations in Free Fall," *Comparative Connections* 22, no. 2 (2020): 25–32.

116. Antony Blinken, "The Administration's Approach to the People's Republic of China," US Department of State, May 26, 2022. https://www.state.gov/the-administrations-approach-to-the-peoples-republic-of-china/; Kurt Campbell and Jake Sullivan, "Competition Without Catastrophe: How America Can Both Challenge and Coexist with China," *Foreign Affairs* 98, no. 5 (2019): 96–110.

117. Keith Bradsher, "China's Leader, with Rare Bluntness, Blames U.S. Containment for Troubles," *New York Times*, March 7, 2023. https://www.nytimes.com/2023/03/07/world/asia/china-us-xi-jinping.html.

Conclusion

1. 中共中央文献研究室, "习近平关于实现中华民族伟大复兴的中国梦论述摘编" [Xi Jinping's selected speeches on realizing the great rejuvenation of the Chinese nation] (Beijing: Zhonggong zhongyang wenxian chubanshe, 2013).

INDEX

Figures and tables are indicated by f *and* t *following page numbers.*

A NOTE ON THE TYPE

This book has been composed in Arno, an Old-style serif typeface in the classic Venetian tradition, designed by Robert Slimbach at Adobe.